iPlanet™ Application Server: Designing and Building J2EE™ Solutions

David F. Ogren and Martin Gee

Wiley Publishing, Inc.

Best-Selling Books • Digital Downloads • e-Books • Answer Networks
e-Newsletters • Branded Web Sites • e-Learning

iPlanet™ Application Server: Designing and Building J2EE™ Solutions

Published by
Wiley Publishing, Inc.
909 Third Avenue
New York, NY 10022
www.wiley.com

Copyright © 2002 by Wiley Publishing, Inc., Indianapolis, Indiana

ISBN: 0-7645-4909-x

Manufactured in the United States of America

10 9 8 7 6 5 4 3 2 1

1B/QT/QX/QS/IN

Published by Wiley Publishing, Inc., Indianapolis, Indiana
Published simultaneously in Canada

For general information on our other products and services or to obtain technical support, please contact our Customer Care Department within the U.S. at 800-762-2974, outside the U.S. at 317-572-3993 or fax 317-572-4002.

Wiley also publishes its books in a variety of electronic formats. Some content that appears in print may not be available in electronic books.

Library of Congress Control Number: 2002103276

Wiley Publishing, Inc. is a trademark of Wiley Publishing, Inc.

Credits

EXECUTIVE EDITOR
Chris Webb

PROJECT EDITOR
Neil Romanosky

TECHNICAL EDITOR
Martin Gee

COPY EDITOR
William A. Barton

EDITORIAL MANAGER
Mary Beth Wakefield

**VICE PRESIDENT AND EXECUTIVE
GROUP PUBLISHER**
Richard Swadley

**VICE PRESIDENT AND EXECUTIVE
PUBLISHER**
Bob Ipsen

EXECUTIVE EDITORIAL DIRECTOR
Mary Bednarek

PROJECT COORDINATOR
Maridee Ennis

**GRAPHICS AND PRODUCTION
SPECIALISTS**
Melissa Auciello-Brogan
Stephanie D. Jumper
Jacque Schneider
Jeremey Unger

QUALITY CONTROL TECHNICIANS
Andy Hollandbeck
Susan Moritz
Carl Pierce

PERMISSIONS EDITOR
Laura Moss

MEDIA DEVELOPMENT SPECIALIST
Greg Stephens

PROOFREADING AND INDEXING
TECHBOOKS Production Services

About the Authors

David F. Ogren is a systems engineer and application server specialist at Sun ONE division of Sun Microsystems. He has been designing and building Java systems for five years and has been working with iPlanet Application Server since 1999 (when it was Netscape Application Server 2.1).

Martin Gee has been an architect/developer for many "J2EE-like" Java application frameworks for many years. Over three years ago, he caught his first glimpse of what now has become a key part of Sun One, Netscape Application Server (NAS) 2.1. Since then, using the iPlanet product suite, he has been involved with architecture plans, development and integration, vendor bake-offs, trouble shooting, mentoring, operations plans, and application framework implementation for enterprise clients in a variety of business verticals. When he's not working with clients he spends a portion of his time at SunED teaching iPlanet Application Server courses.

Chris Buzzetta (author of Chapter 3) is an independent consultant with over 15 years of experience in areas such as object-oriented technologies. His areas of expertise are in Java, C++, and C#. He is a certified iPlanet Application Server instructor and has been working with the iPlanet Application Server since the release of Netscape Application Server version 2.1. His experience with administration and development on many of the leading application server products in the market has given him a unique perspective on planning, configuring, and creating best practices in areas of development to deployment, for true enterprise environments.

Steve DeRidder (author of Chapter 2) has been an independent consultant for the past four years focusing on software testing and configuration management. During the past two years he has been involved in the installation and administration of the iPlanet product suite. He has been testing EJBs on the iPlanet application server using various testing tools from Mercury Interactive's automated tools to test Suites using Junit. Some of his projects involve writing Jakarta Ant build scripts to facilitate in hourly builds and deployment of the applications to the iPlanet application server.

To my father, my inspiration for computing wisdom; to my mother, my inspiration for work ethics; and to my brother, my inspiration for commitment.
– David F. Ogren
To Jodie: Thanks for the infinite support. To Mom and Dad, for giving me the drive to achieve.
– Martin Gee

Preface

Java is Sun Microsystems' platform for developing applications that are portable across many types of computing devices, from Java-enabled cell phones to large multiprocessor Unix-based servers. Java 2 Enterprise Edition (J2EE) is one of the most successful and fastest growing areas of Java. J2EE is a set of technologies designed to aid in the development of Web services and n-tier applications for enterprises.

In addition to defining the J2EE standard, Sun Microsystems also sells a commercial implementation of J2EE under its iPlanet brand: iPlanet Application Server Enterprise Edition (iAS). This book is an insider's guide to developing applications by using iPlanet Application Server. It covers a complete range of topics, from the essentials of the underlying Java technologies to the specifics of developing for and administrating iAS, as well as several best practices for developing J2EE applications.

Who Should Read this Book

Several people would benefit from reading this book, including the following:

- *Java developers looking for an overview of J2EE.* This book presents readers with a survey of the various methods of developing applications in J2EE. These readers should have a general understanding of Java technology but don't need any prior experience with J2EE development.

- *J2EE developers looking for iAS-specific information.* iPlanet insiders wrote this book, and it contains information about iPlanet Application Server that's unavailable anywhere else. Reading this book is essential for developers who are new or experienced with the iPlanet Application Server platform. These readers should have a solid understanding of the J2EE APIs before reading this book so that they can utilize the iAS-specific information herein most effectively.

- *Systems administrators responsible for administrating iPlanet Application Server.* This book presents unique operational guidelines for working with iPlanet Application Server. From an administrator's perspective, this book presents a summary of the underlying technologies of iAS, along with a detailed guide to setting up and utilizing the unique operational features of iPlanet Application Server, such as clustering.

How this Book Is Organized

In general, this book doesn't try to duplicate the reference information that's currently available in the iPlanet documentation. This book takes a more task-oriented, practical approach to both developing and administrating iPlanet Application Server. It also presents critical "under-the-covers" information that can prove helpful to understanding the behind-the-scenes functionality of iAS.

Neither does this book attempt to duplicate the plethora of books that are available on the J2EE APIs. Servlets, JSPs, Enterprise JavaBeans, and JDBC all are complete subjects themselves, and plenty of books are currently available on the market that focus on each of them. This book covers the basics of each of these technologies, as a type of "getting-started" guide, but their details are outside the scope of this book. J2EE developers should utilize this book as an iAS-specific supplement to those product-specific books and not as a replacement.

This book is organized into four major sections, plus two appendixes.

Part I: Getting Started

Part I provides the instructions needed to get your own iPlanet Application Server instances up and running so that you can follow along with the book. Chapter 1 is a lexicon of iPlanet and J2EE terminology and a guidebook to the basic administrative commands. Chapter 2 details the step-by-step instructions of installing your own version of iAS. Chapter 3 walks you through the process of testing your installation and troubleshooting any installation difficulties.

Part II: Fundamentals of J2EE

The next section, including Chapters 4 through 7, provides a survey of the J2EE APIs. The introduction is focused primarily on Java developers that are new to J2EE, but iAS-specific information is also included. This iAS-specific information means that even experienced J2EE developers will want to review this section for the details of iPlanet's implementation. Although these chapters are written for developers, administrators should also have a basic understanding of these chapters' content.

Chapter 4 includes the details of the servlet API, the building block of J2EE applications. Chapter 5 covers application packaging: the process of taking your first basic application and preparing it for deployment. Additional J2EE APIs are presented in Chapters 6 and 7: the Java Server Pages API is presented in Chapter 6 and the Enterprise JavaBean API is presented in Chapter 7.

Part III: Advanced Topics

This section covers iPlanet-specific topics beyond the J2EE specification. You should already be familiar with the basic operation of iPlanet Application Server before beginning this section, as this section assumes that you are already familiar with J2EE and iAS basics. These chapters are designed for both administrators and senior developers.

Chapter 8 covers the process of using Forte for Java and other IDEs with iPlanet Application Server. Chapter 9 provides an in-depth exploration of application deployment, tracing what happens behind the scenes of iAS deployments.

iPlanet Application Server's clustering, load balancing, and failover features are covered in Chapters 10 and 11. Chapter 10 explains how clustering and load-balancing work, while Chapter 11 shows how iAS uses these clustering and load-balancing features to transparently recover from failures.

Chapter 12 is an introduction to SOAP and how iAS can act as both a SOAP service provider and service consumer. The iAS registry is detailed in Chapter 13, generally information on how to work with the registry as well as information about specific registry keys which can be useful to developers and administrators. The iAS log files are explained in Chapter 14, which provides a roadmap to the many places where troubleshooting information can be found.

Part III ends with two chapters on the two most common technologies for remote method invocation within J2EE: RMI/IIOP and Web services. Chapter 15 covers RMI/IIOP, both from a theoretical point of view and from the perspective of iPlanet's implementation, specifically. Chapter 16 presents an overview of Web services technologies and an introduction to using iAS for and with Web services.

Part IV: Best Practices

Part IV is a collection of recommendations for successfully developing and operating iPlanet Application Server applications. (Although much of this advice is generic and is applicable to all types of enterprise development.) The chapters in this section can be read independently of the rest of the book and are designed primarily for developers and system architects.

Chapter 17 is an exploration of iAS production architectures. This chapter explores best practices for network topologies, iAS clustering, and application design. Maintenance strategies, especially application deployment methodologies, are covered in Chapter 18, which debunks many common myths about real-world application deployment.

Two best practices for enterprise application development are covered in Chapters 19 and 20. Chapter 19 addresses daily builds and automated testing. Chapter 20 covers several general strategies for quality assurance, and encourages educated, up-front quality assurance planning.

The last two chapters are directed towards iAS administrators. Chapter 21 is a guide to performing backups and restores on the various iAS components. Chapter 22 is a practical guide to high availability: how and when to remove single points of failure.

Conventions Used in this Book

Throughout the book, `monospace font` is used to designate code and commands. Also, icons are used to set apart information that needs special attention:

The Note icon highlights information that requires special attention and details which are not easy to recognize.

The Caution icon highlights possible trouble spots and common mistakes.

The Tip icon highlights possible shortcuts and recommendations.

The Cross-Reference icon highlights references to other chapters of the book.

Companion CD-ROM

The CD-ROM contains a "Test Drive" evaluation copy of iPlanet Application Server 6.5, so you can follow along with the information provided in this book. The CD-ROM also includes all of the examples from the book, in both source and packaged form, so that you can experiment with the sample applications, as well.

The companion CD-ROM also includes a copy of the Sun's IDE: Forte for Java. Although you can use any IDE to developer Java code for iAS, I discuss Forte for Java in Chapter 8. Although the Community Edition of Forte for Java is included on the CD-ROM, Chapter 8 does refer to some Enterprise edition features. The Community Edition can be upgraded to the Enterprise Edition using the Update Center feature.

Acknowledgments

This book is a summary of years of work with the iPlanet Application Server and its predecessors. It's also the first book that anyone's published that focuses exclusively on iAS. Because of this focus, we expect this book to prove uniquely valuable to everyone interested in working with iPlanet Application Server, and we want to thank everyone who contributed to this book and helped make it possible. Thanks to the team at Wiley, especially Chris, Neil, and Bill. Getting this book from concept to print has been a seemingly endless series of challenges. I appreciate all the hard work they had to do to get over those hurdles; this book has definitely required "above and beyond" efforts from everyone. Special thanks go to Bill, who had to edit all of the work that I did at 3 AM.. Thanks to my friends and family. This book has consumed the last six months or so of my life. Mom, Dad, Chad, Kevin, Nicole, Mike, Bruce, Laura, and everyone: thanks for tolerating my absence and for putting up with my constant deadline desperation. Personal thanks also go to Diana, who not only helped me edit and proofread, but was also there when I needed her. I also owe my appreciation to Ralph Coulter, Tom Abato, Ed DiRocco, Aaron Keuhn, and Dan Lyons. All of my managers at work were supportive of this book. Without their support I couldn't have balanced my work schedule and the book deadlines. Thanks go Tom Barrett, Reggie Carey, John Peiffer, Russ Perry, Jeff Smith, and Orrin Char, Deepak Balakrishna, Chris Kampmeier, Ernie Park, and all of the other iAS gurus (past, present, and future) for all of their insight, knowledge and encouragement. The iAS community has always been very supportive, and I never could have written this book without the knowledge I learned from the mailing lists and conferences. On the iAS engineering and management team I'd like to thank Rohit Valia, Jon Williams, Chris Kampmeier (again), Geoffroy Sejourne, and Curtis Ward. Both for their help facilitating and promoting this book and for all of their assistance in the past. And special thanks go to Martin Gee. When everything else went wrong, he stepped up to the co-author responsibilities and saved the day.
— *David F. Ogren*

Thanks to Dennis Mastin who many moons ago took the personal time and effort to help me get involved in the Netscape Application Server community. Since the Netscape 2.1 days, I have also meet many Netscape/iPlanet friends who I'd like to thank, for they have helped me advance my career in many ways. Thanks, Chris Buzzetta and Steve Deridder for always jumping into the fire with me. Finally, thanks to my family for understanding my desire to get involved with efforts such as this book.

— *Martin Gee*

Contents at a Glance

Contents

Introduction

Neither iPlanet nor the iPlanet Application Server have a simple history. Understanding the history of iPlanet Application Server's can prove helpful in understanding its basic architecture as well as its strengths and weaknesses. The server contains several Java packages, for example, including `com.kivasoft`, `com.netscape`, and `com.sun`. Understanding the history of iPlanet and the iPlanet Application Server enables you determine the age of each of those packages and gives you a clue as to the functionality that each package offers.

Similarly, an understanding of iPlanet's corporate history helps you understand iPlanet's position in the marketplace and its likely future. Kivasoft, Netscape, and Sun all focus on vertical scalability, datacenter manageability, backend integration, and reliability — in other words, features that appeal to Fortune 500 enterprises.

The History of iPlanet

When AOL acquired Netscape in 1999, AOL's primary interest was in the Netscape browser and Netcenter portal. U.S. tax laws, however, prevented AOL from selling the Netscape e-commerce software division without triggering negative tax consequences. As a result, AOL entered into a strategic alliance with Sun Microsystems.

The Sun-Netscape alliance, in summary, was an agreement wherein AOL and Sun would share the revenue and expenses of the Netscape server software for three years. The Sun–Netscape alliance was jointly staffed by both AOL and Sun employees and was to carry the iPlanet brand. At the end of the alliance, both parties would have rights to the software code.

The three years of the alliance are now complete. The majority of AOL employees responsible for iPlanet are now Sun employees. (Netscape retained some employees were for its strategic business-solutions hosting service.) Now that the Sun-Netscape alliance is over, the development, Sun exclusively manages the support and sales of all iPlanet products.

Now that the alliance is complete, iPlanet is a Sun Microsystems brand that encompasses all of Sun's e-commerce software. (Sun also sells software under the Forte, Solaris, Java, and StarOffice brands.) The majority of the iPlanet software, however, including the iPlanet Application Server, originated from the Sun–Netscape Alliance.

The iPlanet Software Stack

The iPlanet brand provides a complete stack of e-commerce software that ranges from basic infrastructure, such as LDAP and HTTP servers, all the way to complete e-commerce software packages, such as online procurement and online bill payment and presentment. iPlanet products are based on a philosophy of open architecture, utilizing open protocols such as J2EE, LDAP, HTTP, SSL, IMAP, and SMTP. iPlanet products are also engineered for extremely high scalability, focusing on high-end customers and data-center deployments.

iPlanet products are currently organized into the following six categories:

◆ *Web and application services (iPlanet Web Server and iPlanet Application Server)* – These products primarily focus on delivering static and dynamic content via HTTP and HTTPS.

◆ *Communication Services (iPlanet Messaging Server and iPlanet Calendar Server)* – These products enable collaboration by Web-based protocols as well as by rich-client protocols such as SMTP, POP, IMAP, and iCalendar.

◆ *Integration Services (iPlanet Integration Server [B2B edition and EAI edition] and iPlanet Message Queue)* – These products are designed to aid integration with legacy systems and trading partners, as follows:

  ■ Integration Server B2B edition enables the secure delivery of documents over the Internet and data transformation of popular business-document formats such as EDI.

  ■ Integration Server EAI edition integrates legacy systems into an XML-based communication hub. The integration server provides data transformation and process management that enables you to integrate the legacy applications into one cohesive business process.

  ■ iPlanet Message Queue is a Java Messaging Service (JMS) provider. JMS is a standard for asynchronous messaging using a Java API. iMQ is a JMS implementation that can provide guaranteed message delivery.

◆ *User Management (iPlanet Directory Server [iDS] plus the Integration Edition and Access Management Edition add-on bundles)* – iDS is the industry's leading LDAP server. The Integration Edition and Access Management Edition supplement the basic LDAP server with additional modules to handle related services such as single sign-on (SSO), delegated administration, and metadirectory services.

◆ *Portal Services (iPlanet Portal Server and its add-on packs)* – iPlanet Portal Server provides personalization, membership management, and other application services. It also provides a frontend that enables you to aggregate, secure, and deliver applications to multiple client types.

◆ *Commerce Services (BillerXpert [standard, B2B, and consolidator editions], MarketMaker, SellerXpert, and TrustBase)* – These packaged applications build on the infrastructure that the rest of the iPlanet software stack provides, including the iPlanet Application Server.

iPlanet products are designed so that using the integrated software stack makes implementing your software easier. iPlanet Portal Server, for example, comes with prebuilt channels for iPlanet Messaging Server and iPlanet Calendar Server. The iPlanet stack doesn't, however, lock customers into using only iPlanet products. To continue the example, customers could easily add iPlanet Portal Server channels to other mail and calendar services.

What Is iPlanet Application Server?

This section describes the history and development of J2EE and iPlanet Application Server.

Java 2 Enterprise Edition

Java provides a wide variety of APIs for developing enterprise applications. EJBs, JSPs, Servlets, JNDI, JMS, JCA, JDBC, and JTA are only a few of the Java APIs currently available. Because each of these APIs has different versions available and different release schedules, however, this multitude of different API versions can potentially become confusing and problematic for both server vendors and customers. Server vendors need to find a way to make all the various APIs work as a cohesive whole. Customers need a standard set of APIs to program against as well as some sort of certification from server vendors to verify that they can successfully provide all the necessary APIs.

Java 2 Enterprise Edition (J2EE) is a way of meeting these needs. J2EE defines a set of APIs that J2EE server providers must provide, along with a required revision level for each API. It also provides a set of compliance tests that vendors must successfully pass to become J2EE certified. The J2EE (version 1.2) APIs are as follows:

- JDBC 2.0

- RMI-IIOP 1.0

- Enterprise Java Beans (EJB) 1.1

- Servlets 2.2

- JavaServer Pages (JSP) 1.1

- Java Message Server (JMS) 1.0

- Java Naming and Directory Interface (JNDI) 1.2

- Java Transaction API (JTA) 1.0

- JavaMail 1.1

- JavaBeans Activation Framework (JAF) 1.0

This certification of J2EE vendors also helps to ensure application portability. If you build your application to the J2EE specification, you can usually port it from one certified vendor to another without difficulty. The J2EE specification doesn't, however, preclude vendors from building proprietary extensions to the specification.

The history of iPlanet Application Server

The iPlanet Application Server's codebase began with a startup company by the name of Kivasoft. Kivasoft built one of the first Web application servers, simply named the Kiva Enterprise Server. Released in 1996, Kiva Enterprise Server was a revolutionary step for server-side Java programming. Because this type of server-based Java computing was new, Kivasoft also needed to develop its own proprietary APIs. (This development occurred long before the introduction of servlets and JSPs.) Although deprecated, these proprietary APIs still exist in current versions of iPlanet Application Server. These proprietary APIs are sure to become unavailable in future versions of iAS.

In December of 1997, Netscape acquired Kivasoft and renamed the Kiva Enterprise Server the Netscape Application Server (NAS). The 2.0 version of Kiva Enterprise Server/Netscape Application Server introduced many of the powerful load-balancing and clustering technologies that iPlanet Application Server still utilizes.

The next major release of Netscape Application Server (version 4.0) came in August 1998. Although version 4.0 included many performance and functionality enhancements, its primary feature was support for the recently released Java standards, including Servlets 2.1, Java Server Pages 0.92, and Enterprise Java Beans 1.0.

In March 1999, the Sun-Netscape Alliance was created. Shortly thereafter, it created the iPlanet brand, and the new alliance focused on transforming the Netscape Application Server into a J2EE application server (Despite the fact that the J2EE specification wasn't finalized until later that year).

In April 2000, iPlanet released iPlanet Application Server 6.0, which the company created from the Netscape Application Server codebase. Although iPlanet Application Server offered several new features (EJB failover, watermarks, graceful shutdowns), its most significant characteristic was its status as the first J2EE-certified application server.

iPlanet Application Server today

iPlanet Application Server is one of the "big three" of J2EE application servers. (The others are BEA's WebLogic and IBM's WebSphere.) Both e-commerce companies and Fortune 500 enterprises widely deploy iPlanet Application Server. (A Google search for the *NASApp* string, which is part of iAS URLs by default, results in approximately 20,000 hits.)

iPlanet Application Server is available on the Solaris, Windows, HP/UX, and AIX platforms. A development license of iPlanet Application Server comes with Sun's Solaris operating system (versions 8 and up). Sun also announced plans to bundle iPlanet Application Server with future versions of the Solaris operating system.

Server-side computing continues to grow. Application servers (whether J2EE-based or .NET-based) are becoming part of the infrastructure of the operating system. Expect to see iPlanet Application Server become more and more integrated with the Solaris environment because of this trend.

Resources for More Information

The following list describes several online sources that you can explore for more information about iPlanet Application Server. Your local iPlanet sales team or iPlanet partner can also help you find information about iPlanet Application Server. A list of local iPlanet offices can be found on the www.iplanet.com website.

- ◆ *Sun software forums* (http://softwareforum.sun.com/) — Web forums for the iPlanet products, including four forums for iPlanet Application Server. Questions that you post here have a reasonable chance of getting answers from other users and/or iPlanet staff. Separate forums are available for performance-tuning, clustering, and installation, as well as a forum for general questions.

- ◆ *iPlanet developer site* (http://developer.iplanet.com/tech/appserver/index.html) — The iPlanet developer site contains the latest official sample code and downloads for iAS. It also contains periodic articles about using iPlanet Application Server. The most recent article, for example, is a basic guide for performance-tuning.

- ◆ *iAS online documentation* (http://docs.iplanet.com/docs/manuals/ias.html) — All the iPlanet documentation is available online. This documentation includes the release notes, which offer a wealth of information about the latest feature additions, as well as the latest bug fixes and known issues. The online documentation also includes the latest administration and programming guides in both HTML and PDF formats.

- ◆ *iPlanet home page* (www.iplanet.com/) — The iPlanet home page is a useful place to look up iPlanet product information, including the latest product announcements, datasheets, and press releases.

- ◆ *J2EE home page* (http://java.sun.com/j2ee/) — You can find the latest J2EE information on the official Sun site, including the J2EE specifications and APIs, as well as links to developer resources. Developer resources include tutorials and blueprints that can prove very helpful for both novice and experienced J2EE developers. All information on the J2EE page is vendor neutral, however, so it doesn't contain any information specific to iAS.

◆ *Java Developer Connection* (http://developer.java.sun.com/) — General Java programming information and help. The articles and advice on the Java Developer Connection site cover all types of Java programming, from embedded systems through enterprise computing.

◆ *J2EE mailing lists* (http://archives.java.sun.com/archives/) — Several mailing lists are available for Java and J2EE discussions. The preceding URL provides links to the individual list archives as well as to information about subscribing and unsubscribing from the mailing lists.

SunONE Branding

Just as this book was being readied for press, Sun announced that it would be terminating the iPlanet brand and transitioning all iPlanet products to use the SunONE brand. SunONE will be the unification of many of Sun's software products including the iPlanet, Forte, and StarOffice brands.

iPlanet Application Server 6.*x* will still carry the iPlanet logo and name, but future versions will be known as SunONE Application Server. The same is true for iPlanet Directory Server (soon to become SunONE Directory Server) and iPlanet Web Server (soon to become SunONE Web Server).

Summary

iPlanet Application Server has a long history as a Java application server. Although iAS was updated to support the J2EE APIs, the core infrastructure is still based on the load-balancing, clustering, and management features inherited from its Netscape and Kiva heritage.

Understanding the basics of the application server's heritage can prove helpful in understanding diagnostic messages. Consider, for example, the following typical stack trace:

```
java.lang.Exception : ServletRunnerInfo not found
at java.lang.Throwable.fillInStackTrace(Native Method)
at java.lang.Throwable.fillInStackTrace(Compiled Code)
at java.land.Throwable.<init>(Compiled Code)
at java.land.Throwable.<init>(Compiled Code)
at
com.netscape.server.servlet.servletrunner.ServletRepository.loadServlet(Unknown
Source)
at
com.netscape.server.servlet.servletrunner.ServletRepository.createInstance(Unkno
wn Source)
```

```
at
com.netscape.server.servlet.servletrunner.ServletRepository.createServlet(Unknow
n Source)
at com.netscape.server.servlet.servletrunner.ServletRepository.execute(Unknown
Source)
com.kivasoft.applogic.AppLogic.execute(Compiled Code)
com.kivasoft.applogic.AppLogic.execute(Compiled Code)
com.kivasoft.thread.ThreadBasic.run(Native Method)
com.kivasoft.thread.ThreadBasic.run(Native Method)
com.kivasoft.thread.ThreadBasic.run(Native Method)
```

The stack trace shows how the `com.netscape.server.servlet.servletrunner` package translates the J2EE servlet request into an equivalent request in the proprietary Kiva AppLogic API. A `com.kivasoft` package that handles the low-level execution and thread management then executes the AppLogic request.

Understanding the past and future of the iPlanet is also helpful in understanding the application server. iPlanet Application Server was designed by a company that focused on the Fortune 500. Netscape maintained that vision and continued to focus on developing features to appeal to the large Fortune 500 datacenter. But now that Sun is positioning iAS as the core of its reference SunONE architecture and integrating iAS with the Solaris operating environment, expect to see new priorities for iAS. The new features that the latest 6.5 version of iAS introduces focus on ease of use and developer support. As J2EE expands outside the Fortune 500, expect to see an effort from Sun to focus on improving the developer experience, especially with its Forte line of developer tools.

Part I

Getting Started

CHAPTER 1
iPlanet Application Server Basics

CHAPTER 2
Installing and Configuring
iPlanet Application Server

CHAPTER 3
Testing Your Install

Chapter 1

iPlanet Application Server Basics

IN THIS CHAPTER

- ◆ J2EE
- ◆ Web servers
- ◆ Web connectors
- ◆ Web containers
- ◆ EJB containers
- ◆ Naming services
- ◆ Application packaging

THE FIELD OF ENTERPRISE JAVA PROGRAMMING is replete with abbreviations and technologies that may prove unfamiliar to some programmers. Even experienced enterprise Java programmers can expect to encounter new concepts and terms as they first start working with iPlanet Application Server (iAS).

This chapter is a lexicon of the various terms and concepts that you need to know to continue with the rest of the book. (Some readers who are already familiar with the basics of iPlanet Application Server and J2EE can skip ahead to the next chapter.) This chapter also includes a basic introduction to the administration and deployment tools that come with iPlanet Application Server. By the end of this chapter, you should have a basic understanding of the various components of iAS and the functions that each provides.

Basic Terminology

Even experienced Java developers must learn many new terms and concepts in programming J2EE applications. In the Foreword to this book, I provide a laundry list of Java technologies that are a part of J2EE: JSP, JDBC, JNDI, JTA, and others. (Many of these technologies I discuss in depth in later chapters of this book.) Before these various abbreviations can become useful to you, however, you need to place them in context. This section describes the basic high-level conceptual terms surrounding iAS – for example, the distinction between a Web *server* and a Web *container.*

Web servers

Although most modern programmers probably have a preconceived idea about the definition of a *Web server*, that definition is rather narrow if you're discussing enterprise Java programming and J2EE. In enterprise Java programming, you typically restrict the definition of a Web server to functions such as listening for HTTP requests and returning such static content as images and unchanging HTML.

Why such a narrow definition of a Web server in J2EE? Because any server that executes code in a J2EE application is generally known as an *application server* rather than a Web server. This terminology can seem confusing to programmers new to J2EE, because almost all commercial Web-server products can function as both an application server and a Web server. Similarly, many commercial application-server products (although not iPlanet Application Server) also include a lightweight Web server.

So regardless of the name of the product, try thinking of any products that receive HTTP requests and serve static content as Web servers and products that execute application code as application servers. Even if you're using a product that can perform both functions, you want to think of the two functions as logically separate.

Web containers

A *Web container* is an application server that executes servlet and JSP Java code to generate dynamic Web content. JSPs and servlets (which I discuss in depth in later chapters of this book) are the primary J2EE APIs for delivering Web content. iPlanet Application Server includes a Web container that's compliant with J2EE 1.2. iAS's J2EE 1.2 certification indicates that it's capable of running Java code written for the 2.2 version of the servlet specification and version 1.1 of the JSP specification.

Web connectors

Because Web servers process only static content and rely on the Web container to process dynamic content, a way must exist for the Web server to communicate with the Web container. After receiving a request for dynamic content, the Web server must have the capability to pass the request to the Web container (in iAS's case, in a separate process), fetch the Web container's result, and return the HTML result to the user's browser.

An application server with a built-in Web server embeds this connection is into the product. If you're using iPlanet Web Server's Web container, for example, you can enable the JSP and servlets just by selecting an option within the administrative console. After doing so, you can process the JSP and servlet requests in the same operating-system process that handles the HTTP requests. Many other products, such as Apache's Tomcat and BEA's WebLogic, also have this capability to combine the functionality of the Web server and the Web container.

Most enterprise architectures separate the Web container and the Web server. Separating the Web server and Web container provides better security (as I explore in Chapter 17), better load balancing, and more customer choice. To enable this separation, application-server vendors provide Web-server plug-ins that enable the Web server to communicate with its application server.

iPlanet calls this Web server plug-in the *Web connector*. (Each vendor has a different name for this plug-in. BEA, for example, calls its plug-in a *proxy plug-in*.) The iPlanet Web connector, available in versions for Microsoft Internet Information Server (IIS), Apache HTTP Server, and iPlanet Web Server, examines each HTTP request that the Web server receives. If the Web connector determines (by examining the URL) that the request is for a JSP or servlet on the application server, it retrieves the results from the application server and returns them to the Web server. The Web server then returns the results to the end user's browser, just as it would if the results were from a file on the Web server itself. The iPlanet Web connector also performs load balancing, failover, and many other functions in retrieving results from the application server.

EJB containers

Just as a Web container is an application server that processes requests for Web components such as JSPs and servlets, the *EJB container* is an application server that processes requests for Enterprise JavaBean (EJB) components.

iPlanet Application Server is an EJB container as well as a Web container. (This setup is relatively common. Many EJB containers can also function as Web containers.) Using an application server that includes both a Web container and EJB container offers many advantages. The most compelling is that a combined Web and EJB container can optimize communication between Web components and EJB components, thereby dramatically improving the performance of EJB calls.

I discuss Enterprise JavaBeans in depth in Chapter 7. You have three major types of EJBs: entity beans, stateful session beans, and stateless session beans. iPlanet Application Server supports all three types, as the J2EE specification requires. iPlanet Application Server currently supports version 1.1 of the EJB specification.

Naming services

One of the services that an application server must provide is a *JNDI (Java Naming and Directory Interface) name service*. Naming services enable you to forge a loose coupling between application components.

As an example of this loose coupling, consider a JDBC datasource pointing to a relational database (RDBMS). To use the JDBC datasource, the developer registers the datasource with the naming service, creating a link between a datasource name and the actual details of the datasource, such as the JDBC driver class, JDBC driver type, and connection details. This way, the JNDI API can shield the application from all the implementation data about the datasource. And if, at a later time, you want to change the implementation information (to change from test to production or from type 4 to type 2 drivers), the application doesn't require any changes. (See Chapter 7 for information about the different types of JDBC drivers.) You just register the new datasource information under the same name, overwriting the old values.

Notice that the application server is necessary to provide naming services, but the implementation of those services isn't specified. iPlanet Application Server doesn't provide a separate JNDI server process. The Web container provides the JNDI naming services directly by using a bundled version of iPlanet Directory Server as the repository for the JNDI information. This repository is transparent to the application developer, because a developer codes only to the standardized JNDI API. But behind the scenes, the iPlanet Directory Server stores the information about components that you name in JNDI (EJBs, JDBC datasources, JMS resources, and any information that you create as part of deployment descriptors), and you can browse it by using the directory-server tools or any other LDAP browser.

The iAS registry

In addition to the JNDI information, the bundled iPlanet Directory Server also holds a large portion of the configuration information for iAS. The remaining configuration information you store locally, in the Windows Registry on the Windows platform or in the `reg.dat` flat file on Unix platforms. These two repositories of configuration information are collectively known as the *iAS registry*. (I discuss the registry in detail in Chapter 13.)

Executing the `kregedit` command enables you to browse the registry information for that iAS instance. The `kregedit` application automatically combines the information from the directory server and the local information.

Application packaging

J2EE introduces a concept that's new to many programmers: that of *application packaging*. Application packaging is the process by which all the various components combine with a series of configuration files known as *deployment descriptors* into a single file in preparation for deployment. (I discuss application packaging in depth in Chapter 5.)

Application packaging offers many benefits. Packaging provides a standard mechanism for including configuration information (an XML-based deployment descriptor) and a standard mechanism for accessing that information (JNDI). Packaging also simplifies the deployment process by reducing the number of files necessary for deployment.

Basic Administration

This section provides a crash course in the administrative tools that come with the application server and the bundled iPlanet products. The following examples assume that you're using the bundled iPlanet Web Server, which you installed into `c:\iws` (on Windows) or `/opt/iws` (on Unix). Similarly, I assume that you've installed the application server into `c:\ias` or `/opt/ias`. The hostname of the machine, I assume, is `myserver`.

Starting and stopping the directory server

Because the application server and Web connector rely on the directory server for configuration information, you must start the directory server before you start any of the other products. Similarly, if you're shutting down your system, the directory server should be the last product that you stop. You should never shut down the directory server while any other application-server component is running, as the Web connector and application server rely on the presence of the directory server.

The iAS installer installs the bundled directory server in the application-server directory, using a subdirectory name combining `slapd` and the name of the host. Using the example installation directories in the preceding section, the iAS installer would install the directory server in `/opt/ias/slapd-myserver` (or `c:\ias\slapd-myserver`). That subdirectory includes all the command-line tools for administrating the directory server, including the start and stop scripts, `start-slapd` and `stop-slapd`.

Thus to start the directory server, just enter the following command (adjusting for your installation directory, operating system, and server name):

```
/opt/ias/slapd-myserver/start-slapd
```

The directory server runs as a single process by the name of `ns-slapd`. You must typically execute the start script as `root` on Unix systems because the default LDAP port is a privileged port. The start script automatically switches the process to the correct owner after starting the process.

Starting and stopping iPlanet Application Server

iAS consists of several processes, each with a specific function. The Kiva Administrative Server (KAS) process handles server administration requests from the command line and GUI tools and also acts as a watchdog to restart failed processes. The Kiva Executive Server (KXS) process handles load balancing and clustering functionality. (See Chapter 10 for the details of iAS's load balancing and clustering.) The Kiva Java Server (KJS) processes act as Web and EJB containers. One specialized type of KJS process, known as a CORBA Executive Server (CXS) bridge, handles RMI/IIOP requests. And finally, the Kiva C++ Server (KCS) processes (if any) handle legacy C++ applications.

The iAS start script (`KIVAes.sh`) starts the KAS process, which, in turn, starts all the other processes. Unlike directory and Web servers, the application server doesn't typically run on privileged ports. You don't need, therefore, to execute the iAS start script as a `root`. In fact, you want to make sure that you *don't* execute the iAS start script as `root`, because the application server runs as the user who executes the start script. (See the following Tip for details.)

Why do you want to make sure that you don't run the application server start and stop scripts (either `KIVAes.sh` or `iascontrol`) as `root`? Starting the server as `root` results in the iAS processes running as `root`. Running the processes as `root` invariably results in `root` owning some files. You may create a new log file with `root` ownership, for example, or you may newly compile a JSP page into `.class` and `.java` files that `root` owns. This situation means not only that the application server is running as the incorrect (overly privileged) user, but also that, if you restart the application server as the correct user, the application server can no longer update these files that have had their ownership inadvertently changed.

If you accidentally start iAS as `root`, therefore, you need to check for any files in the iAS subdirectory that accidentally changed their ownership. Execute the command `find . -user root -print` in the `root` iAS directory to determine whether any files' ownership changed. Change the ownership back to the iAS user, if necessary. If the iAS user is `ias` and the iAS group is `iplanet`, the command `chown -R ias:iplanet /opt/ias` should resolve any ownership problems.

The iAS start/stop script `iascontrol` resides in the iAS binary directory, which is `/opt/ias/ias/bin` (with the installation directory assumptions that I make earlier). `iascontrol` has several functions. Executing `iascontrol` without any arguments gives a detailed list of its uses. Several examples are shown in the following list:

◆ `iascontrol start`: Starts the local copy of iAS.

◆ `iascontrol stop`: Gracefully stops the local copy of iAS, leaving the KAS running so that the server can respond to administration commands.

◆ `iascontrol kill`: Forcefully stops the local copy of iAS, including the KAS. After running this command, you need to use `KIVAes.sh` to start the iAS instance again.

◆ `iascontrol start -host myserver -port 10817 -user admin -password password`: Starts a remote copy of iAS running on the host `myserver`. This command works only if the KAS process is already running on `myserver`.

◆ `iascontrol start -instance iAS1`: Starts a remote copy of iAS, based on the profile `iAS1` that you store in the local `ksvradmin` administration tool. In using the `ksvradmin` tool, you can register iAS instances, including host, port, username, and password. By using the `-instance` flag in `iascontrol`, you can utilize that information from the `iascontrol` command line.

◆ `iascontrol start -host myserver -port 10817 -user admin -password password`: Remotely stops the `myserver` iAS instance.

So, to start your iAS instance, issue the following command:

```
/opt/ias/ias/bin/iascontrol start
```

To stop the instance completely, issue the following commands:

```
/opt/ias/ias/bin/iascontrol stop
/opt/ias/ias/bin/iascontrol kill
```

The `stop` command gracefully stops the application server, enabling requests to finish processing. After waiting a few seconds to enable those requests to finish, you execute the second `kill` command, which stops the remaining KAS process.

Starting and stopping the Web server

The Web-server instance's subdirectory is under the Web server's `root` directory, with the default name `https-myserver.domain.com`. You can find the Web server's start and stop scripts (named simply `start` and `stop`) in this directory. As does the directory server, the Web server typically runs by default on a privileged port (port 80), and thus you need to start it as `root`.

   To start the Web server, execute the following command as `root` (adjusting for installation directory, operating system, and hostname):

```
/opt/iws/https-myserver.domain.com/start
```

The Web server has a multiprocess architecture that uses at least three processes: a `uxwdog` watchdog process, a `ns-httpd` master process running as `root`, and a `ns-httpd` worker process running as the nonprivileged user.

Starting and stopping miscellaneous processes

The directory server and Web server also have administrative-server processes that you can use to manage them remotely. These administrative processes aren't necessary for the operation of the application server, and you often turn them off on production machines.

The following commands start the administrative processes for the Web and directory servers, respectively:

```
/opt/iws/https-admserv/start
/opt/ias/start-admin
```

To turn the administrative servers off, use the following commands:

```
/opt/iws/https-admserv/stop
/opt/ias/stop-admin
```

I don't mention these administrative servers elsewhere in this book. The KAS process is the only administrative process that I discuss any further, and ksvradmin is the only administration tool that I discuss at length.

Deploying an application via the command line

You use the iasdeploy command (which you find in the iAS bin directory /opt/ias/ias/bin) for command-line deployment. As does the iascontrol command, iasdeploy has many suboptions. I discuss deployment and iasdeploy in more depth in Chapters 5 and 9.

You must understand application packaging and deployment in more detail to understand the nuances of the iasdeploy suboptions, but the basic command to deploy an application is as follows:

```
/opt/ias/ias/bin/iasdeploy deployapp myapplication.ear
```

Similarly, the command to remove an application from an iAS instance is as follows:

```
/opt/ias/ias/bin/iasdeploy removeapp myapplication.ear
```

Command-line deployment is, by far, the most common method for deploying applications. You can deploy applications either locally or remotely (by specifying host, port, username, and password).

iasdeploy can sometimes experience difficulty with large (multi-megabyte) EAR files, especially remotely. These large EAR files can exceed a timeout value between the iasdeploy tool and the KAS server. If you encounter this problem, use the deprecated j2eeappreg tool instead of iasdeploy. j2eeappreg, which can operate only locally and, thereby, bypasses the KAS process and the associated timeout.

Deploying an application via GUI

iPlanet Application Server provides a GUI tool to assist in application packaging and deployment. The GUI tool is a Java Swing-based application that you can start with the command `/opt/ias/ias/bin/deploytool`. I discuss this tool in more depth in Chapter 5.

Although command-line deployment is more common for production deployments, the GUI deployment tools that I cover in Chapters 5 and 9 can prove useful as you're learning application packaging and also for use in "quick-and-dirty" deployments.

Summary

Enterprise Java programming is rife with new concepts, new abbreviation, and conflicting vendor terminology. In this chapter, I review the basic J2EE concepts of Web containers, EJB containers, and JNDI. I also clarify iPlanet's vendor-specific terminology and take you on a whirlwind tour of the iPlanet Application Server administrative tools and the tools of the bundled iPlanet products.

Please consult the following sources for more information on the topics that you read about in this chapter:

◆ J2EE terminology and concepts: `http://java.sun.com/j2ee/`

◆ Documentation for all iPlanet products: `http://docs.iplanet.com/`

◆ Application server administration: `http://docs.iplanet.com/docs/manuals/ias/65/admin/contents.htm`

Chapter 2

Installing and Configuring iPlanet Application Server

IN THIS CHAPTER

- ◆ Describing the different types of installs and when to use each one
- ◆ Planning a typical iAS development environment
- ◆ Describing the interactions between the different iAS and related components
- ◆ Performing a typical installation on Unix or Windows NT/2000
- ◆ Configuring common settings in the application server after the installation

IN THIS CHAPTER, you explore the various options and installation methods available when installing iPlanet Application Server (iAS).

Installation Types

The application server environment is very robust and configurable. To meet the needs of most users, iPlanet created five different installation tracks. The five installation types are as follows:

- ◆ Ezsetup
- ◆ Express
- ◆ Typical
- ◆ Custom
- ◆ Silent

Installation methods range from overriding minimal information to overriding just about everything with the installation. The following sections look at each installation type in detail.

Ezsetup

The easiest setup to use is the *Ezsetup* type. With this installation type, most of the settings are defaulted for you. If you simply want to get an environment up and running to use as a prototype or a proof-of-concept environment, this installation type is the one to use. If you do use this installation method, you must make sure that your system meets all the prerequisites before you perform the installation. This installation type asks little of you and assumes that you don't want much in return — it usually neglects to inform you of errors it runs into along the way and continues as if everything is great. The executable for this setup process is named ezSetup on Unix and ezsetup.exe on Windows. The information that the Ezsetup requests is as follows:

- Installation directory
- License key
- Web server instance path (Unix only)

In this type of install, all user IDs and passwords default as follows:

- Configuration Server Administrator — User ID: admin, Password: admin
- Directory Manager — User ID: Directory Manager, Password: DManager
- iPlanet Administration Server — User ID: admin, Password: admin

Reference the iPlanet Application Server Installation Guide for the default port numbers.

In using Ezsetup, make sure that the system meets all the prerequisites (patches, configuration, and so on). The Ezsetup install conveniently neglects to inform you if it runs into problems while attempting to complete the installation. A common problem that it ignores is an incorrect configuration of the install machine's domain name — or no configuration at all. The installation looks as if it completes successfully, but in reality, you just waste about ten minutes. Check the <ias_install_dir>/setup/setup.log file to find errors that occur during the installation.

The remaining installation types share a common installation program. On Unix, it's setup, and on Windows, it's setup.exe.

Express

The next type of installation is an *Express* install. This installation type asks for a minimal amount of input to perform a valid installation while it defaults the rest of the parameters. This installation type enables you to choose the following:

◆ Installation directory

◆ Components to install

◆ Configuration Directory server administrator information

◆ Directory Manager DN/password (if external Configuration Directory asks for host and port)

◆ Web-connector install information such as Web-server type and instance information

◆ iPlanet Application Server administration server authentication information

◆ Internationalization options

◆ License key

Typical

The next type of installation is simply known as *Typical.* It enables you to override many default settings. This installation type enables you to override the following settings:

◆ Installation directory

◆ Components to install

◆ Whether to use internal or external configuration directory (if external, asks for connect parameters)

◆ Whether to use internal or external user directory (if external, asks for connect parameters)

◆ General Directory server settings such as server identifier, server port, and suffix information

◆ Configuration Directory server administrator ID and password (if installing the directory server)

◆ Administration domain for the directory server

◆ Directory manager settings – DN and password

◆ Administration server port

◆ Web-connector install information, such as Web-server type and instance information

◆ iPlanet Application Server administration server authentication information

◆ Internationalization options

◆ License key

Custom

The next type of installation is *Custom*, which enables you to override all the configuration settings (ports for all server processes) and enables you to configure databases, transactions, and resource managers. The installation enables you to supply/override the following settings:

◆ Installation directory

◆ Components to install

◆ Whether to use internal or external configuration directory (if external, asks for connect parameters)

◆ Whether to use internal or external user directory (if external, asks for connect parameters)

◆ General Directory server settings such as server identifier, server port, and suffix information

◆ Configuration Directory server administrator ID and password (if installing the directory server)

◆ Administration domain for the directory server

◆ Directory manager settings – DN and password

◆ Whether to populate directory with sample organization structure and populate database with a sample database

◆ Disable schema checking

◆ Specify bind address for administration server

◆ Administration server port

◆ Global configuration name

◆ Web-connector install information, such as Web-server type and instance information

◆ Number of Java and C++ servers

- ◆ Administration port (KAS), executive port (KXS), ports or Java servers (KJS), ports for C++ servers (KCS)

- ◆ iPlanet Application Server administration server authentication information

- ◆ Database client selection preference order

- ◆ Transaction manager – Global transaction on/off

  - ■ Transaction manager – Mirror directory root

  - ■ Transaction manger – Log volume for engines 1 thru N (using raw partition and information)

  - ■ Third-party JDBC support – whether to use third-party and how many to configure

- ◆ Third-party JDBC driver settings – Driver identifier, driver class name, driver class path, third-party native driver directory (screen for each that you specify in the previous screen)

- ◆ Resource manager – whether to configure resource managers and, if so, how many

  - ■ Resource manager name – Name, database type, datasource, username, password, RM recovery guide and open string, enable/disable (screen for each that you specify in the previous screen)

- ◆ Internationalization options

- ◆ Cluster configuration – Use DSYNC yes/no and cluster name

  - ■ Cluster options – Type of server Sync Server/Sync Local and number of servers to configure

  - ■ IP address, executive server port, and priority (screen for each of the number of sync servers in the previous screen)

- ◆ License key

Silent

The last of the installation methods is the *Silent* installation. Use this installation if you need to perform multiple installations. To complete this type of installation, you run the first installation as one of the Express, Typical, or Custom installation types, except that you pass a -k to the setup process. After the initial installation completes, you have file(s) that you need to copy and modify for each of the following installations. The files are install.inf (located in the <installDir>/setup directory) and, on Unix only, userinput.log (located in the <installDir>/ias directory).

To complete the installation on the other machines, you need to modify some of the values in the files (such as host name, IP address, and so on), copy them to the target installation machine, and run `setup -s -f <full_path_to_the_install. inf>`. For more information on performing Silent installs, refer to the iPlanet Application Server Installation Guide.

 On Unix systems, put the modified `userinput.log` and `install.inf` files in the `/tmp` directory, which is where the installation program looks for the `userinput.log` file.

Now that you've seen the different types of installations available, you can start planning your installation. For development machines where you intend to install everything on a single box, the Ezsetup or the Express installation methods are the easiest to use.

Plan the Install

Planning an iPlanet Application Server environment is probably the most important aspect of building the environment. You must consider many aspects to attain the best possible operating environment. A few points to consider in planning your environment are as follows:

◆ Type of environment – development, test, or production

◆ Reliability of the environment (uptime)

◆ Network topology

◆ Network hardware devices – content switches, local directors, firewalls, and so on

◆ Security – protocols and guidelines

◆ Failover strategy – redundant systems and hardware that provide for high availability

◆ Application requirements

◆ Growth potential of the environment

Many of the preceding topics can fill entire books by themselves, and because the audience of this book consists mainly of developers, I constrain the information here to planning a development environment and the issues that one may face with such an environment.

The first thing to consider is the type of application to develop. If the application that you intend to develop must share state and session information with processes or application components somewhere along the development cycle, you must have a way to test it in a clustered environment – which usually means that you have an integration environment that minimally consists of a simple cluster of two iAS instances sharing DSync information. In such a case, I recommend that each server have two or more KJS servers. The numberone problem that developers face while developing distributed applications is the capability to test them in a distributed environment. This problem usually stems from a lack of an integration-development environment. Because each developer has his own workstation to use in developing, testing in a clustered environment is usually an afterthought – unfortunately, one that comes after the application runs into problems in the test or production environment.

The typical reaction to problems at this stage is that the application servers in the test environment aren't configured correctly. In reality, the application isn't architected correctly to work in a distributed environment. A common problem that arises is that objects that you store in the session aren't serializable. This type of problem usually doesn't cause an issue until two or more Java servers are running (KJS).

For these purposes, I show you how to configure an environment for developers that can act as a standalone server and then show you how you can easily convert this environment to a clustered environment for the final stage of development testing.

The most common development environment is a standalone machine (that is, you install all components on a single machine). I intend to show you how to install and configure such an environment to satisfy all development and integration requirements. You accomplish this task by making modifications to the base configuration to convert the environment to meet the specific need.

Perform the Installation

In this section, I cover the preinstallation tasks. I first review the hardware and software prerequisites for installing the application server. Then I move on to performing the installation. And to wrap up, I show you how to configure the installed software to meet the needs of a developer.

Prepare for the installation

The first step in the installation process is to verify that you've met all prerequisites. The following sections describe the prerequisites for the application-server installation as of this writing. For a list of the most current requirements and any special instructions, refer to the iPlanet Application Server Installation Guide.

SYSTEM REQUIREMENTS

Following are the system requirements for the iPlanet Application Server installation, as of this writing:

◆ For Windows:

- Microsoft Windows NT 4.0 with SP6a, Windows 2000 Professional SP2, Windows 2000 Server SP2, or Windows 2000 Advanced Server SP2

- 400MB free hard-disk space (NTFS)

- 512MB RAM

- One of the following Web servers: iPlanet Web Server, Enterprise Edition 6.0, SP1, SP2, or 6.0.1; iPlanet Web Server Enterprise Edition 4.1, SP7, or later (not supported on Windows 2000); Microsoft Internet Information Server 4.0 or 5.0; Apache Web Server 1.3.19

◆ For Solaris:

- Sun Sparc running Solaris 2.6 or Solaris 2.8

- 400MB free hard-disk space

- 512MB RAM

- One of the following Web servers: iPlanet Web server 6.0, SP1, SP2, or 6.0.1; iPlanet Web Server, Enterprise Edition 4.1, SP7 or later; Apache Web Server 1.3.19

- The patches that I list in Table 2-1

TABLE 2-1   Required Solaris Patches

JDK 1.3.1_02 Patches on Solaris 2.6

105181-29 Kernel update patch

105210-38 libaio, libc and watchmalloc patch

105284-45 Motif 1.2.7: Runtime library patch

105568-23 Libthread patch

105591-11 C++ shared library patch

105633-59 OpenWindows 3.6: Xsun patch

105669-10 libDtSvc Patch

106040-17 X Input and Output Method patch

106125-11 patch for patchadd and patchrm

106409-01 Fixes the Traditional Chinese TrueType fonts

106841-01 Openwin patch

106842-09 Euro support

106429-02 Kernel/drv/mm patch

107733-09 Linker patch

108091-03 ssJDK1.2.1_03 fails with fatal error in ISO8859-01 Locales

JDK 1.3.1_02 patches on Solaris 8

108652-37 X11 6.4.1 patch

108921-13 CDE 1.4 patch

108940-32 Motif patch

Required Solaris 8 OS patches

108528-12 Kernel update patch

108434-04 (32-bit)/ 108435-04 (64-bit) libC patch

108827-12 libthread.so.1 patch

PREREQUISITES FOR INSTALLATION

Following are the general prerequisites for installing iPlanet Application Server:

- ◆ For all platforms:
  - Have administrative privileges
  - Machine has a static IP
  - Have the installation key
  - Correctly configure the domain name
- ◆ For Windows:
  - Correctly set primary DNS suffix
  - Perform special directory server setup if using a remote user or configuration directory (refer to the iPlanet Application Server Installation Guide for details)

◆ For Solaris:

- Unset the `LD_LIBRARY_PATH` in the installation shell

- Create a Unix user and group for the iPlanet Application Server

- Install directory server on a local physical drive (not network mounted)

- For Web-connector installs, must make the user or group the same as the Web server's

Windows NT/2000 installation

This section covers the steps necessary to install iAS on Microsoft Windows NT/2000. Before beginning the actual installation, I discuss how to check some of the prerequisites.

VERIFY THE DOMAIN

To satisfy the domain requirement, you need to verify that the machine's primary domain is set up correctly. The following steps pertain to a Windows 2000 environment:

1. Right-click My Computer icon on the desktop → then select the properties from the pop-up menu .

2. Select the Network Identification tab → Properties, as shown in Figure 2-1.

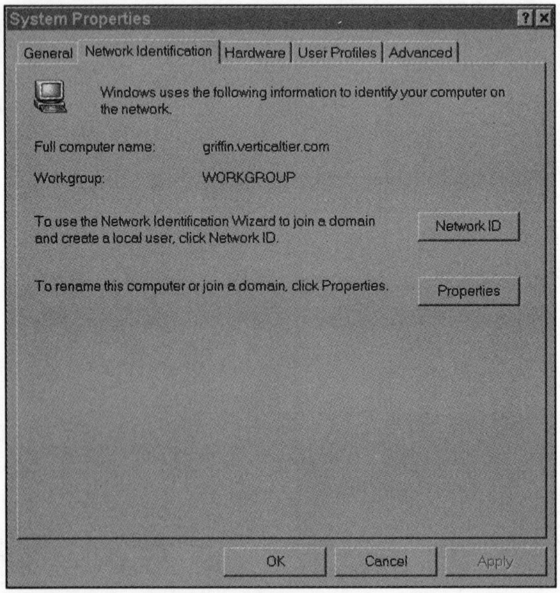

Figure 2-1: Network Identification tab

3. On the Identification Changes window that appears, look at the text below the Computer name: text box. If the Full computer name contains only `Computer` name, your domain isn't set. Click the More button. This will open up a new dialog box to allow you to enter your DNS suffix (see Figure 2-2).

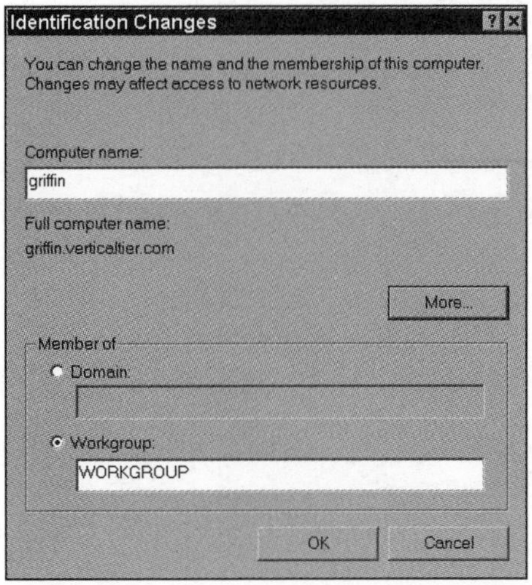

Identification Changes

You can change the name and the membership of this computer. Changes may affect access to network resources.

Computer name:
griffin

Full computer name:
griffin.verticaltier.com

More...

Member of

○ Domain:

⦿ Workgroup:
WORKGROUP

OK   Cancel

Figure 2-2: Identification Changes window

4. On the DNS Suffix and NETBIOS Computer Name dialog box, enter the name of your domain. Make sure that the Change Primary DNS Suffix When Domain Membership Changes check box contains a check mark; if not, click to add it and select the OK button (see Figure 2-3).

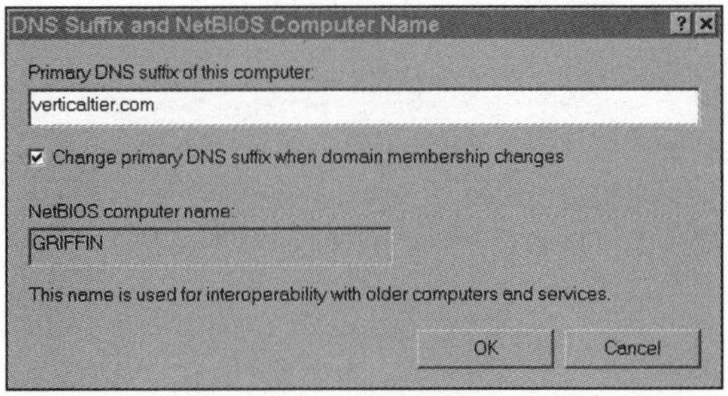

DNS Suffix and NetBIOS Computer Name

Primary DNS suffix of this computer:
verticaltier.com

☑ Change primary DNS suffix when domain membership changes

NetBIOS computer name:
GRIFFIN

This name is used for interoperability with older computers and services.

OK   Cancel

Figure 2-3: DNS Suffix and NETBIOS Computer Name window

5. Select the OK button in the Identification Changes dialog box.

6. Reboot your computer for these changes to take effect. (Notice in Figure 2-4 that the Reboot icon is at the bottom of the dialog box.)

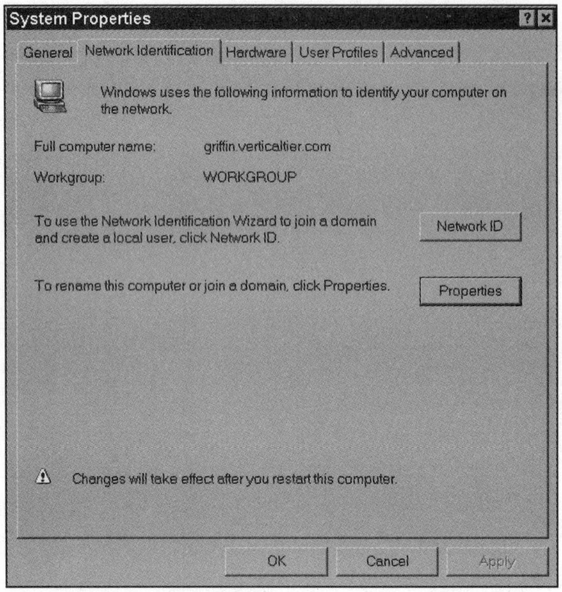

System Properties

General | Network Identification | Hardware | User Profiles | Advanced

Windows uses the following information to identify your computer on the network.

Full computer name: griffin.verticaltier.com

Workgroup: WORKGROUP

To use the Network Identification Wizard to join a domain and create a local user, click Network ID.   [Network ID]

To rename this computer or join a domain, click Properties.   [Properties]

⚠ Changes will take effect after you restart this computer.

[OK]   [Cancel]   [Apply]

Figure 2–4: The Reboot icon

OBTAIN A STATIC IP ADDRESS

For the application server to work correctly, the installation machine must have a static IP address. This requirement is because of how iAS stores and uses configuration information. At certain times, keeping the same IP address just isn't feasible. A situation where this can happen is if you're installing the application server on a laptop. If the laptop connects to different networks, the IP address probably isn't the same for each one, and if the laptop isn't connected to a network at all, the network interface is disabled. A way to circumvent this problem is to use a little known feature of Windows NT/2000, the *Loopback adapter*. The Loopback adapter is essentially a virtual network card that only the local machine can see and use. You normally use loopbacks for testing purposes if you need to test TCP/IP sockets or network programs.

I provide brief instructions on how to install and configure the Loopback adapter here. For detailed information on installing the Loopback adapter, refer to the Microsoft Knowledge Base Article Number Q236869 at http://support/microsoft.com.

You can configure the Loopback adapter two ways. The first way is to give the Loopback adapter its own unique IP address. The second, which I use here, is to assign the same IP as your most commonly used connection (call it the default network) and disable the Loopback adapter after you connect to your default network. You use this second method because you want the capability to enable the server to participate in a cluster in case you need to test your application this way inside of a cluster. If you create a separate IP and use the Loopback only for the application server, remote application servers can't communicate with it because it's local to the machine on which you install it.

The following are the steps necessary to add the Loopback adapter:

1. Right-click the My Computer icon and choose → Properties from the pop-up list.

2. Select the Hardware tab on the System Properties box (see Figure 2-5).

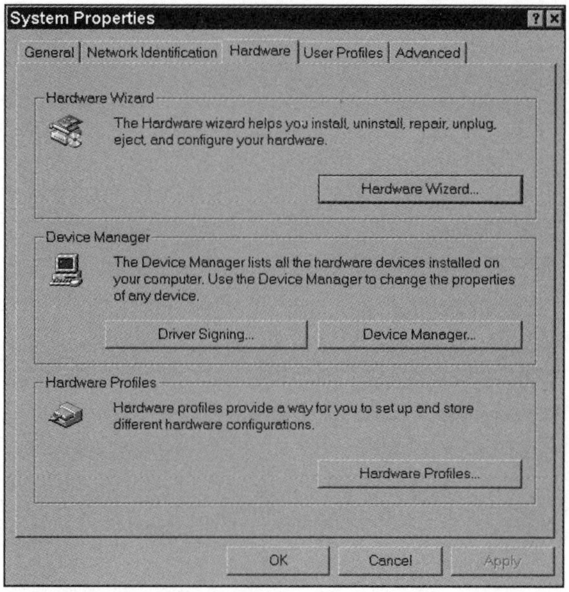

Figure 2–5: Hardware tab

3. Select the Hardware Wizard button.

4. In the new window that appears, click Next (see Figure 2-6).

5. Select the Add/Troubleshoot Device radio button and click the Next button (see Figure 2-7).

Add/Remove Hardware Wizard
Welcome to the Add/Remove Hardware Wizard
This wizard helps you add, remove, unplug, and troubleshoot your hardware.
To continue, click Next.
< Back
Next >
Cancel

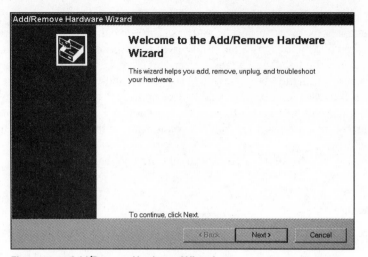

Figure 2-6: Add/Remove Hardware Wizard

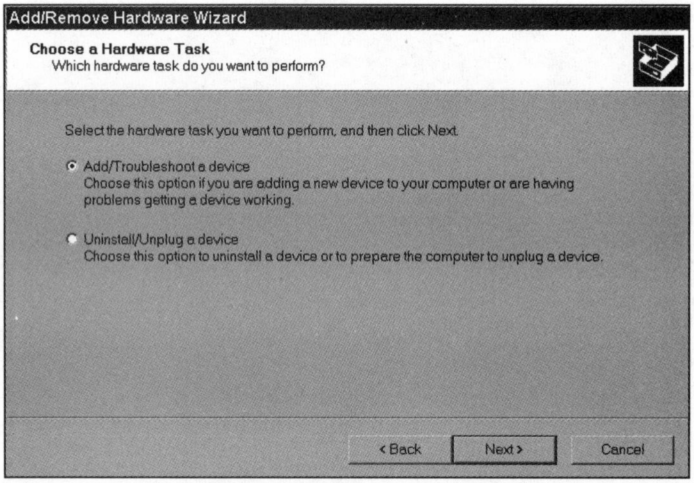
Add/Remove Hardware Wizard
Choose a Hardware Task
Which hardware task do you want to perform?
Select the hardware task you want to perform, and then click Next.
Add/Troubleshoot a device
Choose this option if you are adding a new device to your computer or are having problems getting a device working.
Uninstall/Unplug a device
Choose this option to uninstall a device or to prepare the computer to unplug a device.
< Back
Next >
Cancel

Figure 2-7: The Add/Troubleshoot Device radio button

6. A window appears telling you that it's searching for new hardware; wait for the next window to appear. Select Add a New Device from the list and then click the Next button (see Figure 2-8).
7. Select the "No, I Want to Select the Hardware from a List" radio button and then click the Next button (see Figure 2-9).

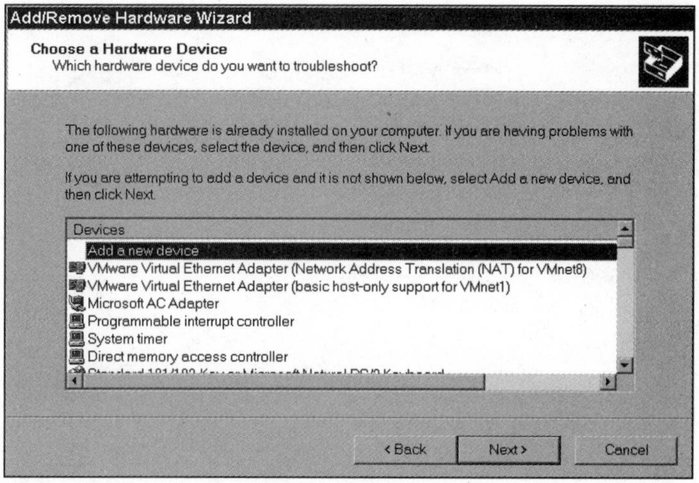

Figure 2-8: Choose a Hardware Device

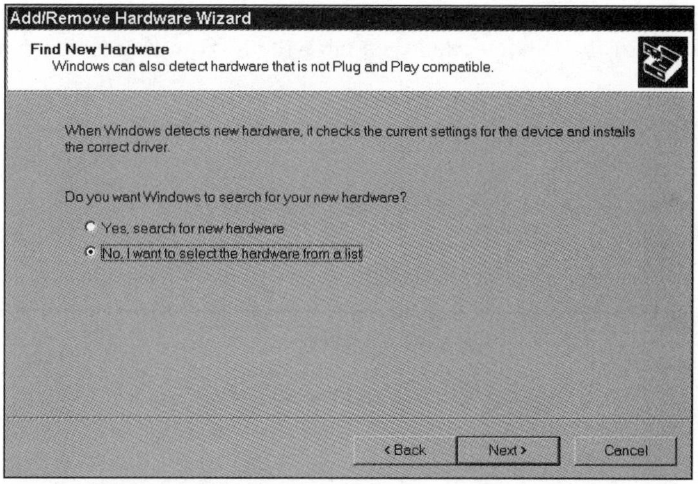

Figure 2-9: Find New Hardware

8. From the Hardware Types list in the new dialog box, select Network Adapters and then click the Next button (see Figure 2-10).

9. Select Microsoft from the Manufacturers list (at the left side of the window that appears).

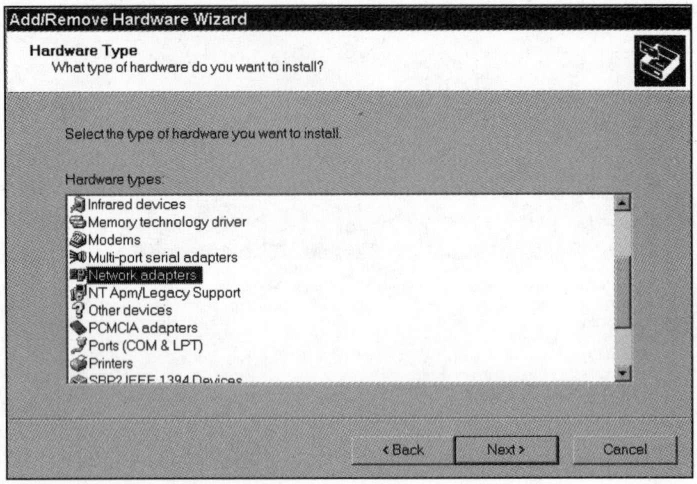

Figure 2-10: Hardware Type

10. Select Microsoft Loopback Adapter from the Network Adapter list (at the right side of the window) and then click the Next button (see Figure 2-11).

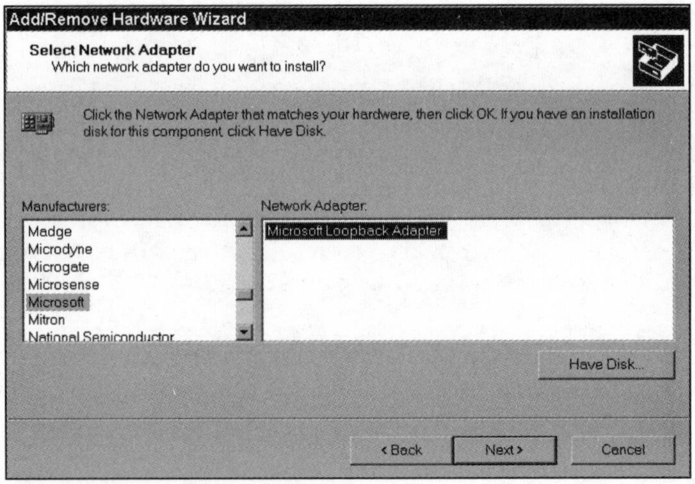

Figure 2-11: Select Network Adapter

11. Click the Next button of the next screen that appears. (I don't know why Microsoft just didn't put the Finish button here.)

12. Click the Finish button (see Figure 2-12).

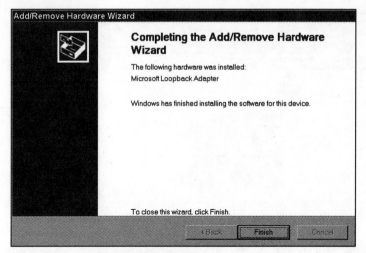

Figure 2-12: Completing the installation

13. Close the System Properties window by clicking on the OK button.

After installing the Loopback adapter, you may want to know how iAS uses it. The next set of steps show how to configure the adapter to give it a static IP. With the Loopback adapter in place, you needn't worry about the IP address changing on the machine or the network services deactivating because it can't find a network connection, as occurs in Windows 2000 if you unplug the network cable.

The following steps show you how to configure the Loopback adapter. This method sets the static IP to the private-network range of IP addresses. (If you need to learn more about private-network address ranges, search for **RFC 1918** in your favorite search engine.) The values that I use in the following example are for informational purposes only, don't use arbitrary numbers in inputting IP addresses. To configure the Loopback adapter, follow these steps:

1. Right-click My Network Places on the desktop and then choose Properties from the pop-up list.

2. In the Network and Dialup Connections window, you should see a Local Area Connection icon. (If you didn't rename your other network connection(s), the name automatically increments.) Right-click the Local Area Connection icon (after ensuring that its Tooltip reads `Microsoft Loopback adapter`), select Rename from the pop-up list, and change the name in the text box to something descriptive, such as **Loopback**. Although this step isn't necessary, it saves confusion later (see Figure 2-13).

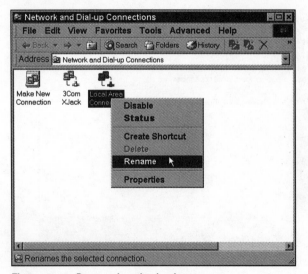

Figure 2-13: Rename Loopback adapter.

3. Right click the Loopback icon and then choose Properties from the pop-up menu.

4. Select Internet Protocol (TCP/IP)from the listbox inside the Loopback Properties dialog box and then click the Properties button.

5. Select Use the Following IP Address radio button.

6. Input a value for the IP address in the text box (using the one that the default network assigns to you, as I describe in the previous section).

7. Subnet Mask should automatically be populated.

8. Input a value in the text box for the Default Gateway.

9. Click OK.

At this point, you may get a warning message reading that the IP address is assigned to another interface and that problems may arise if both are active at the same time. The message box asks whether you want to fix the problem. Click No because you want two adapters with the same IP address. You just need to make sure that both the Loopback and the default network adapters aren't enabled at the same time.

10. Click OK again. (See Figure 2-14 for some values that I use in this example.)

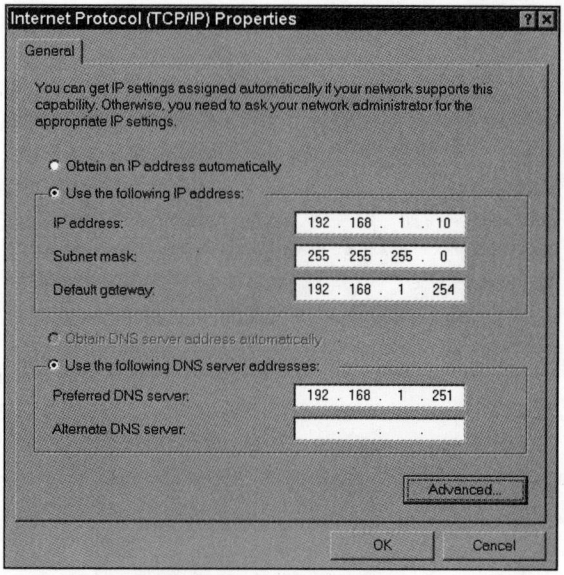

Figure 2-14: TCP/IP Properties

Now, whenever you connect to your default network, simply disable the Loopback adapter. If the default network is unavailable, simply enable the Loopback adapter, ensuring that the IP address that you used to install the application server is available.

INSTALL IAS ON WINDOWS USING EXPRESS SETUP

In examining the contents on the installation software, you notice two setup programs, the `ezsetup.exe` and `setup.exe`. The `ezsetup.exe` is most appropriate for a test drive of iAS, because it has very minimal custom configuration settings. Use this setup if all you want to do is install iAS and use it right away. I concentrate in the following steps on the setup methods in `setup.exe`:

1. From your installation CD or downloaded software, double-click the `setup.exe` program icon. The Welcome screen appears. (You may want to view the `readme` file at this time for any late breaking updates.) Click the Next button to proceed (see Figure 2-15).

2. On the Licensing screen that appears, click the Yes button (see Figure 2-16).

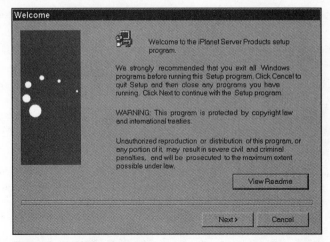

Figure 2-15: Welcome screen

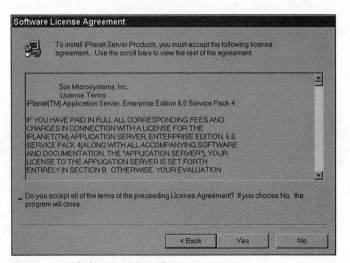

Figure 2-16: Software License Agreement

3. Select Server or Console Installation radio button on the next screen that appears. (You can install the iPlanet Console by itself or with the iAS. Most development installs install the iPlanet Console along with the iPlanet Servers; if you just want to manage other servers from your network, install only the iPlanet Console.) Because you want to install iAS now, select iPlanet Servers (see Figure 2-17).

4. Choose the type of installation to perform. The steps that follow focus on the Typical installation, so select Typical and then click Next (see Figure 2-18).

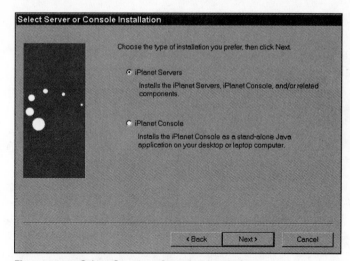

Figure 2-17: Select Server or Console Installation

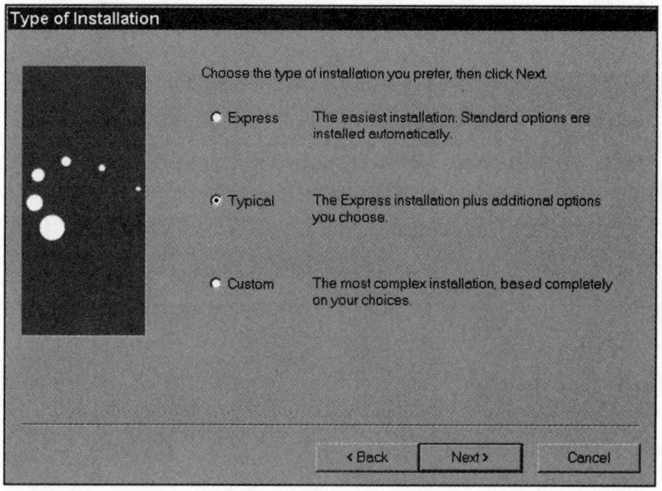

Figure 2-18: Type of Installation

5. On the next screen that appears, choose the directory into which you want to install iAS by either pressing the browse button or accepting the default installation directory. If the directory doesn't exist you see a prompt to confirm the directory creation by pressing the OK button (see Figure 2-19).

6. The next screen asks what components you want to install. Keep the default configuration and click Next to continue (see Figure 2-20).

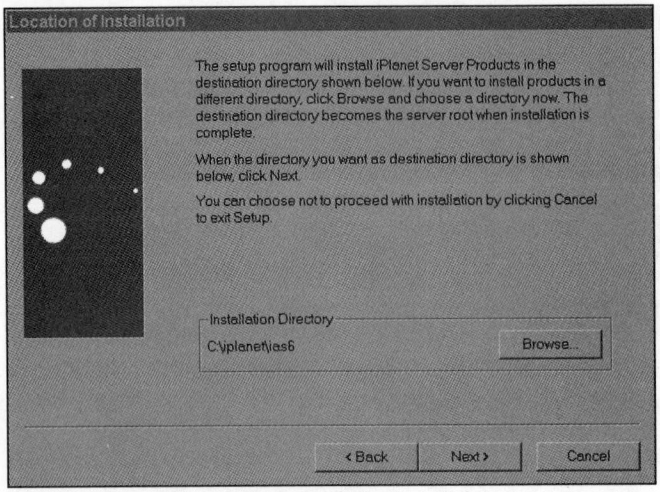

Figure 2-19: Location of Installation

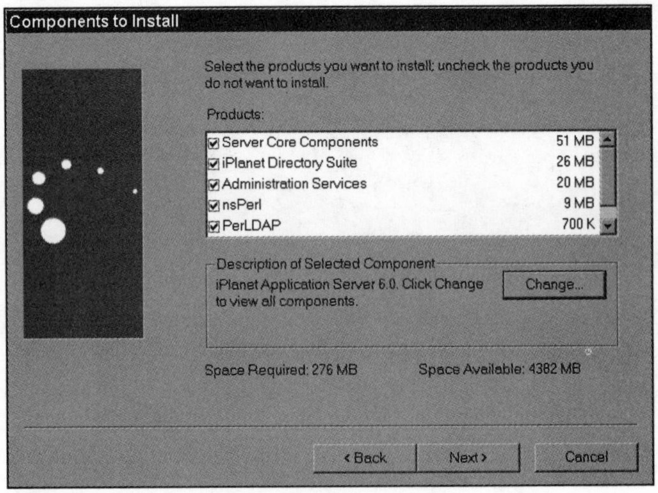

Figure 2-20: Components to Install

7. The next screen that appears is the first of six screens that enable you to configure the directory server. This step sets up where to store the configuration data for this iAS instance. (When you perform an express setup, it is assumed that the iAS will use the new directory server. The directory server setup screens don't appear with an express setup.) Keep the default settings and then click Next to continue (see Figure 2-21).

8. Keep the default settings on the screen that appears now and click Next (see Figure 2-22).

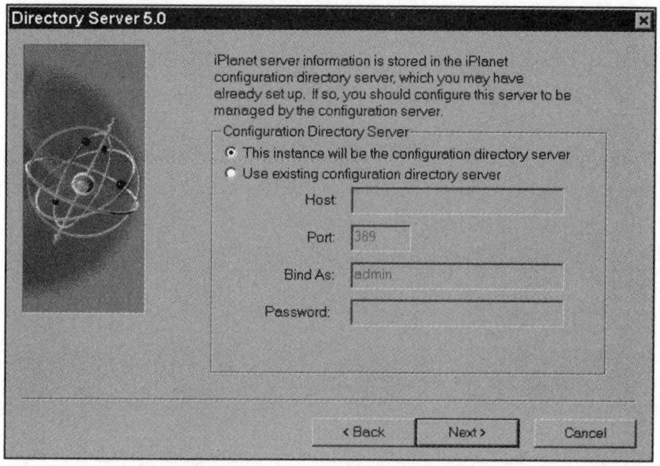

Figure 2-21: Directory Server – Selecting Configuration Directory

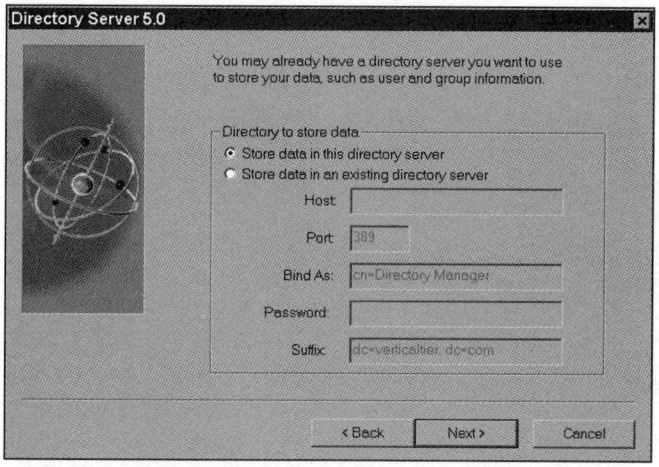

Figure 2-22: Directory Server – Directory to store data

9. This step uses the *hostname.domainname* that you set up per the prerequisites. Verify that this matches your hostname and domain name, if it does not match or is empty do not proceed. (see Figure 2-23).

10. Set the user ID and password for the local-configuration directory server by entering them into the dialog box and click Next to continue (see Figure 2-24).

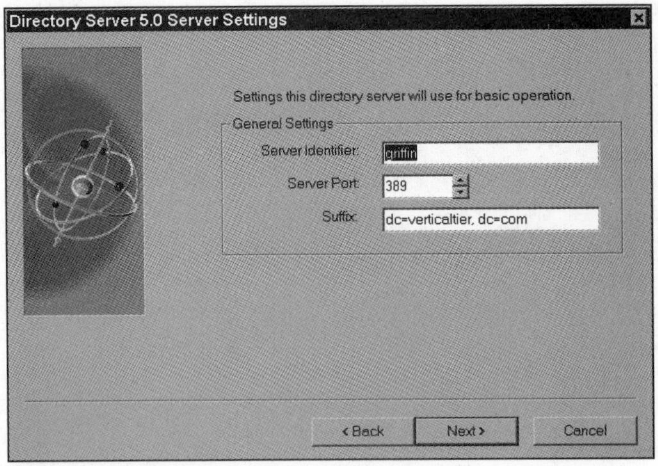

Figure 2-23: Directory Server – Server identifier

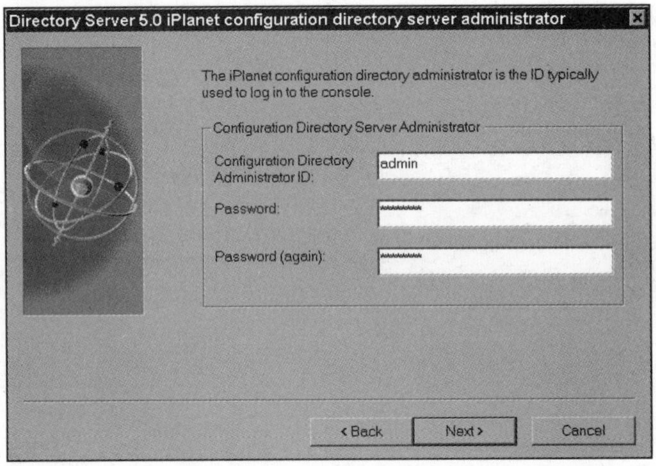

Figure 2-24: Directory Server – Configuring the Administrator

11. Accept the default domain name that appears. If this name doesn't match the domain name that you set up earlier, you didn't set up the domain name correctly, and you may want to exit the installation, as you can't configure it correctly without modification (see Figure 2-25).

12. Set the password for the administrative user for the local configuration-directory server by entering them in the password text boxes (see Figure 2-26).

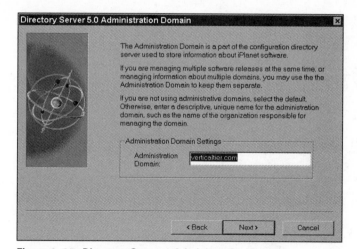

Figure 2-25: Directory Server – Administration Domain

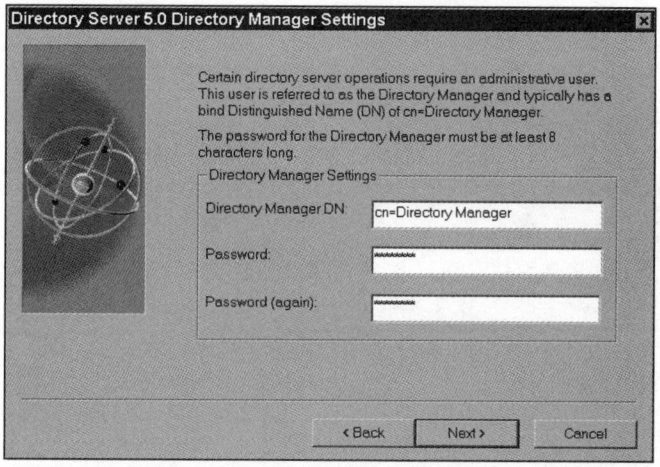

Figure 2-26: Directory Server – Setting the Directory Manager password

13. The administration port is a randomly picked port that isn't in use. Because remembering what port you use during the install may prove difficult, use a value for a port that's not in use (see Figure 2-27).

14. Enter the product key that iPlanet provides you (see Figure 2-28).

You should install a Web server before proceeding with the next step. See your Web server install guide for instructions. If you're doing a Webless install, select the None option.

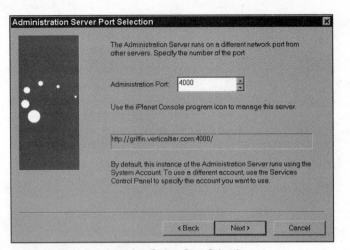

Figure 2-27: Administration Server Port Selection

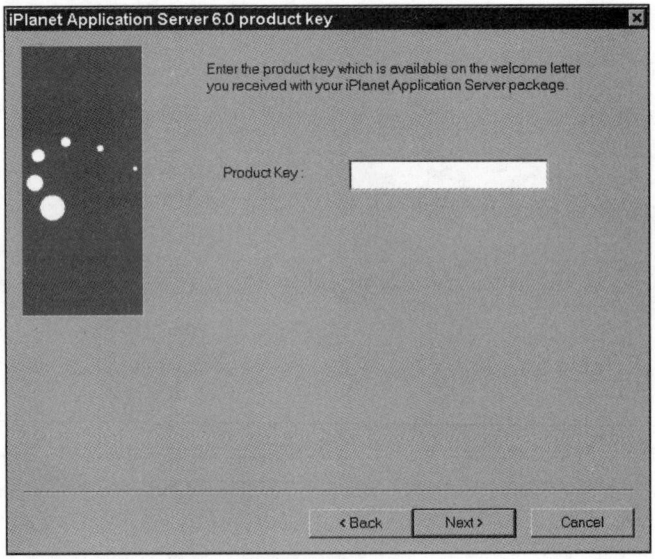

Figure 2-28: Insert Product Key

15. Use the Web server that you installed before the iAS install by selecting it from the radio buttons. Accept the default settings and then click Next (see Figure 2-29).

16. Create a user and password by inserting them in the Username and Password text boxes. Remember the user and password that you use in this step, as you need this information later to further configure iAS by using the iASAT tool (see Figure 2-30).

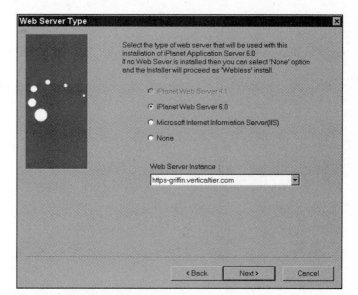

Figure 2-29: Web Server Type

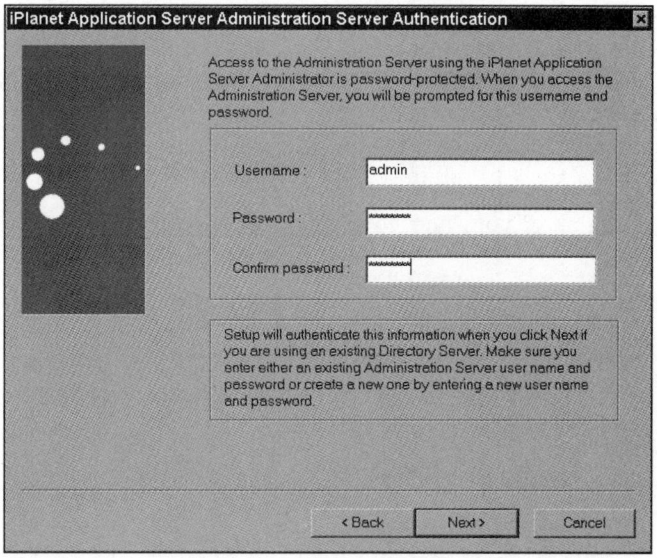

Figure 2-30: iAS Administration Server Authentication

17. You use Internationalization if applications need to support other languages character sets than U.S. English. For most applications, you can set this option to No by selecting the No radio button. Click Next to continue (see Figure 2-31).

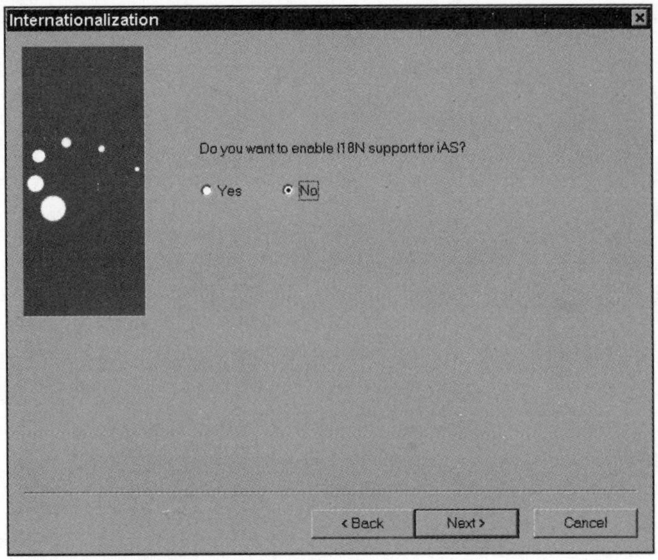

Figure 2-31: Internationalization

18. The Configuration Summary screen that appears next shows you all the settings that you've chosen so far for the install. Highlight and copy all these settings and paste them into a new file; save this file into the base of your iAS install. (This part of the step isn't necessary but can save you a lot of time later if you're trying to figure out ports, usersid(s), and other configuration settings. Click Install to start your installation (see Figure 2-32).

19. Reboot so that all of your new configuration settings are recognized.

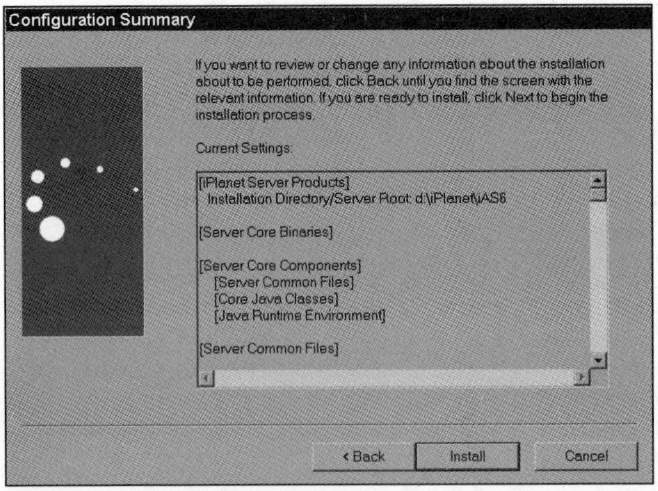

Figure 2-32: Configuration Summary

Solaris installation (custom setup)

This section walks you through a Solaris installation using the custom setup. The custom setup works best on Solaris, because on Solaris, you can have multiple instances of the application server – unlike in Windows, where only a single instance per machine is possible. The capability to have multiple instances per machine enables you to set up a distributed environment using a single machine. I add the following section as a walkthrough of an installation on the Unix platform. Many installation values are specific to the particular environment and you should replace them where necessary.

If you're installing iAS on Solaris, the installer program offers you a multitude of options. You do, therefore, need to engage in some preplanning before the installation. If you're installing iAS for a test drive or light development environment, not much other than satisfying the prerequisites is necessary. For "Web-less" or enterprise installations, you want to consider machine configurations, proxies, firewalls, and DMZ.

Follow these steps to perform the installation on Solaris:

1. Navigate to your iAS installation directory and execute the setup program. The first screen that appears accustoms you to the installation program by teaching you how to navigate the process.

2. Type Yes to agree to the Licensing Agreement so that you can proceed and then press Enter.

3. Type 1 to Select the Components You Would Like to Install prompt to install the iPlanet servers and then press Enter.

4. Type 3 to choose the Custom installation type at the Choose an Installation Type prompt and then press Enter.

5. At the installation directory prompt, type the location where you want to install the application server (for example, /opt/iPlanet/ias6) and then press Enter.

6. At the iPlanet Server Products Components prompt, type All and then press Enter.

7. On the Directory Suite Components screen, type 1,2 to install all the components and then press Enter.

8. On the Administration Services Components screen, type 1,2 to install all the components and then press Enter.

9. On the iPlanet Application Server Suite Components screen, type 1,2,3,4 to install all the components except the PointBase Database server.

TIP If you don't need some of the components (such as the PointBase Database server), omit the number for that component from the list.

10. At the prompt asking for the fully qualified domain name of the computer, type the computer's fully qualified domain name (for example, `blade.icsynergy.com`). (The format is *host.subdomain.domain*, where in the example that I provide, *host*=blade; you have no *subdomain*; and *domain*=icsynergy.com.)

11. At the Choose a Unix User and Group for the Installation prompt, enter the user ID and group that you configured in Prerequisites For Installation section of the Unix installation section or, alternatively, an account and group that you want to use (for example, user ID = appadmin, group = iplanet).

NOTE After you type the user ID, a new line appears on the same screen prompting you for the group.

12. On the Configuration Directory Setup screen, type **No** at the prompt. For the installation example, you're installing the directory server. If an external directory server that you'd rather use is in the environment, type Yes at the prompt instead and then supply the connection information which consists of hostname, port number, user ID, and password.

13. On the User Directory Setup screen, type **No** at the prompt. If an external directory server that you'd rather use is in the environment, type **Yes** at the prompt and supply the connection information, which consists of hostname, port number, user ID, and password.

TIP If your production environment is to have a separated user directory, you're best off configuring the development environment with a separated user directory also.

CAUTION If you're using an external user directory, you must install certain patches. Refer to the iPlanet Application Server Installation Guide for more information.

14. On the Directory Server Setup screen, type the port number that you want the directory server to listen on at the prompt and then press Enter. (For the example installation, use the default LDAP port, 389.)

15. At the Directory Server Identifier prompt, type a unique name for the directory server at the prompt and then press Enter. This name is usually that of the server. (For the example install, use `blade`.)

16. At the Configuration Directory Server Administrator ID prompt, type the user ID that you're using for the configuration directory's administrator at the prompt and then press Enter. (For this example, use `admin`.)

17. At the prompt for the Directory Server Administrator Password, type the password that you chose. (For this example, use `admin001`.)

18. At the prompt `Suffix [dc=icsynergy, dc=com]:`, leave the default, as it should be valid. It consists of the domain of the computer. If it isn't the domain of the computer, the domain isn't configured correctly on the machine. (For these examples, *domain*=`icsynergy.com`, so the chosen suffix is `dc=icsynergy, dc=com`.)

Installations prior to service pack 4 used a 4.*x* directory server, which used a different root scheme. On the 4.*x* directory servers, the root was simply *o*=`icsynergy.com`. On 5.*x* directory servers, the root is separated, as in the preceding step.

19. At the Directory Manager DN prompt, accept the default `cn=Directory Manager`. This user is the equivalent of a root user on Unix; the user is the root user of the directory server.

20. Type the password for the directory manager. (For the example, use `admin001` and repeat it whenever asked.)

21. At the administration domain prompt, type your domain name. (For the example, use `icsynergy.com`.)

22. At the prompt to install sample entries, type **No**.

23. At the prompt to populate your directory instance with data, accept the default. This step creates the default user and group trees in the directory server.

24. At the Disable Schema Checking prompt, accept the default of No. Schema checking makes sure that you're importing valid schema into the directory server.

25. At the Administration Port prompt, enter a port on which the administration server can listen. (For this example, use port number 10555.)

TIP In setting up your environment, you're best off standardizing the port numbers to use for the different elements. Pick these ports in the planning stage for the installation. The default values are randomly generated port numbers.

26. At the Bind IP Address for the Administration Server prompt, type a specific IP address for the administration server to use. (For the example, accept the default.)

27. At the Run Administration Server As prompt, type the account that you want to enable the administration server to run as. (For the example, accept the default of `root`.)

28. At the prompt to Enter the Full Path for the Web Server Instance, type the path to the instance of the Web server. (For the example, iPlanet Web Server is installed at `/opt/iPlanet/iWS/https-blade.icsynergy.com`.)

29. If you're installing the application server with a user ID that's not the same as the owner of the Web server, you're prompted to enable this user ID to access the plug-in libraries that are necessary at runtime. This can cause security problems. Because you're working with a development environment, security constraints are probably a little more relaxed than in a production environment. I recommend, however, that the application-server user and Web-server user belong to the same Unix group. (For the example, to enable the Web server to access the registry and plug-in libraries, type Y at this prompt.)

30. A warning appears regarding the security issue. For the example, acknowledge the warning and continue with the install by typing Y.

31. The next screen enables the installer to override ports for the main servers in the application-server environment. Accept the default ports for the KAS, KXS, and CGI to KXS servers. For the KAS process, the port is 10817; for KXS, the port is 10818; and for the CGI to KXS communication, the default port is 10819.

32. At the prompt for the number of Java servers (KJS) to use, accept the default of 1. This setting creates a single server to handle Java requests.

33. At the prompt for the KJS to KXS communication port, accept the default of 10820.

34. At the prompt for the number of C++ servers (KCS), type 0. Because this application doesn't use C++ components, you don't need the KCS engines.

35. The iPlanet Application Server Administrator Tool (iASAT) requires authentication information to connect to the administration server. Type a user ID and password for this use. (For the example, use user=admin and password=admin001.) Verify the password when asked to do so.)

36. At the prompt asking you to configure data base drivers, type 3. I specify the instructions on how to do this later in the Configure database drivers section. Typically, configuring the database drivers after the install is advisable. Setting up database drivers usually involves a little trial and error and is better suited for when a sample application is available to test the connectivity.

I cover how to configure database drivers in the section "Configure database drivers," later in this chapter.

37. At the prompt for a Full Path for the MirrorDirectoryRoot for the Transaction Manager, accept the default. Because this example install isn't using global transactions, you don't need to configure the transaction-manager properties as you would if you were using global transactions.

In enabling global transactions, you have special considerations for MirrorDirectoryRoot and LogVolumes. You should locate log volumes on different hard drives from the one on which you do the iAS installation. You should also locate the MirrorDirectoryRoot on a different hard drive than those for the iAS installation and the LogVolumes and, if possible, on a separate controller from that of the LogVolumes.

38. At the prompt to configure a resource manager, select n. Resource managers work in conjunction with the transaction manager to facilitate global transactions.

39. At the Enable Internationalization Support prompt, answer N.

40. At the prompt to Automatically Start the Application Server at System Startup, type N. Because you're configuring a development environment, the developer must start the application server.

41. Acknowledge the message that all the information is gathered, and installation begins by pressing Enter.

42. Because you selected a different user name for installing the application server than the one you're installing with, you get a prompt to change the ownership and group to the specified user name and group. Type Y to enable the ownership change during the install.

The installation starts and displays its status as it progresses.

Configure the Environment

In this section I show how to remove one of the default engines that is automatically configured during installation.

Configure the engines (All platforms)

To complete the environment setup, you need to configure the engines. You can do so by adding necessary engines or by deleting unnecessary engines. Unless the application under development uses C++ Applogics (which are legacy application components that iAS supports for backward compatibility), you should remove the KCS engine. If the application doesn't use a rich client, you don't need the CXS process, so you can safely remove it. The following steps remove unneeded engines (assuming, of course, that the application server is running):

1. Start the iASAT tool. (On Unix, run `ksvradmin`; on Windows, choose Start → Run → ksvradmin.)

2. After the iASAT tool starts, click the plus sign next to iAS1 and then click the KCS icon (see Figure 2-33). (*Note:* The iASAT tool should default to logged-in status; if not, log in by using the userid and password that you used during setup; this install used user = `admin` and password = `admin001`.)

3. From the menu bar of the iASAT, choose Edit ⇨ Delete. You see a prompt asking you to verify that you want to delete this process; select Yes from the new dialog window (see Figure 2-34). If you select Yes, the process stops and then removes the KCS engine from the list of engines for the server.

4. If you need rich client support, ignore this step. Otherwise, select the CXS engine icon. From the menu bar, choose Edit ⇨ Delete and then confirm the deletion of the process. If you select Yes, the process stops and then removes from the list of engines for the server.

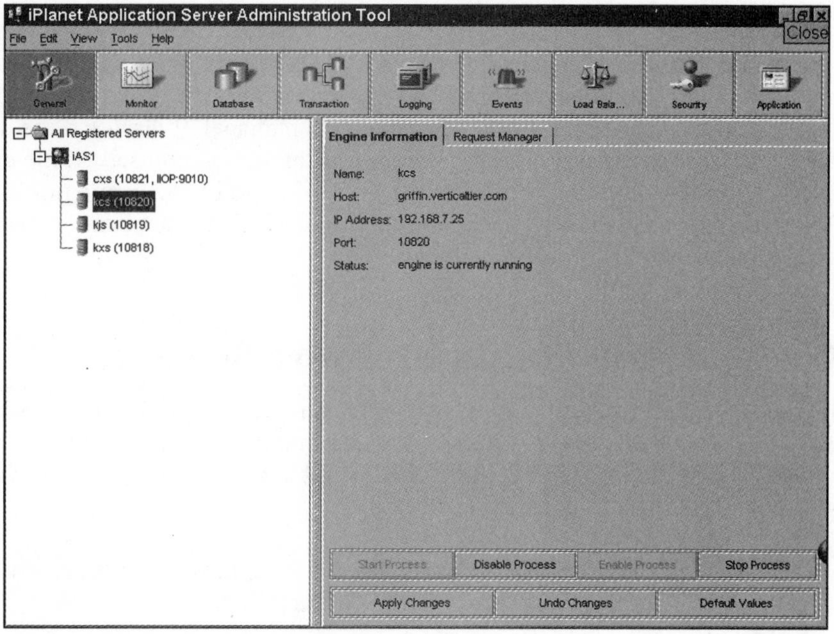

Figure 2-33: iASAT main screen

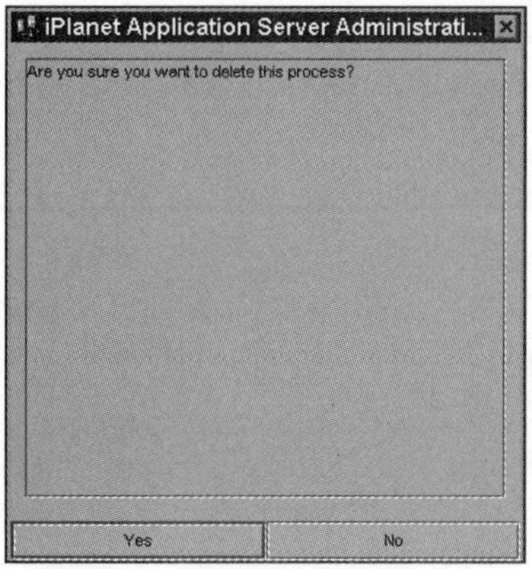

Figure 2-34: Delete this process dialog

CAUTION

In removing engines from a server in a production environment, your best course is to disable the engine first to bleed off any queued requests. After all the queued requests are processed, you can safely remove the engine, and the end users aren't affected.

5. Close the iASAT tool. From the menu bar, choose File → Exit.

6. Verify that the application server is completely stopped and, if so, restart the application server now. You can accomplish this task by using the Unix ps command or the Windows task manager. (I discuss these utilities further in Chapter 3.) After you restart the application server, the only processes running should be the KAS, KXS, and KJS. Turning off unnecessary processes helps the overall performance of the application-server environment.

Configure the CORBA Executive Server (CXS)

If you need RMI/IIOP support in iAS, you need to add and configure the CXS engine. On SP4 onward, a CXS process is automatically added on installation, assuming that the iAS service has started or KAS is running. If not, the following steps show you how to add a CXS process:

1. Start the iASAT tool. (On Unix, run the <ias_home>/bin/ksvradmin, and on Windows, choose Start → Run → ksvradmin.)

2. Select the name of the iAS instance to add the process to from the left side of the iASAT under the All Registered Servers icon. (For the example, select iAS1.)

3. From the menu bar of iASAT, choose File → New → Process. If the Process command doesn't appear on the menu bar, the instance name wasn't selected correctly in Step 2 (see Figure 2-35).

4. A new dialog box will show up, select CXS from the Process Type drop-down list box.

5. Enter a port that's not in use in the Port text box. Usually, you can use a port that's one number higher than the port number of your KJS engine. (If KJS=10819, for example, use 10820.)

6. Use the default setting for the IIOP port and click the OK button on the New Process dialog box. (On Windows, a new DOS window opens; this command window is the new CXS engine that you just set up — see Figure 2-36.)

 The developers writing the rich-client interface need the port number that you select. They use this port to communicate with the application server.

7. In the main iASAT tool window, you should see a new CXS process with the parameters that you entered (see Figure 2-37).

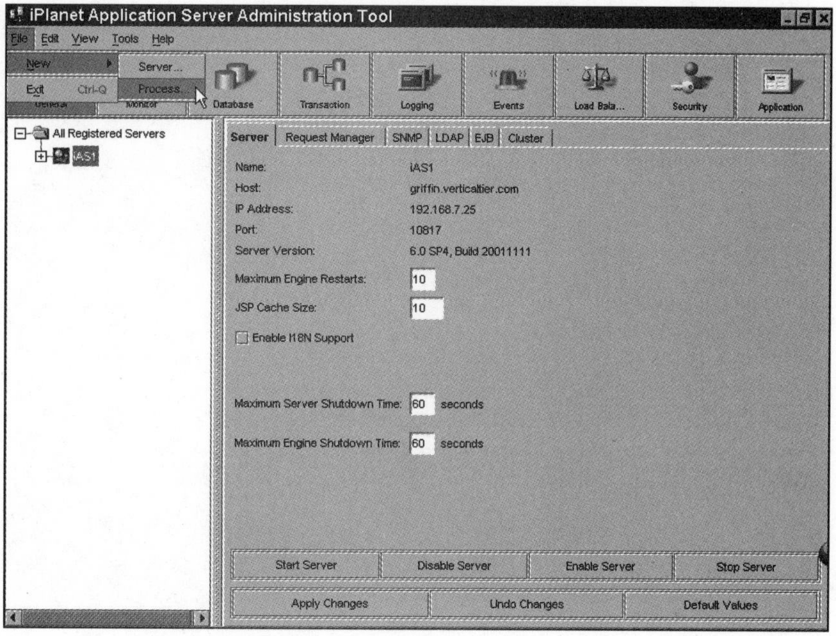

Figure 2-35: iASAT – Adding a new process

8. Close the iASAT tool by choosing File then exit from the menu bar.

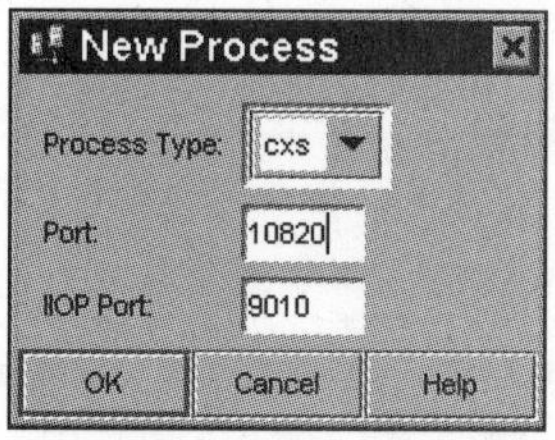

Figure 2-36: New Process dialog box

TIP

To help ease development, you may want to start the engines manually. To do so, open a command prompt window for each of the processes that you want to start. At the command prompt in each window, type the name of the process that you want to start, along with any necessary parameters, as in the following examples:

```
Kxs
kjs
kjs -cset CCSO -eng 2 -iiop -DORBinsPort=9010
```

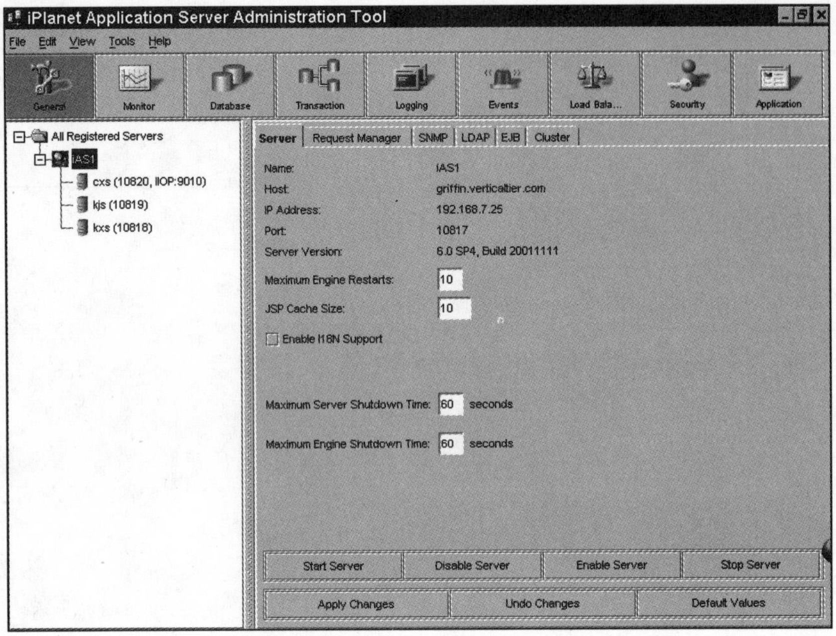

Figure 2-37: iASAT – With the new CXS engine

Configure iAS for Windows NT/2000

After the install is complete, you usually want to make some configuration changes to create a developer-friendly environment. By default, you set up iAS to run as a service. If you want to see the logs whenever iAS starts, you need to enable the service to interact with the desktop. Follow these steps to do so:

1. Choose Start → Run → services.msc (for Windows 2000 and later).

2. In the Services window that appears, locate the iPlanet Application Server 6.0 line, right-click it, and then click Stop. Wait for the service to stop before proceeding (see Figure 2-38).

3. Still in the Services window, locate the iPlanet Application Server 6.0 line, right-click it, and then click Properties.

4. Select the Log On tab of the Properties dialog box that appears and select the Allow Service to Interact with Desktop check box (see Figure 2-39).

5. In the Services window, locate the iPlanet Application Server 6.0 line, right-click it, and then click Start. A window opens for each of the processes that you configured in iASAT. The default processes in this example are KAS, KXS, KCS, KJS, and the CXS (which appears as a KJS).

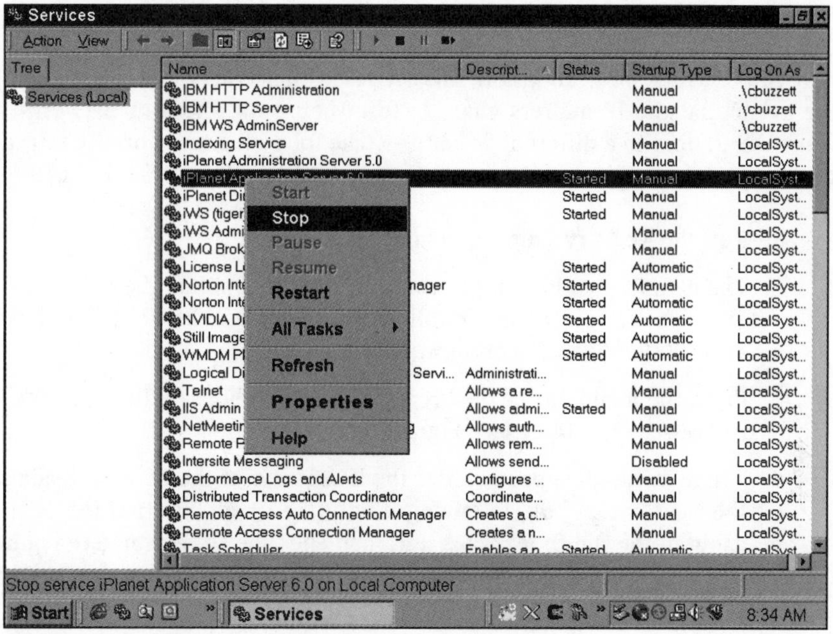

Figure 2-38: Stopping the iAS service

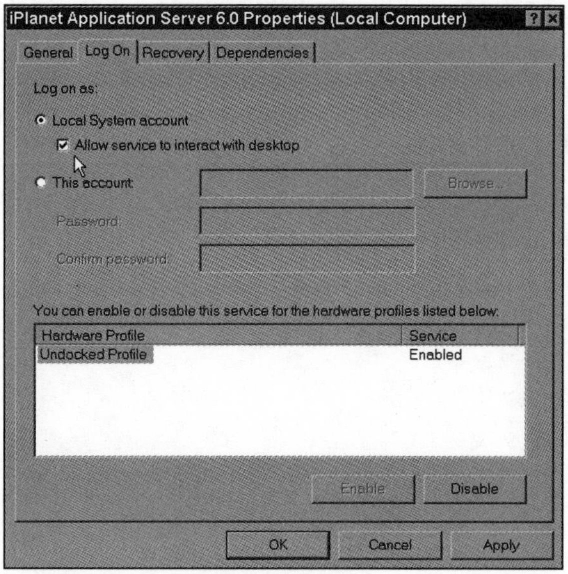

Figure 2-39: iAS6.0 service properties

Using the Express setup doesn't enable you to specify which IP address to use for iAS. If you're not using the Loopback adapter or are content with the IP address that you're using, you can ignore this section. Otherwise, you can use these steps in the event that the IP address changes from being on different networks and you want iAS to bind to a different IP address. The following steps briefly introduce you to the kregedit utility, which you use to change the IP address that iAS uses:

1. Run the Registry Editor by choosing Start → Run → kregedit.

2. The default position on the configuration tree should be set at SOFTWARE\iPlanet icon; if it's not highlighted in the kregedit window, select the SOFTWARE\iPlanet icon now.

3. From the menu bar of the kregedit window, choose Edit → Change IP Addresses in Subtree (see Figure 2-40).

4. A new window appears. Enter the IP address of the Loopback adapter in the New IP text box, following it with the IP address that iAS is currently using in the Old IP text box, and then click the OK button (see Figure 2-41).

5. To verify (or if you don't know what IP address iAS is using): from kregedit, navigate to SOFTWARE\iPlanet\Application Server\6.0\Admin, expand the Admin key by pressing the plus icon, and look for the Host key in the newly expanded Admin tree. This IP address that is listed in the Host= is the address that iAS is binding to (see Figure 2-42).

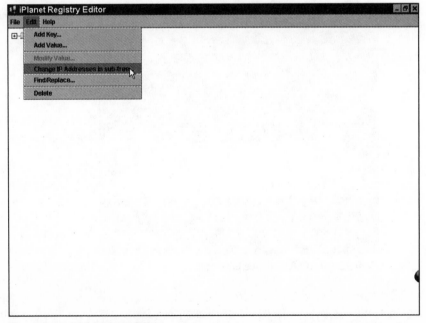

Figure 2-40: iAS Registry Editor

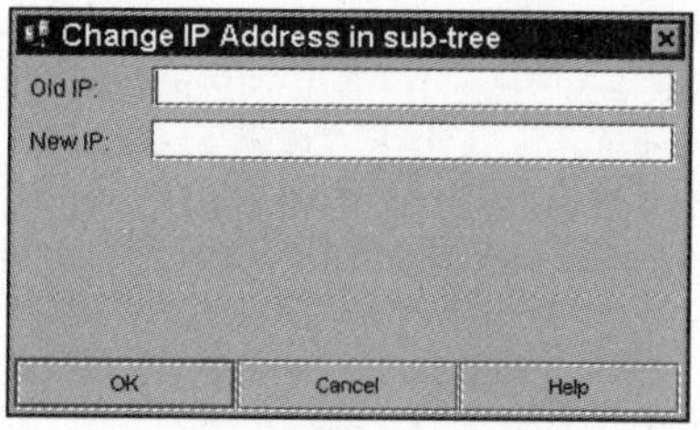

Figure 2-41: Change IP Address in sub-tree

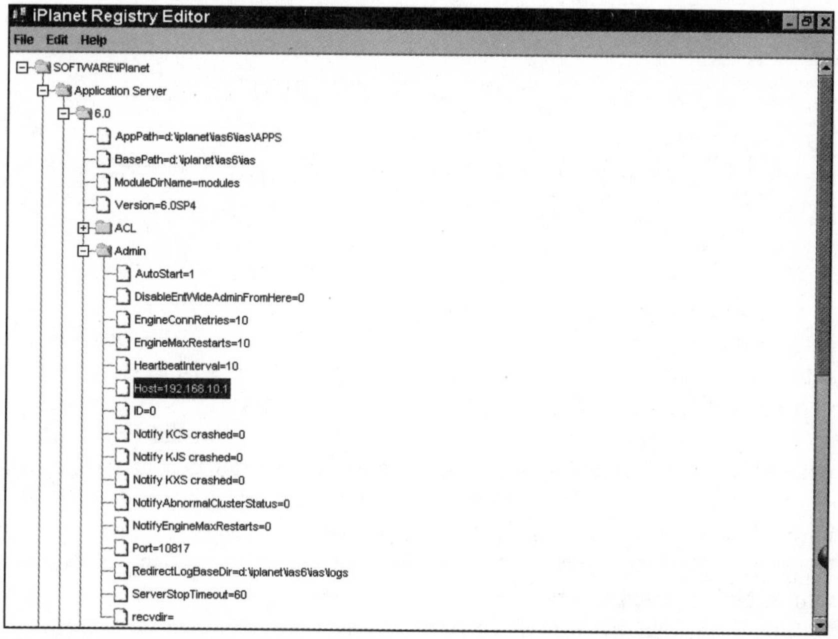

Figure 2-42: iAS Registry Editor – Verifying the current IP address

Configure database drivers

Most applications make use of some sort of datastore. This datastore usually takes the form of a database server (for example, Oracle, Sybase, and so on). For the application server to communicate correctly with the external databases, you must configure a driver for the given database. This section covers the task of configuring database drivers.

iPlanet application server contains built-in native drivers for Oracle, DB2, Sybase, Infomix, and Microsoft SQL Server (the last supported only on NT/2000). In the initial iAS 6.0 release, these were the only drivers supported. The iAS native database drivers were carried through subsequent iAS releases mainly for backward compatibility and global-transaction support. From an iPlanet perspective, the native drivers were fighting a losing battle as the JDBC specification evolved and developers demanded additional features. That the drivers coming from database vendors and companies that specialize in this development should be supported within the application server finally became evident. iAS 6.0 SP1, introduced support for third-party drivers and deprecated the built-in native drivers. The third-party drivers that SP1 onward officially supports are as follows:

◆ Oracle 8.1.6 Type 2 and Type 4

◆ Merant DataDirect Sequelink Java 5.0

◆ Sybase jConnect for JDBC, version 5.2 Type 4

◆ DB2 version 6.1

 Any third-party JDBC driver that correctly implements the `DriverManager` class should work. Cloudscape and PointBase, for example, work with no issues. Virtually any JDBC 2.0 driver should work.

From a developer perspective, support for third-party drivers was seen as a huge benefit, as features and APIs were now in line with the JDBC specifications. The subtle limitation (which isn't an issue with iAS 6.5) was within iAS; third-party drivers could support only local transactions (that is, transactions that ran in a single process and accessed a single data source). What that limitation meant was that if your application needed to use global transactions (that is, transactions that could span multiple processes and/or multiple data sources), you needed to use iPlanet's native built-in drivers. You may ask yourself, "What was the problem with that?" Well, with the introduction of third-party driver support also came some performance enhancements and full JDBC 2.0 support.

One of the benefits that third-party driver support added was connection pooling at the datasource level. Although the built-in drivers supported connection pooling, they supported pooling only at the driver level. What that meant was that all applications needing connections to the Oracle driver needed to share the connections with all the other applications that needed the Oracle driver, which led to a constant flux of connections within the connection pool (that is, connections terminating and recreating themselves as a different user and so on). With drivers implemented at the datasource level, you could now stabilize the connections at the application level, because all connections in the pool contain the same connection information, which eliminates the need for connection stealing This capability enhances performance in regard to creating and destroying connections and by providing a finer grain of tuning for database connection pools.

With the release of iPlanet Application Server 6.5, added support for global transactions with third-party drivers, along with enhanced monitoring and a fine-grained control of transaction-related parameters — as well as improved transaction-recovery capabilities.

The rest of this section demonstrates how to configure database drivers by using the db_setup.sh script for Unix systems and jdbcsetup.exe for Windows NT/2000 systems. You also see how to configure database drivers via the iPlanet Application Server Administrator Tool (iASAT).

For the following examples, you use the following data:

◆ Driver vendor: Oracle

◆ Driver version: 8i

◆ Installation directory of the third-party software for Windows NT/2000: C:\Servers\Db\Oracle8i; for Unix: /Servers/Db/Oracle8i

◆ Driver classpath for Windows NT/2000: C:\Servers\Db\Oracle8i\jdbc\ lib\classes12.zip; for Unix: /Servers/Db/Oracle8i/jdbc/lib/ classes12.zip

◆ Pooled datasource class name: oracle.jdbc.pool. OracleConnectionPoolDataSource

◆ JDBC driver class name: oracle.jdbc.driver.OracleDriver

◆ XA datasource class name: oracle.jdbc.xa.client.OracleXADataSource

CONFIGURE ORACLE DRIVER ON IAS 6.5 (WINDOWS PLATFORM)
Follow these steps to configure a database driver on Windows NT/2000:

1. Start the jdbcsetup.exe too, by choosing Start → Run, and then typing jdbcsetup.exe in the Run dialog box, and clicking OK (see Figure 2-43).

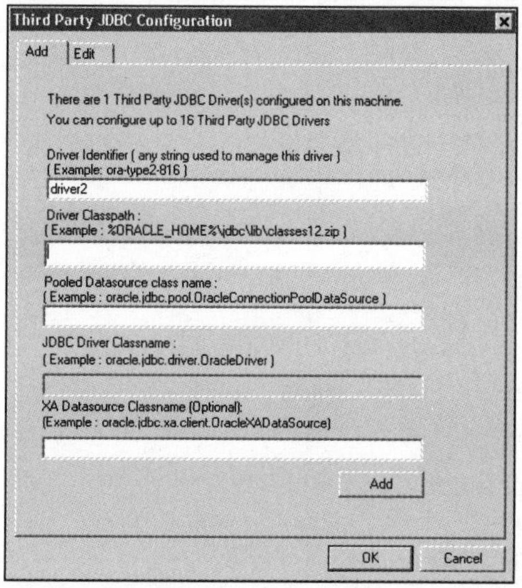

Figure 2-43: jdbcsetup.exe Utility

2. Configure the driver name. This name is just one that you assign to the driver. As you register datasources for your application, you need to specify the driver name for the datasource to use. (See Chapter 5 for more information on creating and registering datasources.) For our example, type **oracle8i** in the Driver Name text box to configure the driver name.

3. Define the driver classpath. This path is where the third-party class files or jar files reside. This name is specific to each third-party vendor, so you may need to check the provider's documentation for this value. For the example, Oracle is installed in `C:\Servers\Db\Oracle8i`, so you enter `C:\Servers\Db\Oracle8i\jdbc\lib\classes12.zip` in the Driver Classpath textbox.

4. Enter the pooled datasource classname. Again, the database provider specifies this name, so consult the vendor's documentation. You're using an Oracle driver with a pooled datasource classname of `oracle.jdbc.pool.OracleConnectionPoolDataSource` in the Pooled Datasource classname textbox.

5. If you don't need global transactions, skip this step. If you do, for the transaction management to work correctly, you need a driver that supports the XA protocol. Fortunately, Oracle supplies such a driver. For the example, add the following: `oracle.jdbc.xa.client.OracleXADataSource` in the XA Datasource Classname textbox (see Figure 2-44).

6. Click the Add button to add the driver so iAS can use it.

7. Click the OK button to exit the jdbc setup utility.

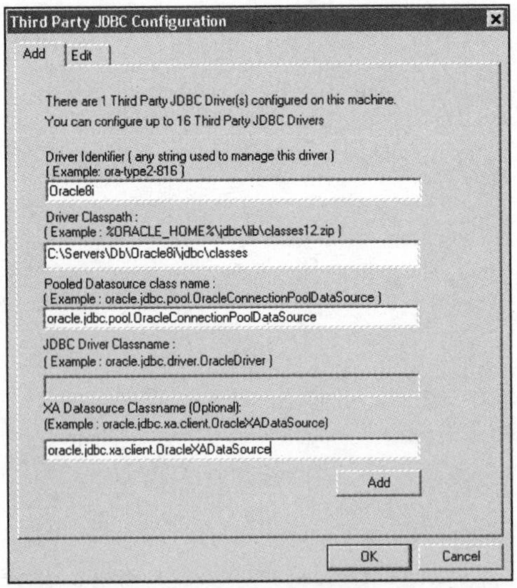

Figure 2-44: Driver configuration

TIP If you need to modify the configuration, click the Edit tab at the top of the utility and modify the values as necessary, clicking the Update button to make the changes.

CONFIGURE THIRD-PARTY DRIVERS ON IAS 6.0 SP1+

Follow the steps below to configure database drivers on Windows NT/2000 for iAS SP1+.

1. Start the `jdbcsetup.bat` tool by choosing Start → Run, and then typing `jdbcsetup.exe` in the Run dialog box, and clicking OK (see Figure 2-45).

```
┌─────────────────────────────────────────────────────────┐
│ Third Party JDBC Configuration                       [x] │
│ ┌─────┬──────┐                                            │
│ │ Add │ Edit │                                            │
│ ┴─────┴──────┴──────────────────────────────────────     │
│                                                          │
│   There are 0 Third Party JDBC Driver(s) configured on this machine. │
│   You can configure up to 16 Third Party JDBC Drivers    │
│                                                          │
│   Driver Identifier ( any string used to manage this driver ) │
│   ( Example: ora-type2-816 )                             │
│   ┌──────────────────────────────────────────────────┐  │
│   │driver1                                           │  │
│   └──────────────────────────────────────────────────┘  │
│                                                          │
│   Driver Classname ( Example: oracle.jdbc.driver.OracleDriver ) │
│   ┌──────────────────────────────────────────────────┐  │
│   │                                                  │  │
│   └──────────────────────────────────────────────────┘  │
│                                                          │
│   Driver Classpath ( Example: C:\jdbc\lib\classes111.zip ) │
│   ┌──────────────────────────────────────────────────┐  │
│   │                                                  │  │
│   └──────────────────────────────────────────────────┘  │
│                                                          │
│   Third Party Native Driver Directory (optional - needed for Type2 drivers ) │
│   ( Example:  c:\orant\bin )                             │
│   ┌──────────────────────────────────────────────────┐  │
│   │                                                  │  │
│   └──────────────────────────────────────────────────┘  │
│                                              ┌───────┐   │
│                                              │  Add  │   │
│                                              └───────┘   │
│                              ┌──────┐   ┌────────┐       │
│                              │  OK  │   │ Cancel │       │
│                              └──────┘   └────────┘       │
└─────────────────────────────────────────────────────────┘
```

Figure 2-45: jdbcsetup.exe Utility on 6.0 SP1 – SP4

2. Configure the driver name. This name is just one that you assign to the driver. As you register data sources for your application, you need to specify the driver name for the datasource to use. (See Chapter 5 for more information on creating and registering datasources.) For the example, type **oracle8i** in the Driver Name textbox.

3. Define the driver classpath. This path is where the third-party class files or JAR files reside. This name is specific to each third-party vendor, so you may need to check the provider's documentation for this value. For the example, Oracle is installed in `C:\Servers\Db\Oracle8i`, so enter `C:\Servers\Db\Oracle8i\jdbc\lib\classes12.zip` in the Driver Classpath textbox.

4. Define the JDBC driver classname. Again, the database provider specifies this name, so consult the vendor's documentation. You're using an Oracle driver with a JDBC driver classname of `oracle.jdbc.driver.OracleDriver` (see Figure 2-46).

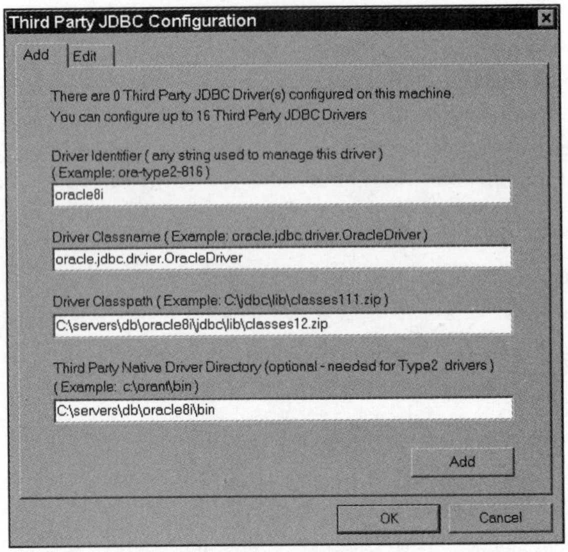

Third Party JDBC Configuration

Add | Edit

There are 0 Third Party JDBC Driver(s) configured on this machine.
You can configure up to 16 Third Party JDBC Drivers

Driver Identifier (any string used to manage this driver)
(Example: ora-type2-816)

> oracle8i

Driver Classname (Example: oracle.jdbc.driver.OracleDriver)

> oracle.jdbc.drvier.OracleDriver

Driver Classpath (Example: C:\jdbc\lib\classes111.zip)

> C:\servers\db\oracle8i\jdbc\lib\classes12.zip

Third Party Native Driver Directory (optional - needed for Type2 drivers)
(Example: c:\orant\bin)

> C:\servers\db\oracle8i\bin

Add

OK   Cancel

Figure 2-46: Driver configuration

5. Click the Add button to add the driver so iAS can use it.

6. Click the OK button to exit the jdbc setup utility.

If you need to modify the configuration, click the Edit tab at the top of the utility and modify the values as necessary, clicking the Update button to make the changes.

CONFIGURE THIRD-PARTY DRIVERS ON UNIX

To configure database drivers on Unix, you use the `db_setup.sh` script in the `<ias_home>/bin` directory.

In configuring database drivers on the Unix platform, you need to make sure that the application-server user is the only user running the setup scripts. Otherwise, you may not have write permissions to write the files that you need to update. Mainly, the <ias_home>/env/iasenv.ksh file will be the file that is updated by the db_setup.sh script. If this happens, you can't create a connection to the database because it doesn't know where to look for the drivers.

To set up third-party database drivers on Unix, follow the steps outlined below.

1. Start the db_setup.sh script by typing <ias_home>/bin/db_setup.sh.

2. Select the type of driver that you want to register. For this example, you register a third-party driver, so type 2 (see Figure 2-47).

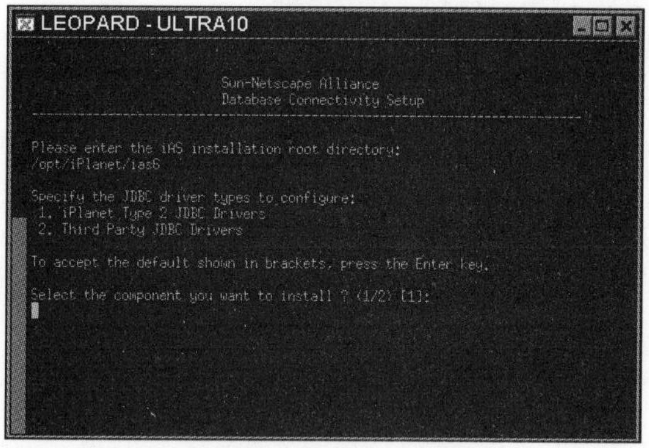

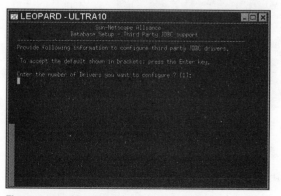

Figure 2-47: jdbc setup utility on UNIX

3. Answer the prompt for the number of drivers that you want to configure. For these purposes, type 1 at the prompt (see Figure 2-48).

Figure 2-48: Number of drivers to configure

4. For the driver name, simply type **oracle8i** at the prompt (see Figure 2-49).

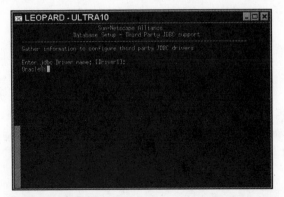

Figure 2-49: Driver name

5. Type the driver class name. For the example, simply type `oracle.jdbc.` `driver.OracleDriver`.

6. Enter the driver classpath. For the example, type `/Servers/Db/Oracle8i/` `jdbc/lib/classes12.zip`.

7. Type the driver library path if necessary (only for Type 2 drivers). For the example, type i `/Servers/Db/Oracle8i/lib` (see Figure 2-50).

Figure 2-50: Gathering information for the third-party JDBC driver

REGISTER AN IPLANET BUILT-IN NATIVE DRIVER
To setup native database drivers on Unix, follow the steps outlined below.

1. Start the db_setup.sh script by typing <ias_home>/bin/db_setup.sh.

2. Select the type of driver that you want to register. For that example, you register a third-party driver, so type 1 (refer to Figure 2-47).

3. At the prompt asking whether you want to install an oracle driver, answer Y.

4. At the prompt asking for the oracle home directory, type /Servers/Db/ Oracle8i (refer to Figure 2-51).

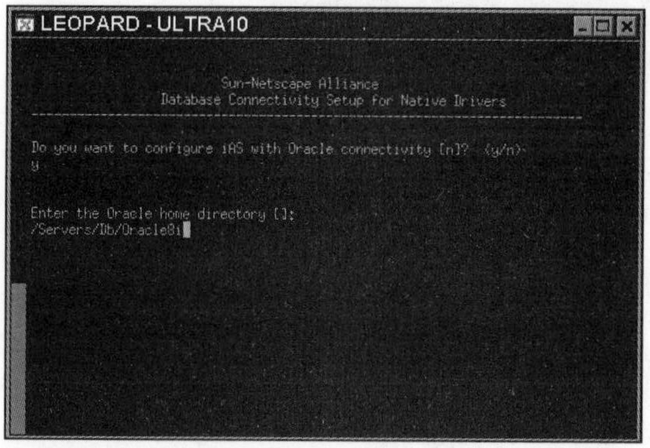

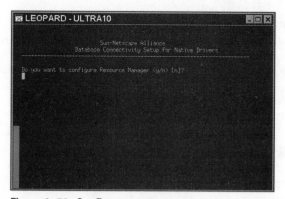

Figure 2–51: jdbc setup for native drivers

5. At the prompt you are asked if you want to configure a Resource Manager. The sample doesn't use global transactions, so you don't need a resource manager; enter N (see Figure 2-52).

Figure 2–52: Configure resource manager

The installation is now complete (see Figure 2-53).

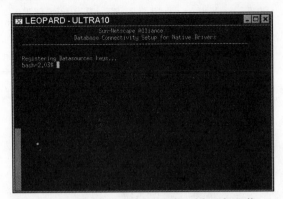

Figure 2-53: Finishing up the native driver install

 If you're mixing driver types (that is, third-party drivers and built-ins) the order in which you install them matters. See the section "Mixing iPlanet's built-in drivers and third party-drivers," later in the chapter. Whichever driver you install last sets the IS3PJDBC flag!

VERIFICATION OF THE DRIVER CONFIGURATION

To verify that the driver is working correctly, you need an application with which to test the connections. To do so, you need to register the application's data-source(s) that use the database drivers that you just configured. I cover creating and registering datasources in detail in Chapter 5.

The only thing that you need to do before registering datasources is to make sure that the environment is updated correctly. On Windows NT/2000, use the kregedit.bat tool to check the Java classpath. Navigate to the Software\ iPlanet\Application Server\[6.0 | 6.5]\Java key and check the classpath value and the libpath values. The CLASSPATH should now reference the driver class name, and the libpath (if you're using a Type 2 driver) should reference the native driver directory.

On Unix, the information to verify resides in the <ias_home>/env/iasenv.ksh script. Because the example deals with configuring an Oracle driver, look for the following lines in the iasenv.ksh file:

```
ORACLE_HOME=/Servers/Db/Oracle8i
ORACLE_SID=
ORCLLIB=${ORACLE_HOME:+$ORACLE_HOME/lib}
```

MIXING IPLANET'S BUILT-IN DRIVERS AND THIRD-PARTY DRIVERS

If you're using a combination of built-in drivers and third-party drivers you need to take care of the order in which you configure the drivers. You must set a special registry entry correctly for the mixture of drivers to work.

If you configure drivers with the application server, you add/modify entries within the registry to maintain these values. Start the `kregedit.bat` file and navigate to the `Software\iPlanet\Application Server\[6.0 | 6.5]\CCS0\` key. Under this key, you find three keys that begin with *DAE*. DAE stands for *Data Access Engine*, and as you may guess, this is where the driver-configuration information is stored. To verify the drivers, at least on the surface, you need to make sure that the settings in these keys look correct. Third-party drivers are stored under the DAE3 key, and the iPlanet native built-in values are stored in the DAE2 key. The tricky part comes in configuring a mixture of driver types. Under the DAE2 key is the value `IS3PJDBC`. A value of 1 for this value means that it uses only local transactions. A value of 0 indicates that it uses local or global transactions. Following is the rundown on what this value should be:

- 1 if it uses only third-party JDBC drivers.
- 0 if it uses only the iPlanet built-in drivers.
- 0 if it uses both types of drivers.

After you visually inspect the settings for correctness, the next step is to try creating an actual database connection through the application.

Summary

In this chapter, you learn about the different installation options available to complete the installation of the application server and some details about each option. Determining which installation is best suited for your environment heavily depends on the type of environment that you need and the type of application you're developing. The purpose of this chapter is to familiarize the developer with how to plan for an installation, check the prerequisites of the machine, perform a typical development install, and configure the environment and the database drivers.

Chapter 3

Testing Your Install

IN THIS CHAPTER

- ◆ Listing all processes in the application server environment and explaining each one's function

- ◆ Listing and using the tools necessary to administer the application server

- ◆ Testing connectivity within the environment

- ◆ Testing load balancing

- ◆ Testing database configuration

- ◆ Testing clustering

- ◆ Testing distributed data synchronization

AFTER THE INSTALLATION is complete, you should test the newly created iAS environment to make sure that it's functioning correctly before you do any more work. This chapter details the components that make up the application-server environment and explains how to verify that each element is running and how to make sure that they're working correctly.

Application Server Components and Internals

The application server consists of a number of components that work in concert to provide a robust, scaleable, and highly available environment. The application server environment consists of the following three main software components:

- ◆ Web server
- ◆ Directory server
- ◆ Application server

The Web server provides the most common entry point into the application server and also serves static content to the client. You install the Web-connector plug-in, or just the *plug-in*, as it's sometimes known, into this layer to provide communication to the application server. The following three different types of plug-ins are available:

◆ Netscape Server Application Programming Interface (NSAPI) plug-in, for iPlanet Web Server

◆ Internet Server Application Programming Interface (ISAPI) plug-in, for Microsoft Internet Information Server

◆ Optimized Common Gateway Interface (CGI) plug-in, for Web servers that implement CGI

The Web server is optimized for serving static content. The benefits to the environment by enabling the Web server to serve static content are as follows:

◆ It decreases internal network traffic (traffic between the Web and application servers)

◆ It increases performance by enabling the Web server to take advantage of its built-in performance features (such as caching)

The directory server holds configuration information for the application server (the *configuration directory*) and stores user information (the *user directory*). The configuration directory and the user directory can reside on the same directory server, or you may separate them onto distinct directory servers, thus enabling enterprise management of such services.

The application server provides the services to run the applications. A number of processes make up the application server. These processes are as follows:

◆ Administrative Server (KAS)

◆ Executive Server (KXS)

◆ Java Server (KJS)

◆ C++ Server (KCS)

◆ CORBA Executive Server (CXS)

The Administrative Server (KAS) receives administrative commands from the iPlanet Application Server Administrator Tool (iASAT) and delegates them to the target subsystem/process. Another important function of the KAS is to act as a watchdog to ensure that all the other processes in the system stay running. The KAS automatically restarts any downed processes. Only one KAS can run per instance of the application server. The Windows NT/2000 process name for the

(KAS) process is kas.exe, of which two are running (one acts as a watchdog while the other acts as the administrative server). The Unix names for this process consist of two parts also. The kas process is a script that acts as the watchdog and sets up the environment to call the actual KAS process, .kas.

 Only one KAS should run per application-server instance. If more than one KAS is running, the results are unpredictable. If this process isn't running, all administration via the iASAT is unavailable, and failover and automatic process restarting doesn't function correctly.

The Executive Server (KXS) is the primary entry point of application requests from the Web connector and the CXS process to the application server. The KXS is responsible for determining what type of application server component was requested by the client, determining load balancing requirements (if you're using iAS-based load balancing), dispatching the request to the correct subsystem for execution or rerouting the request, and delivering the response back to the Web connector. A single KXS process is possible per instance of the application server. The Windows NT/2000 process name is kxs.exe. The Unix process names for this process consist of two parts: The kxs process is a script that sets up the environment to call the actual KXS process, .kxs.

 Again, only one KXS should run per application-server instance. If more than one KXS is running, the results are unpredictable. If the KXS isn't running, Web-connector requests don't forward on to the KJS or KCS process for execution, which usually results in a GX error in the client browser.

The KCS process is responsible for handling requests for C++ components in the application server. You can have 0 or more of these processes per instance of the application server. iPlanet recommends running 1 to 2 of these processes per CPU. The Windows NT/2000 process name for KCS is kcs.exe. The Unix names for this process consist of two parts: The kcs script sets up the environment to call the actual KCS process, .kcs.

 If no C++ components are in use on the system, you don't need a KCS process. So don't install a KCS process, because doing so only wastes finite system resources.

The KJS process is responsible for handling requests for Java components in the application server. You can have 0 or more of these processes per instance of the application server. iPlanet suggests running 1 to 2 of these processes per CPU. The Windows NT/2000 process name for the KJS is `kjs.exe`. The Unix names for this process consist of two parts: The `kjs` script sets up the environment to call the actual KJS process, `.kjs`. The KJS process is essentially the Java virtual machine.

If no JAVA components are in use on the system, you don't need a KJS process. So don't install a KJS process, because doing so only wastes system resources.

The CXS process is an RMI/IIOP bridge for use with applications that support the rich-client architecture. Communication from the rich client to the application server occurs across a single TCP port and uses Remote Method Invocation over Internet Inter-Orb Protocol (RMI/IIOP) to call distributed components on the application server from a rich-client application. Although the CXS is a specific process in the application-server environment, you don't find a `cxs.exe`, `cxs`, or a `.cxs` process as you do with the other processes. The CXS process is just a KJS with two special parameters that pass to it. The first parameter is the `-iiop`. This parameter tells the KJS engine to run as an IIOP to iAS's proprietary communication protocol (KCP) bridge. The second is the `-port` option, which specifies the listening port that connections from the rich-client applications connect.

If you don't need rich-client support, don't create a CXS process because doing so only consumes resources unnecessarily. On SP4 and later, a CXS process is automatically set up, so you will want to delete it via the iPlanet Application Server Administrator Tool (iASAT)

On Unix systems, making sure that the designated application-server user starts all processes is very important. This user should perform all application deployments and should start and stop the application server. Problems can arise if you fail to adhere to this requirement. You find that you can't log on to the application server, for example, or that you can't run the deployed application. Permission-related issues such as these are often very hard to track down.

Verify Running Processes

Now that you have a little background of the application server processes (KAS, KXS, KCS, KJS, CXS) and what functions they perform, you can verify that the installation is currently running as configured. Assuming that you documented the installation, you can normally verify that all processes installed are up and running by using one of several methods. You can, for example, use the operating system's process-monitoring utilities. On Windows NT/2000, you can do this via the taskmgr application (see Figure 3-1). On Unix-based systems, you can accomplish this task by using the ps utility (see Figure 3-2). Another method is to use the ksvradmin tool to verify process states. (I discuss the use of this tool in the section "iPlanet Application Server Administration Tool (iASAT)," later in this chapter.)

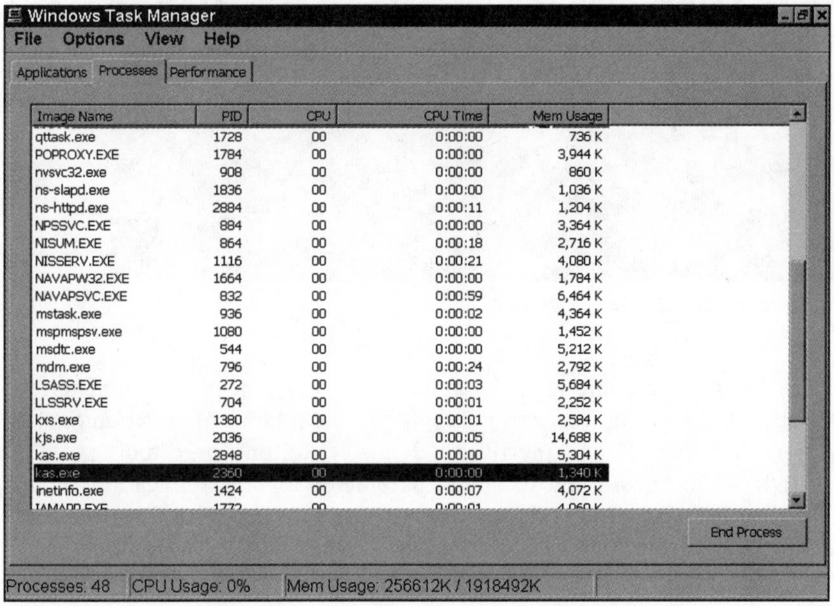

Figure 3-1: The Task Manager application in Windows NT/2000

A couple options are available if you need to monitor the server processes. You usually monitor these processes in a production environment so that you can deal with problems as quickly as possible. The first option – and the easiest to implement – is to set up event notifications for events such as downed processes. (See the Administrators Guide at http://docs.iplanet.com/docs/manuals/ias/60/sp4/ag/admonit.htm#13345 for more information on configuring events.) The next option is to enable Simple Network Management Protocol (SNMP) for the application server so that external processes can monitor the environment via SNMP. For more information on enabling SNMP, refer to the Administrators Guide or visit www.icsynergy.com/ias/HowTo-SNMP.htm.

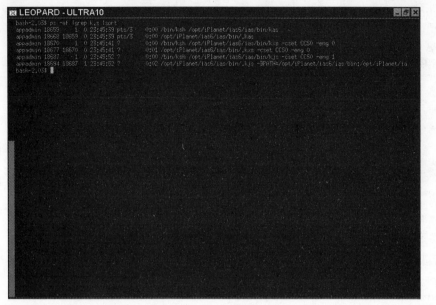

Figure 3-2: The ps utility on Unix

A number of tools that come with the application server help in administering the environment. The two that concern you here are the iPlanet Application Server Administration Tool (iASAT) and the iPlanet Registry Editor. These tools provide graphical interfaces to enable you to adjust parameters of the application server environment. The iASAT tool provides an easy-to-use interface to adjust the most important attributes of the application server—the ones that you use most commonly. The iPlanet Registry Editor provides a more advanced view on the attributes and settings of the application server.

The following two sections briefly explain the tools that you use to administer the application server and how to use them.

iPlanet Application Server Administration Tool (iASAT)

The iASAT tool is a Java Swing GUI that enables you to configure the application-server environment. You can use the iASAT tool to manage local and remote application servers, making management of the application servers convenient and centralized. The tool offers a layout that's intuitive and easy to navigate. The GUI contains many standard components: a menu bar, a toolbar, a tree-view pane, and a ListView pane (see Figure 3-3).

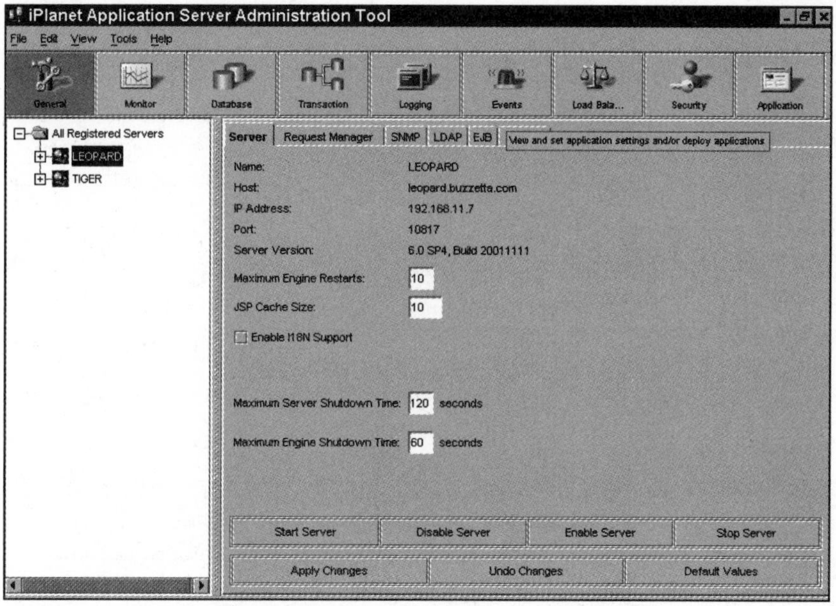

Figure 3-3: iPlanet Application Server Administration Tool (iASAT)

The iASAT consists of the following nine functional areas:

◆ **General:** System-wide settings

◆ **Monitor:** Application-server monitoring configuration

◆ **Database:** Database configuration

◆ **Transaction:** Transaction-management configuration

◆ **Logging:** Application logging configuration

◆ **Events:** Event-notification and processing configuration

◆ **Load Balancing:** Load-balancing configuration

◆ **Security:** Security configuration

◆ **Application:** Application-property configuration

The iPlanet Application Server Administrators Guide covers many of these areas, and they are covered in later chapters, too, so I discuss here only the relevant areas for testing the configuration. The General, Logging, and Application areas should suffice for the purposes of this chapter. Before you can begin using the iASAT, you need to make sure that the KAS process is running, as I describe in the section "Application Server Components and Internals," earlier in this chapter.

Running the iASAT tool is simple. On Unix, you use the executable `ksvradmin`, which you find in the `<IAS_HOME>/bin` directory. On Windows NT/2000 systems, you can launch the tool via the Start menu or run it via the command line, as `ksvradmin.bat`, assuming that the `<IAS_HOME>/bin` directory is in the system path.

One of the first things that you may need to do based on the service pack that you're using, is to register an application server with the iASAT. To register a server, follow these steps:

1. Start the iASAT tool. In Windows NT/2000, use the Start menu to launch the iASAT (Start → Programs → iPlanet Server Products → iPlanet Application Server 6.0 → iAS Administration Tool) or, alternatively, run `ksvradmin.bat` from a command shell. In Unix, run `<IAS_HOME>/bin/ksvradmin` from a shell window.

On Windows NT/2000, use the "Start" menu to launch the iASAT. (Start → Programs → iPlanet Server Products → iAS Administration Tool) or alternatively run "ksvradmin.bat" from a command shell. On UNIX, run <IAS_HOME>/bin/ksvradmin from a shell window, where IAS_HOME is an environment variable that represents the installation directory for the iPlanet Application Server.

2. From the menu bar, choose File → New → Server. A dialog box appears, as shown in Figure 3-4.

3. To add the server on which you're running the iASAT tool to the iASAT tool server list, simply click the Local Host button to the right of the Name text box in the dialog box. These actions populate the text boxes with the current host's information and supplies a password. Otherwise, type the host name and port number in the appropriate text boxes (see Figure 3-5).

I strongly suggest that you give the registered server a meaningful name, because simply using the default name *iAS* can become confusing if you're using iASAT on multiple machines (as iAS may represent different servers).

4. Decide whether iASAT is to connect to the server whenever iASAT starts. Deselect the check box for this option at the bottom of the dialog box just above the OK button if you don't want this connection to occur automatically.

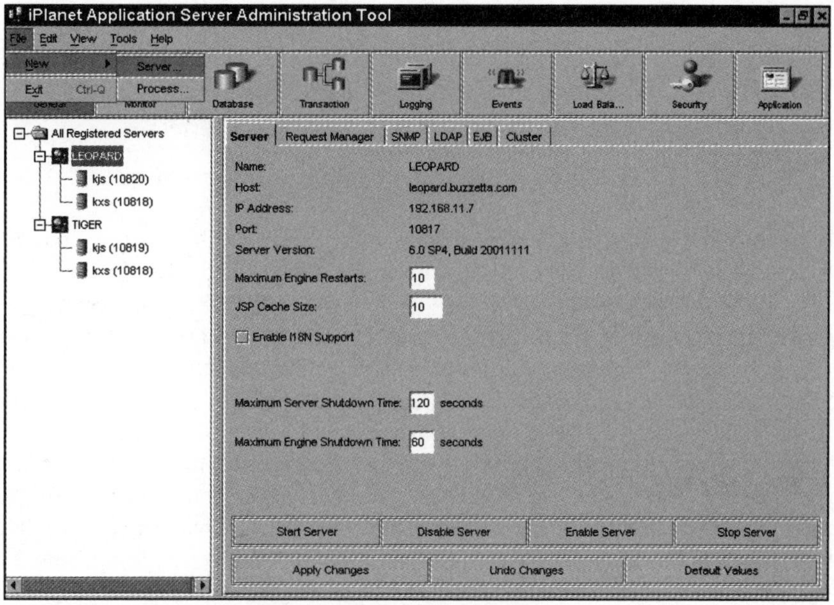

Figure 3-4: Registering an application server with iASAT

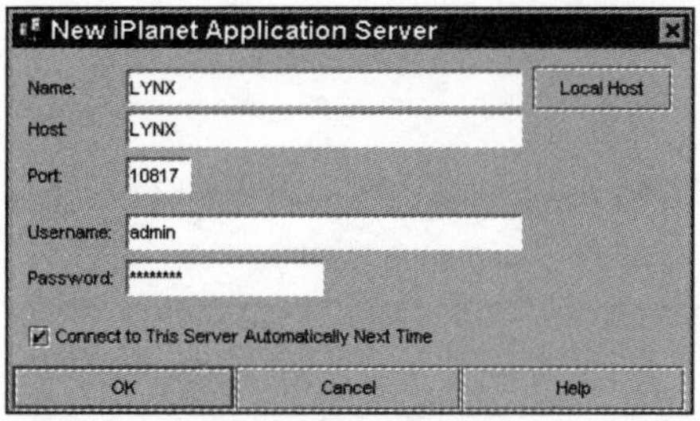

Figure 3-5: Registering server information

Selecting this option enables anyone with permissions to run the iASAT tool to administer the server without a password!

5. Click the OK button to add the server to the iASAT tool server list.

The server should now be registered with the iASAT tool, and you can begin administration.

If you get an error in connecting to the server, check the following items:

◆ Make sure that the target application server is running (KAS process)

◆ Make sure that the username and password are correct

◆ Make sure that the host name and port number are correct

To prepare to test the installed environment, you need to make a few changes in the iASAT tool so that it displays a little more information about what's going on inside of the application-server environment. You make these changes in the General, Logging, and Applications functional areas of the iASAT to help in your testing of the environment, as the following sections describe.

GENERAL FUNCTIONAL AREA

The General section of the iASAT gives you information and enables you to change settings for *servers*, *engines*, and *clusters*, and other important settings, which I don't discuss in this chapter. By clicking the server in the tree-view pane (the left pane), statistics about that server appear, along with some system-wide settings. This area enables you to set and change settings to start, stop, and disable the application-server engines and the application server as a whole. To test your configuration, you can use the status-reporting feature for engines in this section to verify that processes are running as I allude to in the section "Verify Running Processes," earlier in this chapter. Notice the status of the engine in Figures 3-6 and 3-7.

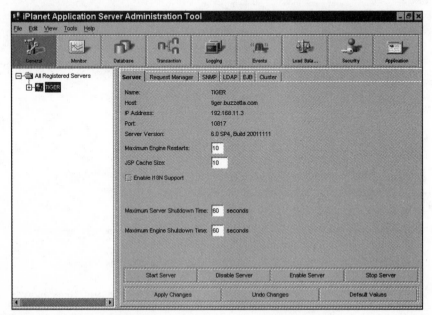

Figure 3–6: General features

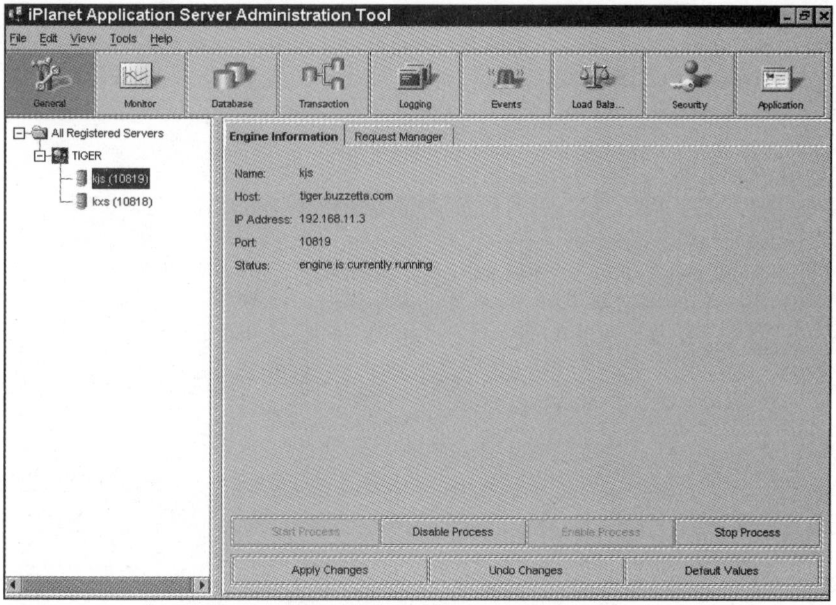

Figure 3-7: Using iASAT to verify process states

LOGGING FUNCTIONAL AREA

Change to this section by clicking the Logging toolbar button. This area enables you to change the logging behavior for the application server. In this section, you can configure the type of information that the application server writes to log files, specify the location in which the application server creates the log files, and specify the log-rotation schedules of the application server. For the current purpose, you want to configure logging to provide information that enables you to determine what's happening in the application server as you start testing the connectivity, load balancing, and clustering of the application server. To set up logging as necessary, follow these steps:

1. Start the iASAT tool (as I describe in Step 1 of the preceding set of steps).

2. Click the Logging button on the toolbar to display the logging options.

3. Enable logging by selecting the "Enable Server Event Log" check box at the top of the right pane of the logging options of the iASAT Tool (see Figure 3-8).

4. Set the message type to All Messages in the "Message Type" drop-down list in the General area of the right pane for the logging options in the iASAT tool (see Figure 3-8).

5. For testing purposes only, set the Write Interval to 10 by typing 10 in the "Write Interval" text box. This setting causes the log-message buffers to write to disk more frequently (see Figure 3-8).

6. Click the Apply button on the bottom of the right pane in the logging options of the iASAT tool. You may have to scroll the right pane of the logging options of the iASAT tool to the bottom using the right scroll bar to view the Apply button.

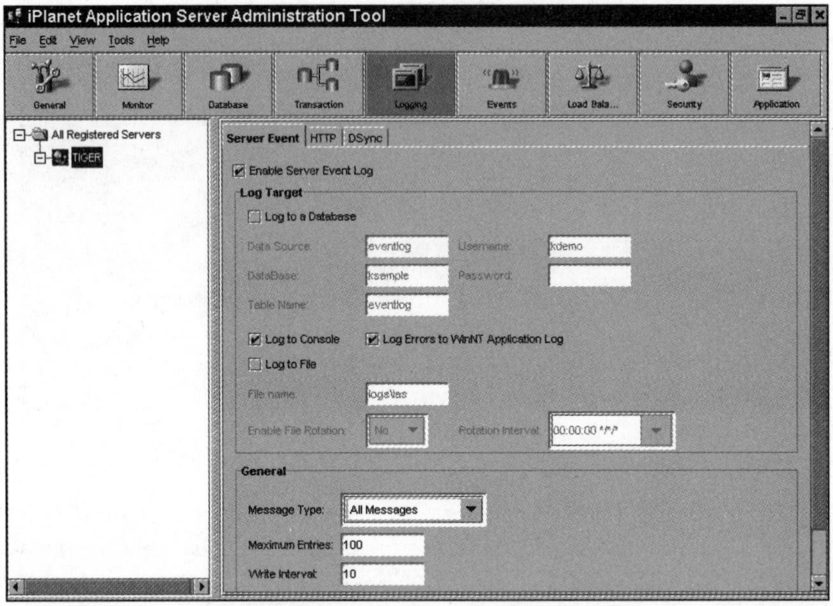

Figure 3-8: Configuring logging options

APPLICATIONS FUNCTIONAL AREA

To finish the preparatory tasks to enable you to test whether the environment is functioning correctly, you need to configure the test application Fortune to make it load balanceable. To do so, follow these steps:

1. Start the iASAT, as I describe in Step 1 of the steps in the section "iPlanet Application Server Administration Tool (iASAT)," earlier in this chapter.

2. Register all the servers involved in the load balancing that you want to test, as I describe in Step 2 of the "iPlanet Application Server Administrator Tool" section regarding registering servers.

3. Select the Applications toolbar button in the iASAT (see the toolbar in Figure 3-9).

4. Expand the server in the left pane of the iASAT window to list the applications registered with that application server (see Figure 3-9).

5. Select the Fortune application in the left pane of the iASAT tool by putting the mouse cursor over the fortune item and click the select mouse button.

6. Select `fortune_FortuneServlet` in the right pane of the iASAT tool and on the Components tab in the section "Servlets in Module fortune" (see Figure 3-9).

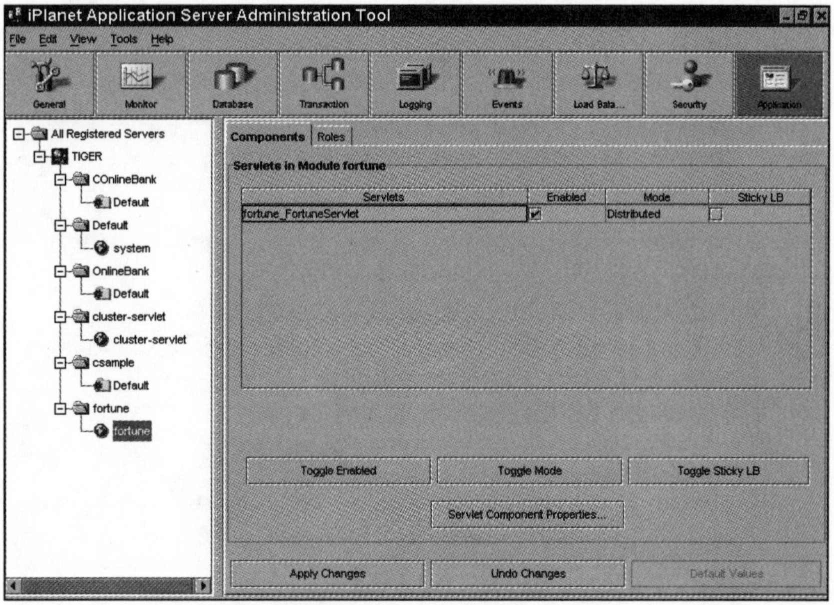

Figure 3-9: Selecting the application servlet's properties

7. Set the Mode to Distributed (if the mode is set differently) by selecting the entry for the servlet in the Mode column (drop down list) in the Servlets in Module fortune section on the Components tab in the right pane of the iASAT window (see Figure 3-10).

Definition of Modes

The different types of modes available for servlets are local, distributed, and global. It is important to know the differences between the modes so I will explain the modes here.

◆ **Local:** The component is available for execution on the current server only.

◆ **Distributed:** The component is available for execution on all the servers registered in the iASAT tool.

◆ **Global:** The component is available for execution on all the servers that have the same multicast parameters as the current server.

8. Click the Servlet Component Properties button at the bottom of the Components tab in the right pane of the iASAT tool.

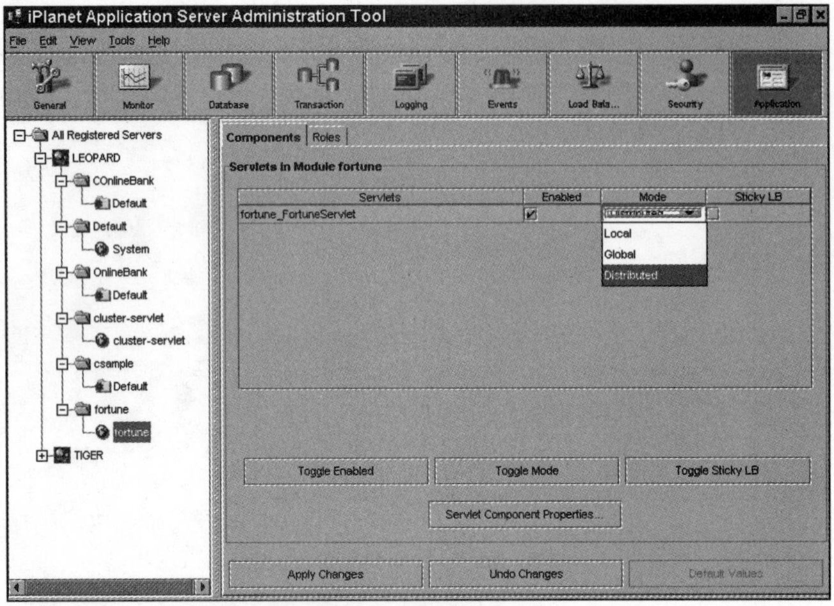

Figure 3-10: Setting the application component's mode

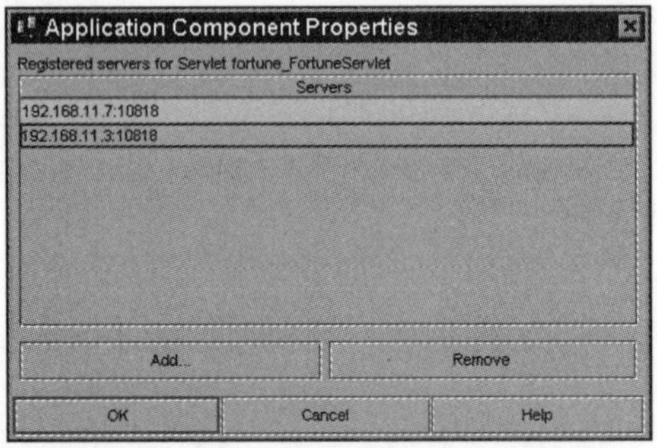

Figure 3-11: Servlet properties

9. A dialog for Application Component Properties will be displayed similar to Figure 3-11. Add the IP address of the servers involved in load balancing, if necessary, by clicking the Add button in the Application Component Properties dialog window. Adding IP address to the component properties tells the application servers where the Fortune servlet can run if you install and enable it.

If the application servers share a configuration directory, you need to perform Step 9 only once. If multiple configuration directories are involved, however, you must perform this step for all the servers with separate configuration directories. For load balancing to work correctly, you must make sure that all the configurations are in sync.

10. Repeat steps 4 through 9 for all the servers participating in load balancing.

iPlanet Registry Editor

The iPlanet Registry Editor provides direct access to the configuration settings of the application server. The iPlanet Registry Editor enables an administrator to make configuration changes that are unavailable in the iASAT tool. For more information on the registry and the iPlanet Registry Editor, see Chapter 13.

Using the iPlanet Registry Editor incorrectly can corrupt the application server's installation. You should use the iPlanet Registry Editor only if you know exactly what you need to change.

To prepare for environment testing, you should make a few advanced changes to help in determining whether the environment is working correctly. The first change is to turn on the logging of the globally unique identifier (GUID) information and routing information for the component in the KXS log for each component executed. To make this change, follow these steps:

1. Start the registry-editor tool. In Unix, type the following command at the shell prompt "`<IAS_HOME>/bin/kregedit`"where `<IAS_HOME>` is replaced by the correct path to the iAS installation directory and then press Enter to run the command. In Windows NT/2000, type the following command at a shell prompt and then type enter to run the command: <IAS_HOME>/bin/kregedit.bat (see Figure 3-12).

2. Navigate the folder view to the `Software\iPlanet\Application Server\6.0\CCS0\Req` key.

3. Change the Debug value to 1 by double clicking on the Debug value in the window and changing the value to 1 in the dialog box that appears and then select the OK button on the dialog box.

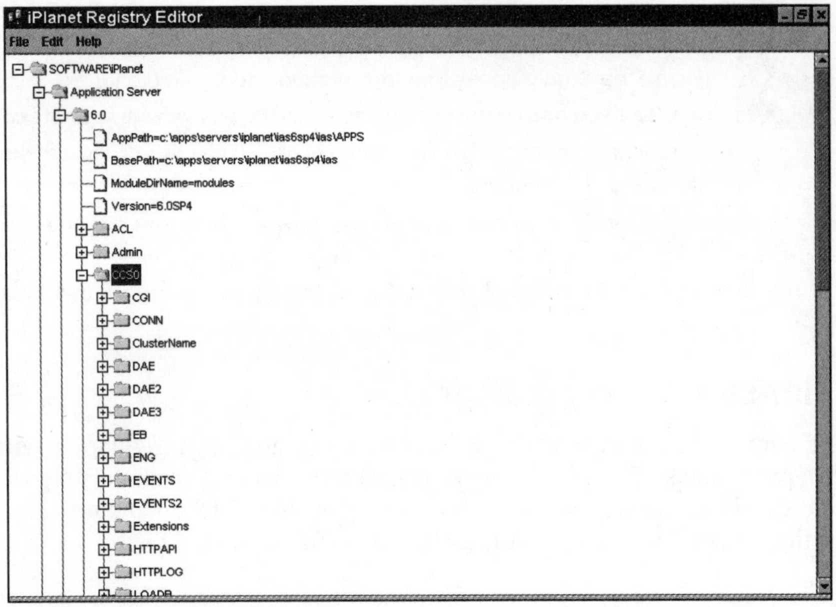

Figure 3-12: The IPlanet Registry Editor

4. Repeat steps 1 thru 3 for all the application servers that you want to test.

5. Restart the application servers.

Testing Functionality

The easiest test to perform on the environment is to check the connectivity of the Web connector (plug-in) and the application server(s). You can accomplish this test by running a sample application that installs by default with the application server. The sample application's name is Fortune. This application consists of a simple JSP file and servlet and returns a whimsical message after you call it — sort of like what you may find in a fortune cookie. You can run Fortune from the iPlanet Application Server Samples Web page that installs along with the application-server Web-connector plug-in. Assuming that you name the Web server www.mywebserver.com, that the Web server uses standard HTTP protocol, and that the document root directory doesn't change after the installation of the Web connector, you can reach the Samples page via the following URL: www.mywebserver.com/ias-samples/.

In the Sample Applications section of the Samples HTML page, locate the Fortune (quick test) entry. To quickly test connectivity between the Web connector and the application server, click the quick test link. This link calls the Fortune application, and if the environment is working correctly, a fortune appears on-screen, similar to the one shown in Figure 3-13.

Figure 3-13: Fortune application

 If the environment consists of two or more application servers, you must check connectivity between the Web connector and all installed application servers. I cover this process in more detail in the following section, "Test Load Balancing."

If a fortune appears on-screen, communication between the Web connector and the application server is working correctly. If the fortune application is successful, skip ahead to the following section "Test Load Balancing." If you receive an error while running the Fortune application, take note of the error (see Figures 3-14 to 3-16) and see Figure 3-17 for a probable cause and resolution.

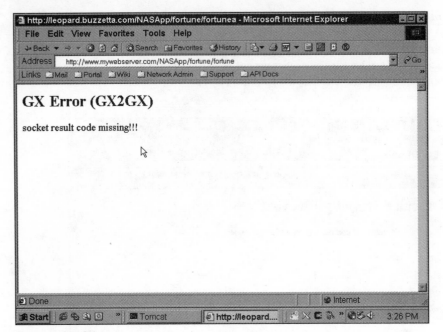

Figure 3–14: GX error

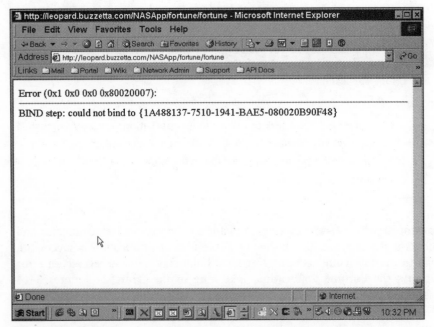

Figure 3–15: Bind error

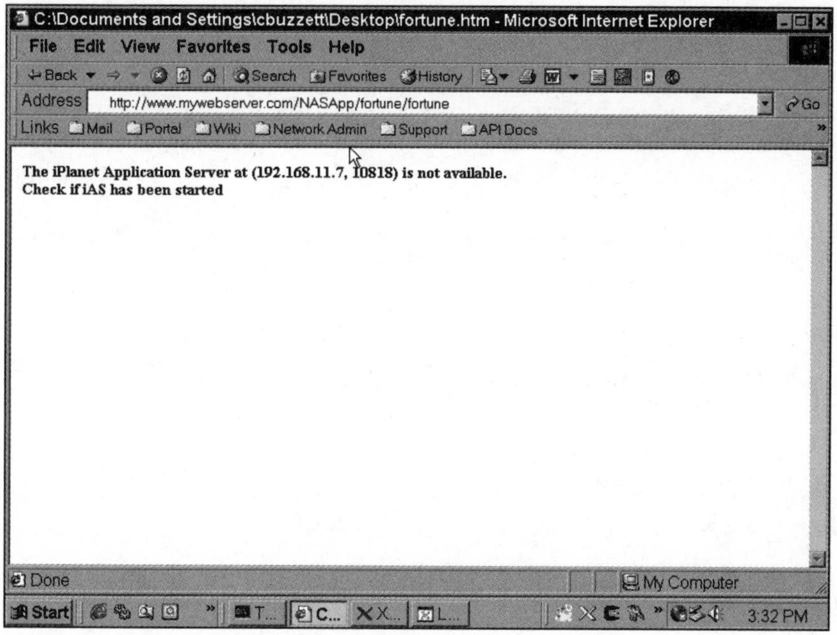

Figure 3-16: Application server unavailable error

Error	Probable Cause	Resolution
The iPlanet Application Server at (192.168.11.9) is not available. Check if iAS has been started.	Application server is not running or communication between the plug-in and application server is not possible	Start the application server or correct any communication issues between the plug-in and application server
GX Error (GX2GX) socket result code missing!!!	The requested component couldn't be resolved usually due to an error registering the application with the application server	Re-register the application
Error (0x1 0x0 0x0 0x80020007): BIND step: could not bind to {1A488137-7510-1941-BAE5-080020B90F48}	There aren't any engines available to handle the request or there are internal communication errors (usually happens when the component is called while an engine is starting but hasn't fully came up yet in debug mode)	Make sure there is an engine running that can handle the component type or restart the application server.

Figure 3-17: Common errors and resolutions

Test Load Balancing

If your installation consists of more than one application server that a Web connector plug-in services, how do you test to make sure that all the backend servers are in use? The following sections discuss how to verify that you're exercising all your application servers.

Load-balancing types

To begin, you need to know the load-balancing scheme that you're using, because this knowledge gives you an indication of what to look for in your testing. I start this section by briefly explaining the different types of load balancing and give you a brief description of each load-balancing type, to provide some functionality background.

The different types of load balancing available with the application server are as follows:

◆ Round robin (Web-connector driven)

◆ Weighted round robin (Web-connector driven)

◆ Per server response time (Web-connector driven)

◆ Per component response time (Web-connector driven)

◆ User-defined criteria (iAS driven)

The most simplistic load balancing scheme is *Round Robin.* The Web-connector plug-in handles the Round Robin load-balancing scheme, which is simply a way to evenly distribute the requests the Web connector receives from a client, one to each application server involved. After all the application servers are assigned a request, the cycle starts over with the first application server.

Weighted Round Robin is a modification of the Round Robin load-balancing scheme, and the Web connector handles it, too. In Weighted Round Robin, each server involved in load balancing is assigned a *weight.* This weight is simply a number of the requests that the application server is to receive. New requests that come in go to a particular server until it receives the weight number of requests, and then the next request goes to the next application server to satisfy its assigned weight and so on in a Round Robin fashion.

The next type of load balancing is *Per-Server Response Time.* In this load-balancing scheme, the Web connector keeps a history (involving the last 128 requests) of all the response times for components that execute on the application server and then averages this number. Each application server gets an average, and the one with the lowest average gets the next request. This load-balancing scheme is the default for an application server.

Per-Component Response Time load balancing is similar to Per-Server Response Time, but for each component request the response time is recorded and grouped by the specific component by the Web connector. The Web connector averages response times on a component-by-component basis for the last 128 calls for the component. This method generally gives you finer-grained control over load balancing but also involves more processing overhead.

The last type of load balancing is *User-Defined Criteria.* The load balancing for this type occurs in the load-balancing service that runs in the KXS process. User-Defined Criteria gives you the greatest control over load balancing but is also the hardest to configure correctly because it heavily depends on your systems and how the applications installed on them behave.

Another type of load balancing that the application server supports is sticky load balancing. Sticky load balancing is a special type of load balancing that you use to force all calls of an application's components that you designate as "sticky" to one server (for a particular session). The initial request of an application for which you set the sticky option is load balanced according to the load-balancing scheme that you configure on the application servers; all subsequent calls to the application components with the sticky bit set for that session, however, are directed to the initial server.

For more information on load balancing, refer to Chapter 10.

Testing load-balancing functionality

To verify that the application server is functioning correctly if two or more application servers are involved in an environment, you need to watch the logs of the application server and make sure that all the servers are getting requests. To do so, you may need to perform some initial steps based on the platform that you're using.

WINDOWS NT/2000

The easiest way to view the iAS logs for a Windows NT/2000 installation is to enable the iAS service to interact with the desktop. To configure the iAS service to interact with the desktop, follow these steps:

1. Open the windows operating system services control utility (see the Windows operating system administrator guides on how to manage services).

2. In the services list, highlight the iPlanet Application Server 6.0 service and double-click to pull up the properties dialog for the service.

3. Click the Log On tab in the properties dialog box.

4. Select the Allow Service to Interact with Desktop check box (see Figure 3-18).

5. Click the OK button.

6. From the Services control utility in Windows, highlight the iPlanet Application Server 6.0 service and then click the stop tool bar button for the service, wait 30 seconds and then click the start tool bar button for the iPlanet Application Server 6.0 service.

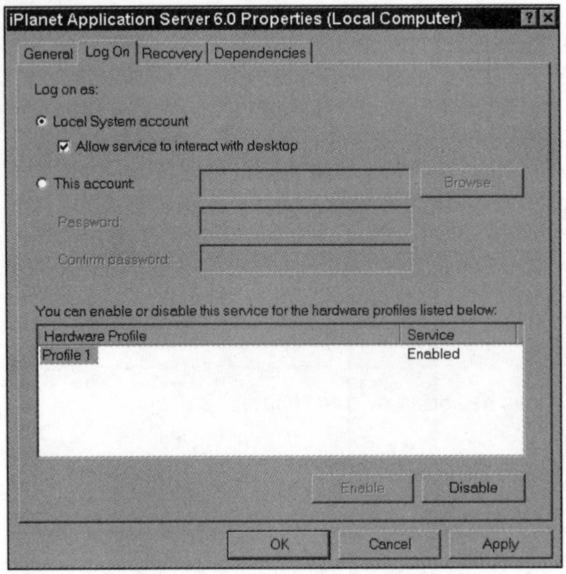

Figure 3-18: Allowing the service to interact with the desktop

On restarting iPlanet, a window for each application server process opens. For this test, only the kxs.exe window concerns you.

Unix

To view the KXS log on Unix systems, navigate to the <IAS_HOME>/logs directory. Run the following command to view the log:

```
tail -f  kxs_0_ccs0
```

Monitor the KXS log files on all the systems that you're testing and run the Fortune application as I describe in the section "Testing Functionality," earlier in this chapter. One of the KXS log files will have a message containing the GUID and the engine number the request was forwarded to for execution by the engine.

The next step is to run the Fortune Application as I describe earlier while viewing the application server KXS logs. To verify that load balancing is working, run the Fortune application repeatedly by hitting the browser's Refresh button. In the KXS log, you should see reqstart and reqexit log messages for the Fortune application requests. You should also see the engine number. The engine number designates to which KJS engine the request is relegated.

In testing situations, you get the best results if you're the only one using the environment. Otherwise, viewing the logs can prove difficult.

Figures 3-19 and 3-20 provide a sample view of the KXS log on Unix and NT/2000, respectively, for reference.

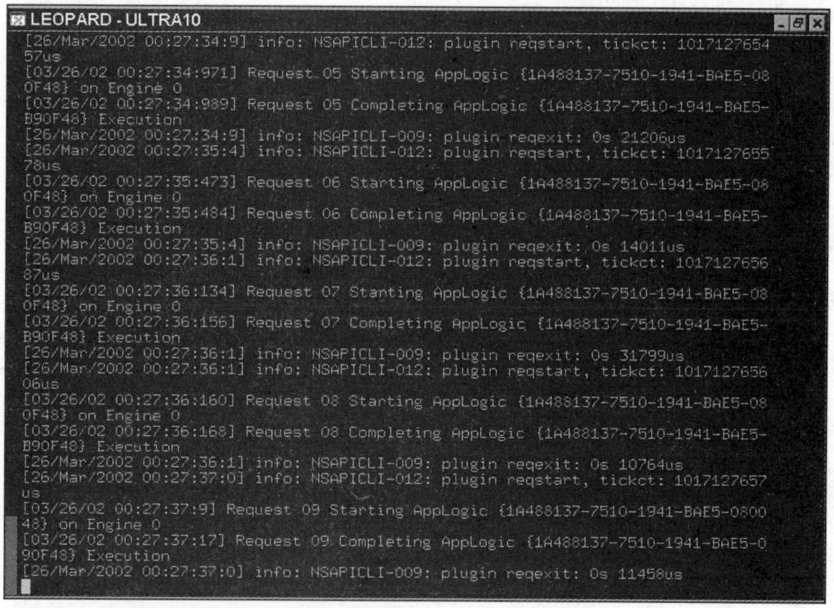

Figure 3-19: Unix KXS log

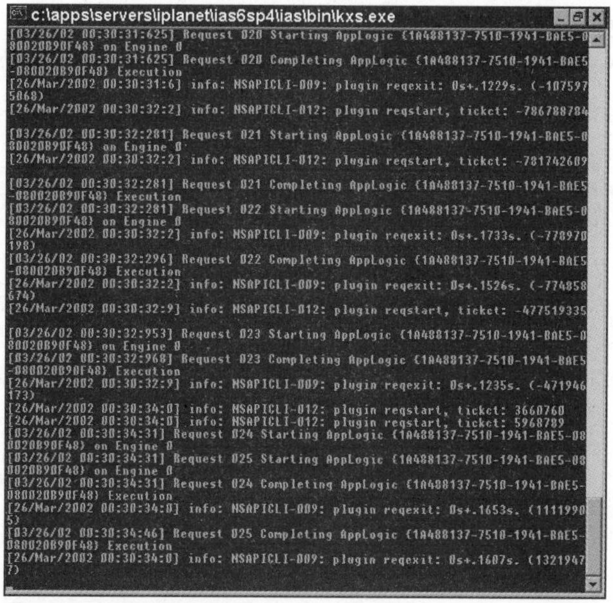

Figure 3-20: NT/2000 KXS log

The GUID for the Fortune application in these examples is {1A488137-7510-1941-BAE5-080020B90F48}. This value may be different on your systems.

The following example represents a log entry for a successful run of the Fortune application:

```
[23/Mar/2002 09:26:31:4] info: NSAPICLI-012: plugin reqstart,
tickct: 1016900791s 448092us
[03/23/02 09:26:31:454] Request 056 Starting AppLogic
{1A488137-7510-1941-BAE5-080020B90F48} on Engine 0
[03/23/02 09:26:31:455] Request 056 Completing AppLogic
{1A488137-7510-1941-BAE5-080020B90F48} Execution
[23/Mar/2002 09:26:31:4] info: NSAPICLI-009: plugin reqexit:
0s 7359us
```

The first line indicates that the KXS has received a request from the Web-connector plug-in and displays the identification number that it assigns to the request (tickct). The next line informs you that the request component's GUID is {1A488137-7510-1941-BAE5-080020B90F48} and that the request passed to engine 0 for processing. The third line informs you that the request was completed. The forth line tells you that the request was sent back to the plug-in along with some timing information on how long the request took to execute.

At the point where the KXS process resolves the component's GUID from the information that the plug-in provides, the following can happen:

◆ The request is successfully handled and a response is generated

◆ The KXS can't resolve the component request

◆ The component generates an error while handling the request

If the KXS can resolve the component request, it forwards the request on to the appropriate engine to handle the request. After the engine completes its processing of the request, it sends the response back to the client.

If the KXS can't resolve the component, it returns an error to the plug-in, and what appears at the client is usually a GX2 error. The error is known as a *Name Translation error*. The html page the client displays when the name translation error is encountered while processing a request for a component, appears in Figure 3-14 in the section "Testing Functionality," earlier in this chapter. An excerpt from the KXS log file is as follows:

```
[23/Mar/2002 09:41:58:6] warning: UTIL-013: GXGUID: NameTrans lookup
failed (Applogic Servlet fortune_fortune)
[23/Mar/2002 09:41:58:6] warning: NSAPICLI-011: socket result code
missing!!!
```

Any of the following can cause this error:

◆ The requested component name is invalid

◆ The requested component isn't registered on the application server

◆ An error occurred while deploying the application

   Another error that can occur is a *bind error*. The major causes of this error are that the requested component is disabled on all the application servers or that the component is registered incorrectly. The error message that appears for this type of error is shown in Figure 3-15 in the section "Testing Functionality," earlier in this chapter. The message written to the KXS log file contains a message similar to the following:

```
[23/Mar/2002 10:19:33:8] error: BINDER-007: GXBindWorker: error
resolving library {1A488137-7510-1941-BAE5-080020B90F48} path
```

 Rarely, the application server gets into a state where it always returns a bind error, or the browser times out on the request. This situation usually occurs in a development environment where you frequently start and stop the application server while a client is making calls to the components. To fix the problem, shut down the entire application server environment and restart it.

   The last type of error that I'm going to discuss is an *application-related error*. The output from this type of error depends on the exact nature of the error or on what type of internal error the application encounters.

   After you test load balancing, only one thing remains for you to verify in the environment. The last functionality to test is whether clustering is working correctly. The following section covers this subject.

Test Clustering Functionality

Clustering in the application-server environment involves two or more application servers connected by a reliable network and working together to handle failure recovery, maintain the integrity of shared state and session data, and enable application code to access session data from distributed sources. You learn more about clusters in Chapter 10. In this chapter, I show you how to determine whether the cluster is working correctly from an application-server point of view and defer the testing of distributed-data synchronization (DSYNC) until Chapter 11.

Server roles in iAS

Before I begin, I need to give you some background information about clusters in the application-server environment. First, I need to discuss the roles that you can assign to servers in the environment. These possible roles are Sync Primary, Sync Backup, Sync Alternate and Sync Local, as the following list describes:

◆ The Sync Primary role is responsible for storing and providing the distributed data to the other servers in the cluster. All distributed data is written to and read from this server. The Sync Primary role also performs the task of updating the Sync Backup's copy of the distributed data store and assigning roles to new application servers joining the environment. Only one Sync Primary can exist per cluster.

◆ The Sync Backup role is responsible for keeping a backup copy of the distributed data store so that it can assume the role of Sync Primary should the Sync Primary fail. You can have one or more Sync Backups in a cluster.

◆ The Sync Alternate role is simply a participant in the cluster that can assume the role of a Sync Backup or a Sync Alternate. You can have any number of Sync Alternates in a cluster.

◆ The Sync Local role is a participant in the cluster that can never assume the role of a Sync Primary. You can have any number of Sync Locals in a cluster.

To test the environment for a correctly functioning cluster, you need only to examine the KXS log. Certain log messages enable you to determine whether the cluster is working correctly in terms of server roles. The easiest way to test this functionality is by stopping all the application servers that are participating in the clustered environment. After you stop all application servers, restart them one at a time and examine the KXS logs for the role that each application server assumes. The next step is to break the cluster to make sure that roles are correctly assigned in the environment automatically.

Test initial roles

Follow these steps to test clustering roles in the application server:

1. Start the first server that can assume the role of a Sync Primary and examine its KXS log. A log message similar to the following should appear, informing you that this server has assumed the role of the Sync Primary:

```
[21/Mar/2002 10:30:31:5] info: DSYNC-039: We(0xc0a80b07:10818),
are coming up as a Primary and max # of hot backup(s)=1
```

2. Start the application server that's to assume the Sync Backup role and examine the KXS log for the Sync Primary and the KXS of the server that you just started. You should find log messages similar to the following:

Look for a similar message in the Sync Primary KXS log:

```
[21/Mar/2002 10:31:26:2] info: DSYNC-079: The Sync Backup,
0xc0a80b03:10818, joined our cluster
```

Look for a similar message in the server just started:

```
[23/Mar/2002 11:50:45:8] info: DSYNC-040:
We(0xc0a80b07:10818), are coming up as a Sync. Alternate and
max # of hot backup(s)=1
...
[23/Mar/2002 11:50:45:9] info: DSYNC-037:
We(0xc0a80b07:10818), have been nominated as a backup by
0xc0a80b03:10818
```

3. Start the Sync Alternates and the Sync Locals. Examine the logs on these servers in the cluster for the following messages:

Look for a similar message in the Sync Primary KXS log:

```
[21/Mar/2002 10:31:26:2] info: DSYNC-079: The Sync Alternate,
0xc0a80b03:10818, joined our cluster
```

Look for a similar message in the server just started log:

```
[23/Mar/2002 12:13:30:9] info: DSYNC-039:
We(0xc0a80b05:10818), are coming up as a alternate and max #
of hot backup(s)=1
```

4. Look for other messages as follows:

If an abnormal cluster is detected (that is, you have no Sync Primary or two Sync Primaries), you see messages similar to the following:

```
[21/Mar/2002 10:30:40:3] error: DSYNC-073: Detected two
primaries (split-brain) in cluster: 0xc0a80b07:10818 and
0xc0a8
0b03:10818. Please shutdown one of them.
[21/Mar/2002 10:31:15:6] info: DSYNC-074: Split-brain
resolved via shutdown of 0xc0a80b03:10818.
```

If the Primary dies, you should see the following message in the log for the new Sync Primary:

```
[21/Mar/2002 13:57:44:0] info: DSYNC-041:
We(0xc0a80b07:10818), are taking over as the Primary and we
have 0 backup(s)
```

If you start a Sync Local, you should see a message similar to the following:

```
[21/Mar/2002 13:59:10:5] info: DSYNC-078: The Sync Local,
0xc0a80b03:10819, joined our cluster
```

If you lose the connection to a Sync Local, you see a message similar to the following:

```
[21/Mar/2002 14:00:11:9] warning: DSYNC-044:
We(0xc0a80b07:10818), lost connection to the Sync Local,
0xc0a80b03:10819
```

If you lose the connection to the Sync Backup, you see a message similar to the following:

```
[21/Mar/2002 14:00:08:3] warning: DSYNC-042:
We(0xc0a80b07:10818), lost connection to the hot backup,
0xc0a80b03:10818
```

For a more in-depth discussion on clusters, see Chapters 10 and 11.

Summary

In this chapter, you learn about some of the tools that you use to administer the application-server environment and the settings that help in determining whether the environment is working correctly. You also learn about the processes that make up the application server, what their responsibilities are, and how to make sure that they're running. You then learn how to determine whether load balancing is working. The last topic that I cover is clustering. You learn what a cluster is, the roles a server can have within a cluster, and how to determine whether the roles are assigned correctly.

Part II

Fundamentals of J2EE

Chapter 4

Writing Servlets

◆ Understanding the role of servlets and the implications of the servlet architecture

◆ Learning the basic application flow of Java servlets

◆ Manipulating session data within a servlet

◆ Introducing the iPlanet Application Server's multiserver and multi-JVM architecture

THIS CHAPTER PROVIDES an introduction to iPlanet Application Server's Web container. This chapter doesn't include an in-depth exploration of the Java Servlets API. We explore enough servlet technology to understand the servlet container of iPlanet Application Server but don't comprehensively explore the details of server-side Java programming with servlets. We explore the topic of iPlanet Application Server servlet deployment in Chapter 5.

HTTP Basics

Before we can discuss how servlets work, you must have a solid understanding of the nature of HTTP (HyperText Transfer Protocol). HTTP is a client/server TCP/IP protocol. A client opens a TCP/IP connection to the server's IP and port, makes a request for a URL, and the server returns a status code and data. (We ignore HTTP Keep-alive for the moment, as the same general principles apply.) Figure 4-1 and the following sections explain this process in detail.

Opening a connection

The first step of an HTTP request is for the client to open the TCP/IP connection between the client and the server. In the simplest case, this process involves a Web browser opening a direct-socket connection to a Web server.

In an enterprise architecture, the process of opening a socket is usually considerably more complex because of the presence of proxies, firewalls, reverse proxies, network address translation, and load balancing. We discuss the effects of these technologies in Chapter 17, but you can safely ignore them for now while considering the basics of servlet architecture.

It is often assumed that the client is a Web browser, such as Internet Explorer or Netscape Navigator but that is not necessarily true. HTTP is now in use for many purposes other than Web browsing, including SOAP and other computer-to-computer interactions. (See Chapter 12 for more information on SOAP.)

Requesting a URL

After opening the socket, the client transmits a request for a URL. The HTTP request goes out in plain ASCII with a blank line marking the end of the request. You can find detailed information on the format of HTTP requests in RFC 2616. We discuss some of the critical elements here, however, by examining the following example of an HTTP request:

```
GET /NASApp/chapter4/AppInfo HTTP/1.1
User-Agent: Mozilla/5.0 (X11; I; SunOS 5.8 sun4u; en-US; 0.8)
Gecko/20010216
Accept: image/gif, image/jpeg, text/*, */*
Cookie: $Version="1";
gx_session_id_="a3f2a9247cc658d9"; $Path="/NASApp/chapter4";
```

The first line of this request shows the type of request we're sending, which we follow with the URL and then the version of the protocol (HTTP/1.1). This part of the request indicates what we're requesting and the format of the request. In this case, we're requesting the /NASApp/chapter4/AppInfo URL, and we're making a GET request over HTTP/1.1.

The rest of the lines provide more details about our request. The second line is a description of the browser that we're using. The third line is a list of all of the MIME types that the client is willing to accept.

The last two lines are a cookie that the client is returning to the server. This gx_session_id cookie is a unique number that iAS automatically generates to identify our session. HTTP is a *stateless protocol.* (*Stateless* means that the protocol doesn't maintain any information about us between requests.) We therefore pass this unique ID to iAS along with each of our requests so that iAS can associate our request with our session information. We discuss sessions in greater detail in the section "Utilizing Sessions" later in this chapter, including alternatives to using cookies to return the unique ID. We also discuss sessions in Chapter 10, where we review the effects of server clustering on sessions.

Server results

After receiving a request, the server returns a response consisting of a status code, status message, and data. The following example illustrates a typical HTTP response.

```
HTTP/1.1 200 OK                              Status Code/Status
Message
Server: Netscape-Enterprise/4.1             MetaData
Date: Tue, 17 Jul 2001 02:37:00 GMT
Content-type: text/html
Last-modified: Tue, 17 Jul 2001 02:36:41 GMT
Content-length: 40
Accept-ranges: bytes
Connection: close
<html>                                       Data
<body>
<h1>Sample
</body>
</html>
```

This HTTP response is an example of a simple successful static HTML request. It contains a status code (200), a status message (OK), metadata (Content-type, Content-length, Last-modified), and the data itself (the HTML). You can find the exact details of the HTTP response format in RFC 2616.

 An important thing to notice about the HTTP response is that the server sends the status and metadata to the client prior to sending the actual data. After our application starts sending data to the client, therefore, the application can no longer change the status code or metadata information.

The Web Connector

With this basic understanding of how HTTP works, we can now examine the differences between returning static content and dynamically returning content that servlets generate. For simplicity, we define *static content* as any content that the application server doesn't generate.

Each Web-server vendor provides an API to enable the third parties to integrate external code with its Web server. The functionality that you implement by using these APIs is known as a *plug-in*. (Apache uses the term *modules* instead of plug-ins, but we use the generic term *plug-in* in this book, even in referring to Apache modules.)

After a Web server receives an HTTP request, the Web server first gives its plug-ins an opportunity to intercept the request. The plug-ins can then modify the request, return the results for the request, or permit the Web server to continue processing the request unmodified. (See the section "For More Information," at the end of the chapter, for links to more information about the plug-in APIs and how they work.)

iPlanet Application Server uses plug-ins to return the results of servlet requests. iAS plug-ins currently are available for iPlanet Web Server 4.1 and 6.0, Apache Web Server 1.3.19, and Microsoft Information Server 4.0 or 5.0. All the plug-ins are functionally identical.

Unlike some other application servers, iPlanet Application Server doesn't include an embedded Web server. You must use a separate Web server even for development.

The iAS Web connector examines each request coming into the Web server and intercepts those for the application server. The Web connector uses a URL path prefix to determine which requests belong to the application server. The default prefix is NASApp, but the administrator can change this prefix to any string value by modifying the iAS registry. (We discuss the details of changing this prefix in Chapter 13.) Thus the Web connector forwards any request that begins with /NASApp to iAS, even if a /NASApp directory is on the Web server; the Web server handles all other requests without interference from the Web connector. Therefore, our earlier example of a request for /NASApp/chapter4/AppInfo will result in the Web connector forwarding the request to the application server for processing.

One commonly asked question is how to avoid using a prefix in iAS URLs. Although changing the prefix is possible, you currently *can't* omit the prefix completely.

After the Web connector determines that the request is an application-server request, it parses the URL path into three parts: the *prefix*, the *context root*, and the *component*. The *prefix* is the string between the initial slash and the second slash. The *context root* is the string between the second and third slashes. The *component* is anything after the third slash, including any additional slashes in the URL. The URL path from the HTTP request in the section "Requesting a URL" earlier in this chapter, for example, is /NASApp/chapter4/AppInfo. NASApp is the prefix; chapter4 is the context root; and AppInfo is the component. The Web connector then searches the component registry for a matching component. The registry has the information needed to process the request, including where the component has been deployed, where the component had been disabled, and the details of the current load balancing parameters. (See Chapter 10 for more information about configuring load balancing.)

The Web connector then transmits the request to the KXS process of the chosen application server. The Web connector includes within its message to the KXS the requested URL, any variables that the HTTP client submits via the post method, any cookies that it sends with the request, the IP of the requesting client, the request method (POST or GET), and a subset of the HTTP headers. The default list of headers is host, referer, and user agent, although the iAS administrator can modify in the registry the list of HTTP headers that the request includes. In summary, however, the Web connector forwards the HTTP headers the application server will need to satisfy the servlet API. If your application needs access to additional headers beyond those available in the servlet API, you will have to configure the Web connector to forward those additional headers. (See Chapter 13 for information about how to change the list of forwarded HTTP headers.)

GET and POST

The HTTP standard provides several "methods" to allow HTTP clients to interact with the HTTP server. The complete list of HTTP 1.1 methods is OPTIONS, GET, HEAD, POST, PUT, DELETE, TRACE, and CONNECT. Not all Web servers implement all of them, however, and as servlet developers we are primarily concerned with the GET and POST methods.

The GET method was originally designed for requests of information from the Web server. When used in combination with HTML forms the browser encodes the form values into the URL. This is both the biggest advantage and disadvantage of the GET method, since the length of the URL is limited.

GET requests can only contain a limited amount of form information. Additionally, since the form values are encoded into the URL, the user can observe the form values directly. For this reason, the GET method is inadvisable for sensitive information such as passwords. The advantage of this URL encoding, however, is that the URL contains all of the information needed to recreate the request. If the user bookmarks the URL, he can automatically pass the same values to the Web server without having to revisit the actual form.

POST requests were originally designed for submission of information from the HTTP client to the Web server. Rather than encoding HTML form elements into the URL, POST requests send form data within the body of the HTTP request. This keeps the data from being casually observed in the URL window of the browser or in the access log of the Web server. (SSL is still required to keep form data from being observed by network sniffers, however.)

You should choose between GET and POST based on the sensitivity of the data and how you want users to interact with your Web site. Passwords and sensitive data should always be sent with a POST request. GETs should be used anytime that you want to allow a user to be able to bookmark the results of a particular request. When in doubt, follow the original guidelines of using the GET method to request information and the POST method to submit information.

It is important to note that iPlanet Application Server expects to be both the Web container and the EJB container. In other words, iAS expects to execute both your servlets/JSPs and your EJBs.

The J2EE specification allows (and almost encourages) the Web and EJB containers to be separated. However, all major application servers, including iAS, can optimize the communication between the Web container and the EJB container. This optimization means that using the same application server for both your Web components and EJB components is *much* more efficient than separating the containers.

The application server's Web container then processes the request and returns the results to the Web connector. The Web connector buffers the results from the application server and streams them back to the client. This result buffering prevents the Web container from needing to wait for the results to go out over a slow connection to the requesting client.

The Servlet Lifecycle

The servlet lifecycle is designed to be extremely efficient. Unlike other methods of generating dynamic content – specifically, CGI – Web containers don't spawn a process for each incoming request. In fact, most Web containers don't even spawn a thread or instantiate a servlet object for each request. Most Web containers, including iPlanet Application Server, keep a pool of worker threads that they assign to incoming requests as necessary. This lifecycle avoids the overhead of continually spawning new threads or processes. Typically, the servlet is created once and continually reused until the server shuts down, the servlet needs to be reloaded, or the server needs the memory that the servlet occupies. An important consideration is that the servlet specification doesn't guarantee that servlets access will be thread-safe unless the developer specifically declares the servlet to implement the `SingleThreadModel` interface. If the developer doesn't implement the `SingleThreadModel` interface, iAS creates only one instance of the servlet, and all the threads in that JVM use that single servlet instance. If you do implement the `SingleThreadModel` interface, iAS creates a pool of servlet instances and manages that pool of instances so that only one thread is using each servlet instance at a time. The default number of instance is ten, but you can define the size of the instance pool in the deployment descriptor for that servlet. In the next chapter we will discuss deployment descriptors and how to customize them.

A more efficient course is to define your servlets without the `SingleThreadModel` interface, because doing so reduces the amount of memory that the servlet container needs and also reduces the amount of overhead managing requests to that servlet increasing the performance and scalability of your application.

If you elect to multithread your servlets, you must make sure that you make your servlets thread-safe, which means that you can't assume that you have exclusive access to the servlet object. You may, for example, need to synchronize access to certain variables or methods of the servlets.

In many applications, synchronizing access to variables isn't a major concern, as the `HttpSession` object (which we describe in the next section, "Utilizing Sessions") enables the developer to store session state safely and application state is often read-only. If you find yourself synchronizing too many methods or variables, however, just using the `SingleThreadModel` may prove more efficient.

When the container needs to instantiate a new servlet (typically because a client has requested the servlet for the first time) the container calls the `init` method of the servlet before allowing clients to access the newly instantiated servlet. This enables the servlet programmer a chance to perform any required initialization.

When creating an `init` method, you must begin your method with a call to the `init` method of the superclass. This ensures that iAS's Web container gets the opportunity to properly initialize the servlet. Omitting the call to the superclasses' init will prevent the servlet from executing. For example, a correctly written init method will look like the following:

```
public void init (ServletConfig config) throws
ServletException {
    super.init(config);
    // You custom initialization code here.
}
```

Init methods are useful to perform one-time initializations of the servlet. Since the `init` method has access to the `ServletConfig`, unlike the object constructor, the `init` method can perform initializations related to the Web container. For example, an init method would be able to initialize a cache, which is based on attributes stored in the `ServletContext`.

Similarly, the container will call the `destroy` method of the servlet before disposing of a servlet instance. The servlet developer can use this method to release resources that `init` allocates. The `destroy` method is used less commonly, however, as the Web container typically destroys servlets only as the server itself is shutting down.

The Initialize on Startup deployment descriptor works differently in iPlanet Application Server than on many other application servers. In iAS, a servlet that you mark to Initialize on Startup initializes when the first user requests the first servlet in the Web application and not as iAS itself starts. Web applications remain dormant until a user requests a servlet or JSP from within that application.

Think of Initialize on Startup as meaning Initialize on Application Startup and not as Initialize on Server Startup. If you need to run initialization code on server startup, use the IStartupClass interface that Chapter 13 of the *iPlanet Programmer's Guide* in the iPlanet documentation set describes.

After initialization, you use the servlet object for all requests for that servlet within that Java engine (KJS). GET requests invoke the doGet method of the servlet object. POST requests invoke the doPost method of the servlet object. Use these methods to implement your servlet functionality.

Many of the sample applications that iAS includes override the service method rather than overriding the doGet and doPost methods of HttpServlet. The service method of the HttpServlet object dispatches incoming requests to the doGet and doPost methods based on the request method. (See the GET and POST sidebar for the differences between the GET method and the POST method.)

Overriding the service method allows you to process requests regardless of the request method used. We recommend that, for portability and flexibility reasons, you override the doGet and doPost methods for production applications rather than overriding service.

If you want to implement identical functionality for both GET and POST requests, use the doPost method to call the doGet method, as we demonstrate in the AppInfo servlet sample for this chapter. The complete source code for the AppInfo servlet can be found in the beginning of the "AppInfo Sample Servlet" section later in this chapter.

In summary, you should override the init, destroy, doGet, and doPost methods of HttpServlet to implement your custom functionality. You should also assume that you can't run your servlet in a thread-safe environment unless you specifically mark it as single threaded in the deployment descriptor and by using the SingleThreadModel interface. Because of the performance penalty of the SingleThreadModel, however, you should make your servlets thread-safe whenever possible.

Utilizing Sessions

One of the first things that the doGet method of AppInfo does is get the HttpSession from the HttpServletRequest object. Conceptually, the HttpSession is a simple API. The HttpSession object provides a way to have the application server store information about a user between the user's requests. Each time that a user makes a request to iAS , the servlet can access the same HttpSession object. (Even though the HTTP protocol is stateless, the application server is able to accomplish this by passing a unique identifier to each user either in the form of a cookie or a hidden field.) The HttpSession object stores information about the user that needs to be preserved for the length of the user's session. The developer could use the session, for example, to store information about the user's privileges or preferences.

 One common example for session usage is to implement shopping cart functionality, where the user will add various products to the HttpSession session objects for later purchase. This is a bad example, however. We discuss later in this section why sessions make a bad implementation for shopping carts.

To use HttpSession effectively, however, you need an understanding of how the server actually implements sessions behind the scenes. Lack of information about how the server implements sessions can result in poorly performing applications, the loss of session information, or even bad HTML results. After discussing the theory of how the server implements sessions in iAS, we discuss in this section and the next how to prevent these problems.

To implement sessions, the application server must have some method of recognizing requests from the same user. We mention earlier in this section that cookies provide one way of recognizing these requests. The application server automatically returns a cookie (which it names gx_session_id_) containing a unique key the first time that a user makes a request to the application server that requires a session. If the user makes subsequent requests, the key value within the cookie identifies the user.

Not all clients support cookies, however, and some users may turn off cookie support in their browsers. (TheCounter.com reported in July 2001 that 11.3 percent of Web users don't have cookie support or disable cookies.) iPlanet Application Server uses *URL rewriting* as an alternative method of identifying these types of users. iAS implements URL rewriting by modifying outgoing HTML to embed the sessionid in all the hyperlinks and forms. iAS uses both URL rewriting and cookies on the user's first request. (If the user's request contains the `gx_session_id_` cookie, iAS knows that the user's client supports cookies and doesn't do URL rewriting on the response to that request.) See the accompanying sidebar, however, for some of the common pitfalls of using URL rewriting.

Beginning with iAS 6.0sp4, there are now options for implementing URL rewriting. If the first option, implicit URL rewriting, is enabled the Web connector automatically rewrites URLs as necessary. The second option, explicit URL rewriting, requires that the user make explicit calls to the server API functions encodeURL and encodeRedirectURL in order to rewrite URLs. (Implicit URL rewriting is the default option and the only option available prior to sp4.)

Implicit URL rewriting is the easiest to implement since it allows the developer to ignore the issues of URL rewriting. However, explicit URL rewriting gives the developer more control and may be necessary if the implicit URL rewriter is not rewriting the URL's correctly (as described in the sidebar). To turn on the explicit URL rewriting option, set the registry value SOFTWARE\ iPlanet\Application Server\6.5\CCS0\HTTPAPI\URLRewrite to "explicit."

You also need to note that iAS stores all session information in-memory and possibly transmits it across the network for high availability. Because of this in-memory implementation of sessions, the `HttpSession` isn't an appropriate location to store large amounts of information. A common guideline is not to store more than a few kilobytes of information in the session. You can best use the session to store small pieces of information, such as user credentials, user preferences, database keys, and the user's current status within the application. Shopping carts and form data are examples of information that you're better off storing in a database rather than in the session. (It's also a bad idea to store shopping cart information in the session because the shopping cart information would be lost if the user's session times out or the user's browser crashes.)

Objects that you store in the `HttpSession` must be serializable if you're enabling distributed (highly available) sessions. Nonserializable objects are lost if you attempt to store them in the session.

You can find information about distributed sessions in Chapters 10 and 11. Distributed sessions enable you to share your session information across an iAS cluster and preserve it in case of a server failure.

URL Rewriting Dangers

URL rewriting is not as foolproof as utilizing cookies, because users who use bookmarks or type URLs directly into their browsers can circumvent the embedded URLs, causing them to lose their sessions. We know of no way to solve this problem other than to warn your users not to navigate to URLs directly. If you expect the user to have a session but detect that he doesn't, you may want to return an error page warning users not to bookmark or type URLs directly.

Additionally, the iAS doesn't recognize URLs in JavaScript code. If you're using JavaScript to open URLs, you must encode the URL's yourself. Use the `HttpServletResponse.encodeURL` method to manually rewrite a URL to include the `sessionid`. This procedure also encodes the sticky cookie, if you've enabled stickiness.

The `encodeURL` method doesn't work in versions of iAS 6.x earlier than sp4. If you're using a version of iAS that predates sp4, you must encode the URL yourself. You can determine the `sessionid` by using the `HttpSession.getID` function. Precede the session with `?GXHC_gx_sessionid_=` to embed this `sessionid` in a URL.

Older versions of iAS (6.0sp2 and earlier) also rewrite JavaScript URLs and other URLs that you don't want rewritten. Workarounds are available to prevent the URL rewriter from breaking your JavaScript, but the better solution is to upgrade to a more recent version of iPlanet Application Server.

If you choose not to support clients without cookies and want to disable the URL rewriter, you can do so by setting the `SOFTWARE\iPlanet\Application Server\6.5\CCSO\HTTPAPI\NoCookie` registry key to the value 2. (For more information about setting registry keys, see Chapter 13.)

To avoid problems using `HttpSession`, therefore, you need to understand the way that the application server maintains your session. Be aware of the limitations of the URL rewriter and of the performance implications of storing large amounts of information in the session object.

Sticky Sessions

"Sticky sessioning" is an iAS feature that allows repeated requests from the same user to always return to the same KJS. The application server accomplishes this by returning a cookie, which the application names GX_jst. This cookie contains an encrypted cookie that contains the host and IP of both the KXS and KJS that should be used to process that user's requests. (If the user has cookies disabled, the server will use URL rewriting to implement the same functionality.)

When the Web connector sees the GX_jst cookie being returned by the browser it decrypts the cookie to determine the KXS where it should forward the request. Similarly, the KXS use the contents of the GX_jst cookie to decide which KJS should process the user's request.

We will discuss sticky sessions in great detail in Chapter 10. We also discuss the benefits of sticky sessions in Chapter 11, when we discover how using sticky sessions increases the performance of high availability sessions.

ServletContext

The ServletContext API allows the developer to interact with the Web container. For example, one common use of the ServletContext is to obtain access to the RequestDispatcher. The RequestDispatcher allows the developer to forward control to another Web container object either temporarily (with the include method) or permanently (with the forward method).

The most common example of this is a servlet forwarding control to a JSP to format results. The following code from iAS's fortune sample is an example of using a JSP to format results:

```
RequestDispatcher dispatcher;
dispatcher = getServletContext().getRequestDispatcher("/fortune.jsp");
dispatcher.include(req,res);
```

The preceding code uses the Servlet method getServletContext to retrieve a RequestDispatcher for the fortune.jsp JSP file. As a final step in the third line of code, the dispatcher is directed to include the results of the JSP into the current output stream. (The req and res arguments are the request object and response object, respectively.)

Another common use of the ServletContext is to store "global" application variables. Like the HttpSession object, the ServletContext is available across all JVMs. (See the following section, "Multi-JVM Considerations.") And like the session object, storing objects in the ServletContext should be used judiciously. Since all changes are kept in-memory and replicated real-time across the network, storing large objects and/or frequent updates to the ServletContext attributes could cause a degradation in application performance.

Multi-JVM Considerations

Many guides to writing servlets assume that you're using a simple, single virtual machine (JVM) Web container. Developers new to iPlanet Application Server, therefore, often make these same assumptions in developing applications for iAS. Because most developers run only a single KJS engine, and therefore a single JVM, on their developer workstations, the consequences of these faulty assumptions often don't surface until the first time that someone deploys the application to a QA or production server configured with multiple JVMs. If you deploy the application with sticky load balancing, the faulty logic may not even surface until you conduct failover tests.

Don't fall into this trap. Don't assume that your code is executing in the same servlet object on every request and don't assume that all the application is executing in the same JVM. The following list describes several commonly made mistakes, as well as some multi-JVM alternatives:

◆ **Don't assume that singleton patterns are unique.** *Singletons* are a simple construction pattern that ensures that one – and only one – instance of the created class exists. You implement most singleton patterns by storing the object instance in a static variable of the class itself. You then use a static method to control access to the variable and to limit the class to one instantiation. (For more information on patterns, see the links in the section "For More Information," at the end of this chapter.)

Realizing that static variables and methods are unique to the classloader, however, and not unique across the entire application-server cluster is important. So traditional singleton patterns create one instance of the class per KJS engine and not one instance per cluster. If your application assumes that singletons are completely unique (for example, to create unique database keys), therefore, your application fails if you deploy it to a multi-JVM environment.

Having singleton objects that are truly unique across the cluster is theoretically possible. (One implementation is to use an EJB with a handle that you share via the ServletContext.) Because that object resides in only one JVM, however, you must access it via remote invocation. Additionally, that single object becomes a severe bottleneck for the entire application. You want, therefore, to avoid this type of "true" singleton.

The better solution to this challenge is to design your code so that it doesn't depend on the complete uniqueness of a singleton. In the preceding situation, for example, you could allocate the unique keys out of the database itself.

◆ **Do not use static variables to pass information between sessions.** A similar problem occurs if programmers attempt to use static variables as a method of communication between sessions. Imagine, for example, a simple chat server running on a single JVM. You can place the chat messages in a hashtable that you store in a static variable of the servlet. Each request could use synchronized methods to read and add messages to the hashtable.

In a multi-JVM environment, however, multiple JVMs can't share the hashtable static variable between themselves. As requests load-balance across the cluster, the user sees only the chat messages that the request's JVM stores.

You also can't use the servlet object for sharing information. Each JVM has its own instantiation of the servlet object. Counters in the servlet object (such as the `unsafeCounter` in the `AppInfo` sample from this chapter), for example, don't increment sequentially if you deploy them in a clustered environment.

One way to share data between sessions safely in a multi-JVM environment is to use the `ServletContext` object. Attributes that you store in the `ServletContext` are globally accessible by other Web container objects in the cluster via the distributed-sessions mechanism (*DSYNC*). You can obtain the `ServletContext` by using the `getServletContext` method of the servlet object. You can then use the `setAttribute` and `getAttribute` methods to add and retrieve data objects.

Another, more scalable way to share information in a multi-JVM environment is to use a central backend system such as a database or JMS publisher. `ServletContext` is better suited to information with less frequent updates. For example, `ServletContext` would not be a good datastore for our chat server example.

◆ **Don't use sticky load balancing to avoid these limitations if you have failover requirements.** Using sticky load balancing forces repeated requests from the same session to go to the same JVM every time. Sticky load balancing can therefore enable you to avoid some of the multi-JVM issues by ensuring that the same JVM always processes your session. This would theoretically enable you to take advantage of static variables and servlet instance variables to store state information in between requests.

If your JVM fails, however, this information is lost. If your JVM were to fail, the sticky property of your request would be ignored so that it can route the request to a working JVM. This new JVM doesn't contain the expected state information for your session, probably causing a disruption in the user's experience.

Session state information belongs in the `HttpSession`. Global application state information belongs in the `ServletContext`. Attempting to store state elsewhere, such as in the servlet object or in static variables, is likely to cause long-term problems in designing multiple JVM architectures. (Stateful EJB's are another possible location to store state information. We will discuss the advantages and disadvantages of storing state this way in chapter 7.

You have valid reasons to use static variables and servlet instance variables — for example, to create a shared pool of resources or a local cache of information. However, the system architect must remain aware that these pools and caches are implemented per JVM, and a session's requests aren't always processed on the same JVM.

AppInfo Sample Servlet

We mention the AppInfo sample servlet several times earlier in this chapter, in discussing how to override `doGet` and `doPost`. We now examine AppInfo in more detail to demonstrate the basics of writing a servlet. The complete source code for AppInfo is shown below in Listing 4-1. We will explain each section of the source code in detail as we progress through this section.

Listing 4-1: Complete AppInfo source code

```
/*
 * Copyright 2001 HungryMinds Inc.
 */
package com.hungryminds.ias.chapter4;

import java.io.*;
import java.util.*;
import javax.servlet.*;
import javax.servlet.http.*;
import java.net.*;


/**
 * A simple servlet to demonstrate how servlets handle threads and
 * the basics of servlet operation.
 *
 * @Author David F. Ogren
 */
public class AppInfo extends HttpServlet {

    String myHostName;
    int unsafeCounter;

    /**
     * The init method gives us the opportunity to perform one-time
     * initialization of the servlet object.
     * <p>
     * We perform four operations:<br>
     *    1. Allowing the superclass to perform its initializations<br>
     *    2. Logging the initialization<br>
     *    3. Initializing the "unsafeCounter" variable<br>
     *    4. Initializing the hostname variable<br>
     *
     * @param config ServletConfig object required by superclass
     */
```

Continued

Listing 4–1 *(Continued)*

```java
public void init (ServletConfig config) throws ServletException {

    super.init(config);
    System.out.println("Chapter4 : init method of AppInfo");

    try {
        InetAddress theAddress = InetAddress.getLocalHost();
        myHostName = theAddress.getHostName();
    }
    catch (Exception e) {
        myHostName = "N/A";
        System.out.println("Hostname not available");
    }

    unsafeCounter=1;
}

/**
 * The doGet method is used to process requests made to the servlet
 * <p>
 * We handle requests by returning some basic status information about
 * the request back to the user. We return the following information
 *    1. The name of the servlet and application.
 *    2. The hostname (of the application server)
 *    3. The sessionid
 *    4. Session creation time.
 *    5. Session last accessed time.
 *    6. User Agent string
 *    7. The value of a counter variable in the servlet (unsafe counter)
 *    8. The value of a counter variable in the session (safe counter)
 *
 * @param req    HttpServletRequest object required by superclass
 * @param resp   HttpServletResponse object required by superclass
 */
public void doGet(HttpServletRequest req,
                  HttpServletResponse resp)
    throws IOException, ServletException {

    //Log requests
    System.out.println("Chapter4 : AppInfo processing request");

    //Get objects from request and session
    HttpSession session = req.getSession();
    PrintWriter out = resp.getWriter();
```

```
        Integer safeCounter = (Integer) session.getAttribute("safecounter");
        String userAgent = req.getHeader("User-Agent");
        if (safeCounter==null) {
            System.out.println("Chapter4 : Initializing safeCounter");
            safeCounter=new Integer(1);
        }
        if (userAgent==null) {
            userAgent="No User Agent HTTP header provided.";
        }

        //Send results to client
        resp.setContentType("text/html");
        out.println("<html>");
        out.println("<head><title>Chapter4 : AppInfo</title></head>");
        out.println("<body bgcolor=\"white\">");
        out.println("<h1>Chapter4 Sample</h1>");
        out.println("<h3>Host : " + myHostName);
        out.println("<h3>User Agent : " + userAgent);
        out.println("<br>Session ID: " + session.getId());
        out.println("<br>");
        out.println("Session Start: ");
        out.println(new Date(session.getCreationTime()) + "<br>");
        out.println("Session Last Accessed: ");
        out.println(new Date(session.getLastAccessedTime()));
        out.println("<br>");
        out.println("<br>Safe Counter :" + safeCounter.toString());
        out.println("<br>Unsafe counter :" + unsafeCounter);
        out.println("</body></html>");
        out.close();

        // Update counters
        unsafeCounter++;
        safeCounter=new Integer(safeCounter.intValue()+1);
        session.setAttribute("safecounter",safeCounter);

        System.out.println("Chapter4 : AppInfo finished processing request");
    }

/**
 * This sample makes no distinction between GET and POST requests,
 * forwarding all doPost requests to doGet for processing.
 *
 * @param req    HttpServletRequest object required by superclass
 * @param resp   HttpServletResponse object required by superclass
```

Continued

Listing 4–1 *(Continued)*

```
*/
public void doPost(HttpServletRequest req, HttpServletResponse resp)
    throws IOException,ServletException {
    doGet(req,resp);
}
```

You can find all the sample code on this book's CD-ROM. Under the samples directory, you find a subdirectory for each chapter. In that directory, you find an EAR file ready for deployment to your server, as well as subdirectories containing the source code, compiled classes, and javadocs for that sample. The file-system layout is the same as the iAS sample applications use.

If you register your server in the Administration tool, as we describe in Chapter 2, you can use the included Ant build files to build, package, and deploy the samples. You can find information on deployment in Chapter 5.

For the sake of brevity, we may omit some white space in the code listing excerpts in the book. They're functionally identical, however, to the complete listings on the CD-ROM.

AppInfo is a simple servlet that demonstrates some basic functionality of the Web container. If called, the servlet returns an HTML page that lists the following information:

◆ Static information, including the name of the servlet and sample.

◆ The host name of the application server.

◆ The client's user agent string (an identifier that the browser provides to the Web server).

◆ The `sessionid` (an identifier that the application server uses to identify the interactions between that user and the application server cluster).

◆ The creation time and last accessed time for that `sessionid`.

◆ The current value of two different counters, one of which is a "safe" counter that the `HttpSession` stores. The other is an "unsafe" counter that the servlet object stores.

Listing 4-2 shows sample output from the AppInfo servlet. (The application server was running on a server named `chico.thirdnotice.com`, and it was accessed via a Netscape browser running on Solaris 8.)

Listing 4-2: Sample Output from AppInfo

```
Chapter4 Sample

Host : chico.thirdnotice.com

User Agent : Mozilla/4.7 [en] (x11; I; SunOS 5.8 sun4u)
Session ID: f102508f3182c013
Session Start : Tue Jul31 19:25:24 EDT 2001
Session Last Accessed : Tue Jul 31 19:25:24 EDT 2001

Safe Counter :1
Unsafe Counter :1
```

Definition of AppInfo

The AppInfo servlet is just an ordinary Java class, as can be seen in the beginning of the AppInfo source code.

```
package com.hungryminds.ias.chapter4;

import java.io.*;
import java.util.*;
import javax.servlet.*;
import javax.servlet.http.*;
import java.net.*;

public class AppInfo extends HttpServlet {
```

This excerpt from the beginning of the servlet shows how the AppInfo servlet imports the relevant servlet packages (javax.servlet.* and javax.servlet.http.*) along with the other required Java packages. The `AppInfo` servlet extends the HttpServlet superclass that provides the access to the Web container APIs.

More complicated inheritance models are, of course, possible. Servlets are free to implement additional interfaces, or extend subclasses of `HttpServlet` rather than extending `HttpServlet` directly. For example, some applications will define an abstract subclass of `HttpServlet` that implements business logic common to all servlets within the application.

Initializing AppInfo

AppInfo performs three tasks in its `init` method. The source code for the `init` method is shown below in Listing 4-3. (The init method also calls the superclass' `init` method, as you should always do in overriding the `init` method of `HttpServlet`. The superclass's init method is required to allow the Web container to properly initialize the servlet.) As we mention in the section "The Servlet Lifecycle" earlier in this chapter, the `init` method is called only once: as iAS receives the first request for the AppInfo servlet.

The first task that AppInfo performs is to write a log message out to `System.out.println`. This simple log message enables you to easily verify that the `init` method is called only once. iPlanet Application Server writes these `System.out` messages into the KJS log of the JVM handling the request. If you need help finding or reading this log, you can find more information about iAS logging in Chapter 14.

The next task is to determine and save the hostname of the application server and store it in a variable of the servlet for future use. Because the hostname of the application server never changes, looking it up once during initialization is more efficient than looking up the hostname for each request.

The final task is to initialize the "unsafe counter." (We call it an unsafe counter for two reasons: Because you store the counter as a variable of the servlet, all the requests that are using that JVM share it. Repeated requests to the counter, therefore, don't always yield consecutive results, because other users are incrementing the same counter. We discuss the second reason that we call it unsafe when we discuss the `doGet` method in the next section.)

Listing 4-3 shows the code for the `init` method of AppInfo, implementing the functionality that we list in the preceding four paragraphs.

Listing 4–3: Init method of AppInfo servlet

```
public void init (ServletConfig config) throws ServletException {
    super.init(config);
    System.out.println("Chapter4 : init method of AppInfo");
    try {
        InetAddress theAddress = InetAddress.getLocalHost();
        myHostName = theAddress.getHostName();
    }
    catch (Exception e) {
        myHostName = "N/A";
        System.out.println("Hostname not available");
    }
    unsafeCounter=1;
}
```

The first line calls the superclasses `init` method, as required to allow the servlet to properly initialize. The method then prints a log statement, gets the host name of the server by using the InetAddress class, and then initializes the `unsafeCounter` variable. A try/catch block is also included to account for any problems encountered obtaining the host name.

Handling requests

AppInfo processes all incoming requests by using the doGet method; doPost merely forwards incoming POST requests to the doGet method. (This is a common implementation for servlets that respond to GET and POST methods identically.) The doGet method gathers information from the HttpServletRequest object, the HttpSession, and the actual servlet object to create an HTML response that returns to the client.

Servlets use the HttpServletRequest object that the Web container passes to them as an argument as their view into all the incoming information. AppInfo demonstrates two HttpServletRequest methods: getSession and getHeader. Other methods exist to enable the developer access to all the information available about the incoming request, including the fields of HTML forms.

Similarly, servlets use the HttpServletResponse object to tell the Web container how to build the response back to the client. AppInfo uses HttpServletResponse very simply, setting the content type to HTML and obtaining an output stream for the generated HTML.

The AppInfo code generates the HTML simply by concatenating strings together. It builds HTML line by line by combining the static content strings with the dynamic data and outputting the results with println statements. (We discuss more sophisticated methods of generating HTML results as we discuss JSPs in Chapter 6.)

Listing 4-4 shows the code that you use to process incoming requests: the doGet and doPost methods of AppInfo.

Listing 4-4 : Processing Requests in the AppInfo servlet

```
public void doGet(HttpServletRequest req, HttpServletResponse resp)
    throws IOException, ServletException {
    //Log requests
    System.out.println("Chapter4 : AppInfo processing request");

    //Get objects from request and session
    HttpSession session = req.getSession(false);
    PrintWriter out = resp.getWriter();
    Integer safeCounter = (Integer) session.getAttribute("safecounter");
    String userAgent = req.getHeader("User-Agent");
    if (safeCounter==null) {
        System.out.println("Chapter4 : Initializing safeCounter");
        safeCounter=new Integer(1);
    }
    if (userAgent==null) {
        userAgent="No User Agent HTTP header provided.";
    }

    //Send results to client
```

Continued

Listing 4-4 *(Continued)*

```
resp.setContentType("text/html");
out.println("<html>");
out.println("<body bgcolor=\"white\">");
out.println("<head><title>Chapter4 : AppInfo</title></head>");
out.println("<body>");
out.println("<h1>Chapter4 Sample</h1>");
out.println("<h3>Host : " + myHostName);
out.println("<h3>User Agent : " + userAgent);
out.println("<br>Session ID: " + session.getId());
out.println("<br>");
out.println("Session Start: ");
out.println(new Date(session.getCreationTime()) + "<br>");
out.println("Session Last Accessed: ");
out.println(new Date(session.getLastAccessedTime()));
out.println("<br>");
out.println("<br>Safe Counter :" + safeCounter.toString());
out.println("<br>Unsafe counter :" + unsafeCounter);
out.println("</body></html>");
out.close();

// Update counters
unsafeCounter++;
safeCounter=new Integer(safeCounter.intValue()+1);
session.setAttribute("safecounter",safeCounter);
System.out.println("Chapter4 : AppInfo finished processing request");
}

public void doPost(HttpServletRequest req, HttpServletResponse resp)
   throws IOException,ServletException {
   doGet(req,resp);
}
```

One subtle flaw exists in the doGet method. As we mention in the section Initializing AppInfo," earlier in this chapter, the unsafeCounter increments with each request to the servlet. The flaw is that unsafeCounter doesn't print to the output simultaneously with incrementing the counter. unsafeCounter prints first and then increments several lines later in the code. Another thread could use this thread at the same time and print the old value a second time.

In such a case, you can make the unsafeCounter thread-safe by incrementing the counter within a synchronized block. The consequences of the unsafe threading are very minor, however, because the counter becomes accurate again after the second thread updates it. But in a scenario where updating the variable is more complex, you must synchronize access to the variable.

The following is an example of what a more threadsafe version of the unsafeCounter would look like:

```
out.println("<br>Safe Counter :" + safeCounter.toString());
synchronize(AppInfo) {
    out.println("<br>Unsafe counter :" + unsafeCounter);
    unsafeCounter++;
}
out.close()
```

In this code, the reference to AppInfo serves as a lock. After printing the safe counter, all of the threads that are executing AppInfo must stop and "wait in line" to get the AppInfo lock before continuing to printing and incrementing the unsafe counter. After completing the println and increment the threads leaves the synchronized block and releases the lock on AppInfo. This synchronization adds some additional overhead to the method as the JVM must keep track of the lock and the list of threads waiting for the lock. But it ensures that the unsafe counter is incremented automatically and is much more efficient than synchronizing access to the entire method.

Using HttpSession

AppInfo uses HttpSession to store the safeCounter variable. It also returns several pieces of information about the session that it receives by using HttpSession method calls.

By storing the safeCounter variable in the session, AppInfo can count the number of times that a specific user accesses the servlet. Calling AppInfo several times results in both the safeCounter and unsafeCounter incrementing. Closing your browser and reopening it causes your browser to get a new session. Returning to the AppInfo servlet after reopening your browser makes it appear that the safeCounter is reset, because you have a new session. (The old HttpSession object continues to exist, inaccessible, until it times out.) The unsafeCounter continues to increment the old value, however, because the actual servlet object stores the unsafeCounter.

The servlet gets the HttpSession object from the HttpServletRequest object in the beginning of the doGet method, storing it in a method variable for easy access. The developer then uses the HttpServlet object to get the session information that it needs for the HTML results and to get and put the safeCounter attribute. The session is essentially a hashtable where you can store objects by associating them with a string key value. (As we mention in the section "Utilizing Sessions," earlier in this chapter, all the stored objects should be serializable if you intend to use distributed sessions.)

Summary

This chapter offers a whirlwind tour of servlets, the basic building block of Web-based Java applications. From an administrative point of view, you've learned the basics of how the Web server receives HTTP requests, , and how the Web connector intercepts requests and forwards them to the iAS Web container. You've also learned the basics of how the Web container handles threading and servlet objects.

From a programmer's perspective, we've shown you the basics of the four most important objects for handling requests: HttpServlet, HttpServletRequest, HttpServletResponse, and HttpSession. You've also learned some of the common pitfalls of designing enterprise (multi-JVM) applications and examined a basic sample of servlet programming.

Understanding how servlets work is critical in understanding Web-application development in Java. Following are links to more information, should you need a refresher on the Servlet API or Java-based Web programming. Sun's servlet resources page (which we include among those links) provides a comprehensive list of where to find the best servlet information.

You should also be considering the weaknesses of the servlet development model, however. If developers were to create their HTML results by using println statements in servlets, Java applications would be very difficult to maintain. Java programmers would be required in order to make even the slightest change to the HTML results. We will examine some of the weaknesses in the servlet model, as well as ways to address these weaknesses in Chapter 6.

You can find additional information on servlets and the topics that we discuss in this chapter in the following places.

- ◆ Internet RFCs

  - ■ http://www.cis.ohio-state.edu/cgi-bin/rfc/rfc1738.html, "Uniform Resource Locators (URL): www.cis.ohio-state.edu/cgi-bin/rfc/rfc1738.html

  - ■ RFC 2396, Uniform Resource Identifiers (URI): Generic Syntax: www.cis.ohio-state.edu/cgi-bin/rfc/rfc2396.html

  - ■ RFC 2616, Hypertext Transfer Protocol – HTTP/1.1: www.cis.ohio-state.edu/cgi-bin/rfc/rfc2616.html

  - ■ RFC 2965, HTTP State Management Mechanism: www.cis.ohio-state.edu/cgi-bin/rfc/rfc2965.html

- ◆ Web-server plug-in APIs

  - ■ Online NSAPI documentation for iPlanet Web Server: http://docs.iplanet.com/docs/manuals/enterprise/41/nsapi/contents.htm

  - ■ Online documentation of the Apache API: http://httpd.apache.org/docs/misc/API.html

- ■ Online ISAPI documentation for Microsoft Internet Information Server: `http://msdn.microsoft.com/library/default.asp?url=/library/en-us/iisref/html/psdk/asp/isgu6j5f.asp`

◆ Servlet documentation

- ■ Online Servlet Documentation from Sun: `http://java.sun.com/products/servlet/2.2/javadoc/`

- ■ Sun's list of Servlet Resources: `http://java.sun.com/products/servlet/resources.html`

- ■ iPlanet Application Server Programmer's Guide: `http://docs.iplanet.com/docs/manuals/ias/60/sp3/JavaProgGuide/jpgserv1.htm#11284`

- ■ iPlanet Application Server Samples (Servlets and JSPs): `http://developer.iplanet.com/appserver/samples/docs/servlet-jsp.html`

◆ Miscellaneous

- ■ TheCounter.com Global Browser Statistics: `http://www.TheCounter.com/stats/`

- ■ Patterns and Anti-Patterns: `http://dmoz.org/Computers/Programming/Methodologies/Patterns_and_Anti-Patterns/`

- ■ Sun Java Tutorial: `http://java.sun.com/docs/books/tutorial/`

Chapter 5

Packaging

IN THIS CHAPTER

◆ Learning the importance of the J2EE packaging process

◆ Understanding how XML descriptors support packaging

◆ Picking the best-suited assembly tool

IN THIS CHAPTER, I cover what some perceive as one of the most important portions of the J2EE standard — *packaging*. Packaging, sometimes referred to as *assembly,* is a vital step in the application lifecycle. Packaging applications in a standards-based fashion enables you to deploy them to any J2EE-certified application server.

The Lifecycle of J2EE Applications

At the end of the day, you want your application to execute in the Application Server. To get there, you must first understand the lifecycle of a J2EE application. Figure 5-1 depicts this lifecycle.

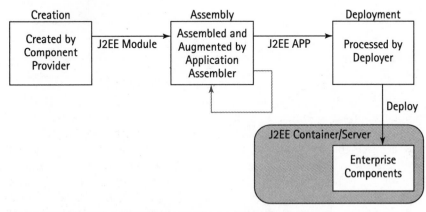

Figure 5-1: Lifecycle of a J2EE application and the roles involved

The J2EE platform specification contains the reference material for packaging and deployment. You can download at the PDF `http://java.sun.com/ j2ee/download.html#platformspec`.

Component creation

A *component* is a reusable piece of functionality or building block that you can use in combination with other components. Simply put, in a J2EE context, the frequently used components are servlets, Java Server Page (JSP) files and Enterprise JavaBeans (EJB). You clearly want to use these types of components together in your applications. JSP pages and Servlets are classified as Web components, and EJBs themselves are EJB components. For completeness, I mention applets and client applications as the remaining J2EE component types. Typically, you deal with Web and EJB components. With the advent of Web services, however, the exact definition of client application components may take a slightly different form.

In the application lifecycle, developers are responsible for creating components such as EJBs or Servlets. A developer in this position is acting in the *Component Provider* Role (as the J2EE specification defines it). The developer uses development tools such as Integrated Development Environments (IDEs) to aid in the creation of components (see Figure 5-2).

Chapter 8 reviews Forte for Java and other IDEs that can assist with component creation.

Assembly

The goal of the assembly stage within the application lifecycle is to package components into manageable units — *modules* — and, from there, assemble into an enterprise application (as in Figure 5-2). A J2EE module is a combination of one or more like components (e.g., servlet and JSP pages) and a *deployment descriptor.* I discuss the deployment descriptor in more detail in the section "Deployment Descriptors," later in this chapter. For now, you just need to know that the deployment descriptor is a well-formed XML file that defines settings about the particular module and the components that it contains. In Figure 5-2, the DD refers to a deployment descriptor within a module or an application. You classify modules as either Web Application Archive (WAR) or Enterprise JavaBean Archive (EJB-JAR) files.

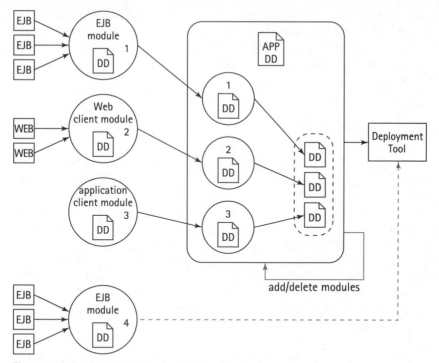

Figure 5-2: The composition of a J2EE application

A *component provider* produces components and modules. An *application assembler* (a role that the J2EE specification defines) produces an Enterprise Application Archive (EAR) file. The application assembler uses a tool to package one more module and an application deployment descriptor into the EAR file. The application assembler may then modify or adjust settings in the appropriate deployment descriptors to resolve any dependencies and naming conflicts.

Deployment

Deployment is the act of taking an assembled application or module and making it available for execution on the application server (the J2EE platform). In the *application deployer* role, tools that the J2EE product provider (the application server) supplies you use for installation and configuration, for the execution of the newly deployed application or module. The deployer then correlates settings (for example, security roles) within the application with the target deployment environment.

To summarize, a J2EE application consists of several building blocks. The first building block is a *component*. Next, you can define *modules* as the aggregate of one or more components along with a deployment descriptor. Finally, *applications* consist of an assembly of one or more modules along with the application deployment descriptor. The J2EE specification defines the roles of the *component provider*, *application assembler*, and *application deployer*. These roles can be equated to specific personnel that perform specific tasks within the lifecycle of a J2EE application. If you're a manager, defining these roles helps you identify staffing needs for a J2EE-based project.

J2EE Archives

The J2EE archives (EJB-JAR, WAR, EAR) are really just well-formed JAR files. A Jar file itself is just like a Windows ZIP file or Unix tar file that is optionally a compressed set of files that may contain an internal directory structure. What make the J2EE archives special are the specific internal directory structure, the inclusion of deployment descriptors, the component file, and other resources in predefined locations. The J2EE specification details the structure of any J2EE archive.

Basing your deployment of modules and applications archives on specific industry standards solves the age-old problem of deploying predictably and repeatability to multiple platforms. For years, software developers have lamented the necessity of building software that's hard to package and deploy in diverse environments. The J2EE specification puts into place standards for both the developers and the J2EE vendors so that packaging and deployment can involve nothing more than using an automated tool. In the following sections, I review the J2EE archives, WAR, EJB-JAR, and EAR.

WAR

A Web Application Archive (WAR) file is simply a well-formed file with a .war extension that contains one or more components of the Web container type. A WAR module conforms to a specification that enables you to deploy it to any J2EE Web container with minimal effort.

 A *Web container* is the runtime environment for Web components.

A WAR file can contain the following elements:

◆ Servlets

◆ JavaServer Pages (JSPs)

◆ Utility classes

◆ Static documents (HTML, images, sounds, and so on)

◆ Client-side applets, beans, and classes

◆ Deployment descriptors

 You find detailed information about Web Application Archive and its related deployment descriptor in the servlet specification.

Listing 5-1 presents a sample structure of an iAS WAR file. Notice the iAS-specific descriptor, ias-web.xml. Table 5-1 explains the WAR file structure.

Listing 5-1: Contents of a sample WAR file

```
/index.html
/com/acme/login.jsp
/WEB-INF
/WEB-INF/web.xml
/WEB-INF/ias-web.xml
/WEB-INF/classes/com/acme/util.class
/WEB-INF/lib/dbClasses.zip
```

TABLE 5-1 WAR FILE STRUCTURE

Directory	Description
/	This base directory is sometimes known as the document-root of the WAR file. JSPs and static content typically root here. An internal directory structure is commonly present — for example, com/acme/index.jsp.
/WEB-INF	WEB-INF directory has special significance. The Web-application deployment descriptor web.xml must be present in this directory for the WAR file to be valid. As with iAS, an ias-web.xml must currently be present as well. You also commonly use the WEB-INF directory to package .tld files (taglib descriptors). (See Chapter 6 for more information about JSP pages and taglibs.)

Continued

TABLE 5-1 WAR FILE STRUCTURE *(Continued)*

Directory	Description
/WEB-INF/classes	Any servlets or supporting utility Java classes that you use for this Web application are typically packaged in this directory, respective of their Java package structure. Optionally, you can JAR CLASS files and place them in the lib directory, which the next entry covers. Property files and other files that need to be resolved via your CLASSPATH can be placed within this directory as well.
/WEB-INF/lib	This Web application may depend on some JAR or ZIP files supporting application functionality. You should package these files in the lib directory. An option to using this lib directory is to share the JAR and ZIP files for other Web applications by putting them in the application server CLASSPATH. JAR and ZIP files that are packaged within the WAR file are not to be shared with other Web applications.

EJB-JAR

An Enterprise JavaBean Archive (EJB-JAR) is a well-formed file with a .jar extension. This module contains one or more EJBs as well as a deployment descriptor. The objective of the EJB module is to be deployable to any EJB container. Depending on the EJB container (the runtime environment for EJBs), support classes known as *stubs* must be generated for each EJB component within a module. Stubs are necessary for the EJB container to perform remote-method invocations and specific lifecycle behaviors for the EJB (among other things). Tools that the EJB vendor supplies generate the stubs that are packaged within any particular module. (I cover the EJB tools in Chapter 7.)

You find detailed information on Enterprise JavaBean Archive and its related deployment descriptor in the EJB specification.

Listing 5-2 shows an example of an iAS EJB-JAR file structure. Notice the iAS-specific descriptor, ias-ejb-jar.xml. The <EJB stubs and skeletons> denotes about nine archaically long filenames. Table 5-2 describes the EJB-JAR file structure.

Listing 5-2: Contents of a sample EJB-JAR file

```
/com/acme/Person.class
/com/acme/PersonEJB.class
/com/acme/PersonHome.class
/com/acme/<EJB stubs and skeletons>
/dbClasses.jar
/META-INF/ejb-jar.xml
/META-INF/ias-ejb-jar.xml
```

Table 5-2 EJB-JAR FILE STRUCTURE

Directory	Description
/	You may package EJBs, stubs, and utility classes off the root of the EJB archive. You must package CLASS files respective of their Java package structure. JAR or ZIP files that the particular module uses you can also place off the root.
/META-INF	As with the WEB-INF directory covered in the WAR section above, the META-INF directory has special significance to the EJB archive. The deployment descriptors ejb-jar.xml, ias-ejb-jar.xml, and, optionally, any container-managed persistence (CMP) XML files must be packaged with the META-INF directory. The ias-ejb-jar.xml is the iAS-specific descriptor.

Client archive

An *application client* is a J2EE module that runs in its own Java main and JVM. In iAS terms, you can refer to an application client as a *rich client*. A rich client is a command-line or GUI program that can interact remotely with EJBs. With iAS, you have no requirement to package a client archive to enable rich-client functionality. In fact, doing so isn't really encouraged because of the minimal benefit that you gain from all the addition complexity and questionable portability. You can simply execute a rich client by setting up the CLASSPATH path appropriately. Also a viable alternative to a rich client is using a SOAP client as described in Chapter 12 (SOAP). Listing 5-3 shows the contents of a sample client archive. Table 5-3 describes the client archive structure.

Listing 5-3: Contents of a sample client archive file

```
/myEjbStubs.jar
/META-INF/app-client.xml
/META-INF/ias-app-client.xml
```

TABLE 5-3 CLIENT ARCHIVE STRUCTURE

Directory	Description
/	This root directory can package dependent Jar and Zip files used for this client archive.
/META-INF	As with and EAR and EJB archive the META-INF directory contains the deployment descriptors. In this case the descriptors mainly are used to declare EJB references.

You can find information on the application-client descriptor in the J2EE specification. Also check `<iAS  HOME>  \ias\docs\JavaProgGuide\jpgrichc.htm` .

EAR

The Enterprise Archive (EAR), as I discuss earlier in this section, consists of one or more J2EE modules and application deployment descriptors. It has an .ear exten-sion. Listing 5-4 shows the structure of an application archive packaged with a WAR and EJB-JAR module. Table 5-4 explains the EAR file structure.

Listing 5-4: Contents of a sample EAR file

```
/PersonEJB.jar
/Person.war
/META-INF/application.xml
/META-INF/person.war.altdd.xml
/META-INF/ias-person.war.altdd.xml
```

TABLE 5-4 EAR FILE STRUCTURE

Directory	Description
/	WAR and EJB modules, client archives, and dependent JAR/ZIP files can be packaged off the root directory of the EAR file. The modules contained within the EAR file can be in a nested directory structure, too.

Directory	Description
/META-INF	The `META-INF` directory contains the mandatory `application.xml` file. It can also contain alternative deployment descriptors. You can use alternatives to override a descriptor packaged in one of the application modules, preserving the original signing of the module. The alternate deployment descriptor can be packaged in the root directory as well.

 You can find information on the application deployment descriptor in the J2EE specification.

Deployment Descriptors

You can think of *deployment descriptors* as a contract between a J2EE runtime container and a component. A container can't possibly execute your component without any knowledge of your component's name, dependent files and so on. You use the deployment descriptor to declare information about your components. After deployment and registration of your application or module, the application server contains information about your application, modules, and components, all via the deployment descriptors. Finally, as you run your application, the container now knows all the details necessary to find and execute your components.

Deployment descriptors provide a valuable function for the component provider, application assembler, or application deployer. A *component provider* initially creates the descriptors as it creates components. The provider can then use the descriptor not only to declare components, but also environmental settings, security roles, EJB references, and so on. The important thing to notice is that the descriptor provides a nonhard-coded place for component and application settings. An application assembler generally uses a GUI to assemble a series of modules and an application deployment descriptor to create an EAR file. The assembled application then passes on to the application deployer, and the deployer may modify the values in the deployment descriptors to match the target deployment environment. To perform their duties, these roles indeed need to know the features and capabilities of a deployment descriptor.

In this section and those that follow, I review both the J2EE and iAS deployment descriptors that are necessary for each J2EE archive. I detail the iAS-specific descriptors with a little more depth than the well-documented J2EE descriptors.

Finally, I run you through the remaining iAS-specific descriptors. I don't cover all deployment descriptor settings because the iPlanet documentation does a fine job of this task.

 All the deployment descriptor document type definitions (DTD) that you use within iAS you find installed in the <IAS-HOME>/ias/dtd directory. The DTDs contain very useful comments.

WAR file descriptor

You primarily use a Web-application deployment descriptor to declare servlet and JSP components. Other notable elements are ejb-ref that is used to create a naming alias to an EJB, init-param that supply a place to externalize parameters that are to be passed to a component, and auth-constraint used for security definitions. To a developer, the deployment descriptors may seem to get a little more feature-rich with each subsequent release of the J2EE specification. I advise that you keep up to date with the specifications so that you're not always re-inventing the wheel. The sample descriptor in Listing 5-5 shows the declaring of the GreeterServlet servlet.

Listing 5-5: Snippet of a J2EE Web descriptor

```
<web-app>
  <display-name>helloworld</display-name>
  <servlet>
    <servlet-name>GreeterServlet</servlet-name>
    <servlet-class>
      samples.helloworld.servlet.GreeterServlet
    </servlet-class>
    <load-on-startup>0</load-on-startup>
  </servlet>
...
</web-app>
```

Listing 5-5 is the iAS-specific descriptor for the helloworld Web module. Notice how the servlet-name elements match from both descriptors (in Listing 5-5 and 5-6). The iAS descriptor includes a globally unique identifier (GUID) that iAS uses for internally naming this component. Chapter 13 explains how a GUID is used for internal component naming within iAS.

The majority of the remaining settings are iAS value-added features beyond what's necessary within the J2EE specification. Some interesting elements are encrypt, sticky-lb, caching, and session_info. *Encrypt* ensures that communication between this servlet and the Web connector occurs via an encrypted connection. *Sticky-lb*, as I describe in Chapter 3, ensures that this servlet always runs on the server and on JVM, which serves it or other related components in the application with the sticky-lb option set first for the user session. *Caching* enables you to define some criteria to avoid the regeneration of content via a particular Web component. The *session-info* element defines advanced session settings – for example, whether the session for this Web application is highly available or not. In Listing 5-6, I show the iAS specific descriptor that declares the GreeterServlet servlet along with the GUID.

The iAS online Developer's Guide includes very complete descriptions for all the iAS deployment descriptor settings at `http://docs.iplanet.com/docs/manuals/ias/65/devguide/jpgdeplo.htm`.

Listing 5-6: Corresponding iAS descriptor

```
<ias-web-app>
  <servlet>
    <servlet-name>GreeterServlet</servlet-name>
    <guid>{bd498e61-3c98-11d4-a006-0010a4e78552}</guid>
    <servlet-info>
      <sticky>false</sticky>
      <encrypt>false</encrypt>
      <number-of-singles>10</number-of-singles>
      <disable-reload>false</disable-reload>
    </servlet-info>
  </servlet>
  <session-info>
    <impl>lite</impl>
    <dsync-type>dsync-distributed</dsync-type>
    <timeout-type>last-access</timeout-type>
    <secure>false</secure>
    <domain></domain>
    <path></path>
    <scope></scope>
  </session-info>
  ...
</ias-web-app>
```

EJB-JAR

You mainly use the EJB deployment descriptor to declare EJB component settings such as type, EJB name, and support classes. Beyond the actual component, transaction settings take the most interest. Chapter 7 covers EJBs and transactions in more detail. Listing 5-7 shows the typical deployment descriptor elements used to declare the stateless session bean, TheGreeter.

Listing 5-7: Snippet of a J2EE EJB descriptor

```
<ejb-jar>
  <enterprise-beans>
    <session>
      <display-name>TheGreeter</display-name>
      <ejb-name>TheGreeter</ejb-name>
      <home>samples.helloworld.ejb.GreeterHome</home>
      <remote>samples.helloworld.ejb.Greeter</remote>
      <ejb-class>samples.helloworld.ejb.GreeterEJB</ejb-class>
      <session-type>Stateless</session-type>
      <transaction-type>Bean</transaction-type>
    </session>
  </enterprise-beans>
  <assembly-descriptor>
    <container-transaction>
      <method>
      <ejb-name>TheGreeter</ejb-name>
      <method-name>*</method-name>
      </method>
      <trans-attribute>NotSupported</trans-attribute>
    </container-transaction>
  </assembly-descriptor>
</ejb-jar>
```

Listing 5-8 supplies the corresponding iAS descriptor for Listing 5-7. The iAS EJB descriptor has a few value-added features such as `failoverrequired`, `persistence-manager`, and `iiop`. `Failoverrequired` enables stateful session beans to become highly available, where an EJB's state can survive a server crash. `Persistencemanager` enables definition of a pluggable persistence framework for CMP beans. `IIOP` indicates that a bean can be used with a rich client.

Listing 5-8: Corresponding iAS descriptor

```
<ias-ejb-jar>
  <enterprise-beans>
    <session>
      <ejb-name>TheGreeter</ejb-name>
      <guid>{bd498e60-3c98-11d4-a006-0010a4e78552}</guid>
      <pass-timeout>0</pass-timeout>
      <is-thread-safe>false</is-thread-safe>
```

```
        <pass-by-value>false</pass-by-value>
        <session-timeout>0</session-timeout>
      </session>
    </enterprise-beans>
</ias-ejb-jar>
```

EAR

The Enterprise Application Archive's deployment descriptor is pretty simple. You primarily use it to declare modules, which you package within the EAR file. An example is shown in Listing 5-9 where helloworld.war is declared. Currently, it has no iAS-specific application descriptor.

Listing 5-9: Application descriptor

```
<application>
  <display-name>HelloWorld</display-name>
  <module>
    <web>
      <web-uri>helloworld.war</web-uri>
      <context-root>helloworld</context-root>
    </web>
  </module>
  <module>
    <ejb>helloworldEjb.jar</ejb>
  </module>
</application>
```

 TIP   The iAS Deployment Tool offers excellent online Help documentation for descriptor settings.

Client application

As I discuss in the section "J2EE Archives," earlier in this chapter, packaging a client module is pretty rare. But if you do choose to package the client module, you need to include the client-application descriptors. These deployment descriptors are extremely simple, with a primary feature of declaring an EJB reference. This simplicity and lack of value-adds of this descriptor should help you determine whether packaging the client archive is important for your client application. Listing 5-10 shows the J2EE client-application descriptor.

Listing 5-10: J2EE client-application descriptor

```
<application-client>
   <display-name>converter-acc</display-name>
   <description>
   Currency Converter Application Client Container Sample
   </description>
   <ejb-ref>
      <ejb-ref-name>SimpleConverter</ejb-ref-name>
      <ejb-ref-type>Session</ejb-ref-type>
      <home>j2eeguide.converter.ConverterHome</home>
      <remote>j2eeguide.converter.Converter</remote>
      <ejb-link>Test</ejb-link>
   </ejb-ref>
</application-client>
```

Listing 5-11 shows the iAS-specific descriptor necessary for the client module. It really just completes the EJB reference to map the SimpleConverter name to the internal iAS JNDI name.

Listing 5-11: iAS descriptor for the client module

```
<ias-java-client-jar>
   <ejb-ref>
      <ejb-ref-name>SimpleConverter</ejb-ref-name>
      <jndi-name>ejb/MyConverter</jndi-name>
   </ejb-ref>
</ias-java-client-jar>
```

Resource descriptor

You use *resource descriptors* to describe the iAS resources JDBC datasources, Java Mail, URLs, or JMS. This descriptor enables you to externalize connection-related information such as user/password, host, and so on. After you register a resource, the resource is available to application modules for descriptor referencing or JNDI lookup within the application server. The EJB and WAR descriptors have the element *resource-ref* that you use to declare a module's dependency on a resource.

The tools iasdeploy and resreg can register resource descriptors. Chapter 13 discusses these tools in more depth.

The `resource-ref` element in a Web or EJB deployment descriptor enables a module to have a level of indirection from the actual resource name and particulars. For example, this capability can prove convenient for applications that you develop by using one database resource and deploy to another for production. The fact that the application is looking up the resource using an alias for the real resource name allows the particulars or the name of the actual resource to change without affecting the application code. Listing 5-12 shows the descriptor entries and Listing 5-13 is a code snippet using the `resource-ref` element.

From a security perspective, you can set the *res-auth* element to either `application` or `container`. *Application* specifies that the module code authenticates programmatically to the resource. *Container* specifies that it signs on to the resource on behalf of the application. The container setting is most convenient to use so that the application code doesn't need to maintain authentication information.

Listing 5-12: Snippet from a module descriptor declaring a resource

J2EE descriptor
```
<resource-ref>
   <description>This database is used for customer data</description>
   <res-ref-name>BankDataSource</res-ref-name>
   <res-type>javax.sql.DataSource</res-type>
   <res-auth>Container</res-auth>
</resource-ref>
```

iAS descriptor
```
<resource-ref>
   <res-ref-name>BankDataSource</res-ref-name>
   <jndi-name>jdbc/bank/BankDB</jndi-name>
</resource-ref>
```

Listing 5-13: Java code snippet used to look up the declared resource
```
InitialContext ctx = new javax.naming.InitialContext();
DataSource ds =
   (DataSource) ctx.lookup("java:comp/env/BankDataSource");
Connection dbConn = ds.getConnection();
```

Resource descriptors bring an elegant solution to the task of containing connection-related information for resources. Applications no longer need to worry, for example, about maintaining database connection information. They simply look up a datasource by its name and then use it. An application `deployer` can make sure that the datasource is registered and functional for the deployed components.

Listing 5-14 shows the most common usage (database connection) for the resource descriptor from the `Bank` sample application (which you find in `<IAS-HOME>/ias/ias-sample/bank`). Please see Chapter 2 for setting JDBC features for iAS. In this listing, the important elements to notice are the `jndi-name`, `drive-name` (if used), and user/password. The other connection pooling elements are best left to the presented defaults and configured and tuned by an administrator.

Listing 5-14: iAS 6.5 resource descriptor declaring a JDBC data source

```
<ias-resource>
     <resource>
       <jndi-name>jdbc/bank/BankDB</jndi-name>
       <jdbc>
         <user>bank</user>
         <password>bank</password>
         <driver-name>db2-type4</driver-name>
     <databaseName>sample</databaseName>
     <portNumber>50001</portNumber>
         <conn-pooling>
           <initialPoolSize>1</initialPoolSize>
           <waitQueueEnabled>true</waitQueueEnabled>
           <reclaimTime>600</reclaimTime>
           <maxPoolSize>30</maxPoolSize>
           <maxIdleTime>120</maxIdleTime>
           <queueLength>30</queueLength>
           <trace>disable</trace>
           <stat>disable</stat>
           <waitTimeInQueue>120</waitTimeInQueue>
           <tableBasedSanity>false</tableBasedSanity>
           <isSanityRequired>true</isSanityRequired>
           <incrementPoolSize>1</incrementPoolSize>
           <minPoolSize>1</minPoolSize>
         </conn-pooling>
       </jdbc>
     </resource>
</ias-resource>
```

The 6.5 release of iAS enhances the resource descriptor to better support third-party database drivers. Connection-pool parameters, global-transaction support, and debug elements are just a few of the new features. The iAS tools `iasdeploy` and `resreg` can convert old resource descriptors to the new format.

Listing 5-15 is a sample from a JSP that demonstrates acquiring a database resource with the purpose to create a database connection.

Listing 5-15: shows a JSP snippet using the datasource

```
<%@ page import="javax.naming.*" %>
<%@ page import="javax.sql.*" %>
<%@ page import="java.sql.*" %>
<%
  InitialContext ctx = new InitialContext();
  DataSource dbSource = (DataSource) ctx.lookup("jdbc/bank/BankDB");
  Connection dbConn = dbSource.getConnection();
  // use the database connection
  // make sure to close the database connection
%>
```

Listing 5-16 is an example mail-resource descriptor, and Listing 5-17 puts it to the test.

Listing 5-16: Resource descriptor example for an e-mail resource

```
<ias-resource>
  <resource>
    <jndi-name>mail/MyBox</jndi-name>
    <mail>
      <host>mail.earthlink.net</host>
      <name>martin</name>
      <address>martin.gee@icsynergy.com</address>
    </mail>
  </resource>
</ias-resource>
```

Listing 5-17: Code snippet from a JSP that uses the mail resource

```
<%@ page import="javax.naming.*" %>
<%@ page import="javax.mail.internet.*" %>
<%@ page import="javax.mail.*" %>
<%@ page import="java.util.*" %>
<%@ page import="java.text.*" %>
<%
  InitialContext ctx = new InitialContext();
  javax.mail.Session mSession =
    (javax.mail.Session) ctx.lookup("mail/MyBox");
  Message msg = new MimeMessage(mSession);
  msg.setFrom();
  msg.setRecipients(Message.RecipientType.TO,
    InternetAddress.parse("customer@sale.com", false));
  msg.setSubject("Test Message");
```

Continued

Listing 5-17 *(Continued)*

```
DateFormat dateFormatter = DateFormat.getDateTimeInstance(
  DateFormat.LONG, DateFormat.SHORT);
Date timeStamp = new Date();
String messageText = "Thank you for your order."+
  "We received your order on " +
  dateFormatter.format(timeStamp) + ".";
msg.setText(messageText);
msg.setHeader("X-Mailer", "my-mailer");
msg.setSentDate(timeStamp);
Transport.send(msg);
out.println("EMAIL MESSAGE SENT!");
%>
```

As of iAS 6.5, the JMS and URL resource-descriptor elements aren't yet implemented.

Packaging and Deployment Tools

As I discuss in the preceding sections, the roles of component provider, application assembler, and application deployer figure in the lifecycle of a J2EE application. Clearly, each role needs a tool that helps that person best perform his duties. Component providers are developers. Their interests lie in tools that aid the development process, such as syntax checking, compiling, deployment-descriptor creation, and component deployment. Application assemblers' interests lie in tools that aid with the assembly and configuration of an EAR file. Finally, the interests application deployers lie in tools that can securely deploy/undeploy applications to local or remote iAS instances.

In this section, I contrast the function that iAS command line tools such as Ant, and the GUI tools iAS Deployment Tool and IDEs can play within the lifecycle roles.

See Chapter 19 for the virtues of packaging and deployment.

iAS command-line tools

A typical iAS installation provides the tools that I list in this section as the lowest common utility to support the J2EE platform roles. These command-line tools are typically best suited for those individuals who use scripting or are at home on the command line. You find the iAS deployment- and packaging-related command-line tools in the `<IAS-HOME>/ias/bin` directory.

Table 5-5 provides context on which iAS command-line tools you can use within the J2EE platform roles.

TABLE 5-5 IAS COMMAND-LINE TOOL USAGE FOR J2EE PLATFORM ROLES

Role	Tool Usage
Component provider	`ejbc` - Creates and compiles the stubs necessary for an EJB. Chapter 7 provides more details on this tool.
	`jspc` - Syntax-checks and compiles JSPs. Chapter 6 supplies details on JSPs.
	`deploytool` - Launches iASDT GUI. Creates deployment descriptors for components and can deploy components.
	`iasdeploy` - Deploys components to appropriate containers for execution and unit testing.
	Summary: These tools help streamline the assembly and deployment cycles by validating that components can pass syntax, compile and dependency checks before application assembly and deployment. The `deploytool` (iASDT) is useful to a component provider by supplying deployment-descriptor creation and editing capabilities. I discuss iASDT in the following section.
Application assembler	`deploytool` - Launches the iASDT GUI. Supplies facilities to manage components to validate and assemble EAR files.
	Summary: Assembly can prove tedious and error prone. The `deploytool` supplies a remedy to requiring the assembler to hand-edit scripts and deployment descriptors, which, of course, can prove an error-prone and time-consuming task. The down side of iASDT is that you can't script it for automatic packaging or deployments.
Application Deployer	`iasdeploy` - Deploys and undeploys WAR, EJB-JAR and EAR files. Also supports datasource and startup class.
	Summary: Best suited for administrator types who are at home on the command line. Good because you can script it.

These tools deploy applications to an iAS instance. Make sure that you have rights and policy in place if recoverability of the iAS instance is necessary. See Chapter 21 for more details.

An iAS instance ships with other command-line tools that I don't discuss in the preceding table. The remaining deployment tools are mostly deprecated and ship merely for backward compatibility. For a complete reference, Table 5-6 provides a quick description and example of these iAS command-line tools.

The supplemental docs in the `<IAS HOME>/ias/docs` directory document iAS command-line tools.

TABLE 5-6 IAS COMMAND-LINE AND GUI TOOLS

Tool	Description

iasdeploy	Performs local or remote deploy, redeploy, and undeploys of J2EE archives. Can only deploy datasources and startup classes.
	
	Examples:
	
	`> iasdeploy deployapp helloworld.ear`
	
	`> iasdeploy deplpyapp -user admin -password admin -host 192.168.1.4 -port 10817`

deploytool	Launches iASDT GUI. On NT/2000, choose Start → Programs → iPlanet Application Server 6.X → iAS Deployment Tool. Alternatively, can state it via the command line.
	
	Examples:
	
	`> deploytool`
	
	`> deploytool <a J2EE archive>`

deploycmd (*deprecated*)	Deploys J2EE modules on iAS 6.X. Use `iasdeploy` instead. Example: `> deploycmd.bat -deploy -f helloworld.war -s admin:admin@192.168.1.4:10817`

Tool	Description
beanreg (*deprecated*)	Performs deploy and remove of NAS 4.0 EJBs within iAS. Migrate your EJBs to 6.X and use `iasdeploy` with the `deploymodule` option instead.
j2eeappreg (*deprecated*) iAS 6.X	Performs local deploy and undeploy of J2EE archives to iAS 6.X. Although deprecated, this tool still has utility. The replacement tool, `iasdeploy`, requires you to run the KAS process for usage. `j2eeappreg` can perform a local deploy a little quicker than `iasdeploy` can, because the archive doesn't ship over the wire to the KAS process. In fact, the `iasdeploy` tool uses the `j2eeappreg` tool under the covers to deploy your archive from the `<IAS-HOME>/ias/JAR directory` (which is the archive repository for the `iasdeploy` tool).

Example:

```
> j2eeappreg helloworld.ear
```

Tool	Description
resreg (*deprecated*) iAS 6.X	Registers an iAS 6.X data source XML descriptor with a local iAS instance. See the section on deployment descriptors, earlier in this chapter, for an explanation of the resource XML file.

Use `iasdeploy` instead.

Example:

```
> resreg.bat myDataSource.xml
```

Tool	Description
webappreg (*deprecated*)	Deploys a WAR archive to a local iAS instance. Use `iasdeploy` with the `deploymodule` option instead.

Example:

```
> webappreg helloworld.war
```

Tool	Description
servletReg (*deprecated*)	Perform deploy of NAS 4.0 servlet descriptor. Migrate your servlet to iAS 6.X and use `iasdeploy`.
kreg (*deprecated*)	Deploys AppLogics. AppLogics are the component type previous versions for iAS support. Currently iAS remains backward compatible with application modules supported before J2EE.

Example:

```
> kreg myapp.gxr
```

See Chapter 9 for behind the scenes of deployment. In this chapter you see the after affect of using the iAS deployment tools.

IAS Deployment Tool

The *iAS Deployment Tool* (*iASDT*) is a Java Swing-based GUI tool that you install in typical iAS installations. The main strengths of this tool are the graphical aid of descriptor creation and editing, module and application packaging and deployment.

As I discuss in the section "Deployment Descriptors," earlier in this chapter, iAS modules have an iAS-specific descriptor as well as a J2EE descriptor. iASDT supplies a graphical interface over a module so that any descriptor edits are synchronized across the appropriate descriptors.

The iASDT (`deploytool`) offers an excellent online tutorial that provides a walkthrough of how to package an Enterprise Application Archive (EAR file). You can access the tutorial by clicking the Tutorial button in the `deploytool`'s Welcome dialog box.

iASDT provides wizards and utilities to streamline the task of packaging a module or application. CLASS-file validation and EJB-stub generation are just a few of the implicit utilities that this process involves. After archive creation, iASDT can use your archives as project files so that you can reopen them at any time for modification. Finally, iASDT also can deploy your archive to any registered iAS instances. Figure 5-3 shows iASDT with the helloworld WAR descriptor open.

Table 5-7 contrasts the capabilities of iASDT for the J2EE platform roles.

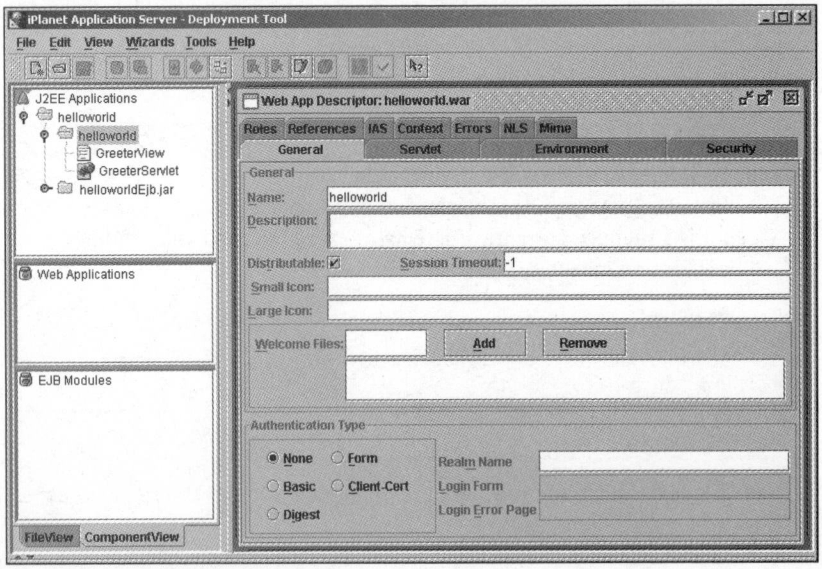

Figure 5-3: Deployment tool GUI

TABLE 5-7 DEPLOYMENT TOOL USAGE FOR J2EE PLATFORM ROLES

Role	Tool Usage
Component provider	Developers find the iASDT tool helpful for creating baseline deployment descriptors (DD) for their J2EE applications. iASDT enables you to view the DDs so that you can easily copy and save them to become part of your source control. If additional components need declaration, iASDT can open your last WAR or EJB-JAR archive for additions. Then you can again save the latest DDs. Eventually, developers get familiar enough with DD entries as to negate the need for iASDT. Most developers are likely to get frustrated with the lack of automation that iASDT supplies. Every time that packaging and assembly is necessary, iASDT is necessary. Ideally, developers prefer automated packaging and assembly such as Ant or a development IDE supplies.
Application assembler	Assemblers should find iASDT well-suited for their role. The graphical nature of the tool enables quick assembly of modules and adjustments to deployment descriptors.
Application deployer	A deployer is likely to use iASDT to finalize EAR file edits — for example, matching declared security roles to those available in the deployment environment. From there, actual deployment depends on the situation. The following constraints may factor into your decision whether to use iASDT for deployment: Unlike with `iasdeploy`, you can't script iASAT for unmanned deployments; because iASDT is a GUI, availability of an X manager may dictate that you use the alternative `iasdeploy`; deployers are sometimes more at home using command-line tools.

TIP iASDT has the capability to insert iAS specific descriptors into archives not created for iAS. When you open an archive that doesn't have iAS deployment descriptors, iASDT will prompt you for the creation of these additional descriptors.

Ant

Ant is a Java-based build tool provided under the open source Jakarta project umbrella. Its main claim to fame is the simplistic XML dialect that it uses to describe the build process. Being Java, Ant is portable across any platform that has a JVM. So, in all practicality, a build file that you create on one platform, such as Windows NT/2000, can run seamlessly on another – for example, Unix. The Ant build file that contains all your build instructions is an XML document – typically, build.xml. I detail the structure of a build file later in this section.

 iAS ships with Ant 1.2. Go to http://jakarta.apache.org/ant/ index.html to get Ant 1.4.1.

Ant itself contains such baseline functionality as Java-source compiling, dependency checking between build targets, and JavaDoc generation. From there, the developer community's taken advantage of the extendibility of Ant to supply value-added "tasks" such as J2EE packaging and deployment, source-control integration, and so on. Table 5-8 reviews how you can use Ant to satisfy the J2EE platform roles and provide you with some examples.

TABLE 5-8 ANT USAGE FOR J2EE PLATFORM ROLES

Role	Tool usage
Component provider	Ant is well-suited for developers in the basic fact that builds reside in a tool that's neutral to any IDE or developer editor. A sign of a mature development organization is that you can automate and build and make them scriptable across development deployment platforms. The combination of baseline Ant functionality and Ant extensions makes easy work of compiling source trees and packaging and deploying J2EE projects. See the examples later in this section for details.
Application assembler	Depending on how knowledgeable an assembler is with deployment descriptors, Ant may or may not add value. Ant can make easy work of packaging modules or applications. But obviously, Ant supplies no utility to edit deployment descriptors.

Role	Tool usage
Application deployer	Ant supplies no facility to edit deployment descriptors. iASDT is more suitable for that task. Ant does add lots of value with deployment for a deployer. You can easily script secure deployment and undeployment to one or more iAS instances within Ant. The iAS Ant extensions example that follow supply a few scenarios to illustrate this capability.

Go to `http://www.icsynergy.com/downloads/index.html` to download Ant extensions for iPlanet. You find the online documentation for Ant at `http://jakarta.apache.org/ant/manual`.

Following are a few Ant examples, which cover some of the basic steps involved with a J2EE application. The topics that I cover in these examples are compiling source, building EJB stubs, packaging modules, and, finally, deployment. I create these examples using Ant 1.4.1.

Listing 5-18 gives us a reference point for a simple Ant script that can compile source code. This example assumes that you have some Java source code in an `src` directory parallel to the directory where you run this build script. The results of the compile go into a `classes` directory. Notice that Ant automatically looks for a `build.xml` file in the location in which you execute it.

Setting up Ant involves setting the `ANT_HOME` environment variable to the location of your Ant install directory. Next, add `ANT_HOME/bin` to your system path. Simply run `ant` at the command line to see the command-line options for the Ant tool.

From the example in Listing 5-18, you can see the simple XML structure of an Ant build file. First, the root element is a `project`. A `project` includes the following attributes: `name`, `default`, `basedir`. The name attribute typically correlates to the actual software project that you're creating. Ant enables you to reference this value as a property the same as you do any other property, via the `${ant.project.name}` syntax. The `default` attribute sets the default target to execute in running this build file. The `basedir` attribute specifies the relative directory location of this build file. Notice that I reference the `basedir` value in Listing 5-16 by using `${basedir}`.

Next you see that targets primarily compose the build file. You can execute targets individually or you can set them up to depend on other targets. You refer to the contents of the targets as `tasks`. Tasks can perform functions such as compiling source code and packaging a WAR file. Ant contains a wealth of tasks that you can use for any particular occasion.

The examples following Listing 5-18 are snippets of targets that you can insert into a build script such as what you see in Listing 5-18.

Listing 5-18: Basic Ant example

```
<project name="helloworld" default="compile" basedir=".">
<!-- ===================================================== -->
<!--                    INIT                             -->
<!-- ===================================================== -->
<target name="init">
  <property name="build.compiler" value="classic"/>
  <property name="debug" value="on"/>
  <property name="optimize" value="off"/>
  <property name="deprecation" value="on"/>
  <property name="src" value="${basedir}"/>
  <property name="classes" value="${basedir}/classes"/>
</target>


<!-- ===================================================== -->
<!--                   COMPILE                           -->
<!-- ===================================================== -->
  <target name="compile" depends="init" >
    <echo message="Compiling ${ant.project.name} Source Tree" />
    <mkdir dir="${classes}"/>

    <javac
        classpath="${classpath}"
        destdir="${classes}"
        deprecation="${deprecation}"
        optimize="${optimize}"
        debug="${debug}" >
      <src path="${src}" />
        <include name="**/*.java"/>
    </javac>
  </target>
</project>
```

In Listing 5-19, I demonstrate an Ant snippet that uses the ICSynergy Ant extensions. This example creates stubs for the entire list of EJBs that you declare within the `ejb-jar.xml` descriptor. Without getting into the specifics of the `ejbc` task, you can see that the target `ejbc` depends on the compile target. In short, the compile target must run successfully before the `ejbc` can execute.

 The documentation for the ICSynergy Ant extensions comes bundled with the CD-ROM in this book. Alternatively, you can find the online docs at `www.icsynergy.com/downloads/iplanetAnt/antExtDocs.html`.

Listing 5-19: Ant task that you use to build EJB stubs

```
<target name="ejbc" depends="init, compile" >
  <iplanet-ejbc debug="on"
    srcdir="${src}/com/acme"
    destdir="${classes}">
      <include name="META-INF/ejb-jar.xml" />
  </iplanet-ejbc>
</target>
```

Listing 5-18 packages `myEjb` by using the `iplanet-ejbjar` task. This task implicitly includes the `ias-ejb-jar.xml` descriptor. The `myEjb.jar` file then includes the classes and stubs from the `classes` directory (as specifies via the `fileset`).

Listing 5-20: Packaging an Ejb-jar module

```
<target name="ejb-jar" depends="init, stubs">
  <iplanet-ejbjar jarfile="${build}/myEjb.jar"
    ejbxml="${src}/com/acme/META-INF/ejb-jar.xml">
    <fileset dir="${classes}">
      <include name="com/acme/ejbs/**" />
    </fileset>
  </iplanet-ejbjar>
</target>
```

Listing 5-21 shows an example packaging a WAR module. This target again depends on successful completion of the `compile` target. Notice that the `iplanet-war` task makes no mention of the `ias-web.xml` file. This task implicitly includes that iAS dependent descriptor. The important thing to notice here is the Ant extensions supply all the constructs needed to assemble the WAR file. The war target could, in fact, prove useful to an application assembler.

Listing 5-21: Packaging a WAR module

```
<target name="war" depends="init, compile">
  <iplanet-war warfile="${build}/myWar.war"
    webxml="${src}/com/acme/WEB-INF/web.xml">

    <webinf dir="${src}/com/acme/WEB-INF">
      <include name="struts-config.xml" />
      <include name="ics-tags.tld" />
    </webinf>

    <lib dir="${src}/com/acme/WEB-INF/lib">
      <include name="*.jar" />
    </lib>
  </iplanet-war>
</target>
```

Listing 5-22 creates the Enterprise Application Archive. The added Ant echo task creates a file, which you can include in your EAR archive for version information.

Listing 5-22: Packaging an Enterprise application

```
<target name="ear" depends="init, ejb-jar, war">
  <echo message="Build Date ${TODAY} at ${TSTAMP}&#xOA;
    &#xOA;Using Environment:
    &#xOA;====================
    &#xOA;JDK: ${java.version}
    &#xOA;Compiler: ${build.compiler}
    &#xOA;Op Sys: ${os.name}
    &#xOA;Built By: ${user.name}"
    file="${build}/version"/>

  <ear earfile="${build}/$myEar.ear"
    appxml="${src}/com/acme/META-INF/application.xml">
    <fileset dir="${build}" >
      <include name="version" />
      <include name="myEjb.jar" />
      <include name="myWar.war" />
    </fileset>
  </ear>
</target>
```

Listing 5-23 deploys the EAR file to the local iAS instance. The iplanet-deploy task also enables you to deploy to one or more iAS instances.

Listing 5-23: Deploying EAR file to an iAS instance

```
<target name="deploy" depends="war, ejb-jar">
    <iplanet-deploy>
        <application name="${build}/myEar.ear" />
        </iplanet-deploy>
</target>
```

 TIP Ant 1.4.1 supplies iAS `ejbc` and `ejbjar` tasks as an optional download at http://jakarta.apache.org/builds/jakarta-ant/release/v1.4.1/bin/jakarta-ant-1.4.1-optional.jar. Place this JAR file in the ANT_HOME/lib directory to use these tasks.

Ant 1.4.1 does include some optional iPlanet tasks. It bundles these tasks with Ant's optional JAR file. The iPlanet tasks line up beside the other J2EE application server-specific tasks bundled with Ant. You can use the ICSynergy Ant tasks in combination with the optional Ant tasks. Listings 5-24 and 5-25 demonstrate the optional tasks.

Listing 5-24: ejbc task

```
<iplanet-ejbc ejbdescriptor="ejb-jar.xml"
  iasdescriptor="ias-ejb-jar.xml" dest="${build.classesdir}"
  iashome="${ias.home}" >
  <classpath>
    <pathelement path="." />
    <pathelement path="${build.classpath}" />
  </classpath>
</iplanet-ejbc>
```

Listing 5-25: ejbjar task

```
<ejbjar srcdir="${build.classesdir}" descriptordir="${src}"
  basejarname="helloworld" >
  <iplanet destdir="${assemble.ejbjar}" iashome="${ias.home}">
    <classpath>
      <pathelement path="." />
      <pathelement path="${build.classpath}" />
    </classpath>
  </iplanet>
  <include name="**/ejb-jar.xml"/>
  <exclude name="**/*ias-*.xml"/>
</ejbjar>
```

In summary, Ant seems to add a little something for each role. Developers (component providers) can pick up very nice productivity gains and add maturity to their development practices. Application assemblers can pick up the Ant scripts from the developers and script the assembly of the enterprise application. And, finally, a deployer can script deployments to one or more application server. In practice, making sure you can pass the Ant scripts between roles can prove quite effective, because all the roles can exchange a common build file. Each role can emphasize the important aspects of the build file to the other roles. This portability usually turns out to be a good thing.

Integrated Development Environment (IDE)

IDEs are typically best suited for developers in that they integrate source editing, version control, and productivity wizards into a common tool. In Chapter 8, I detail IDEs that integrate in some fashion into iAS. The common theme that you see is that IDEs can also aid in packaging and deployment. These productivity gains, however, don't mean that an IDE is best suited for application assemblers or deployers. Table 5-9 contrasts the roles.

TABLE 5-9 IDE USAGE FOR J2EE PLATFORM ROLES

Role	Tool Usage
Component Provider	As long as you, as a developer, like using IDEs (that's another long story), IDEs can help you rapidly create your modules and components. Forte, for example, has excellent iAS support and can package, deploy, execute, and debug your components.
Application Assembler	An application assembler is likely to use the `deploytool` instead of an IDE. `Deploytool` is very vertical in its features, package, and deploy. An IDE typically has too many bells and whistles for assemblers.
Application Deployer	Just as for the application assembler, IDEs are more than likely a distraction and overkill for the deployer's job. The `deploytool` with Ant or `iasdeploy` should suit deployers best.

See Chapter 8 for Forte packaging and deployment walkthrough.

As I state at the beginning of this section, IDEs are built for developers. Yet, in certain situations, an IDE is ideal for all the roles. An IDE is a good place to learn and experiment with the details of deployment descriptors, packaging, and deployment. The graphical nature of the IDE gives quick results and is usually pretty well documented. Application assemblers and deployers can use the IDE as a springboard into detailed knowledge of descriptors, `deploytool`, Ant, and `iasdeploy`.

Deployment Planning

I cover deployment thoroughly in Chapter 9. But it's worth reviewing in this section, considering all the context that I've built on packaging within this chapter. The application deployer role, of course, performs deployment. The deployer makes the application available for execution within the runtime environment by using the deployment tools that I describe in the preceding sections. Before starting the deployment process, however, visualizing how this application is to run in the grand scheme of things is usually a good idea.

The application server creates a separate class loader for each deployed enterprise application. Class loaders, in this context, isolate and partition applications. In short, any class or component that you deploy within one application isn't available to any other application. This situation exists by design. The J2EE specification prompts it as a way to make sure applications can be isolated from one another. From a re-use perspective, however, an archive that you deploy as module is reusable by other modules and by any enterprise application. The planning comes in making sure that you're deploying reusable components as modules. In all practicality, you should try to deploy only application-specific functionality in the form of an enterprise application and try to take advantage of reusable modules. Listing 5-26 shows how this setup may look within an iAS instance, where `myApplication` can use the components that you deploy to the modules directory.

Listing 5-26: Listing an iAS APPS directory structure

```
<IAS HOME>/ias/APPS/myApplication
<IAS HOME>/ias/APPS/modules/<reusable components>
```

Of course, maintaining an inventory of modules isn't simple. This task involves strict versioning and the appropriate support. In today's rapid development cycles, whether to invest in the personnel necessary to make an inventory of components available to all your applications is usually a business decision. The fallback procedure is simply to use enterprise applications (EAR files) as your default deployment units to ensure the correct partitioning between applications.

Refer to Chapter 9 for perspective on how deployments affect the application server and its application directories.

Summary

In this chapter, I take you on a tour of the application lifecycle for a J2EE application. Fundamentally, you've seen that the J2EE archives are packaged into specific formats known as *modules* and *applications*. You must package each of these archives with an appropriately well-formed deployment descriptor. The chapter also describes the roles of component provider, application assembler, and application deployer and how these roles provide a division of labor within the lifecycle of an application. Finally, the chapter defines the responsibilities of these roles and the tools that you can best apply for each role.

Chapter 6

Adding JSPs

IN THIS CHAPTER

- ◆ Understanding how JSPs work behind the scenes
- ◆ Using JSPs as an alternative programming model
- ◆ Using JSPs as a templating system
- ◆ Learning the iPlanet JSP extensions

JAVA SERVER PAGES (JSPs) offer many features that can make your development process easier. This chapter doesn't explore the JSP API in depth. As do the chapters about servlets and EJBs, this chapter gives you enough of an introduction to the topic that I can discuss the details of JSPs that are specific to iPlanet Application Server.

What Is a JSP?

JSP is a common abbreviation for *Java Server Page*, which is a Java technology for creating Web-based applications. Java Server Pages are designed to enable the easy development of dynamic Web content while still maintaining the power and flexibility of Java. Similar to scripting technologies such as Active Server Pages and PHP, Java Server Pages enable you to integrate application code directly into HTML. But unlike scripting languages, JSP APIs encourage a clean separation between application code (which Java developers create) and presentation (which HTML designers create). JSPs are not limited to generating HTML, however. JSPs can also be used to generate XML, WML, or any other content type.

---

 iPlanet Application Server 6.x supports version 1.1 of Java Server Pages.

JSPs from a developer's point of view

Any regular HTML page is also a valid JSP page. Simply renaming an HTML page from an .html extension to a .jsp extension converts it into a valid JSP page. This type of JSP isn't very interesting, however, because it always returns exactly the same content with every request. JSPs enable developers to make their pages return dynamic content by enabling them to embed Java code either programmatically — that is, by including Java code between special JSP tags.

From the developer's point of view, JSPs are merely a combination of plain HTML, special JSP tags, and embedded Java code. The JSP tags and Java code generate dynamic content to combine with the static HTML, which then returns to the end user as a normal Web page. (Of course, the Java code can also perform any other function that Java is capable of. The JSP can, for example, update a database.)

Listing 6-1 is a simple example of a Java Server Page that combines Java code and HTML.

Listing 6-1: A simple JSP page

```
<html>
<head><title>Chapter6 : TestJSP</title></head>
<body bgcolor="white">
<h2>iPlanet Application Server Enterprise Development</h2>
<h2>Chapter 6 : Simple JSP</h2>
<p>This simple JSP will be used to demonstrate interlacing HTML and
Java in a JSP.</p>
<p>Today's date is :
<% out.println(new java.util.Date()); %>
</p>
</body></html>
```

This simple JSP shows how you can embed Java code into ordinary HTML by using a *scriptlet*. A scriptlet is a section of Java code that you enclose within <% and %> tags. The scriptlet in the simple JSP retrieves the current date and sends it to the output. This output inserts the current date into the returned HTML in place of the scriptlet. The output of simple.jsp is similar to the code in Listing 6-2.

Listing 6-2: Output from simple.jsp

```
<html>
<head><title>Chapter6 : TestJSP</title></head>
<body bgcolor="white">
<h2>iPlanet Application Server Enterprise Development</h2>
<h2>Chapter 6 : Simple JSP</h2>
<p>This simple JSP will be used to demonstrate interlacing HTML and
```

```
Java in
a JSP.</p>
<p>Today's date is :
Tue Aug 21 17:38:25 EDT 2001
</p>
</body></html>
```

Notice that the ordinary text that the Java code produces replaces the contents of the scriptlet. I discuss other ways of embedding Java into JSPs throughout the rest of this chapter, but the key concept is that all JSP processing occurs at the server tier.

Behind the scenes with JSPs

New J2EE developers often struggle with the relationship between servlets and JSPs, perceiving them as competing technologies. This perception isn't true, however, as JSPs are just an alternative method of authoring servlets.

Whenever a user requests a JSP page, the server actually converts the JSP code into a servlet before execution. This conversion process happens automatically the first time that someone requests each JSP. The JSP compiler "compiles" the JSP code into the source code for an equivalent Java servlet. The regular `javac` Java compiler then compiles the Java servlet code into Java bytecode.

We discuss the JSP compilation process in more detail in Chapter 9. Understanding how the JSP compiler compiles JSPs into servlets can help you debug your JSP code.

Because JSPs are compiled into servlets before use, the JSP API is just an alternative way of writing servlets. JSPs provide a much more elegant alternative than using `println` statements to send HTML to an output stream within servlet code.

JSP strategies

JSPs employ a very flexible technology that you can use in many ways to assist J2EE development. In the sections "Model I – JSPs as Servlets" and "Model II – JSPs as Templates" later in this chapter, I explore two common JSP methodologies that the Java community refers to as Model I and Model II. These models are general strategies that use JSP technology, which development teams can further refine. Some development teams, for example, may use the Struts framework, which is an extension of Model II. Other teams may use a JavaBean library to extend their Model I strategies.

Even if you choose to use Model I exclusively, understanding Model II can help you separate presentation and business logic. And even if you use Model II exclusively, Model I can teach you good strategies for componentizing your JSPs.

The JSP API

The JSP API is very sophisticated. Although you can pick up the basics of JSPs very quickly, the JSP API exhibits considerable depth in the flexibility that enables it to support the development of large applications.

I remind you that the following sections serve only as an introduction to the JSP API so that I can move on to the details of JSPs that are specific to iPlanet Application Server. If you need more information about the JSP API, many books are available that focus completely on JSP development, such as *JSP: JavaServer Pages*, by Barry Burd (Hungry Minds, 2001 0-7645-3535-8). Several links at the end of this chapter lead to JSP resources, including the JSP specification and online JSP tutorials.

Implicit objects

One of the advantages of the JSP API is that it relieves the author of some of the tedious aspects of authoring servlets. One example of a benefit of JSP-based development is *implicit objects*. Implicit objects are a set of objects that the JSP compiler automatically creates for you, including the following:

◆ `application` — A wrapper around the `ServletContext` object.

◆ `config:` — A `ServletConfig` object.

◆ `exception` — Used by the Web container to wrap the `Throwable` object that an error-handling JSP is processing.

◆ `out` — A buffered output stream.

◆ `pageContext` — An object encapsulating the page environment.

◆ `request` — An `HttpServletRequest` object.

◆ `response` — An `HttpServletResponse` object.

◆ `session` — An `HttpSession` object.

The request and response objects are necessary because they're your only interface to the `HttpServletRequest` and `HttpServletResponse` objects that the `doGet()` or `doPost()` method of the generated servlet receives. The other objects are just for the developer's convenience — for example, saving the developer the lines of code necessary to create a buffered output stream from the `response` object.

The simple JSP shown in Listing 6-1 uses the implicit out object to return the current date and time. The scriptlet example in the next section also uses implicit objects.

Scriptlets

Scriptlets provide a straightforward way of performing the basic function of including Java code within HTML. You've already examined a simple example of a scriptlet in Listing 6-1. The scriptlet in Listing 6-1 looks up the current time and embeds the results in a simple HTML page.

Using scriptlets is as simple as including your own Java code within <% and %> tags. You can even use scriptlets to place flow-control and conditional statements around your HTML code. Listing 6-3 provides an example of how you can use scriptlets for more complex purposes, such as including conditional processing of HTML blocks.

Listing 6–3: conditional.jsp

```
<html>
<head><title>Chapter6 : Conditional Scriptlet JSP</title></head>
<body bgcolor="white">
<h2>iPlanet Application Server Enterprise Development</h2>
<h2>Chapter 6 : Conditional Scriptlet JSP</h2>
<p>This JSP demonstrates several elements of scriptlets, including
how
scriptlets can be used for conditional processing of HTML
blocks.</p>

<p>The random number (1-4) generated for this page view is:
<% /* This scriptlet generates a random number.
    * Some parts of the JSP are conditionally processed based on the
    * generated number. */
   java.util.Random randomGenerator = new java.util.Random();
   int randomNumber = randomGenerator.nextInt(4)+1;
   out.println(Integer.toString(randomNumber)); %></p>
<p>The following will be printed once per value of the random
number:</p>
<blockquote>
<% /* Looping scriplet */
   for (int i=0;i<randomNumber;i++) { %>
   <em>This line is printed once per value of the number.</em><br>
<% } %></blockquote>
<p>The following is conditional based on the value of the
```

Continued

Listing 6-3 *(Continued)*

```
number:</p>
<blockquote><em>
<% /* Conditional scriptlet */
   switch (randomNumber) {
   case 4: %>
       Four calling birds<br>
<% case 3: %>
       Three French hens<br>
<% case 2: %>
       Two turtledoves<br>
<% case 1: %>
       A partridge in a pear tree<br>
<% break; } %>
</blockquote></body></html>
```

The interesting point to notice about the code in Listing 6-3 is that blocks of code can span more than one scriptlet. This capability enables you to include HTML in loops and conditionals that you create within the scriptlets. The `conditional.jsp` code includes a loop that prints a line of HTML a random number of times and a select statement that prints lines from *The Twelve Days of Christmas* that it bases on the random number.

Expressions

One common purpose of a scriptlet is to get some piece of dynamic data, such as a customer name, and include it in the HTML results. As you've seen in Listing 6-1 from the "JSPs from a developer's point of view" section, you can use the `out` implicit object as one way to accomplish this task.

The expression tag (<%= %>) is a shortcut that enables developers to avoid repeatedly typing `out.println`. In `simple.jsp`, for example, the scriptlet-based method of output is as follows:

```
<% out.println(new java.util.Date()); %>
```

You can also write the same line of code using an expression tag as follows:

```
<%= new java.util.Date() %>
```

The <%= expression tag marks the enclosed Java code as an *expression* rather than a scriptlet. The JSP compiler automatically generates the code necessary to output the Java fragment to the output stream. Both lines of JSP code generate the same Java code in the compiled servlet.

Strong Typing and Weak Typing

One difference between JSPs and other similar technologies is that JSP is strongly typed. Strong typing means that you must declare your variables before using them along with the type of data that they will store. Strong typing is the opposite of weak typing, where variables are automatically created by the container as needed and variables can store any type of information.

The following is an example of a PHP script. PHP is a weakly typed Web scripting language.

```
<?php
$myvar = 5        //The variable $my var does not have to be
                  //declared beforehand. It is automatically created.


$myvar = "hello" //Even though $myvar was originally used to store
                 //and integer, it can also be used to store other
                 //datatypes. Such as strings.

?>
```

There are advantages to both strong typing and weak typing. Weak typing is obviously more convenient, since developers do not need to worry about variable declarations and type conversions. Strong typing, however, helps improve code quality by insuring that the variable types used by the container are the types that the developer intended. A strongly typed language compiler will automatically prevent type conversions not explicitly declared by the developer.

One additional advantage of using expressions is that you don't need to worry about converting the results of your Java fragments to Strings. To make JSP expressions as easy to use as more weakly typed scripting languages, the JSP compiler automatically accepts and converts primitives to Strings. The following expression, therefore, is valid:

```
<%= new java.util.Random().nextInt(10)+1 %>
```

Notice that, if you use expressions, you don't need a semicolon.

You can find both expressions on the `conditional.jsp` file in the sample code on the CD-ROM.

Declarations

JSP *declarations* provide a place to initialize variables and methods that you use later in other declarations, expressions, and scriptlets. Declarations must include one or more complete Java statements.

Declarations can't directly send data to the page results, unlike expressions or scriptlets. Also, unlike scriptlets the scope of variables in a declaration are global to all threads of the JSP within the JVM.

Scriptlets add their enclosed code to the methods that the `service` method of the generated servlet calls. Variables declared within a scriplet, therefore, have a scope that extends only to the current request. Declarations add their enclosed code directly to the generated servlet class itself. Declaration variables, therefore, have a scope that extends visibility to all servlet requests within the current JVM.

Declarations use a beginning delimiter of `<%!` and an ending delimiter of `%>`. The following is an example of a simple JSP declaration element:

```
<%! Date myDate = new Date(); %>
```

This simple declaration defines a variable that is stored within the generated servlet object. The variable is accessible from any page request, but the variable initializes only once (per JVM) and any modifications that you make to the variable are visible to all requests.

Developers must give the same considerations to variables scoped with JSP wide visibility as they give to variables scoped with servlet wide visibility. Specifically, you must consider both threading issues and multi-JVM issues. Declarations, as is true of any variables with the scope of the servlet object, have a scope only within the current JVM. If you use the preceding declaration (`<%! Date myDate = new Date(); %>`) in a JSP that you run in a multi-JVM or multiserver environment, each JVM has its own copy of the `myDate` variable. Notice that the definitions that you enclose in declaration tags must end in a semicolon.

Because the Web container compiles JSPs into servlets, the threading issues and multi-JVM considerations involve exactly the same issues that I address in examining servlets in Chapter 4.

In that chapter, the section "The Servlet Lifecycle" describes the multi-threaded nature of servlets and, therefore, JSPs. It includes details on several strategies to use to manage threading issues.

The section "Multi-JVM Considerations" describes the additional complexity that designing applications to operate in multiserver and multi-JVM environments can involve. Multi-JVM environments are critical to designing high availability applications, but they require additional forethought on the part of application architects.

JSP directives

JSP directives provide a way of customizing the behavior of the JSP compiler, similar to what a pragma does in the C programming language. The following list describes the JSP 1.1 directives:

- `include` — The directive that you use to include static files into the JSP. The `include` directive causes the JSP compiler to insert external files in the generated servlet at translation time. (The `include` action has a similar affect, but the included files are evaluated at run time by the Web container.)

- `page` — Sets several attributes specific to the page. You can have multiple `page` directives for a JSP page, as long as you don't set any attribute twice. Following is a partial list of page attributes that you can set. (You can find the complete list of page directive attributes in section 2.7 of the JSP 1.1 specification. A hyperlink to the specification can be found at the end of this chapter.):

  - `buffer`: The attribute that you use to define the size of the out implicit variable's output buffer.

  - `errorPage`: The URL of a page to forward control to if the JSP page throws an unhandled exception. Notice, however, the limitations of the `forward` action. Heeding this directive may prove impossible if results were already sent to the client.

  - `isErrorPage`: The attribute that you use to indicate that a JSP is for the purpose of handling errors. Enables the construction of the `exception` implicit variable, which contains the `Throwable` object that was thrown.

  - `import`: The attribute that you use to add packages to the import list. The default import list is `java.lang.*`, `javax.servlet.*`, `javax.servlet.jsp.*`, and `javax.servlet.http.*`. Unlike with other attributes, you can define multiple `import` attributes.

  - `session`: Indicates whether to create the `session` implicit object. It's `true` by default, but you should set it to `false` if no interaction with the `HttpSession` is necessary.

- `Taglib`: The directive/attribute that you use to indicate the location of a `taglib` definition. I discuss `taglib`s in the section "JSP Tag Libraries," later in this chapter.

The JSP directive syntax is `<%@ directive { attr="value" }%>`. Listing 6-4 shows the use of several directives.

Listing 6–4: directive.jsp

```
<%@ page buffer="64k" %>
<%@ page session="false" %>
<%@ page import="java.util.*" %>
<html>
<head><title>Chapter6 : Directive JSP</title></head>
<body bgcolor="white">
<h2>iPlanet Application Server Enterprise Development</h2>
<h2>Chapter 6 : Directive JSP</h2>
<p>This JSP demonstrates the use of directives.</p>
<p>Today's date is :
<% out.println(new Date()); %>
</p>
<%@ include file="footer.html" %>
</body></html>
```

The directive.jsp code includes four directives. The first directive (page buffer=
"64k") changes the size of the output buffer from the default of 8K to 64K. Because
this page is small, this directive ensures that the Web container buffers the entire
page before sending it to the client. The second directive (page session= "false")
prevents iAS from needlessly generating the session object. The third directive
(page import= "java.util.*") includes the java.util package so that the JSP code
doesn't need to explicitly qualify the Date object. The final directive (include
file= "footer.html") includes a small HTML file at the bottom of the JSP.

Always make sure that you set the page:session attribute equal to false
if you're not going to interact with the HttpSession. Leaving the session
value equal to true can lead to unnecessary performance overhead if
you're not using the session object. This advice is especially true for small
JSPs that you use as includes in other JSPs and of JSPs that you use only for
templating.

JSP actions

One key to keeping JSPs readable and maintainable is to minimize the actual
amount of Java code within the JSPs. *Actions* are prebuilt functions that you can
call via JSP tags. They enable you to minimize the actual amount of Java code and
enable you to construct JSPs by simply scripting together prebuilt Java components.

This capability increases readability, especially to the HTML-page designers who may have little understanding of Java. Encapsulating Java functionality into tags enables JSP-page designers and authors to utilize business functionality without exposing them to the implementation details.

Seven standard action tags are available in the JSP 1.1 API, as the following list describes:

◆ useBean — A useBean action associates an instance of a JavaBean to a given id. You can adjust the scope of the JavaBean to the application, the session, the page, or the tag by changing the scope attribute. If an instance of the JavaBean with the specified id doesn't already exist within the scope, the container creates a new instantiation. (See the links at the end of this chapter for information about JavaBeans.)

◆ setProperty — A setProperty action invokes a setter method on a JavaBean that the name property specifies. The name property must correspond to the id of a JavaBean that is specified earlier in the JSP page.

◆ getProperty — A getProperty action invokes a getter method on a JavaBean that the name property specifies and places the results from the method into the JSP results. The name property must correspond to the id of a JavaBean that the developer specified earlier in the JSP page.

◆ include — An include action inserts another HTML or JSP page into the JSP. Unlike the include directive, the include action operates at run time, enabling the inclusion of dynamic content.

◆ forward — The forward action transfers control to an alternate JSP. If any output has already returned, this output raises an IllegalStateException. If output was buffered, but not yet returned, the container clears that buffer before passing control to the alternate JSP.

◆ param — The param action adds name/value pairs to the request object and is designed for use in combination with the include, forward, or plugin actions.

◆ plugin — You use the plugin action to generate the HTML that the browser needs to invoke the Java plug-in to execute a JavaBean or Java Applet (which is either the OBJECT or EMBED tag, depending on the user's browser). The plugin tag has the params and fallback subelements. The params subelement encloses the param action tags that you use to pass parameters to the Applet/JavaBean. The fallback subelement encloses alternative content that the Web container returns to clients that can't support OBJECT/EMBED.

Use some discretion in utilizing the `include` action. Reinitializing the JSP container to handle the included JSP involves a certain amount of overhead, as does dispatching the included request.

You can minimize the overhead by using the `session="false"` page direction (to minimize the overhead of recreating the session implicit variable) or, if possible, by substituting the `include` directive to enable processing at compile time instead of run time.

Listing 6-5 shows how elegant JSP actions can be. The JSP shown in the listing calls a JavaBean that performs a CRC-32 hash on a String. (CRC is a method for creating hashes of data, often for error-checking purposes. For more information, see the links at the end of this chapter.)

Listing 6-5: action.jsp

```jsp
<%@ page session="false" %>
<%@ page errorPage="customerror.jsp" %>
<jsp:useBean
  id="CRC"
  class="com.hungryminds.ias.chapter6.web.CRCBean"
  scope="request" />
<jsp:setProperty
  name="CRC"
  property="hashString"
  value="iPlanet Application Server Enterprise Development"/>
<html>
<head><title>Chapter6 : Action JSP</title></head>
<body bgcolor="white">
<h2>iPlanet Application Server Enterprise Development</h2>
<h2>Chapter 6 : Action JSP</h2>
<p>This simple JSP will be used to demonstrate using JavaBeans via
action tags.</p>
<p>The following value is a CRC-32 hash of "iPlanet Application
Server
Enterprise Development" that has been calculated with a server-side
JavaBean.
</p><blockquote><em>
CRC-32 Hash = <jsp:getProperty name="CRC" property="hashValue" />
</em></blockquote>
</body></html>
```

This code is easily readable because the process of performing that actual CRC calculations have been encapsulated into a JavaBean. The JSP merely instantiates the bean with a `useBean` tag, places the String that it's going to hash into the JavaBean by using a `setProperty` tag, and then retrieves the resulting hash value into the results by using a `getProperty` tag.

This version of the JSP is very self-documenting. Even a nonprogrammer unfamiliar with Java can discern that basic purpose of the `useBean`, `setProperty`, and `getProperty` tags.

Be careful with case in using JavaBean properties, as the case of the property is somewhat nonintuitive. A property with the `getter` method of `getABCCompany`, for example, has the property name of `aBCCompany` and not `ABCCompany`! The first letter of the property name is always the opposite case of the name that the `getter` and `setter` methods use.

You can turn off this strict enforcement of case by adding the `-DIAS_JSP_ IGNORECASE=true` argument to the KJS. You can do so by modifying the last line of the KJS script (on Solaris) or adding it to the `\\(SOFTWARE\ iPlanet)\Application  Server\6.5\JAVA\JavaArgs` registry key (on NT).

Listing 6-6 shows the JavaBean code that the JSP is accessing. The `CRCBean.java` code includes a default constructor, two `getter` methods, one `setter` method, and three private methods that perform the actual CRC-32 calculations.

Listing 6-6: CRCBean.java

```
package com.hungryminds.ias.chapter6.web;
/**
 * JavaBean to calculate CRC hashes of Strings.
 * This code is based on public domain code created by Michael
Lecuyer.
 */
public class CRCBean
{
    int CRCTable[];   // CRC Lookup table
    private String hashString;
    private int hashValue;
    private int crc;
```

Continued

Listing 6-6 *(Continued)*

```java
public CRCBean()
{
    buildCRCTable();
}

public void setHashString(String newValue) {
    hashString=newValue;
    hashValue=crc32(newValue);
}

public String getHashString() {
    return hashString;
}

public int getHashValue() {
    return hashValue;
}

private void buildCRCTable()
{
    final int CRC32_POLYNOMIAL = 0xEDB88320;
    int i, j;
    int crc;
    CRCTable = new int[256];
    for (i = 0; i <= 255; i++)
    {
        crc = i;
        for (j = 8; j > 0; j--)
            if ((crc & 1) == 1)
                crc = (crc >>> 1) ^ CRC32_POLYNOMIAL;
            else
                crc >>>= 1;
        CRCTable[i] = crc;
    }
}

private int crc32(String buffer)
{
    return crc32(buffer.getBytes(), 0,buffer.length(),0xFFFFFFFF);
}
```

```
    private int crc32(byte buffer[], int start, int count, int
lastcrc)
    {
        int temp1, temp2;
        int i = start;
        crc = lastcrc;
        while (count-- != 0)
        {
            temp1 = crc >>> 8;
            temp2 = CRCTable[(crc ^ buffer[i++]) & 0xFF];
            crc = temp1 ^ temp2;
        }
        return crc;
    }
}
```

As you can see in the CRCBean example, JavaBeans that the `useBean` action includes don't need to strictly adhere to the JavaBean specification. Specifically, you don't need to package them in JAR by using a bean manifest, and they don't need to implement the `serializable` interface.

To utilize the `useBean` action, the JavaBean must only provide public `getter` and `setter` methods for its properties and provide a public constructor without arguments.

Although iPlanet Application Server doesn't enforce the `serializable` interface requirement, JavaBeans must implement `serializable` if you add them to the session. This requirement includes JavaBeans that you declare by using a session scope.

Including this code within the JSP detracts greatly from the readability of the JSP. Even using scriptlets to instantiate the JavaBean and to call the CRC function isn't as readable as the useBean tag to someone who isn't proficient in Java. But even a nonprogrammer can cut and paste the `setProperty` and `getProperty` tags to perform a second CRC hash on a second string.

JSP Tag Libraries

Tag libraries, often called *taglibs*, are a method of building custom actions. Taglibs enable you to encapsulate functionality even more elegantly and descriptively than you can just by using a JavaBean with the `useBean` action.

As an additional benefit, taglibs also enable developers much more flexibility. Unlike JavaBeans, taglibs are aware of the state of the JSP engine, can interact with the JSP environment, and can nest. Taglibs are an essential tool for implementing significant custom functionality in the Model I JSP development methodology.

Because of the extra flexibility of taglibs, however, they're more complex than other methods of encapsulation, such as JavaBeans. Implementing a tag library involves the following four steps:

1. Implement the custom functionality in one or more *tag handlers*. Tag handlers are JavaBeans that implement either the `Tag` interface or the `BodyTag` interface. (`BodyTag` is a more complex interface that gives the tag handler access to the content of the JSP between the start and end of the custom tag.) The collection of tag handlers is known as the *Tag Library*.

2. Create a *Tag Library Descriptor* (*TLD*). The TLD is an XML document that describes and documents a Tag Library. It includes information about the tags and attributes implemented, as well as information about the library as a whole.

3. Use a `taglib` directive to link the TLD to the JSP page. The `taglib` directive declares that a JSP page uses a given Tag Library and associates that Tag Library with a `tag` prefix. This prefix enables each tag library to have its own XML `tag` namespace and prevents name conflicts between different Tag libraries.

4. Invoke the taglib within the JSP. You invoke the `taglib` by using an XML syntax. The tag name that you need to invoke a custom action is the declared tag prefix, a colon, and then the action name in the Tag Library. Listings 6-9 and 6-13 later in this section are examples of using tag libraries within JSPs.

Taglibs are the most powerful tool that you have for developing components for use in JSPs. Developing simple taglibs is relatively straightforward. Developing tag libraries becomes more complex, however, as you implement the more advanced features such as composite tags, new objects, and body processing.

In this chapter, I examine two examples of custom tag actions. One is a simple HelloWorld tag that inserts a fixed string in the place of the custom tag. The second is a CRC tag that performs a CRC hash of the enclosed text. This taglib gives you an even more elegant way of implementing CRC calculations than the CRC JavaBean from Listing 6-5.

IMPLEMENTING A SIMPLE TAG HANDLER

The first custom tag that I show you is a `HelloWorld` application that returns a simple fixed string. The following sections demonstrate the four steps of implementing that custom tag.

BUILDING THE CUSTOM TAG HANDLER   Tag handlers must implement either the `Tag` or `BodyTag` interface, depending on whether they need to process the contents of the body of the tag. Because you're going to implement your `HelloWorld` as an empty tag so that you have no body contents to process, you therefore must implement the simpler Tag interface.

The JSP API also provides two corresponding base classes, TagSupport and BodyTagSupport, that you can optionally use as superclasses in developing custom tag handlers. Although optional, these classes simplify the process of developing tag libraries. You must extend the TagSupport base class to implement your HelloWorld tag.

Listing 6-7 shows the implementation of the HelloWorld tag handler. You override three methods in this implementation: the constructor, doStartTag, and doEndTag. Your only addition to the constructor is a simple System.out.println call to log when the JVM invokes the constructor. Your only modification to the doEndTag method is to return the constant to indicate that JSP processing is to continue normally after completion of the tag. The doStartTag method is where you actually add the Hello World message to the JSP results.

Listing 6-7: HelloTag.java

```java
package com.hungryminds.ias.chapter6.web.taglibs;

import java.io.*;
import javax.servlet.jsp.*;
import javax.servlet.jsp.tagext.*;

public class HelloTag extends TagSupport {

    public HelloTag() {
        System.out.println("Chapter6 : HelloTag constructor");
    }

    public int doStartTag () throws JspTagException {
        try {
            pageContext.getOut().print(
                "<blockquote>Hello World!</blockquote>");
        }
        catch (IOException e) {
            throw new JspTagException(e.getMessage());
        }
        System.out.println("Chapter6 : HelloTag Start Tag");
        return EVAL_BODY_INCLUDE;
    }

    public int doEndTag () {
        System.out.println("Chapter6 : HelloTag End Tag");
        return EVAL_PAGE;
    }
}
```

BUILDING THE TAG LIBRARY DESCRIPTOR   The tag library descriptor (TLD) contains the information that you need to document the tag library and the custom actions available within it. For the `HelloWorld` custom action, you need a `<tag>` element with the following three subelements:

◆ The `name` subelement, which names the action. You use this name in the actual action tag, so try to keep it short and descriptive.

◆ The `tagclass` subelement that tells the JSP compiler where to find the tag handler for the custom action. This subelement is the fully qualified class name of our `HelloTag` class.

◆ The `bodycontent` subelement, which declares whether the custom tag has a body. For `HelloWorld`, a tag body is meaningless, so you specify the empty option to indicate that you expect an empty XML element — that is, `<ch6:HelloWorld />` and not `<ch6:HelloWorld>body</ch6:HelloWorld>`.

The TLD file also includes standard information such as the XML version, DTD link, and JSP version, as well as information about the entire tag library, such as the tag library's name, description, and version. Listing 6-8 shows a TLD that describes your `HelloWorld` custom action.

Listing 6-8: chapter6.tld (excerpt)

```
<?xml version="1.0" encoding="ISO-8859-1" ?>
<!DOCTYPE taglib
        PUBLIC "-//Sun Microsystems, Inc.//DTD JSP Tag Library
1.1//EN"
        "http://java.sun.com/j2ee/dtds/web-jsptaglibrary_1_1.dtd">
<taglib>
  <tlibversion>1.0</tlibversion>
  <jspversion>1.1</jspversion>
  <shortname>chapter6</shortname>
  <info>
    Sample JSP taglib used in Chapter 6 of iPlanet Application
Server
    Enterprise Development
  </info>
  <tag>
    <name>HelloWorld</name>

<tagclass>com.hungryminds.ias.chapter6.web.taglibs.HelloTag</tagclass>
    <bodycontent>empty</bodycontent>
  </tag>
</taglib>
```

USING THE TAG LIBRARY   As I mention in the "JSP Tag Libraries" section, utilizing a tag library involves two steps. First, you create a link between your JSP page and the tag library by using a `taglib` directive. Second, you invoke the actual custom action with an XML tag by using the prefix that the taglibs directive defines and the action name that the TLD defines.

Listing 6-9 shows a simple example of a JSP using the `HelloWorld` custom tag.

Listing 6-9: hello.jsp

```
<%@ page session="false" %>
<%@ taglib prefix="ch6" uri="/WEB-INF/tlds/chapter6.tld" %>
<html>
<head><title>Chapter6 : Hello TagLib JSP</title></head>
<body bgcolor="white">
<h2>Chapter 6 : Hello TagLib JSP</h2>
<p>Hello Test</p>
<blockquote><ch6:HelloWorld /></blockquote>
</body></html>
```

Notice that the `taglib` directive defines the prefix for the tag library, and, therefore, the prefix can be different in each JSP that invokes the tag library. This ability to map taglibs to prefixes dynamically prevents any prefix naming conflicts between tag libraries. Having two custom actions with the same name causes no problems, because they have different XML tag prefixes.

A taglib URI can optionally be defined in the web.xml file. Defining a taglib URL in the deployment descriptor allows you to avoid hardcoding the path of the TLD into all of the JSPs that utilize that taglib. The following is an example of a web.xml taglib definition:

```
<taglib>
<taglib-uri>/ch6</taglib-uri>
<taglib-location>/WEB-INF/tlds/chapter6.tld
</taglib-location>
</taglib>
```

If this element exists in the web.xml file, the taglib directive in hello.jsp could be abbreviated to:

```
<%@ taglib prefix="ch6" uri="/ch6" %>
```

This allows the physical location of the TLD to be stored in only one location (the descriptor) instead of being repeated in each JSP that used the taglib.

By examining the results of the JSP compiler, you can observe the interaction between the JSP container and the tag handler. The Java code that the JSP compiler for `hello.jsp` generates is shown in Listing 6-10.

 You can find information on where deployment environment stores the compiled JSPs in Chapter 9.

Listing 6-10: hello.java (excerpt)

```
out.write("\r\n<html>\r\n<head><title>Chapter6 : Hello TagLib
JSP</title></head>\r\n<body bgcolor=\"white\">\r\n<h2>Chapter 6 : Hello TagLib
JSP</h2>\r\n<p>Hello Test</p>\r\n<blockquote>");
                // end
                // begin
[file="/export/home/apps/ias1/ias/APPS/chapter6/chapter6/hello.jsp";from=(7,12);
to=(7,30)]
                    /* ---- ch6:HelloWorld ---- */
                    com.hungryminds.ias.chapter6.web.taglibs.HelloTag
_jspx_th_ch6_HelloWorld_0 = new
com.hungryminds.ias.chapter6.web.taglibs.HelloTag();
                    _jspx_th_ch6_HelloWorld_0.setPageContext(pageContext);
                    _jspx_th_ch6_HelloWorld_0.setParent(null);
                    try {
                        int _jspx_eval_ch6_HelloWorld_0 =
_jspx_th_ch6_HelloWorld_0.doStartTag();
                        if (_jspx_eval_ch6_HelloWorld_0 == BodyTag.EVAL_BODY_TAG)
                            throw new JspTagException("Since tag handler class
com.hungryminds.ias.chapter6.web.taglibs.HelloTag does not implement BodyTag, it
can't return BodyTag.EVAL_BODY_TAG");
                        if (_jspx_eval_ch6_HelloWorld_0 != Tag.SKIP_BODY) {
                            do {
                            // end
                            // begin
[file="/export/home/apps/ias1/ias/APPS/chapter6/chapter6/hello.jsp";from=(7,12);
to=(7,30)]
                            } while (false);
                        }
                        if (_jspx_th_ch6_HelloWorld_0.doEndTag() == Tag.SKIP_PAGE)
                            return;
```

You can observe several interesting things in this compiled JSP. First, the beginning of the custom `taglib` is well commented. These comments enable you to use the compiled JSP as a debugging tool for taglib interactions. You can also observe the JSP container evaluating the return values from your tag handler methods – for example, you can see that, if your doEndTag method returns a SKIP_PAGE response, the JSP service method immediately exits with a return statement.

 TIP You can invoke the JSP compiler from the command line by using the jspc command. (Execute jspc without any arguments for the complete syntax.) This command enables you to inspect the generated Java code and check the syntax of your JSPs without going through a complete deployment cycle.

BUILDING A TAG HANDLER WITH A BODY

Next, you get to build a tag handler that processes the body of a custom tag. You create a tag handler that takes the body between the starting and ending tags and performs a CRC-32 hash of the contents. It then returns the results of the hash in place of the body contents.

BUILDING THE CUSTOM TAG HANDLER   Because you need to interface with the body of the tag, you must implement the BodyTag interface and (optionally) extend the BodyTagSupport class. In addition to the methods that you implement in the HelloWorld tag, you also implement the doAfterBody method, which the JSP container calls after the body of the custom tag is evaluated. You retrieve the contents of the tag body in this method and hash it by using the same CRC hashing method that you use in your earlier CRC JavaBean from Listing 6-6.

Listing 6-11 shows the code that you use to implement the CRC tag handler. (I omit the CRC methods for brevity, as they're the same methods that you use in Listing 6-6). Notice the general similarity to the HelloWorld example. You respond to callbacks from the JSP container and take advantage of the JSP API to interact with the calling JSP. In this case, you're using the BodyContent object to retrieve the contents of the tag body for processing and using the getPreviousOut method to get the out method of the surrounding page.

Listing 6-11: CRCTag.java (excerpt)

```
package com.hungryminds.ias.chapter6.web.taglibs;

import java.io.*;
import javax.servlet.jsp.*;
import javax.servlet.jsp.tagext.*;

public class CRCTag extends BodyTagSupport {
```

Continued

Listing 6-11 *(Continued)*

```java
int CRCTable[];   // CRC Lookup table
private int crc;

public CRCTag() {
   buildCRCTable();
}


public int doStartTag() {
   return EVAL_BODY_TAG;
}


public int doAfterBody() throws JspTagException {
   BodyContent bc = getBodyContent();
   String data = bc.getString();
   int hash;

   bc.clearBody(); // We do not want to show the raw data.
   hash=crc32(data.getBytes(),0,data.length(),0xFFFFFFFF);
   try {
      getPreviousOut().print("CRC-32 Hash : " +
         Integer.toString(hash));
   }
   catch (IOException e) {
       throw new JspTagException(e.getMessage());
   }
   return SKIP_BODY; //This indicates that we are done processing body.
}


public int doEndTag () {
   return EVAL_PAGE;
}
private void buildCRCTable()
{
   final int CRC32_POLYNOMIAL = 0xEDB88320;
   int i, j;
   int crc;
   CRCTable = new int[256];
   for (i = 0; i <= 255; i++)
   {
      crc = i;
      for (j = 8; j > 0; j--)
         if ((crc & 1) == 1)
             crc = (crc >>> 1) ^ CRC32_POLYNOMIAL;
```

```
        else
            crc >>>= 1;
        CRCTable[i] = crc;
    }
}
private int crc32(String buffer)
{
    return crc32(buffer.getBytes(), 0,buffer.length(),0xFFFFFFFF);
}

private int crc32(byte buffer[], int start, int count, int lastcrc)
{
    int temp1, temp2;
    int i = start;
    crc = lastcrc;
    while (count-- != 0)
    {
        temp1 = crc >>> 8;
        temp2 = CRCTable[(crc ^ buffer[i++]) & 0xFF];
        crc = temp1 ^ temp2;
    }
    return crc;
}
}
```

Notice the return codes that you're passing back to the JSP container. You return a value of EVAL_BODY_TAG in doStartTag to indicate that you're processing the contents of the tag body. You return a value of SKIP_BODY in doAfterBody to indicate that you're done processing the body. (Iterative tags may want to process the body multiple times, returning EVAL_BODY_TAG until they complete their processing.) Returning a value of EVAL_PAGE enables normal processing to continue after your doEndTag method, just as in the HelloWorld example.

BUILDING THE TAG LIBRARY DESCRIPTOR   Now that you've built the tag handler for your custom action, you can update your existing TLD with the information for your new tag, as shown in Listing 6-12.

Listing 6-12: chapter6.tld

```
<?xml version="1.0" encoding="ISO-8859-1" ?>
<!DOCTYPE taglib
        PUBLIC "-//Sun Microsystems, Inc.//DTD JSP Tag Library 1.1//EN"
        "http://java.sun.com/j2ee/dtds/web-jsptaglibrary_1_1.dtd">
```

Continued

Listing 6-12 *(Continued)*

```
<taglib>
    <tlibversion>1.0</tlibversion>
    <jspversion>1.1</jspversion>
    <shortname>chapter6</shortname>
    <info>
        Sample JSP taglib used in Chapter 6 of iPlanet Application Server
        Enterprise Development
    </info>
    <tag>
      <name>HelloWorld</name>
      <tagclass>com.hungryminds.ias.chapter6.web.taglibs.HelloTag</tagclass>
      <bodycontent>empty</bodycontent>
    </tag>
    <tag>
      <name>CRC</name>
      <tagclass>com.hungryminds.ias.chapter6.web.taglibs.CRCTag</tagclass>
      <bodycontent>tagdependent</bodycontent>
    </tag>
</taglib>
```

The only difference between your new CRC XML element and the existing `HelloWorld` element is the `bodycontent` subelement. The `tagdependent` value for the subelement indicates that you expect to utilize this tag with a body, and that you expect to interpret the body of the tag directly. (Other custom tags may indicate that the body content is more JSP code, enabling you to nest the JSP tags.)

USING THE TAG LIBRARY   The end benefit of your CRC tag is a very simple way to perform CRC-32 hashing within a JSP page. Compare Listing 6-13 with Listing 6-5, which uses your CRC JavaBean to perform CRC-32 hashing.

Listing 6-13: taglib.jsp

```
<%@ page session="false" %>
<%@ taglib prefix="ch6" uri="/WEB-INF/tlds/chapter6.tld" %>
<html>
<head><title>Chapter6 : TagLib JSP</title></head>
<body bgcolor="white">
<h2>iPlanet Application Server Enterprise Development</h2>
<h2>Chapter 6 : TagLib JSP</h2>
<p>This page demostrates the use of custom tag libraries.</p>
<p>Today's date is :
<% out.println(new java.util.Date()); %>
<p>Hello Test</p>
<blockquote><ch6:HelloWorld /></blockquote>
```

```
<p>CRC Test</p>
<blockquote><ch6:CRC>
This is a String that will be hashed. (This String will not be included in
the actual results passed to the browser.)
</ch6:CRC></blockquote>
</body></html>
```

After you link the TLD with the JSP by using the `taglib` directive, hashing a value is as simple as enclosing the value with the `<ch6:CRC>` XML tags. This is even more intuitive and obvious than the `setProperty` and `getProperty` tags that you need if you use the `useBean` action, as you do in `action.jsp`.

PACKAGING JSP TAG LIBRARIES Using tag libraries is a great way to build reusable functionality. Some tag libraries, however, you develop for a specific application, so such libraries have no purpose outside that application. How you package your tag libraries depends on how you intend on using them.

If you're developing a tag library that you plan on using in multiple applications or that you're providing for use as a generic component in other applications, your best course is to package your Tag Library as a standalone module. If, on the other hand, your `taglib`'s functionality is specific to your application, package your tag library inside your application's WAR file.

STANDALONE TAG LIBRARY PACKAGING The JSP specification instructs that, in packaging a tag library as a standalone JAR file, you must include the TLD in the /META-INF subdirectory of the JAR, and you must name the TLD `taglib.tld`.

Listing 6-14 shows an excerpt from the Chapter 6 Ant build script. This excerpt builds a standalone `taglibs` JAR file for the `HelloWorld` and CRC tags.

Listing 6-14: build.xml (excerpt)

```
<target name="taglib" depends="clean_taglib,compile">
<mkdir dir="${assemble.taglib}/${taglib.pkgprefix}"/>
<copy todir="${assemble.taglib}/${taglib.pkgprefix}">
   <fileset dir="${build.classesdir}/${taglib.pkgprefix}/"
       includes="**/*.class"/>
</copy>
<copy file="${src}/tlds/chapter6.tld"
   tofile="${assemble.taglib}/META-INF/taglib.tld" />
<jar jarfile="${assemble.taglib}/${taglib}"
   basedir="${assemble.taglib}" />
</target>
```

In working with a tag library that you package as a standalone JAR, you can reference the JAR file in the `taglib` directive instead of the TLD. The JSP container automatically looks in the META-INF directory of the JAR to find the TLD.

The JSP specification encourages you to place your tag library JAR files in the WEB-INF/lib directory of your WAR file. The iAS deployment process, however, automatically unJARs all the files in the WAR file. This situation prevents JSPs from referencing taglib JARs directly in a taglibs directive if they're deployed as part of a WAR. You can still deploy tag handlers in WEB-INF/lib, but you must reference the TLD directly.

Alternatively, you can manually copy the taglib JAR into the appserver file system. (You can copy it anywhere, even to WEB-INF/lib, as long as the taglib directive points at the correct location.) This method is especially useful if you're sharing tag libraries across multiple applications, because all applications can share the tag library files.

In short, self-contained tag library packaging is useful to enable you to share JSP components across multiple applications. For components that you're going to use in only a single application, however, the added deployment and packaging complexity often isn't worth the additional effort.

WAR FILE PACKAGING

If you don't intend to use your tag library across multiple applications, just packaging the tag library along with your application is easier than self-contained packaging. This packaging strategy is what the sample application in Chapter 6 uses. That application compiles and packages all the tag-handler classes along with the rest of the class files and also includes the TLD is under the WEB-INF directory in a directory that it calls tlds.

Including your tag libraries in a separate Java package is still advantageous. Doing so enables you to change your file-packaging strategy later without needing to worry about the visibility of your objects. The sample application in Chapter 6 places all its tag library classes in a taglibs subpackage of the main com.hungryminds. ias.chapter6.web package that you use for the rest of the application.

In packaging the taglib classes along with the application in the WEB_INF/classes directory, your only question is where to place the TLD files. The logical location is somewhere in or beneath the WEB-INF directory, because doing so prevents the Web container from making the TLD URL-addressable. In Chapter 6's sample application, you place the TLDs in a tlds subdirectory of WEB-INF. The build.xml Ant script in the WAR file automatically creates this directory so that a corresponding directory is automatically created on the application server during deployment.

Including your tag libraries in your WAR file is a simple and easy method to distributing tag libraries that are application-specific. Keeping tag libraries logically separate, however, is important in maintaining the portable nature of these libraries.

Component Model Comparison

The preceding sections examine several methodologies for integrating Java code into your JSPs. These methodologies range from the very simplistic, such as using scriptlets to embed Java code between delimiter tags, to custom action components that you tightly integrate with the JSP container. Each of these methodologies has its advantages and disadvantages, and you should use each one whenever appropriate.

Scriptlets and expressions enable you to integrate code directly into the JSP page. Very quick and simple, they require no additional packaging or componentization. You're best off using them in "quick-and-dirty" applications and in situations where you need to integrate only a few lines of code, such as including a date or simple variable in the JSP results. Scriptlets and expressions aren't very reusable and also can increase the complexity of the JSP code, so don't use them to implement complex functionality.

JavaBeans enable you to separate Java code from the HTML code in the JSPs. They also enable a better separation between business logic and presentation logic. You can even use business logic that you implement in JavaBeans in other non-JSP applications. JavaBeans are a great way to componentize the Java code that a JSP is to utilize, but the useBean, setProperty, and getProperty action tags are somewhat limiting. You still need scriptlets to invoke nondefault constructors, perform nonstandard type conversions, and invoke methods other than property getters and setters. This limitation eliminates the readability and elegance benefits of the JavaBean model. JavaBeans provide a good way to implement reusable components in JSPs but only if you can implement their functionality by using the useBean, setProperty, and getProperty actions.

Typically, tag libraries provide you with the most flexible and elegant way of implementing Java code in JSPs. They're well integrated into the JSP engine and enable complex interactions with the JSP page. They support a rich component model and are easily portable to other JSP pages and other JSP applications. In comparison to the other component models, however, tag libraries require a reasonable amount of setup and planning time. Additionally, you can't easily reuse them outside the JSP model.

Figure 6-1 summarizes the high-level comparison between the various JSP component models. Each development model is appropriate for some situations, and application architects should base their choice of the appropriate methodology on the amount of componentization that they want and the complexity of the code that they require.

jspInit and jspDestroy

All the JSP APIs that the preceding sections examine give the same results as equivalent overriding the service method of a servlet. But what if you have initializations to performed only once? In a servlet, you merely override the init and destroy. To support this type of functionality in JSPs, however, the JSP API enables you to create two special methods in your JSP: jspInit and jspDestroy.

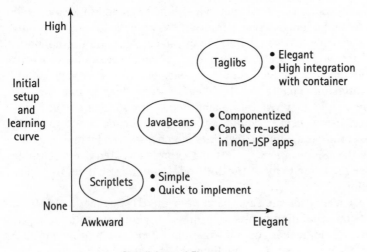

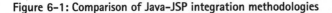

Figure 6-1: Comparison of Java–JSP integration methodologies

If you implement these methods the JSP compiler calls them in the `init` and `destroy` methods, respectively, of the generated servlet. You can then perform whatever initializations are necessary in the `jspInit` method and release those resources in the `jspDestroy` method.

As you do the servlet equivalents, you must use the `jspInit` and `jspDestroy` methods with several considerations in mind. First, you invoke the `jspInit` method once per JVM. Because JSPs compile into servlets, you must take into consideration the same multi-JVM issues that you evaluated in creating servlets.

Similarly, you must take into account the same multithreading issues that you consider in developing servlets. If you initialize a variable in the `jspInit` method, all the threads in that JSP container utilize that variable unless you specify the JSP as single threaded.

Finally, you must remember that, as with the servlet `destroy` method, you have no guarantee that the `jspDestroy` method will get called, especially if the JSP is destroyed because of a server shutdown. For example, `jspDestroy` methods are a good place to release resources that the `jspInit` method initializes, because releasing the resources helps make sure that the you don'trun out of shared resources such as database connections. An example of a poor use of the `jspDestroy` method, is recording the time of application shutdown, as `jspDestroy` may not get called at shutdown.

Listing 6-15 provides a simple example of a JSP that implements `jspInit` and `jspDestroy` methods. The `jspInit` method records the time that the JSP is initialized. This value then appears following each request for the page.

Listing 6-15: jspinit.jsp

```
<%@ page import="java.util.*" %>
<%@ page import="java.text.*" %>
<%!
  String initDate;
  public void jspInit() {
     initDate=DateFormat.getDateTimeInstance(
        DateFormat.FULL,DateFormat.FULL).format(new Date());
  }
  public void jspDestroy() {
     System.out.println("Chapter6 : JspDestroy called.");
  }
%>
<html>
<head><title>Chapter6 : JspInit JSP</title></head>
<body bgcolor="white">
<h2>iPlanet Application Server Enterprise Development</h2>
<h2>Chapter 6 : JspInit JSP</h2>
<p>This simple JSP will be used to demonstrate interlacing HTML and Java in
a JSP.</p>
<p>Today's date is :
<%= new Date() %>
</p>
<p>This JSP was initialized on :<br><%= initDate %>
</p></body></html>
```

Of course, this example is a trivial one that you can as easily handle by using a simple initializer for the `initDate` variable. But it does illustrate how the JSP compiler interacts with the `jspInit` and `jspDestroy` methods. Assuming a single JVM, the `jspInit` is called only once, during the initialization of the JSP, and the initDate variable, therefore, always contains the time of the JSP's initialization.

iAS Custom Tags

iPlanet Application Server includes a number of custom tag libraries. You can use these tag libraries the same way that you access any tag library. Some of the iAS tag libraries, however, utilize proprietary features of the application server, and so you can't use them in a different Web container. (Licensing issues would also prohibit you from using these custom taglibs outside of iPlanet Application Server.)

The following five public tag libraries come with iAS:

◆ **Database query library** – Includes custom actions to execute queries, loop through result sets, and retrieve data from the queries into the JSP results.

◆ **LDAP library** – Includes tags to authenticate against LDAP directories, perform LDAP searches, and iterate through the search results.

◆ **Conditional tag library** – Provides custom actions to enable you to use select statements and other conditionals.

◆ **Attribute tag library** – Aids you in retrieving and placing values in the attributes of the page, request, session, or application.

◆ **JSP caching library** – Provides tags that enable you to indicate which content to cache and the properties of the JSP cache.

Inspecting the $IAS_ROOT/ias/APPS/jsp_extensions directory turns up two other iAS tag libraries as well. These additional libraries (RegexpLib.tld and GX.tld) are for internal use by iAS only.

Database query library

The database query tag library (rdbmstags6_0.tld) provides seven tags to assist in the manipulation of relational databases. By using this library, authors can open database connections and process the returned result sets.

TIP

The database query library provides an easy way to retrieve data from a database and directly insert the results into HTML. If you must process the database results, however, a better strategy is to move the database query logic into a JavaBean, servlet, or custom tag library.

Moving this query processing out of the JSP supports a cleaner separation between presentation logic and business logic. See the following sections on the "Model I" and "Model II" best practices for more ideas on how to separate business logic and presentation logic.

The sample applications that iPlanet Application Server provides include an example application utilizing the database query custom tags. You can find the EAR file for the sample in the $IAS_ROOT//ias/ias-samples/iastags/rdbms directory. You can find instructions for installing and using the sample online at http://developer.iplanet.com/appserver/samples/iastags/docs/index.html.

Query Files

The iAS database tags introduce the concept of query files that store the SQL statements for use in useQuery tags. Query files are a part of the NAS heritage of iPlanet Application Server. The query file format used by the iAS database tags is the same format as used by the proprietary AppLogic API used by NAS. Query files have the following purposes:

◆ To prevent SQL code (data logic) from cluttering JSP code (presentation logic).

◆ To enable you to reuse SQL queries.

◆ To provide better division of labor. Providing database administrators a separate file in which to store their SQL code enables them to more easily control and maintain source code.

Each application can have multiple query files, and each query file can have multiple named queries. Queries have the following syntax, and blank files delimit them:

```
query queryname is SQLQuery
```

Queries can use parameters that you specify at run time. To denote a parameter, place a colon in front of the parameter name that you want to use as a placeholder for a run-time value. Following is an example of a query file with two parameterized queries:

```
query customerlist is select * from customer where :customerfilter


query customerdetail is
  select customer.cust_id, customer.cust_name, customer.primarycontact_id,
    contact.contact_name
  from customer, contact
  where customer.primarycontact_id=contact.contact_id AND

    customer.cust_id=:customerid
```

USEQUERY TAG

The useQuery tag opens a connection to a database and readies an SQL query. The tag can also execute if the execute attribute is set to true. It can provide the SQL query either directly in the command attribute or indirectly by using a flat file that it specifies in the queryFile and queryName attributes. (See the accompanying sidebar for information on the format of query files.) If the tag specifies a `queryFile` but defines no `queryName` attribute, it uses the `useQuery`'s `id` attribute as the default `queryName`.

The page author specifies the database to connect to by using a `dataSourceName` attribute (or a `url` attribute for ODBC sources). The tag attributes can also change the default scope of request to any of the other standard JSP scopes: page, session, or application.

The following is an example of a `useQuery` tag that establishes a simple, single table query:

```
<rdbm:useQuery id="cust_list" command="select cust_id, cust_name from customer"
dataSourceName="jdbc/custDB"></rdbm:useQuery>
```

PARAM TAG

You use the `param` tag to bind run-time values to parameters in the query that you specify in the `query` attribute. You can specify a named parameter in a query by placing a colon in front of a placeholder, which you can then replace at run time by using the `param` tag.

You specify the name of the parameter to fill by using the `name` attribute. You specify the value to use in place of that parameter either by using the `value` attribute or, more commonly, in the body of the tag. You must also provide a `type` attribute to support the correct type conversion. (You also provide a `format` attribute to assist with Date type conversions.)

The following example uses a `param` tag and a parameterized query to retrieve a specific customer row (in which a variable that you retrieve by using an expression determines the exact row to retrieve):

```
<rdbm:useQuery id="cust_detail" command="select * from customer where
cust_id=:custid" dataSourceName="jdbc/custDB"></rdbm:useQuery>
<rdbm:param query="cust_detail" name="custid" type="Int">
<%= custID %></rdbm:param>
```

LOOP TAG

You use the `loop` tag to iterate through the rows of a `Resultset`. The `query` attribute indicates the query to iterate through. An optional `start` tag can indicate the starting row, which you can specify as a constant, an attribute, or as the special value of `last`. You can also use the optional value of `max` to limit the number of rows that the row set iterates through. (Programmers often use the combination of `start` and `max` attributes to enable a user to scroll between JSP pages that list only a few rows of data at a time.)

You can also adjust the scope of a `loop` tag to any of the standard JSP scopes: page, request, session, or application. If the `execute` attribute is set to `true`, the query executes before the loop begins.

The following is an example of a `loop` tag. Notice that, because I haven't introduced the `field` tag yet, you're not printing any of the actual data. The `loop` tag merely prints one static string for each customer in the `resultset`.

```
<rdbm:loop id="myloop" query="cust_list" execute="true">
This string is printed once per customer in the database.<br>
</rdbm:loop>
```

FIELD TAG

The `field` tag enables you to actually retrieve and display data from the `result-set`. You specify the `resultset` by using the `query` attribute, and you specify the database column (or alias) by using the `name` attribute. If the column doesn't exist (is null), the body of the tag returns instead.

The `field` tag also provides several useful features to help with formatting the retrieved data, as the following list describes:

- ◆ As do JSP expressions, types automatically convert into strings.

- ◆ You can use the `format` attribute to perform simple string, number, and date formatting.

- ◆ The `urlEncode` attribute causes the results to automatically URL-encode if the attribute is set to `true`. (This attribute causes nonprinting and special characters to escape to URL-safe values.)

The following example of the `loop` tag modifies the previous `loop` example to actually return the customer names. Notice how the tag body provides a default value in case the value of the column is null.

```
<rdbm:loop id="myloop" query="cust_list" execute="true">
<rdbm:field query="cust_list" name="cust_name">
Customer Name Not Provided</rdbm:field><br>
</rdbm:loop>
```

GORECORD TAG

The `goRecord` tag seeks to a particular row of a `resultset`. The `start` attribute specifies the record to seek to, which is a constant, an attribute, or the special value of `last` (similar to what the `start` attribute of a `loop` tag does). As you can do with several other tags in this library, you can set the `execute` attribute to true to execute the query before the tag performs its action.

The following example of the `goRecord` tag skips to the last row of a `resultset`:

```
<rdbm:goRecord query="cust_list" start="last" />
```

EXECUTE TAG

The `execute` tag explicitly executes a query that you specify in the `query` attribute. Notice that many other tags in this library have `execute` attributes that enable them to implicitly execute queries as well. The following example explicitly executes a query by using an `execute` tag.

```
<rdbm:execute query="cust_list"/>
```

CLOSE TAG

The `close` tag closes a `resultset` and releases the associated resources. Because the database tag library utilizes database connections that iPlanet Application Server's database-pooling mechanism manages, explicitly closing database resources so that other threads can reuse them is very important.

The following `close` tag example closes the query that I opened in the `useQuery` example:

```
<rdbm:close resource="cust_list" />
```

LDAP library

In addition to the custom tag libraries that it provides to query relational databases, iAS includes a tag library to query LDAP databases. The LDAP tag library enables you to bind against LDAP databases, execute LDAP queries, and process the returned results. (A link to the LDAPv3 specification is provided at the end of this chapter.) iPlanet Directory Server, the market leading enterprise directory server, is bundled with iPlanet Application Server and is an excellent combination with the iAS LDAP tags.

The sample applications that iPlanet Application Server provides include an example of the LDAP tag library. You can find the EAR file for the sample in the `$IAS_ROOT//ias/ias-samples/iastags/ldap` directory. You find instructions for installing and using the sample on the same instructions page as the database tags (at `http://developer.iplanet.com/appserver/samples/iastags/docs/index.html`).

USEQUERY

Just as in the database taglib, you use the `useQuery` tag to define the query URL that you intend to use. (If you're unfamiliar with the LDAP query URLs, you can find information on building LDAP queries in RFC 1959. RFC 1959 is available online at `www.cis.ohio-state.edu/cgi-bin/rfc/rfc1959.html`.)

This `useQuery` tag has a very similar format to the database `useQuery` tag. You can store queries in query files (and access them by using the `queryFile` and `queryName` attributes) or define them directly in an attribute (by using a `url` attribute).

The container makes the results of the query available to other JSP code by using the `id` of the `useQuery` tag and with the scope that you specify by using the `scope` attribute. You also often use subtags such as `authenticate`, `password`, and `param` to modify the `useQuery` tag.

The following is an example of a `useQuery` tag that retrieves the telephone number for the user `ogren` from the fictional LDAP server at `chico.hungryminds.com`. Notice that LDAP queries do contain some information that you don't find in SQL queries, such as the name of the server that you're querying.

```
<ldap:useQuery id="tele_num" url="ldap://chico.hungryminds.com:389/uid=ogren,
ou=People,o=hungryminds.com?telephoneNumber">
</ldap:useQuery>
```

AUTHENTICATE

The `authenticate` tag modifies a query by designating the user who should execute the query. You specify the distinguished name of the designated user in the `url` attribute. You specify the password for the authentication by using the `password` subtag or in the `password` attribute.

The process of authenticating to an LDAP server is known as *binding*. Binding is optional in LDAP version 3 (the latest and most common version of LDAP), as portions of the directory data are often available to anonymous access.

The following example shows how you can use the `authenticate` tag to add binding information to an LDAP query. This query uses a hardcoded LDAP user and password, which is useful if you create an entry specifically for the application's use.

```
<ldap:useQuery id="tele_num" url="ldap://chico.hungryminds.com:389/uid=ogren,
ou=People,o=hungryminds.com?telephoneNumber">
<ldap:authenticate query="tele_num" url="ldap://chico.hungryminds.com:389/
uid=myapplication,ou=People,o=hungryminds.com" password="thepassword">
</ldap:authenticate></ldap:useQuery>
```

CONNECTION

The `connection` tag is just an alias to the same tag handler that you use for the `authenticate` tag. The two tags are synonymous, and you can use either tag name to create an authenticated connection to the LDAP server.

AUTHORIZE

The `authorize` tag uses a proxied authorization control to modify an LDAP query. A proxied authorization control enables an existing connection to make LDAP queries by using the credentials of different users.

The LDAP client binds once and then uses the proxied authentication control to execute queries on behalf of various users. (The directory server administrator must create special privileges on the account to enable it to use proxied authorization.) Not all LDAP servers support proxied authorization. (The iPlanet Directory Server bundled with iPlanet Application Server does support proxied authorization. See Chapter 5 of the iDS 4.x Administrators Guide for information about setting up proxied authorization.)

To use proxied authentication with an `authorize` tag, submit the `dn` of the user whose credentials you want to use in the `dn` attribute of the `authorize` tag. The following code example uses `authorize` to modify a query. A connection that binds to the server as the user `myapplication` then uses an `authorize` command to execute the query as the user `ogren`.

```
<ldap:useQuery id="tele_num" url="ldap://chico.hungryminds.com:389/uid=ogren,
ou=People,o=hungryminds.com?telephoneNumber">
<ldap:authenticate query="tele_num" url="ldap://chico.hungryminds.com:389/
uid=myapplication,ou=People,o=hungryminds.com" password="thepassword">
</ldap:authenticate>
<ldap:authorize query="tele_num" dn="ldap://chico.hungryminds.com:389/
uid=ogren,ou=People,o=hungryminds.com"></ldap:authorize>
</ldap:useQuery>
```

PASSWORD

You use the `password` tag to pass the value of a password to an enclosing `authenticate` tag. You should provide the actual password in the body of the `password` tag. This tag enables you to dynamically provide the password at run time by using an expression or some other means. (You can also assign the password to the value of a `password` attribute if you know the password at creation time.)

The following example uses the `password` tag to forward a password to an `authenticate` tag at run time:

```
<ldap:useQuery id="tele_num" url="ldap://chico.hungryminds.com:389/uid=ogren,
ou=People,o=hungryminds.com?telephoneNumber">
<ldap:authenticate query="tele_num" url="ldap://chico.hungryminds.com:389/
uid=myapplication,ou=People,o=hungryminds.com" >
<ldap:password><%= session.getAttribute("ldap_password") %>
</ldap:password></ldap:authenticate></ldap:useQuery>
```

PARAM

The `param` LDAP tag provides the same functionality as the `param` database tag: It replaces parameters in queries with actual values. You specify the name of the parameter that you're replacing in the `name` attribute and give the value to substitute for it in the `value` attribute or in the body of the `param` tag.

The following shows a parameterized LDAP query. Because the `:389` in the LDAP URL precedes the DN of the URL, it isn't considered a parameter.

```
<ldap:useQuery id="tele_num" url="ldap://chico.hungryminds.com:389/
uid=:employee,
ou=People,o=hungryminds.com?telephoneNumber">
<param name="employee"><%= session.getAttribute("emp_username") %>
</ldap:param></ldap:useQuery>
```

FIELD

The `field` LDAP tag provides similar functionality as the `field` database tag: It returns data from the executed query. You specify the name of the attribute to return in the `attribute` field and you specify the query to retrieve the value in the `query` field.

Notice that the LDAP tags handle looping through results differently than do the database tags. LDAP entries can have more than one value for each attribute, which can complicate the process of retrieving values. A user's LDAP entry, for example, may contain several `committeeMembership` entries designating dynamic groups that the user belongs to.

You should use the `field` tag whenever you need to retrieve single-valued attributes from a single entry that you've retrieved — for example, to retrieve the name, mailing address, and e-mail address that correspond to a DN. The following example uses the `field` tag to print the e-mail address of a user with a known DN:

```
<ldap:useQuery id="tele_num" url="ldap://chico.hungryminds.com:389/uid=ogren,
ou=People,o=hungryminds.com?telephoneNumber"></ldap:useQuery>
Email address = <ldap:field attribute="mail" query="tele_num">
No email address available</ldap:field>
```

LOOPENTRY

The LDAP `loopEntry` is similar in function to the database `loop` tag, although quite different in implementation. The `loopEntry` tag enables you to iterate through the set of entries that returns from an LDAP search.

The `query` attribute indicates which search results are iterating. The `id` and `scope` variables define a new attribute, which you use to export the LDAP entry for the current loop iteration. As with the `loop` database tag, you can define `max` and `start` attributes for `loopEntry` to set the maximum number of entries that return and the starting entry.

You can also use virtual list views (VLV) by defining the `useVL`, `pre`, and `jump` attributes. (For information about virtual list views and how they can help you manage searches, consult the Directory Server documentation links at the end of this chapter.) Other LDAP servers, however, may not support virtual list views.

The following example of a `loopEntry` tag iterates over a list of users:

```
<ldap:useQuery id="user_list" url="ldap://chico.hungryminds.com:389/ou=People,
o=hungryminds.com?cn,
telephoneNumber,mail?sub"></ldap:useQuery>
<ldap:loopEntry id="user_loop" query="user_list" scope="request">
<%= request.getAttribute("user_loop") %>
</ldap:loopEntry>
```

LOOPVALUE

Because LDAP entries can contain multiple values with the same attribute name, the LDAP tag library must provide a way to iterate through the attributes of an entry. The `loopValue` provides this functionality and operates similarly to the way that `loopEntry` iterates through entries.

The `loopValue` can iterate either through the first entry that a query returns (by specifying the `query` attribute) or through the current entry of a `loopEntry` loop (by specifying the `id` of the loop in the `entry` attribute). As for the `loopEntry` tag, the `id` and `scope` attributes define the exported attribute and the scope of that attribute. Optionally, you can also use the `max` attribute to limit the number of attributes to iterate.

The following example uses `loopValue` to iterate through the object classes of a user's entry:

```
<ldap:useQuery id="user_classes"
url="ldap://chico.hungryminds.com:389/uid=ogren,ou=People,
o=hungryminds.com?objectclass"></ldap:useQuery>
<ldap:loopValue id="user_obj" query="user_classes" scope="request">
<%= request.getAttribute("user_obj") %>
</ldap:loopEntry>
```

CLOSE

The LDAP tags automatically use a self-maintained pool of LDAP connections. (Look in the KJS log for status messages about the pool creation.) To prevent the pool from exhausting its connections, therefore, you must clean up your queries after you finish with them. Use the `close` tag with the `resource` attribute set to the `id` of your query to close the query and free the associated resources.

The following example demonstrates the syntax of the `close` tag:

```
<ldap:useQuery id="tele_num" url="ldap://chico.hungryminds.com:389/uid=ogren,
ou=People,o=hungryminds.com?telephoneNumber"></ldap:useQuery>
<% // Some commands that use the query here %>
<ldap:close resource="tele_num"/>
```

Conditional tag library

The *conditional tag library* provides case and switch statements and the comparison tags to support them. You have the following three general categories of conditional tags:

◆ **Switch tags** — Switch tags establish a type of conditional to consider and evaluates the `case` tags that the tag encloses.

◆ **Case tags** — Case tags represent one possible result of a switch statement and contain an expression that the Web container evaluates at run time. If case's expression is the first to evaluate `true`, the results include the `case` tag's body. Otherwise the `switch` tag discards the body of the case statement without evaluating it.

◆ **Dynamic evaluation tags** — The conditional tag library provides additional tags to enable comparisons to dynamically generate at run time. The dynamically generated values pass into `switch` and `case` tags.

SWITCH TAGS

The `switch` tag itself is the basic switch conditional. The `switch` tag establishes a type of comparison in the `type` attribute and, for some comparison types, a value with which the cases are evaluated in the `value` attribute. The following list describes the six possible switch types:

◆ `value` — A simple comparison to a fixed value. The default type of comparison.

◆ `parameter` — A comparison with a page parameter.

◆ `attribute` — A comparison with an attribute in the request, page, session, or application.

◆ `role` — An evaluation if the current remote user has membership in a role.

◆ `rowset` — An evaluation of the state of a named rowset from a database tag (for example, if the rowset exists or is on the last row).

◆ `ldap` — An evaluation of the state of a search result from an LDAP tag.

Each of the switch types, other than the default value type, also has a shortcut form. You can also express the `<cond:switch type="parameter" value="param">` tag, for example, as `<cond:parameter name="param">`. Notice that all the shortcut forms use the attribute `name` rather than the `value` attribute that the `switch` tag uses.

CASE TAGS

`Case` tags evaluate a conditional, but the types of valid conditionals vary depending on the type of `switch` tag. A `<` comparison, for example, isn't meaningful in comparing strings, and an `isLast` comparison is useful only in examining a database `rowset` search result. An invalid comparison type throws a run-time exception. The `operation` attribute selects the operation type, and the `value` attribute specifies the second operand, if necessary.

The following list describes all the available case operations:

◆ numerical comparisons — All the standard numerical comparisons are valid operations ($<$, $>$, !=, =, and so on).

◆ `equals` — The `equals` operation is a string comparison (as compared to the = operation, which is a numerical comparison).

◆ `equalsIgnoreCase` — The `equals` operations performs a case-insensitive string comparison.

◆ exists — The exists comparison is useful for determining the existence of an attribute, parameter, or other object.

◆ notEmpty — This comparison returns true if the database rowset contains at least one row.

◆ executeNotEmpty — This comparison returns true if the database rowset has at least one row. It automatically executes the query before evaluation.

◆ isLast — This comparison returns true if the rowset is positioned on the last row.

◆ connected — This comparison returns true if the LDAP search has an active connection.

◆ authenticated — This comparison returns true if the LDAP search has authenticated.

◆ else — This comparison returns true. It enables the specification of an else case that executes if no other case is true.

As do the switch cases, all the cases other than the numerical comparisons also have shortcut equivalents. You can also express <cond:case operation= "equalsIgnorecase" value="foo">, for example, as <cond:equalsIgnoreCase value="foo">.

The following example shows a simple case statement using JSP tags:

```
<cond:attribute session="user_type">
<cond:equals value="admin">
  Some text that should only be displayed for admins
</cond:equals>
<cond:equals value="guest">
  some text that should only be displayed for guest accounts
</cond:equals>
</cond:attribute>
```

DYNAMIC EVALUATION TAGS

One unfortunate feature of the conditional tags is that you must specify the comparison values in attributes. This feature prevents the container from dynamically evaluating the values at run time. iAS provides two additional tags to support changing case and switch value attributes at run time.

The value tag exports its body into the value attribute of its parent tag. Thus <cond:switch><cond:value>5</cond:value></cond:switch> is functionally equivalent to <cond:switch value="5"></cond:switch>.

Unfortunately, only the switch and dynamicValue tags can receive the value attributes dynamically. To export a value into a case tag, you must use a dynamicValue tag. The dynamicValue tag should contain one value tag and any number of case tags to which you should export the value tag's value. This format is somewhat awkward but is the only method flexible enough to enable dynamic comparisons.

The example in Listing 6-16, which comes from the sample application, demonstrates a dynamic comparison of two numeric parameters (as well as a simpler case statement with fixed string comparisons and an existence check of the numeric parameters).

Listing 6-16: condtags.jsp

```
<%@ page session="false" %>
<%@ taglib prefix="cond" uri="/WEB-INF/tlds/condtags6_0.tld" %>
<html>
<head><title>Chapter6 : Conditional JSP Tags Sample</title></head>
<body bgcolor="white">
<h2>iPlanet Application Server Enterprise Development</h2>
<h2>Chapter 6 : Conditional JSP Tags Sample</h2>
<p>This sample demonstrates the JSP conditional tags.</p>

<h3>Parameters:</h3>
<blockquote>
The msg parameter passed was = <%= request.getParameter("msg") %><br>
The value1 parameter passed was = <%= request.getParameter("value1") %><br>
The value2 parameter passed was = <%= request.getParameter("value2") %>
</blockquote>

<h3>msg switch statement evaluates to : </h3>
<blockquote><cond:parameter name="msg">
<cond:equalsIgnoreCase value="msg1">
  This is the first message.
</cond:equalsIgnoreCase>
<cond:equalsIgnoreCase value="msg2">
  This is the second message.
</cond:equalsIgnoreCase>
<cond:exists>
  An invalid message has been selected.
</cond:exists>
<cond:else>
  No message has been selected.
</cond:else>
</cond:parameter></blockquote>
```

Continued

Listing 6-16 *(Continued)*

```
<h3>dynamic comparison statement evaluates to : </h3>
<blockquote>
<cond:parameter name="value1">
<cond:exists>
  <cond:parameter name="value1">
    <cond:dynamicValue>
    <cond:value>
       <%= request.getParameter("value2") %>
    </cond:value>
    <cond:case operation="<">less than</cond:case>
    <cond:case operation="=">equals</cond:case>
    <cond:case operation=">">greater than</cond:case>
    </cond:dynamicValue>
  </cond:parameter>
</cond:exists>
<cond:else>
  No dynamic comparison parameters
</cond:else>
</cond:parameter>
</blockquote>

<p>Use the following links to select interesting parameters (or enter your
own in the URL)</p>
<ul>
<li><a href="condtags.jsp?msg=msg1">
Message 1</a></li>
<li><a href="condtags.jsp?msg=msg2">
Message 2</a></li>
<li><a href="condtags.jsp?msg=foo&value1=4&value2=5">
Invalid Message, but dynamic case lt</a></li>
<li><a href="condtags.jsp?msg=foo&value1=5&value2=4">
Invalid Message, but dynamic case gt</a></li>
<li><a href="condtags.jsp?msg=msg1&value1=5&value2=5">
Message 1 and dynamic case equals</a></li>
<li><a href="condtags.jsp">
No parameters</a></li>
</ul></body></html>
```

Attribute tag library

The *attribute tag library* provides several simple tags for getting parameter, attribute, and user information. Implementing the same functionality by using expressions or scriptlets is easy, but these tags provide a way to access these properties without using Java code, thereby improving your JSP code readability.

The following four tags are in this library:

- `getAttribute`

- `setAttribute`

- `getParameter`

- `getRemoteUser`

GETATTRIBUTE

The `getAttribute` tag retrieves attributes from the request, page, session, and application. You specify the name of the attribute to retrieve in the `name` attribute and specify the parent object (request, page, session, or application) in the `scope` attribute. You can also use the `format` attribute to specify a simple formatting template by using the same syntax as you do for the database `field` tag.

The following statement retrieves a `user_firstname` property from the session to customize a page:

```
Welcome <attr:getAttribute name="user_firstname" scope="session">
New User</attr:getAttribute>
```

This statement is functionally equivalent to the following scriptlet. Notice that, although the `getAttribute` tag is very simple, it does noticeably improve the readability of the code.

```
Welcome
<%
    if (session.getAttribute("user_firstname") {
        out.println(session.getParameter("foo"));
    } else {
        out.println("New User");
    }
%>
```

SETATTRIBUTE

As does the `getAttribute` tag, the `setAttribute` tag makes working with object attributes more convenient and readable. You specify the name of the attribute in the `name` attribute, the object to which the attribute belongs in the `scope` attribute, and the new value for the attribute in the body of the tag, as in the following example:

```
<attr:setAttribute name="user_type" scope="session">admin</attr:setAttribute>
```

GETPARAMETER

The `getParameter` tag is a convenient way to retrieve parameters from the request object. You specify the name of the parameter in the `name` attribute, and the body should contain the default value to return if the parameter doesn't exist, as the following example demonstrates:

```
<attr:getParameter name="color">white</attr:getParameter>
```

GETREMOTEUSER

The `getRemoteUser` tag returns the username of the user if the user is authenticated; otherwise, the body of the tag returns. The following is a simple example:

```
Welcome <attr:getRemoteUser>Guest</attr:getRemoteUser>
```

JSP caching library

iPlanet Application Server provides *JSP caching* as a method of increasing the performance of your application. JSP caching is different from results caching. JSP caching utilizes caches stored in the JVM and are specified using JSP tags. In contrast, result caching happens in the KXS process, before the request is even assigned to a JVM. Result caching parameters are specified in the `ias-web.xml` deployment descriptor.

The JSP cache enables you to store content, which a JSP dynamically generates in a configurable cache for later use. This capability prevents you from needing to regenerate the content with every request.

Consider, for example, a portal application that displays news headlines that it retrieves from a wire service. The process of retrieving the headlines may prove a time-consuming process, and retrieving the headlines with every request is inefficient because they change only every few minutes. You could instead use a JSP cache to cache the headlines for five minutes at a time. Doing so would minimize the number of calls to the wire service and would increase the performance of the JSP that generates the headline page.

CACHING IMPLEMENTATION DETAILS

The JSP cache is stored within the KJS engine, and each KJS has its own independent cache of results. Additionally, each JSP page has its own cache, enabling each application to have multiple cached JSP pages (for example, a technology headlines page, a sports headlines page, and a business headlines page).

Unlike in result caching, each JSP can cache only one result. If you need to cache the technology page and sports headline page separately, you should create them as two different JSP pages rather than as one JSP page that determines its contents based on a parameter.

JSP CACHING TAGS

Four tags are in the JSP cache library. Together, they indicate what content to cache, under what conditions to return the cache, and how long to keep the cache before rebuilding the content. The following list describes these four tags:

◆ The `cache` tag encloses the other JSP caching tags. The presence of the `cache` tag indicates that the container needs to cache the page. (The container caches the entire page and not just the contents of the `cache` tag.)

◆ The `check` tag designates a class to use to determine whether to use the JSP page cache. The class must support a method with the signature `public Boolean check(ServletRequest req, Servlet servlet)`. The JSP caching mechanism calls the check method with the appropriate arguments while evaluating the JSP. If the class returns `true`, the cache is used. This feature gives developers great flexibility in deciding when to use the cached values.

◆ The `param` tag is a much simpler alternative method of determining whether to use a cache. The parameter or attribute that you specify in the `name` and `scope` attributes of the `param` tag must be in the range that you specify in the `value` attribute for the page to return from the cache. If the `value` attribute is set to `*` the page returns from the cache if the current parameter (or attribute) matches the value of the cached page.

◆ The `criteria` tag sets a cache timeout. You specify the timeout in seconds in the `timeout` attribute. After the timeout period expires, the cache for that page is discarded.

JSP CACHING RECOMMENDATIONS

The JSP caching tags work well in combination with the `include` action. You can break up a JSP into individual subpages that can have their own caching criteria. A "master" page can then use `include` actions to aggregate the subpages.

Consider, for example, the portal page that I describe earlier in this chapter. You may want to customize the look and feel of the page for each user. You can do so by placing the page formatting code in one JSP page, the content in another JSP page, and a standard footer in another JSP page. You can cache the content page by using the JSP caching tags without the customizations that you make for each user in the header affecting the page itself. The code for the master JSP would look something like what you see in the following example:

```
<%@ taglib prefix="cond" uri="/WEB-INF/tlds/condtags6_0.tld" %>
<%-- Include a header that has a customized style sheet, background and
     welcome message for each user. */ --%>
```

```
<jsp:include page="header.jsp" flush="true">
<%-- Include content based on user's preferences (stored in session) --%>
<cond:attribute name="show_headlines">
<cond:exists><jsp:include page="headlines.jsp" flush="true"></cond:exists>
</cond:attribute>
<cond:attribute name="show_sports">
<cond:exists><jsp:include page="sports.jsp" flush="true"></cond:exists>
</cond:attribute>
<%-- Include a standard footer. Since the footer is static it uses an include
     directive so that it can be processed at compile time. --%>
<%@ include file="footer.jsp" %>
```

Model 1 – JSPs as Servlets

The Model I approach to JSP development involves using JSPs as a complete replacement for servlets. The end user requests the JSP page directly, and the JSP code includes both the business logic and presentation logic. The Model I methodology relies on several methods for encapsulating business logic, such as taglibs and JavaBeans, to try to prevent business logic from cluttering the JSP pages. Figure 6-2 shows the ideal Model I architecture.

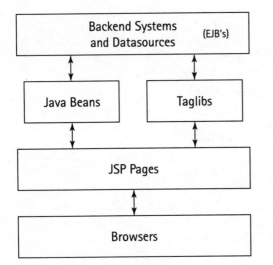

Figure 6-2: Model I architecture

Advantages of the Model 1 approach

The primary goal of Model I is simplicity. Model I focuses on simplifying the process of creating and maintaining user interfaces. Model I offers the following benefits:

- ◆ Each URL maps to one JSP page. This feature makes understanding the program flow very straightforward.

- ◆ An HTML designer can examine and understand each JSP page so that you don't need a Java coder to make cosmetic changes to JSP pages.

- ◆ If the business functionality is well encapsulated in JavaBeans and taglibs, creating a JSP is as simple as creating a webpage with a scripting language.

- ◆ You can implement many elements of functionality declaratively by using JSP directives instead of needing to implement them by hand in Java code. This often requires significantly less lines of code than by building the servlet without a JSP.

Disadvantages of the Model 1 approach

The very simplicity of the Model I approach can also prove its undoing. Keeping business logic cleanly separate from the presentation can prove difficult, even if you're using taglibs and JavaBeans. And because you control the program flow for each page within the JSP itself, JSPs commonly become cluttered with conditional code.

Imagine, for example, the type of scenario where you want to create a different look and feel to your webpage depending on the user type. If you use Model I, the JSP page ends up cluttered with conditional logic for determining the look and feel of the page. (The JSP author could instead abstract the presentation logic into JavaBeans, but this course would prevent HTML designers from maintaining the presentation logic.)

The Model I approach becomes difficult to implement in complex applications, because JavaBeans and taglibs can prove insufficient in separating business logic and presentation logic. If your Model I JSP pages are too complex for your HTML designers to understand and maintain, therefore, you may want to consider using Model II instead. (Model II is discussed below in the section "Model II - JSPs as Templates".)

Using Model 1

The Model I framework provides a powerful model for rapid development. The JSP API includes several features that make programming a JSP simpler than coding the equivalent servlet. The JSP API also has several features that provide for very strong componentization of applications, including JavaBeans and tag libraries. This combination of strengths can enable the very rapid development of applications.

Using Model I effectively for large applications, however, can require a great deal of forethought. If business logic isn't well componentized, the JSP code can become cluttered and difficult to maintain. The simplicity of the Model I approach can become deceiving, because an enterprise Model I application requires extensive effort in planning the application flow and component model.

The keys to successfully writing Model I applications include the following:

◆ **Using the full range of tools available in the JSP API:** A complete understanding of the JSP API is necessary, because the advanced JSP features, such as taglibs, are the features that you need to support large-scale application development under Model I.

◆ **Managing application flow effectively:** Supporting scenarios with conditional application flow can prove a challenge in Model I, because you can't forward control to an alternative JSP after data returns to the client. Handling exception cases can prove equally difficult. You can solve these challenges by using custom tags to handle the conditional flow and by testing for all exception conditions before returning data.

◆ **Spending upfront design time to develop tag libraries:** Providing effective tag libraries is the key to enabling effective Model I application development. By thoroughly defining these libraries early in the development process, you can develop tag libraries concurrently with the actual JSP pages.

You often encounter extensive conditional program logic in applications that must support multiple client-types (such as wireless devices) or multiple user-types (such as different branding styles). One method of handling such situations is to surround all content with custom tags that can adapt to the client type and/or user type — for example, a `<branding:logoimage>` tag that returns an `IMG` tag with the appropriate branding image for the user and client.

Another method is to use custom tags to forward the user to a JSP page appropriate to the user and client. This method is less desirable, because you must maintain one JSP page for each user-interface style. It's sometimes necessary, however, if the user interface changes too significantly.

Model II – JSPs as Templates

The Model II methodology implements a Model-View-Controller pattern by using Java components as *models*, JSPs as *views*, and servlets as *controllers*. (See the accompanying sidebar for background on the Model-View-Controller pattern.) Figure 6-3 illustrates the typical Model II architecture and its relationship to MVC.

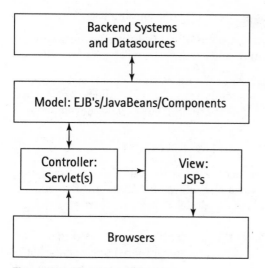

Figure 6-3: Model II architecture

In Model II, the browser makes its requests to the URL of a servlet. The servlet performs "controller" logic, such as authenticating the user, validating the request, and determining which model and view components to access. The servlet then invokes whatever model components that it needs to process the request.

You can implement model components as Enterprise Java Beans, JavaBeans, or ordinary Java classes. The model components perform the business logic necessary to complete the request and pass results (typically in the form of a JavaBean) back to the controller.

The controller then takes the results and passes them to the JSP that's acting as the view component. The JSP then interacts with the forwarded result objects to format the HTML for presentation back to the browser. Because you use JSPs only for presentation logic rather than to invoke business-logic components, JSPs in Model II function largely as templates that merge the model's data with HTML.

Advantages of the Model II approach

The primary focus of the Model II approach is building applications that encourage reusability and long-term maintenance. Using an architecture that you base on Model II has the following benefits if you use it correctly:

◆ Model components are reusable in other applications – even applications with completely different user interfaces and client types (PDAs, browsers, phones).

◆ The user interface is easy to modify, even by nonprogrammers.

◆ The controller logic provides a single point of control for enforcing common business logic, such as logging and security.

◆ The division of labor is very clean between the various components. The JSP authors can work very independently from the Java coders. The loose coupling between components enables very efficient parallel development.

Disadvantages of the Model II approach

The Model II approach relies on a strong definition of the interfaces between the model, view, and controller. If you don't use a prebuilt Model II framework, you can spend a significant amount of time building a Model II infrastructure to manage and define these interfaces.

Additionally, the program flow of Model II is much more complicated than that of Model I. Logical control passes from the servlet to one or more components, back to the servlet, and then to a JSP. This complex flow makes the learning curve for Model II steeper than for Model I. This amount of indirection can also amount to overkill for simple applications (such as reports) that involve little business logic.

Using Model II

A common and effective way to implement a Model II architecture, is to use a pre-built Model II framework such as Struts, Turbine, WebMacro, or JATO. This approach enables you to take advantage of a rich framework with prebuilt functionality, as well as enabling you to avoid spending time developing the interface layer between your components. Prebuilt frameworks can also help you avoid developer learning curves, because these frameworks are gaining popularity in the developer community.

After you select or build your development framework, building your application is relatively straightforward. The framework itself helps you enforce your programming model, typically making any violation of the MVC paradigm difficult. And because your code must interface with other components via a well-known interface, developer mistakes are often localized and easier to fix.

JSP Alternatives

Although the JSP API is very powerful, J2EE doesn't mandate the use of JSPs. Several alternative methodologies for generating Web content exist, and you should also consider those methods in evaluating the benefits of JSPs.

Templating languages

One common criticism of JSPs is that the API is *too* rich. Because the full flexibility of the Java language is available within JSPs, business logic and presentation logic can become intertwined. This complexity can make maintenance difficult and readability poor. The JSP API also has some limitations because JSPs eventually compile into servlets. This servlet compilation step also makes development with JSPs more awkward, since your JSP must be parsed into a servlet before execution or debugging.

Proponents of templating alternatives suggest that using a tool dedicated specifically toward templating can enable the presentation code to become more elegant and easy to maintain than the equivalent JSP code. And if you remove the requirement that JSPs support the complete Java language and compile into servlets, templating languages can become higher performing and lighter in weight than JSPs.

Model–View–Controller

Model-View-Controller (MVC) is a design pattern originally developed as part of Smalltalk at Xerox PARC. MVC is one of the most successful design patterns and is widely used in all types of computer application design. The essential concept of the MVC pattern is that data logic, presentation logic, and controller logic are all separate from one another. The data logic is the *model*; the presentation logic is the *view*; and the controller logic is the *controller*.

By keeping this separation, you can minimize the effects of changes in one component. You can accommodate changes in the underlying data structure by updating the model component without affecting the resulting view. You can make updates to the look and feel without needing to change the program logic or the data structures.

Another valuable benefit from MVC is reusability. By decoupling business logic from presentation logic, the business logic becomes reusable outside its original context. A Java component that accepts a part number and returns an HTML table with the sales history for that part is useful only for that one application and only as long as the format for the HTML table doesn't change significantly.

If you build that Java component according to MVC standards, however, the data logic (getting the sales data) remains separate from the presentation logic (building the HTML table from the data). This separation enables you to reuse the data logic in other applications. The same data logic component may prove reusable, for example, in a sales-analysis tool that may not have an interactive GUI at all.

These arguments are very valid. If you're using a Model II based architecture, JSPs offer significantly more functionality than you need. The additional functionality does add complexity and increase the chance for developer error. If an HTML author inadvertently removes a semicolon from scriptlet code, for example, the JSP compiler usually returns an obscure and nonintuitive error.

The question to consider is whether the benefits of using a templating language are worth the loss of functionality. Another factor that you must consider is that templating languages such as Velocity and WebMacro are generally less known than JSPs. Because the J2EE developer is likely to have a knowledge of JSPs but not of Velocity, using a templating language instead of JSP involves an added learning curve.

XML/XSLT

As more and more applications use XML (eXtensible Markup Language) for data interchange and data storage, you can also expect to see a rise in the use of XSLT (eXtensible Stylesheet Language Transformations) for the transformation of XML data. XSLT enables you to transform XML documents into different formats based on a set of rules that an XSLT stylesheet defines.

One common use of XSLT is the transformation of XML data into HTML. Consider, for example, an EJB that returns purchase-order information formatted in an XML dialect. Imagine, too, that you have an XSLT template that can convert those XML purchase orders into HTML documents. Now you can use any XSLT processor to automatically convert those purchase orders into Web pages without requiring any JSPs or other code. As an added benefit, you could have different XSLT templates for different client types. You could render the XML into HTML for browsers, but present lightweight WML for PDAs.

XSLT has the advantage of supporting very clean delineation between business logic and presentation logic. It also is very standards-based and easy to maintain. Using an XML/XSLT approach, however, essentially requires that you complete all business logic before generating the XML document. (XSLT can perform some basic processing but is limiting and awkward in comparison with Java processing.) It also doesn't provide a good mechanism for generating Web pages other than those representing data (for example, a page that gathers information from the user). XSLT processing is also very CPU and memory intensive in comparison to JSPs and other templating languages. Using XSLT as the primary HTML generation technology will have a significant affect on system performance.

Using XSLT to present Web information is sure to become more commonplace as XML becomes more prevalent. XSLT-generated HTML, however, is likely to remain a supplement rather than a replacement for Java Server Pages.

Summary

JavaServer Pages remain a somewhat controversial topic. This controversy stems from the fact that JSPs have many different types of developers, each with very different expectations about the technology. Developers that expect JSPs to be similar to ASP or PHP are often disappointed by the strict Java syntax. Developers that are using Model I often become overwhelmed by the complexity of the taglib component model. And developers using the Model II often yearn for a simpler solution that better separates presentation and business logic.

Despite this wide focus, JavaServer Pages are still the most common tool for creating presentation logic in J2EE applications. They can be a very powerful and flexible tool if used wisely. JSPs can help isolate your business logic from your presentation logic, speed your development process, and enable your developers to use effective development patterns.

You can find additional information about the topics that I cover in this chapter in the following places.

JavaSoft documentation

◆ JSP Specifications: http://java.sun.com/products/jsp/download.html

◆ Online JSP Tutorial: http://developer.java.sun.com/developer/onlineTraining/JSPIntro/contents.html

◆ TagLibs Tutorial: http://java.sun.com/products/jsp/tutorial/TagLibrariesTOC.html

◆ JavaBeans Tutorial: http://java.sun.com/docs/books/tutorial/javabeans/

LDAP information

◆ LDAP URL Specification: http://www.cis.ohio-state.edu/cgi-bin/rfc/rfc1959.html

◆ LDAP v3 Specification: http://www.ietf.org/rfc/rfc2251.txt

◆ iPlanet Directory Server Proxied Authentication Instructions: http://docs.iplanet.com/docs/manuals/directory/41/admin/acl.htm#998718

◆ iPlanet Directory Server Virtual List View Instructions: http://docs.iplanet.com/docs/manuals/dirsdk/jsdk40/controls.htm#2848467

Other documentation

◆ *JavaWorld* Article on Model 2 Methodology, by Govind Seshadri:
www.javaworld.com/javaworld/jw-12-1999/jw-12-ssj-jspmvc.html

◆ WhatIs.com explanation of CRC hashing: http://whatis.
techtarget.com/definition/0,,sid9_gci213868,00.html

◆ Online sample documentation for iAS JSP tag extension samples:
http://developer.iplanet.com/appserver/samples/iastags/docs/
index.html

◆ Jakarta Taglibs Home Page: http://jakarta.apache.org/taglibs/
index.html

◆ Struts Home Page: http://jakarta.apache.org/struts/

◆ Turbine Home Page: http://jakarta.apache.org/turbine/index.html

◆ Velocity Home Page: http://jakarta.apache.org/velocity/
index.html

◆ WebMacro Home Page: www.webmacro.org/

◆ XSLT Resource Site: www.xslt.com

Chapter 7

Adding EJBs

IN THIS CHAPTER

◆ Reviewing Enterprise JavaBeans (EJBs) architecture and services

◆ Discussing transaction capabilities for EJBs

◆ Giving case-point scenarios of EJB usage

IN THIS CHAPTER, I present an overview of Enterprise JavaBeans (EJBs) and discuss creating, configuring, deploying, and using EJBs in the iPlanet Application Server environment. This discussion isn't a detailed coverage of Enterprise JavaBeans; rather, the objective of this chapter is to give you a high-level overview of EJBs and then dive into the process of creating, configuring, accessing, and deploying EJBs into iPlanet Application Server.

What Are Enterprise JavaBeans?

The *Enterprise JavaBean* (*EJB*) is an architecture for building server-side, distributed components. These components are configurable, distributed business objects that services within the application server implicitly support. A 500-page specification document (available from Sun Microsystems at `http://java.sun.com/products/ejb/index.html`) defines the EJB technology at its current revision. The specification not only is in writing, but it also defines an API as a set of Java interfaces. Acting as the J2EE Product Provider, the iPlanet Application Server supplies its own implementations of these interfaces, producing a certified set of J2EE services for building and deploying EJBs. Figure 7-1 gives you a high-level view of the EJB topology, where a client makes a remote method call to an EJB with the EJB container.

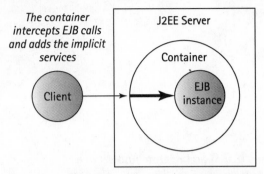

Figure 7-1: EJB within a container in an application server

Working with Enterprise JavaBeans

While working with EJBs, users can assume various roles. The EJB specification defines the following roles to enable a division of responsibility for your EJB projects. The following list briefly describes these roles:

- *Provider* – Builds EJB modules for use in enterprise applications.

- *Assembler* – Builds EJB modules into enterprise applications.

- *Deployer* – Specializes in deployment of beans in development and/or production environments.

- *Administrator* – Monitors and tunes the EJB environment.

- *Container/server provider* – Builds application servers and component containers.

The focus in this chapter is on the development aspects of EJBs, which can include the provider, assembler, and deployer roles. (In Chapter 5, I also discuss these roles, but with emphasis on packaging and assembly.)

EJB Architecture

The vision behind EJBs is to provide an industry-standard execution environment for enterprise business objects. The *execution environment*, also known as an *EJB container*, provides a scalable, transactional, and multiuser-secure environment for business objects. Application-server (J2EE Product Provider) vendors, such as iPlanet, provide implementations of the EJB container as well as a Web container. iPlanet Application Server (iAS) 6.0 implements the 1.1 version of the EJB container.

As an EJB component provider, you want to focus your energy on business logic for your application and not the run-time architecture and services for your components. Everyone knows that defining business logic is hard enough at times. As the EJB specification defines it, you can rely on the container to supply implicit and programmatic value-added services for your components.

Implicit services supply value-added dynamics for EJB components. The J2EE and EJB specification require that the product provider supplying the EJB container provide these services. The added value to developers is that taking advantage of these services requires little effort. Whenever you invoke EJB methods, the container automatically applies these services. The container accomplishes this task by intercepting invocations of EJB business methods and providing implicit services to the EJBs, based on the bean type and descriptor settings. Figure 7-1 (in the section "What are Enterprise JavaBeans," earlier in this chapter) depicts the scenario where the container doesn't permit an EJB client to directly interact with an EJB instance. Follow up this situation by looking at Figure 7-2, where you can see the variety of J2EE technologies that support these services.

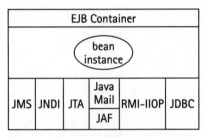

Figure 7-2: Implicit EJB services

To reiterate, the type of EJB and the values declared within a component's deployment descriptors define the manner in which the container applies its implicit services to an EJB component. The EJB specification is your guide for the exact rules and language for the services that I describe in the following section.

Implicit container services

The following list describes the implicit services and capabilities that the EJB container supplies with no or minimal effort on your behalf:

◆ *Concurrency* — EJB instances permit only one call at a time.

◆ *Remote access* — Works via Remote Method Invocation (RMI) (and considered implicit because the standard RMI process is hidden).

◆ *Lifecycle* — Depending on the type of EJB (session, entity, or message), the container automatically calls lifecycle methods at the appropriate times.

◆ *Persistence* — The EJB container triggers storing/retrieving of state from the persistent store. Additional instructions are necessary for entity beans in relational mappings to data stores.

◆ *Transactions* — Configurable transaction management applies on each method call via the deployment descriptor (DD).

◆ *Security* — The EJB container checks configurable security authorization on each method call via the DD.

Programmatic container services

These programmatic services consist merely of the implementation of standard J2EE technology APIs. The following services are directly available as APIs to both the container and the components executing within the container:

◆ Remote Method Invocation/Internet Inter-ORB Protocol (RMI/IIOP)

◆ Java Naming and Directory Interface (JNDI)

◆ Java DataBase Connection (JDBC)

◆ Java Transaction API (JTA)

◆ Java Messaging Service (JMS)

◆ JavaBeans Activation Framework and Mail Service (JAF/JavaMail)

As a developer, you may need more control or functionality than you can get via the deployment descriptor-based declarations. You may find that you need to create and manage your own transactions, for example, rather than leave this task for the container to automatically perform. JTA enables you to access the transaction manager within the container in a fashion that you've not tied to a particular application server.

To summarize, an EJB gains exposure to these services either programmatically, via APIs, or declaratively, via deployment descriptors. In the sections following "How to Access Session EJBs," later in this chapter, I present examples that leverage the deployment-descriptor settings. Figure 7-3 depicts an EJB within an EJB container.

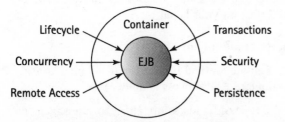

Figure 7-3: EJB container and J2EE services

The distributed EJB environment

EJBs are *distributed objects*, which use Remote Method Invocation (RMI) to access the remote bean that's running on a server. An RMI object and, therefore, an EJB consists of a *server object*, a *server skeleton*, and a *remote stub*. As shown in Figure 7-4, a client accesses the remote stub as a proxy to the server object. The stub has the same API as the server object, but its methods bundle method parameters, send the request to the server, and reply with any return parameters.

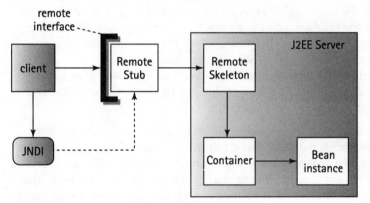

Figure 7–4: Interaction with EJB via client

 iAS uses Kiva Communications Protocol (KCP) as the underlying Remote Method Invocation facility. KCP is a simple TCP/IP-based protocol that's optimized for streaming.

Types of EJBs

The EJB specification (2.0) provides four types of EJBs. Two of these are *session beans*, which are components held in memory and that don't permanently persist their state between method invocations or server crashes. The remaining two are the *entity bean*, which does permanently store its state, and the *message-driven bean*, which responds to asynchronous events. The four EJBs are as follows:

♦ *Stateless session beans* (*SLSBs*) are components that don't maintain state on behalf of the client. Each SLSB method call should produce consistent and expected results, even if a client makes the call that the container routes to a separate bean instance. In fact, the container generally pools

SLSBs, and subsequent calls to an SLSB can access different instances in the pool. These EJBs can contain class attributes as long as these attributes don't reflect state between method calls (that is, by holding a database connection or socket).

◆ *Stateful session beans* (*SFSBs*) are components that do maintain state on behalf of only one client. These EJBs are less desirable in a highly scalable Web application because the EJB container doesn't pool them. Again, by definition, an SFSB holds state for one client only. The state within an SFSB doesn't persist to permanent storage (that is, a database) and is available to the client only for a specific period of time. The SFSB's state is lost after the time period of bean inactivity expires, until the EJB container stops (gracefully or not), or the client removes the bean instance. The EJB container holds an SFSB's client's state in memory, and you shouldn't use it for holding critical information. An SFBS client accesses its SFBS instance by using a serializable handle that uniquely identifies this bean instance within the container.

◆ *Entity beans* (*EBs*) are components that save state to a permanent store, usually a relational database. Each EJB instance associates to a unique identifier known as a *primary key*. The primary key must uniquely identify a record in the permanent store so that the container can find, load, and store the entity's state. Finder methods enable a client to get a reference to the entity bean. Behind the scenes, the container invokes an entity bean-finder method to try to identify the record in the database that this entity is to represent. After the record is uniquely identified and the entity bean has its primary key, the server/container determines when to access the database, leaving the client to set properties on the entity bean. Entity beans go into a pool if they're not assigned to a primary key. The pool size can configure in the deployment descriptor or in the administration tools.

◆ *Message-driven beans* (MDBs) are components that receive asynchronous messages from a JMS queue or topic. EJB 2.0 introduced them to provide an adapter from JMS to session and entity EJBs. They have no remote or home interface and are accessible from clients only by sending a JMS message.

iAS 6.5 implements the EJB 1.1 specification with the addition of the EJB 2.0 message-driven beans (MDBs) feature.

Makeup of an EJB

EJB components consist of a series of interfaces, implementation classes, and stub/skeleton classes. The EJB specification supplies interfaces that the component provider implements, depending on the desired EJB type. iAS supplies an EJB compiler tool that checks to make sure that your EJB classes conform to the EJB syntax rules (for example, implementing the same business-method signature from your remote interface in the bean implementation class) and creates the appropriate stub/skeleton classes as well.

Finally, you use an XML deployment descriptor to declare the EJB name and the essential EJB classes. As I describe in Chapter 5, in addition to the J2EE deployment descriptor, iAS mandates an additional descriptor that you use to declare the iAS internal name and iAS value-added features. These classes and descriptors are to be packaged into an EJB-JAR archive, which represents the EJB module. You use modules for deployment and application assembly.

Session and entity EJBs consist of the following Java files:

- ◆ Remote interface

- ◆ Home interface

- ◆ Bean class

- ◆ Stubs and skeletons

As developers, you create the classes in the preceding list, with the exception of the stubs and skeletons, which I describe in the following section.

Stubs and Skeletons

An EJB container is responsible for taking your EJB component and making it accessible and callable by a client. You can't simply access and run your EJB classes without the accompanying stubs and skeletons. The application server supplies you with tools such as `ejbc` and the iAS Deployment Tool to generate the stubs and skeletons so that you can deploy your EJBs to the EJB container.

The stubs and skeletons are necessary to supplement to your EJB classes. The stubs and skeletons transparently enable your EJB to access the EJB container services and such features as RMI capabilities, lookups, security, transactions, lifecycle, and so on. Without the aforementioned functionality, your EJBs aren't too useful. The stubs and skeletons facilitate the perception that the remote EJB object is actually running locally with the client. Your EJB container's vendor can also use the stubs and skeletons to introduce value-added features such as persistence and high availability.

The ejbc tool first sanity-checks your EJB classes for integrity rules such as method signatures and exceptions. Then it produces the necessary stubs and skeletons. ejbc also provides command-line options that enables high availability for your EJB, RMI/IIOP, and generation of the stub and skeleton source files.

In the following lists, I give some reference to the additional classes that the ejbc tool generates for the Greeter EJB after it runs without errors.

The additional classes for the home interface are as follows:

- ◆ ejb_stub_GreeterHome
- ◆ ejb_kcp_stub_GreeterHome
- ◆ ejb_kcp_skel_GreeterHome

The additional classes for the remote interface are as follows:

- ◆ ejb_stub_Greeter
- ◆ ejb_kcp_stub_Greeter
- ◆ ejb_kcp_skel_Greeter

The additional classes for the bean class are as follows:

- ◆ ejb_skel_samples_helloworld_ejb_GreeterEJB
- ◆ ejb_fac_samples_helloworld_ejb_GreeterEJB
- ◆ ejb_home_samples_helloworld_ejb_GreeterEJB

The additional classes in using a rich client (IIOP) are as follows:

- ◆ ejb_RmiCorbaBridge_Greeter
- ◆ ejb_RmiCorbaBridge_Greeter_Tie
- ◆ ejb_RmiCorbaBridge_GreeterHome
- ◆ ejb_RmiCorbaBridge_ Greeter Home_Tie
- ◆ GreeterHome_Stub
- ◆ Greeter_Stub

Message-driven beans (MDBs) consist only of a bean class.

All iAS EJBs require two deployment descriptors, ejb-jar.xml (generic J2EE EJB settings) and ias-ejb-jar.xml (iAS-specific settings). In Figure 7-5, you can see the relative positioning of these descriptors in the META-INF directory of the invoicemgrEJB.jar.

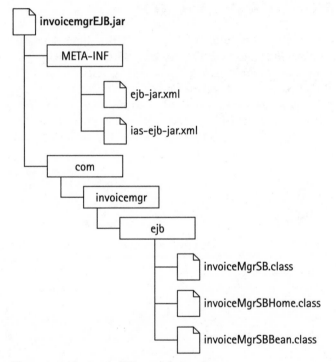

Figure 7-5: A sample EJB-module topology

Before you can deploy and execute your EJB, you must package the EJB module. The packaging stage involves simply using a tool to assemble one or more EJB components and associative stubs and skeletons with the descriptors in the preceding list and then creating an EJB-JAR file.

Chapter 5 covers packaging, deployment descriptors, and tools that facilitate packaging.

Now that you're aware of the basic elements of EJBs and their types, you get to dive in the following sections into an example that exposes you to the various developer tasks necessary for creating EJBs.

How to Access Session EJBs

You're going to explore in this section a simplified example of a developer scenario that covers all the aspects involving adding EJBs into an iAS environment. The problem revolves around a company invoice manager, InvoiceMgr (see Figure 7-6), which includes several EJBs as well as a JavaBean accessor. You start with the accessor class so that, as you build the EJBs, your test class becomes ready. This pattern, known as a *service locator*, encapsulates the EJB access away from the client and enables Java Server Pages (JSP) to access EJBs especially easily without a lot of code in the JSP.

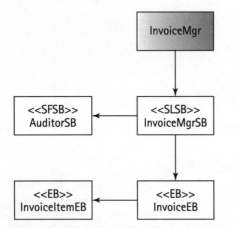

Figure 7-6: Topology of the invoice manager

You find many good J2EE examples in the <IAS-HOME>/ias-samples directory. You can use these examples as a primer for your applications.

In this example, InvoiceMgr is the access class, and it handles all your access by using the InvoiceMgrSB stateless session bean. As you can see in Listing 7-1, this class serves as a JavaBean proxy to your EJB and, therefore, mirrors the EJB's methods.

Listing 7-1: Signatures on the InvoiceMgr accessor class

```
public class InvoiceMgr
{
    public void createInvoice()
    public InvoiceVO getInvoiceByID(int id)
    public Iterator getInvoiceByDate(String date)
    public Iterator getInvoiceByCompany(String company)
    public void deleteInvoice(InvoiceVO inv)
    public void updateInvoice(InvoiceVO inv)
}
```

In Listing 7-2, you focus on creating an invoice, so you need to take a look at that method. The first step is to get the home interface from JNDI. Because your access could be remote, you have exceptions on which you want to manage the message. After you have the home interface, you create the remote object. Notice that you must always refer to the remote object as the remote interface, because you don't want your client to use the actual bean implementation or you negate the services that the container provides. Next, you narrow the remote object by using the RemoteObject.narrow static method. You must do so in case the remote object is actually a CORBA object. Then you're ready to access the business methods of the EJB. In this case, you call createInvoice() on the EJB.

Listing 7-2: JNDI lookup of invoice EJB

```
public class InvoiceMgr
{
    public void createInvoice() throws Exception
    {
        Context ctx = new InitialContext();
        Object obj = ctx.lookup("ejb/invoicemgrEJB/InvoiceSBMgr");
        InvoiceMgrSBHome home = (InvoiceMgrSBHome)
            PortableRemoteObject.narrow(
                obj, InvoiceMgrHome.class);
        InvoiceMgrSB ejb = home.create();
        ejb.createInvoice();
        ejb.remove();
    }
}
```

To review, your process for accessing the `InvoiceMgr` stateless session EJB involves just a few steps, as follows:

1. Get the home interface from JNDI.

2. Create the remote instance.

3. Narrow the instance by using `PortableRemoteObject`.

4. Call EJB methods (in your case, the `createInvoice` method).

5. Remove the bean reference.

In building the client access code for your EJB, you just need the EJB classes that you supply in your CLASSPATH. The stubs and skeletons are necessary only for deployment.

Create a Stateless Session EJB (SLSB)

The preceding section shows you how to create your client-access JavaBean. Now you're ready to create your first EJB, the `InvoiceMgr` stateless session bean (see Figure 7-7). In Listing 7-3 you begin with the remote interface. This step is a good place to start, because the interface is defining your business methods for the EJB, so it's a natural first step in the implementation. You need two packages: `javax.ejb` and `java.rmi`. Your interface is public and extends `EJBObject`. The interface is remote, so you must make all method parameters and return values serializable, and they must at a minimum throw `RemoteException`.

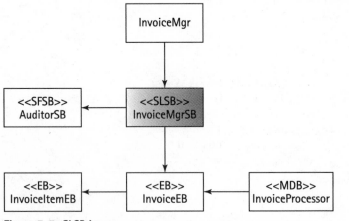

Figure 7-7: SLSB in use

Listing 7–3: InvoiceMgrSB.java

```java
import java.rmi.*;
import javax.ejb.*;

public interface InvoiceMgrSB extends EJBObject
{
    public void createInvoice() throws RemoteException;
    public InvoiceVO getInvoiceByID(int id) throws RemoteException;
    public void deleteInvoice(InvoiceVO inv) throws RemoteException;
    public void updateInvoice(InvoiceVO inv) throws RemoteException;
}
```

As Listing 7-4 shows, the second step is to create the home interface. It's a natural second step, because again, the home is an interface and so it's easy, and because the home interface provides access to your bean. The home interface must extend the EJBHome interface. It's also remote and so needs all parameters serializable and all methods to throw RemoteException. Since this is a stateless session bean, the interface must declare a create method that returns the remote interface, as the implementation of the create method returns the remote reference to the client. Because this EJB is a stateless session bean, the create() method must have no arguments. All create() methods must also throw CreateException.

Listing 7–4: InvoiceMgrSBHome.java

```java
import java.rmi.*;
import javax.ejb.*;

public interface InvoiceMgrSBHome extends EJBHome
{
    InvoiceMgrSB void create() throws CreateException, RemoteException;
}
```

The third step is to create the bean class. The container instantiates and runs this class, and only the container calls it. It's not remote and, therefore, shouldn't implement the remote interface. Yet it does need to contain all the business methods with the exact signature (without throwing RemoteException). Using the remote interface as a guide to which methods you must implement in your bean class is useful. This class needs to implement the javax.ejb.SessionBean interface and needs to implement the methods that I list in Table 7-1 from that interface as well.

TABLE 7-1 METHODS THAT YOUR SESSION BEAN IMPLEMENTS

ejbActivate()	Called if a bean instance activates after it's passivated.
ejbPassivate()	Called if a bean instance is passivated.
ejbRemove()	Called before this bean is removed.
setSessionContext()	Called if the SessionContext for this bean is created.
ejbCreate()	Called if a bean instance is created. You need one of these for every create method in the home interface, with matching parameters.

EJB passivation is the process wherein the application server reclaims resources on EJBs that aren't accessed for a period of time. On stateful session beans, the EJB state is serialized to a store on passivation automatically, after the ejbPassivate() method returns. After an EJB is passivated, the server activates it the next time that a client calls it. During activation, the container restores the EJB's state and then calls the ejbActivate method to perform tasks such as opening any necessary resource connections.

Listing 7-5 is the bean class for your InvoiceMgr. Notice that this class provides implementations for the methods that I list previously.

Listing 7-5: InvoiceMgrSBBean.java

```java
import javax.ejb.*;
import javax.naming.*;
import java.rmi.*;
import java.util.*;

public class InvoiceMgrSBBean implements SessionBean
{
    protected SessionContext _context = null;

    public void setSessionContext(SessionContext ctx)
    {
        _context = ctx;
    }
```

```
public void ejbActivate()
{
    // ...
}

public void ejbPassivate()
{
    // ...
}

public void ejbRemove()
{
    // ...
}

public void ejbCreate()
{
    // ...
}

//
//    Business methods
//
public void createInvoice(InvoiceVO vo)
{
  try
  {
    Context ctx = new InitialContext();
    Object obj = ctx.lookup("ejb/invoicemgrEJB/InvoiceEB");
    InvoiceEBHome home =
        (InvoiceEBHome)PortableRemoteObject.narrow(
             obj, InvoiceEBHome.class);
    InvoiceEB ejb = home.create();
    ejb.setValues(vo);
    }
    catch (Exception e)
    {
throw (new InvoiceMgrException("Error creating Invoice"));
    }
}

public InvoiceVO getInvoiceByID(int id)
{
```

Continued

Listing 7-5 *(Continued)*

```
        return null;
    }

    public void deleteInvoice(InvoiceVO inv)
    {
    }

    public void updateInvoice(InvoiceVO inv)
    {
    }
}
```

Methods in the bean class can throw both system exceptions and application exceptions. A *system exception* is either EJBException or an exception class that you create that extends EJBException. These exceptions indicate that an error exists in the system — for example, you can't access JNDI or a resource within the EJB. An *application exception* is an exception that extends Exception, and your code may throw it to indicate a business-logic error condition.

The final step before deployment is to create your deployment descriptors. I include the creation of these descriptors with the development tasks, and as such, you focus on the bare essential settings in the descriptors to get your stateless session bean ready for deployment. The first descriptor is the generic J2EE EJB descriptor ejb-jar.xml. This file is portable across application servers and minimally defines the elements and type of your bean. Listing 7-6 shows your entry for the InvoiceMgrSB.

Listing 7-6: ejb-jar.xml

```
<ejb-jar>
    <enterprise-beans>
        <session>
            <ejb-name>InvoiceMgrSB</ejb-name>
            <home>com.invoicemgr.ejb.InvoiceMgrSBHome</home>
            <remote>com.invoicemgr.ejb.InvoiceMgrSB</remote>
            <ejb-class>com.invoicemgr.ejb.InvoiceMgrSBBean</ejb-
class>
            <session-type>Stateless</session-type>
            <transaction-type>Container</transaction-type>
        </session>
    </enterprise-beans>
    <assembly-descriptor>
        ...
    </assembly-descriptor>
</ejb-jar>
```

Your minimal settings include an element for the session bean, which contains children elements configuring the package-qualified class names for the remote interface, home interface, and bean class. You also see an element indicating whether the session bean is <stateful> or <stateless>.

The final thing that you must do is set the JNDI name of the EJB. This name in JNDI is what clients need to look up the home interface. You set this name in the ias-ejb-jar.xml file, as shown in Listing 7-7.

Listing 7-7: ias-ejb-jar.xml

```
<ias-ejb-jar>
  <enterprise-beans>
    <session>
      <ejb-name>InvoiceMgrSB</ejb-name>
      <guid>{620F2AF8-AF0A-4B65-8046-45D52B93DA32}</guid>
      <pass-timeout>0</pass-timeout>
      <is-thread-safe>false</is-thread-safe>
      <pass-by-value>false</pass-by-value>
      <session-timeout>0</session-timeout>
    </session>
  </enterprise-beans>
</ias-ejb-jar>
```

You explore other settings in the section "Configure Transactions," later in the chapter, but the preceding descriptors get your SLSB to a deployable state.

How to Create a Stateful Session EJB (SFSB)

The preceding section shows you how to successfully build an SLSB, so now you take a look at what you need to do to build a stateful session bean. AuditorSB is your stateful session bean (see Figure 7-8) and accumulates logs until you choose to post them. This approach isn't one that I suggest for log management, but you may use it to emphasize the state that your stateful session bean can retain.

Your remote interface in Listing 7-8 follows the pattern of your previous SLSB, so you can move on to the home interface in Listing 7-9. You have your default create() method, and you add a create(String appname) method to pass in the application name. Now that your EJB can have state, you can pass in arguments on creation of the bean that the bean can maintain.

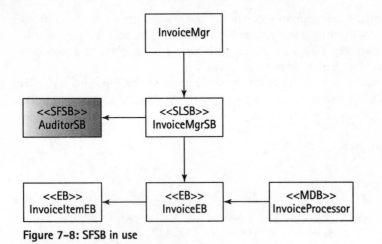

Figure 7-8: SFSB in use

Listing 7-8: AuditorSB.java

```
import java.rmi.*;
import javax.ejb.*;

public interface AuditorSB extends EJBObject
{
    public void log(Date date, String msg)
throws RemoteException;
    public void postLogs() throws RemoteException;
}
```

Listing 7-9: AuditorSBHome.java

```
import java.rmi.*;
import javax.ejb.*;

public interface AuditorSBHome extends EJBHome
{
    AuditorSB void create() throws
CreateException, RemoteException;
    AuditorSB void create(String appname) throws    CreateException,
RemoteException;
}
```

Your bean class now has attributes to hold the bean state. Notice in Listing 7-10 that your `ejbActivate()` and `ejbPassivate()` methods don't contain anything explicit. The server saves the bean state, so the only thing that you need to do is to open and close any resource connections. In this bean, however, you don't have any resource connections to manage.

TIP If you don't have any functional code to put in the EJB methods, putting in a log statement at a debug level is a good idea. That way, as you're debugging, you can see what sequence of state changes in the log.

Listing 7-10: AuditorSBBean.java

```java
import java.rmi.*;
import javax.ejb.*;

public class AuditorSBBean implements SessionBean
{
    private String _appname = "";
    private List _logs = new ArrayList();

    public void ejbActivate()
    {
        // ...
    }

    public void ejbPassivate()
    {
        // ...
    }

    public void ejbRemove()
    {
        // ...
    }

    public void ejbCreate()
    {
        // ...
    }

    public void ejbCreate(String appname)
    {
        _appname = appname;
    }

    //
    //    Business methods
    //
```

Continued

Listing 7-10 *(Continued)*

```
public void log(Date date, String msg)
{
    _logs.add(new MyLog(_appname, date, msg));
}

public void postLogs()
{
    //    save logs with EntityBean or log4j, etc
    _logs.clear();
}
}
```

In Listing 7-11, you now add a `<session-bean>` element to the `ejb-jar.xml`. You set the type as `<stateful>`. In Listing 7-12, you configure the `<JNDI-name>` in the `ias-ejb-jar.xml` descriptor, and you're ready to test the stateful session bean.

Listing 7-11: ejb-jar.xml

```
<ejb-jar>
    <enterprise-beans>
        <session>

            ...

        </session>
    </enterprise-beans>
    <assembly-descriptor>

        ...

    </assembly-descriptor>
</ejb-jar>
```

Listing 7-12: ias-ejb-jar.xml

```
<session>
    <ejb-name>AuditorSB</ejb-name>
    <guid>{B6B4CFFD-A0CD-4D53-9942-0E5A8FF70C51}</guid>
    <pass-timeout>0</pass-timeout>
    <is-thread-safe>false</is-thread-safe>
    <pass-by-value>false</pass-by-value>
    <session-timeout>0</session-timeout>
</session>
```

As a reminder, the container pools stateless session beans. The container doesn't pool stateful session beans because they contain state that's specific to the client. The container, therefore, creates a new SFSB instance on the server every time that a client calls a `create()` method on the home interface. A client can conceivably send a remote reference handle to another client, giving them both access to the same SFSB. This type of situation, however, most likely results in concurrency problems, as only one client can access the bean's methods at a time.

Deploy EJBs to IAS

In this section, you take a look at the deployment process. The first step in deployment is to compile your files. The next step is to create the stubs and skeletons for the EJBs that you define in the preceding descriptor. You create the stubs by using the Ant tool with the target stubs, as follows:

```
ant stubs
```

 I review Ant in Chapter 5 in the context of packaging.

You can call your file `invoicemgrEJB.jar`.

Now you must package the deployment descriptors in the `/META-INF` folder and the EJB classes and stubs into the JAR. If you're using Ant, your command is as follows:

```
ant jar
```

Next, you deploy to the iPlanet Application Server by using the following command:

```
ant deploy
```

Use EJB References

One of the most common clients of an EJB is another EJB. As frameworks grow, components need to access one another to effectively perform their tasks. Although this requirement doesn't necessarily pose a problem, it does reduce the level of component pluggability that the designers of EJBs intended. If clients are hardwired to the JNDI names of the components that they use, accommodating naming conventions between servers becomes more difficult, and the effort necessary to effectively version EJBs increases.

EJB references provide the solution to this problem. These references provide a lookup *alias* that you configure in the deployment descriptor of the bean itself. The effect isn't tremendous, but it's effective. Client beans can access EJBs by looking up a reference to the target EJB rather than explicitly coding the JNDI name in the bean code. This capability provides the flexibility to change components at deployment time (that is, no Java code changes are necessary—only XML descriptor changes), giving a deployer the capability to control the system. This capability can prove effective in making components highly portable across application servers, which may implement different JNDI naming conventions. It also can reduce the necessary maintenance efforts that deployment involves, because the JNDI name doesn't tightly couple to the client bean code.

In the example in Listing 7-13, you add EJB references to the `InvoiceMgrSB` EJB for the EJBs that it accesses.

Listing 7-13: ejb-jar.xml

```
<ejb-jar>
    <enterprise-beans>
        <session>
            <ejb-name>InvoiceMgrSB</ejb-name>
            <home>com.invoicemgr.ejb.InvoiceMgrSBHome</home>
            <remote>com.invoicemgr.ejb.InvoiceMgrSB</remote>
            <ejb-class>com.invoicemgr.ejb.InvoiceMgrSBBean</ejb-
class>
            <session-type>Stateless</session-type>
            <transaction-type>Container</transaction-type>
            <ejb-ref>
        <ejb-ref-name>ejb/AuditorSBHome</ejb-ref-name>
                <ejb-ref-type>Session</ejb-ref-type>
                <home>invoicemgr.AuditorSBHome</home>
                <remote>invoicemgr.AuditorSB</remote>
            </ejb-ref>
            <ejb-ref>
        <ejb-ref-name>
ejb/ InvoiceEBLocalHome</ejb-ref-name>
                <ejb-ref-type>Entity</ejb-ref-type>
                <local-
home>com.invoicemgr.ejb.InvoiceEBLocalHome</local-home>
                <local>com.invoicemgr.ejb.InvoiceEBLocal</local>
            </ejb-ref>
        </session>
        <session>
            <ejb-name>AuditorSB</ejb-name>
            <home>com.invoicemgr.ejb.AuditorSBSBHome</home>
```

```
            <remote>com.invoicemgr.ejb.AuditorSBSB</remote>
            <ejb-class>com.invoicemgr.ejb.AuditorSBBean</ejb-class>
            <session-type>Stateful</session-type>
            <transaction-type>Container</transaction-type>
        </session>
    </enterprise-beans>
    <assembly-descriptor>
    </assembly-descriptor>
</ejb-jar>
```

Configure Transactions

Transaction management is a basic aspect of almost every enterprise application. Transactions basically define atomic sets of operations, which behave as a single operation. To achieve this atomic behavior, either all the operations within the transaction must succeed or all operations must "roll back" to remove any trace of their execution. Seems simple enough, right? Well, as usual, it's simple only until you start adding some complexity. Figure 7-9 gives you some context on the transaction manager that I discuss in the following paragraphs.

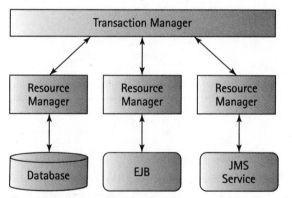

Figure 7-9: Transaction manager

So why do EJBs need transactions anyway? If you're using a transactional data-source (javax.sql.XADataSource), don't transactions support your data? The answer is yes, but you then must explicitly demarcate your transactions manually, and you're limited to local transactions. These transactions can involve only one resource manager, such as the datasource driver, and they don't involve the behavior that you code within your EJB. So if your EJB sends a JMS message and stores some data to the database and then rolls back the transaction, the data isn't committed to the database — yet you have no way to unsend the JMS message. The same situation exists if you're accessing two different databases within the scope of your desired transaction.

The solution is to define a *distributed transaction*. This type of transaction is capable of mediating transaction-state changes via the XA protocol. It involves using a two-phase commit, with the first phase ending as each resource manager prepares to commit and the second phase containing the actual commit.

With the release of iAS 6.5, iPlanet has replaced the Encina transaction manager with the Java Transaction Service Reference Implementation (JTS RI). iAS 6.5 also includes the JDBC 2.0 Standard Extension's `XADatasource`, `PooledDataSource`, global transaction support for third-party JDBC drivers, and more.

Transaction management determines the demarcation of transactions, and you can set it to *bean managed* (*BMT*) or *container managed* (*CMT*). You set it in the EJB-JAR deployment descriptor of each EJB. Session beans must demarcate their own transactions explicitly or rely on their clients to demarcate transactions. The example in Listing 7-14 shows how to demarcate a transaction by using the `UserTransaction`.

Listing 7-14: Creating your own user transaction

```
Context jndi = new InitialContext();
UserTransaction tran = (UserTransaction)jndi.lookup(
    "java:comp/UserTransaction");
tran.begin();
...
tran.commit();
```

Whenever you select container-managed transactions in a session or message-driven bean, the container begins a transaction (based on the transaction attribute, which I discuss in the following paragraph) at the beginning of an EJB method call and commits the transaction at the end of the method call. In message-driven beans, transactions can't span invocations of `onMessage()`. Entity beans are always set to container-managed transactions. If a system exception is thrown during execution of the method, the transaction rolls back at the end of the method. Be careful, however, as application exceptions don't roll back the transaction but permit the transaction to commit normally.

The *transaction attribute* determines how a container-managed transaction behaves for a method if you're using CMT. You can configure this attribute for each method or for a group of methods on the EJB. The following list describes each of the attributes and how the container manages the transaction. The two relevant states concerning the container are those having an active transaction and not having an active transaction, as follows:

♦ Supports — If a transaction is active, this method and any EJB calls participate in the transaction. If the client provides no transaction, however, no transaction is used. This attribute is the default CMT attribute (see Figure 7-10).

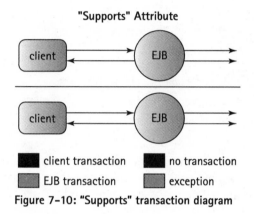

Figure 7-10: "Supports" transaction diagram

♦ NotSupported — If a transaction is active, the transaction is suspended until the method completes. The caller's transaction resumes after the method completes. If no client transaction is active, no transaction is used (see Figure 7-11).

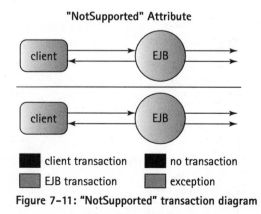

Figure 7-11: "NotSupported" transaction diagram

◆ Required — If a transaction is active, this method and any EJB calls participate in the transaction. If no transaction is active, however, a transaction starts and commits/rolls back at the end of the method. The container guarantees that this method executes in a transaction (see Figure 7-12).

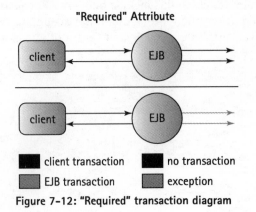

Figure 7-12: "Required" transaction diagram

◆ RequiresNew — A new transaction starts at the beginning of the method and commits/rolls back at the end of the method. If an active transaction exists at the beginning of the method, it is suspended and resumes at the end of the method (see Figure 7-13).

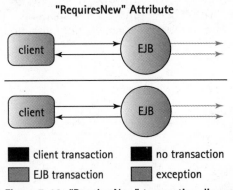

Figure 7-13: "RequiresNew" transaction diagram

◆ Mandatory — If an active transaction exists, the method participates in the transaction. If no transaction is active, however, an exception is thrown — TransactionRequiredLocalException, if local, or TransactionRequiredException, if remote (see Figure 7-14).

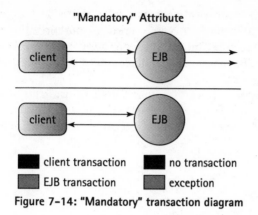

"Mandatory" Attribute

■ client transaction   ■ no transaction

■ EJB transaction   ■ exception

Figure 7-14: "Mandatory" transaction diagram

◆ Never — If an active transaction exists, an exception is thrown (RemoteException, to remote clients, or EJBException, to local clients). If no active transaction exists, the method performs without intrusion (see Figure 7-15).

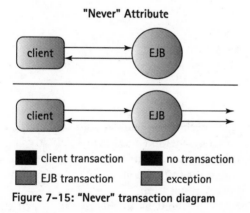

"Never" Attribute

■ client transaction   ■ no transaction

■ EJB transaction   ■ exception

Figure 7-15: "Never" transaction diagram

 The EJB 2.0 specification strongly advises that CMP 2.0 entity beans use only the Required, RequiresNew, and Mandatory transaction attributes, which ensure that all database access occurs within the context of a transaction.

Configure Security

EJB security occurs through access control. The other explicit services in J2EE provide other aspects of security, such as authentication and secure communications.

Authentication, for example, can occur within servlets, JSPs, and/or in JNDI whenever clients look up EJB home interfaces. Access control or authorization limits users' access to resources. EJB methods, in this case, are based on the role of the user. The security settings for EJBs are set in the deployment descriptors, so you need to know how the process works.

Your first task is to create security roles that your EJBs can use, and then you need to map the bean methods to these security roles. The `ejb-jar.xml` deployment descriptor defines these roles via the `<security-role>` element, as follows:

```
<security-role>
    <description>
        This is an example security role.
    </description>
    <role-name>Guest</role-name>
</security-role>
```

Next, you need to associate these roles to EJB methods by using the `<method-permission>` tag, as follows:

```
<method-permission>
    <role-name>Guest</role-name>
    <method>
        <ejb-name>IvoiceMgrSB</ejb-name>
        <method-name>*</method-name>
    </method>
</method-permission>
```

Notice here that you're including all methods by using a wild card as the method name. You can also include one or more method names to explicitly map each method to a role. This access control is implicit, requiring no code to check authorization. If you specify method permissions in the deployment descriptor, the container checks these permissions on every invocation.

As of EJB 2.0, you can also declare methods as *unchecked*, in which case the container permits any and all access to these methods, as the following example shows:

```
<method-permission>
    <unchecked/>
    <method>
        <ejb-name>AuditorSB</ejb-name>
        <method-name>*</method-name>
    </method>
</method-permission>
```

Also as of EJB 2.0, you can specify that all the methods on an EJB are invoked as a specific principal by using the `<run-as>` tag. This strategy is useful if the EJBs or resources that they use require a principal that's different than the calling principal, as shown in the following example:

```
<enterprise-beans>
    ...
    <entity>
        <ejb-name>InvoiceEB</ejb-name>
        ...
        <security-identity>
            <run-as>
                <role-name>Guest</role-name>
            </run-as>
        </security-identity>
    </entity>
```

The final step is to map principals to the logical roles that you define. You perform this final step by declaring the following descriptor elements in the `ias-ejb-jar.xml` descriptor (and for another example, see the Java Pet Store example that you find at `<IAS HOME>/ias-samples/jps1.1.2`):

```
<role-mapping>
  <role-name>Guest</role-name>
  <role-impl>
      <group>EstoreAdmin</group>
  </role-impl>
</role-mapping>
```

Access Entity EJBs

Entity EJBs reflect persistent data within your business model. As you consider your other stateful EJB (the stateful session bean), you can see that you basically need to add a way to "find" existing beans. Entity beans are components in memory that reflect an entry in a persistent store, and you therefore need a way to find the entry in the persistent store and create an EJB in memory that reflects its values. These entries are *finder methods*. But because the relationship between an entity bean and its persistent store also effects EJB creation, I first need to discuss EJB identity.

Primary keys are values that uniquely identify an entity EJB instance. You need to make the primary key serializable, and you can represent them by classes such as `java.lang.String`, `java.lang.Integer`, or `java.lang.Double` and so on. Primary keys can also exist as custom classes that developers build to encapsulate single or multiple values (in which case, they're known as *compound keys*). Primary key classes must implement java.io.Serializable and must provide equals() and hashCode() methods. The class must have a default constructor. Listing 7-15 shows an example of a compound key.

Listing 7-15: Compound key

```
import javax.ejb.*;
import java.rmi.*;

public class InvoicePK implements java.io.Serializable
{
    private Integer _number = null;
    private String _company = null;

    public InvoicePK()
    {
    }

    public InvoicePK(String company, Integer number)
    {
        _number = number;
        _company = company;
    }

    public Integer getNumber()
    {
        return _number;
    }

    public String getCompany()
    {
        return _company;
    }

    public boolean equals(Object obj)
    {
        boolean result = true;
        if ((obj == null) || !(obj instanceof InvoicePK))
            result = false;
        InvoicePK other = (InvoicePK)obj;
        if ((result == false) ||
```

```
(!other.getNumber().equals(_number))
      || (!other.getCompany().equals(_company)))
          result = false;
      return result;
  }

  public int hashCode()
  {
      return _number.hashCode() + _company.hashCode();
  }
}
```

You use primary keys to find a unique EJB instance, and you need to generate them whenever you create a new EJB instance. The following section describes how to create an entity EJB.

Create Entity EJBs

As you begin to create your entity EJB, you start with the remote interface, as you do with your session beans. The remote interface for an entity EJB follows all the same rules as — and is no different from — your session EJB remote interfaces.

EJB 2.0 introduces *local interfaces*. These interfaces are for accessing EJBs that are in the same application server as the client. Entity beans offer a good place to introduce these interfaces, mainly because creating and using your entity beans locally is more efficient than using them remotely. Because your database server (where the data persists) is probably remote, you gain very little by accessing your entity beans remotely. Local interfaces are optional for both session and entity beans, and you begin by creating a local interface, as in Listing 7-16.

Listing 7-16: IvoiceItemEBLocal.java

```java
import javax.ejb.*;
import java.rmi.*;

public interface InvoiceItemEB extends EJBLocalObject
{
    public InvoiceItemVO getValues() throws EJBException;
    public void setValues(InvoiceItemVO vo) throws EJBException;
    public Integer getItemNumber() throws EJBException;
    public String getItemName() throws EJBException;
    public Double getPrice() throws EJBException;
    public Integer getQuantity() throws EJBException;
    public Double calcTotal() throws EJBException;
}
```

Notice that you extend `javax.ejb.EJBLocalObject` instead of `EJBObject`, and your methods throw `EJBException` instead of `RemoteException`. To use your local interface, you must create a local home interface, as shown in Listing 7-17.

Listing 7-17: InvoiceItemEBHomeLocal.java:

```
import java.rmi.*;
import java.util.*;

public interface InvoiceEBHomeLocal extends EJBLocalHome
{
    public void create() throws CreateException, RemoteException;
    public InvoiceEB findByPrimaryKey(Integer id)
throws FinderException, RemoteException;
}
```

 iAS 6.5 doesn't support local interfaces. The preceding examples serve as a primer for iAS 7.0.

In your local home interface, you declare both `create` and `finder` methods. Your `create` method has an `Integer` parameter that's a part number (the primary key). You have one `finder` method, findByPrimaryKey(Integer pk). All entity EJBs require it, and it returns the local interface in the same manner that the remote home returns the remote interface. One aspect of local interfaces to consider is that arguments may pass by reference instead of passing by value. Changes within the bean to a parameter Java instance, therefore, modifies the parameter instance. Because remote interfaces serialize parameters, these instances always pass by value. References are especially tricky, because the subtlety occurs in the bean class but is relevant to whether the client accesses the EJB via local or remote interface.

Entity beans support two types of persistence: *bean-managed persistence* (*BMP*) and *container-managed persistence* (*CMP*). In a BMP entity bean, the developer writes the persistent code and can pretty much control how the bean persists. In CMP beans, the container handles the persistence, and the developer/deployer merely configures persistence settings in the deployment descriptors. Your `InvoiceItemEB` is BMP.

Create a BMP entity EJB

Now that you've created a local interface and local home, I'm going to skip showing you the remote interface and remote home, because they're very similar to their local counterparts and you worked through that process with your session beans. So in this section, I discuss the bean class. Figure 7-16 shows the entity beans involved in the preceding paragraphs.

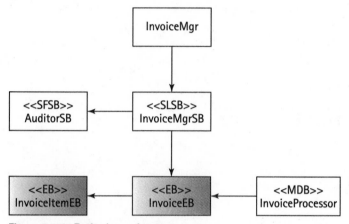

Figure 7-16: Entity beans in use

The first thing to notice about your bean class in Listing 7-18 is that you implement `javax.ejb.EntityBean` instead of `SessionBean`. You need method stubs for the following methods: `ejbActivate()`, `ejbPassivate()`, `setEntityContext()`, and `unsetEntityContext()`. This last method calls right before your bean gets garbage-collected.

Listing 7-18: InvoiceItem entity bean

```
import java.rmi.*;
import java.util.*;

public class InvoiceItemEBBean implements EntityBean
{
    protected EntityContext context        = null;
    public Integer number = null;
    public Integer invnumber = null;
    public String name = null;
    public Integer quantity = null;
    public Double price = null;

    public void setEntityContext(EntityContext ctx)
    {
        _context = ctx;
    }
```

Continued

Listing 7-18 *(Continued)*

```
    public void unsetEntityContext()
    {
        context = null;
    }

    public void ejbActivate()
    {
        // ...
    }

    public void ejbPassivate()
    {
        // ...
    }
...
}
```

Now you need to take a look at the persistence methods. First, you have your create method. Your bean class in entity beans must have both an ejbCreate() and ejbPostCreate() method for every create method in the home (or LocalHome) interface, all with matching parameters. You call ejbCreate to perform the insert, and you can use the ejbPostCreate method for inserting any aggregated values that depend on rows that you insert in ejbCreate(). The ejbPostCreate() method isn't particularly useful in BMP entity beans but proves more valuable in CMP entity beans. Listing 7-19 shows the BMP code for creating an invoice.

Listing 7-19: Bean class ejbCreate implementation

```
public void ejbCreate(Integer invoice_number)
    {
        number = (int)System.currentTimeMillis() +
(int)(Math.random()*1000);
        invnumber = invoice_number;

        Connection        con = null;
        PreparedStatement  ps = null;

        try
            {
            con = getConnection();
            ps = con.prepareStatement("insert into InvoiceItem
(number, invnumber, "
                        + "name, price, quantity) values (?, ?,
```

```
?, ?, ?)");
            ps.setInt(1, number);
            ps.setInt(2, invnumber);
            ps.setString(3, name);
            ps.setDouble(4, price);
            ps.setInt(5, quantity);

            if (ps.executeUpdate() != 1)
                {
                throw new CreateException("JDBC did not create any
row");
                }

            return number;
            }
        catch (CreateException ce)
            {
            throw ce;
            }
        catch (SQLException sqe)
            {
            throw new CreateException(sqe.getMessage());
            }
        finally
            {
            try
                {
                ps.close();
                con.close();
                }
            catch (Exception ignore)
                {
                }
            }
    }

    private Connection getConnection() throws SQLException
        {
        InitialContext initCtx = null;
        try
            {
            initCtx = new InitialContext();
            DataSource ds = (javax.sql.DataSource)
                initCtx.lookup("java:comp/env/jdbc/InvoiceMgrDS");
```

Continued

Listing 7-19 *(Continued)*

```
            return ds.getConnection();
            }
        catch(NamingException ne)
            {
            String msg;
            msg = log("ERROR getConnection() from InoivceMgrDS! ");
            throw new EJBException(msg + ne);
            }
        finally
            {
            try
                {
                if(initCtx != null)
                    initCtx.close();
                }
            catch(Exception ne) {}
            }
        }
```

You're using JDBC in Listing 7-19 to perform your entity create. You use a resource reference to access a DataSource. From DataSource, you get the connection and perform a pretty standard SQL insert statement. If you want your DataSource to support "global" transactions, you need to configure a resource manager and associate the DataSource as you configure the descriptor for the JDBC resource. A DataSource generally points to a pool of database connections that support your requests. Next, in Listing 7-20, you need to create an ejbLoad() method that does a basic read (or SELECT) for the attributes of the EJB. The container calls this method automatically if a read from the database is necessary.

Listing 7-20: Bean class load implementation

```
public void ejbLoad()
{
    try
    {
        refresh((Integer) context.getPrimaryKey());
        }
    catch (FinderException fe)
    {
        throw new EJBException(fe.getMessage());
    }
}

    protected void refresh(Integer pk)
    {
```

```
        if (pk == null)
            {
            throw new EJBException("InvoiceItemEB: Primary key
cannot be null");
            }
        Connection          con = null;
        PreparedStatement   ps = null;
        try
            {
            con = getConnection();
            ps = con.prepareStatement("select * from InvoiceItem
where Number = ?");
            ps.setInt(1, pk);
            ps.executeQuery();
            ResultSet   rs = ps.getResultSet();
            if (rs.next())
                {
                number = pk;
                invnumber = rs.getInt("INVNUMBER");
                name = rs.getString("NAME");
                price = rs.getDouble("PRICE");
                quantity = rs.getInt("QUANTITY");
                }
            else
                {
                throw new FinderException("InvoiceItemEB.Refresh: ("
+ pk
                + ") not found");
                }
            }
        catch (SQLException sqe)
            {
            throw new EJBException(sqe.getMessage());
            }
        finally
            {
            try
                {
                ps.close();
                con.close();
                }
            catch (Exception ignore)
                {
                }
            }
        }
```

After taking care of create and read, you need to look at update. In Listing 7-21, you handle updating your entity state in the ejbStore() method, which the container calls automatically if a write to the database is necessary.

Listing 7-21: Bean class store implementation

```
public void ejbStore()
{
    Connection           con = null;
    PreparedStatement    ps = null;

    try
        {
        con = getConnection();
        ps = con.prepareStatement("update InvoiceItem set
NUMBER=?, INVNUMBER=?, NAME=?, PRICE=?, QUANTITY=? where ID = ?");
        ps.setInt(1, number);
        ps.setInt(2, invnumber);
        ps.setString(3, name);
        ps.setDouble(4, price);
        ps.setInt(5, quantity);

        int i = ps.executeUpdate();
        if (i == 0)
            {
            throw new EJBException("Error: InvoiceItemEB ("+
number + ") not updated");
            }
        }
    catch (SQLException sqe)
        {
        throw new EJBException(sqe.getMessage());
        }
    finally
        {
        try
            {
            ps.close();
            con.close();
            }
        catch (Exception ignore)
            {
            }
        }
}
```

To recap, the previous examples involve creating, loading, and storing your entity. That leaves removing or deleting your entity. As shown in Listing 7-22, you accomplish this task by implementing the ejbRemove() method. The job of this method is to actually remove the record from permanent storage that this entity represents. So make sure that, if you call this method, you really mean it.

Listing 7-22: Bean class remove implementation

```
public void ejbRemove()
{
    Connection          con = null;
    PreparedStatement   ps = null;
    try
        {
        con = getConnection();
        Integer pk = (Integer) context.getPrimaryKey();
        ps = con.prepareStatement("delete from InvoiceItem where
ID = ?");
        ps.setInt(1, pk.id);
        int i = ps.executeUpdate();
        if (i == 0)
            {
            throw new RemoveException("InvoiceItemEBBean..." +
pk.id + " not found");
            }
        }
    catch (SQLException sqe)
        {
        throw new RemoveException(sqe.getMessage());
        }
    finally
        {
        try
            {
            ps.close();
            con.close();
            }
        catch (Exception ignore)
            {
            }
        }
    }
```

The last feature that you add to your entity is the finder method(s). You must implement the findByPrimaryKey method so that you can find your entity bean after you create it. As you may recall from Listing 7-17, you define this finder method in the home interface. In Listing 7-23, I supply your implementation of this method. Notice that I return the pk from this method. Returning the pk here tells the container the entity bean's identity.

Listing 7-23: Bean class finder implementation

```
public Integer ejbFindByPrimaryKey(Integer pk)
                            throws FinderException
    {
    if (pk == null)
        throw new FinderException("primary key cannot be null");
    refresh(pk);
    return pk;
}
```

The ejbFindByPrimaryKey method is using the same common database code as ejbLoad(), except that you're passing the primary key as an argument instead of already having it in the bean class. This pattern is a common one with BMP entity beans.

After you implement all your persistence and EJB methods and after your business methods are complete, you just need to construct your initial deployment descriptors and test the entity bean.

You really don't have much new in the deployment descriptor, except that you're defining a resource reference for your datasource. Notice in Listing 7-24 that you define a local interface and a local home, which you must configure.

Listing 7-24: ejb-jar.xml

```
<entity>
<ejb-name>InvoiceItemEB</ejb-name>
<home>invoicemgr.InvoiceItemEBHomeRemote</home>
<remote>invoicemgr.InvoiceItemEBRemote</remote>
<ejb-class>invoicemgr.InvoiceItemEBBean</ejb-class>
<local-home>invoicemgr.InvoiceItemEBHomeLocal</local-home>
<local>invoicemgr.InvoiceItemEBLocal</local>
<persistence-type>Bean</persistence-type>
<prim-key-class>java.lang.Integer</prim-key-class>
<reentrant>false</reentrant>
</entity>
```

Create CMP entity EJBs

The purpose of *container-managed persistence* (*CMP*) is to move all the tedious and repetitive JDBC database code into the container and away from the EJB developer. CMP sounds like a dream, so why would you ever use BMP entity beans? Well, to turn persistence to a configuration task occurring in the deployment descriptors, you have some restrictions and complexities in mapping CMP entity beans to relational databases. In dealing with simple relational-table and primary-key-to-entity mappings, CMP works very well, but in introducing complex relationships, such as many-to-many, inheritance, composition, and composite keys between tables, CMP typically becomes hard to manage, configure, and optimize. Handling these complexities sometimes is better dealt with by using BMP code. All in all, CMP entity beans are still very useful, especially if you're using a course-grained EJB approach to a normalized database model.

For your example, you build `InvoiceEB` as a CMP entity bean. You're looking at both the CMP 1.1 and the CMP 2.0 approach to entity beans. Just as with your `InvoiceItemEB` entity bean in Listing 7-25, you begin with the local interface, which is pretty straightforward and doesn't present anything new to your CMPs.

Listing 7-25: InvoiceEBLocal.java

```java
import javax.ejb.*;
import java.rmi.*;

public interface InvoiceEB extends EJBLocalObject
{
    public InvoiceVO getValues()                     throws
EJBException;
    public void setValues(InvoiceVO vo) throws EJBException;
    public void createItem(String name, Double price, Integer
quantity) throws EJBException;
    public Collection getItems() throws EJBException;
    public Date calcDueDate() throws EJBException;
}
```

Next, you have your remote-home and local-home interfaces. You have two `create` methods, one default `create` method and one that enables you to specify a number (which is the primary key in this case). You also have two `finder` methods: `findByPrimaryKey()` and `findByCompany()`. Notice that the `findByCompany()` returns a `Collection` of all the invoices for the specified company string. This `Collection` contains local interfaces (or remote interfaces, if you call it from the remote home). Now you're ready to tackle the bean class in Listing 7-26, where CMP entity beans start to differ from BMP entity beans.

Listing 7-26: InvoiceEBHomeLocal

```
import java.rmi.*;
import java.util.*;

public interface InvoiceEBHomeLocal extends EJBLocalHome
{
    public void create() throws    CreateException, EJBException;
    public InvoiceEB findByPrimaryKey(Integer id) throws
FinderException, EJBException;
    public Collection findAll()    throws    FinderException,
EJBException;
}
```

Create a CMP 1.1 entity bean

In your CMP 1.1 entity bean, you implement `javax.ejb.EntityBean` and need to implement the methods that it defines. Before you start into the methods, however, you need to create public attributes for all the container-managed fields. These fields map to columns in a relational table. In Listing 7-27, as you implement your `ejbMethods`, notice that you're required only to stub out the methods. I suggest that you put log statements into `create`, `load`, `store`, and `remove` methods to assist in debugging, but doing so isn't a requirement.

Listing 7-27: Bean class BMP implementation

```
import java.rmi.*;
import java.util.*;

public class InvoiceEBBean implements EntityBean
{
    protected EntityContext _context      = null;
    //
    //    cmp-fields
    //
    public Integer number;
    public Date    date;
    public Integer    terms;
    public String     company;

    public void setEntityContext(EntityContext ctx)
    {
        _context = ctx;
    }
```

```
public void unsetEntityContext()
{
    _context = null;
}

public void ejbActivate()
{
    // ...
}

public void ejbPassivate()
{
    // ...
}

public void ejbRemove()
{
    // ...
}

public void ejbLoad()
{
    // ...
}

public void ejbStore()
{
    // ...
}

//
//    Create Methods
//
public Integer ejbCreate()
{
    // ...
    return null;
}

public void ejbPostCreate()
{
    // ...
```

Continued

Listing 7-27 *(Continued)*

```
    }

    //
    //      Business methods
    //
    public InvoiceVO getValues()
    {
    InvoiceVO    vo = new InvoiceVO();
    vo.setNumber(this.getNumber());
    vo.setDate(this.getDate());
    vo.setTerms(this.getTerms());
    vo.setCompany(this.getCompany());
    }

    public void setValues(InvoiceVO vo)
    {
    this.setNumber(vo.getNumber());
    this.setDate(vo.getDate());
    this.setTerms(vo.getTerms());
    this.setCompany(vo.getCompany());
    }

    public Date calcDueDate()
    {
        Calendar due = new GregorianCalendar();
        due.setTime(this.getDate());
        due.add(Calendar.DAY_OF_YEAR, this.getTerms().intValue());
        return due.getTIme();
    }
}
```

Now you move on to the ejbCreate() methods in the preceding listing. Notice that, just as with BMP entity beans, you need both ejbCreate() and ejbPostCreate(). The ejbCreate() method returns the primary key type, and the container calls it before the database insert occurs. Notice that your method just returns null, which occurs to enable the container vendor to implement the persistence methods itself. You don't return a value, because the persistence occurs in the container. The container calls the ejbPostCreate() method after the database insert, and it returns void. You can use it to set up any aggregations that require the invoice row insert to already have occurred.

You're now done coding the bean class. Notice that you didn't need to code the EJB methods, but you did need to stub them out. All you do in ejbCreate() is set the primary key field, but you return a null and have the container return this value. Notice, too, that you don't need any `ejbFindBy` methods, as they all implement in the container. Before you look at configuring CMP entity beans, you next need to look at the CMP 2.0 bean class implementation.

Create a CMP 2.0 entity bean

Just as with the CMP 1.1 bean class, you start in 2.0 by implementing the `javax.ejb.EntityBean`. But instead of adding public attributes for container-managed fields, you must add abstract accessor methods to your class, as shown in Listing 7-28. You also stub out the other entity-bean methods, just as you do with CMP 1.1.

Listing 7-28: EJB 2.0 version of the InvoiceEBBean class

```
public class InvoiceEBBean implements EntityBean
{
    protected EntityContext        _context        = null;

    public void setEntityContext(EntityContext ctx)
    {
        _context = ctx;
    }

    public void unsetEntityContext()
    {
        _context = null;
    }

    public void ejbActivate()
    {
        // ...
    }

    public void ejbPassivate()
    {
        // ...
    }

    public void ejbRemove()
    {
        // ...
    }
```

Continued

Listing 7–28 *(Continued)*

```
public void ejbLoad()
{
    // ...
}

public void ejbStore()
{
    // ...
}

//
//    Create Methods
//
public Integer ejbCreate()
{
    // ...
    return null;
}

public void ejbPostCreate()
{
    // ...
}

//
//    Property setters and getters
//
public abstract Integer getNumber();
public abstract void     setNumber(Integer arg);
public abstract Date     getDate();
public abstract void     setDate(Date arg);
public abstract Integer    getTerms();
public abstract void     setTerms(Integer arg);
public abstract String   getCompany();
public abstract void     setCompany(String arg);
public abstract Collection getItems();
public abstract void addItem(InvoiceItemEBLocal item);

//
//    Business methods
//
```

```
public InvoiceVO getValues()
{
InvoiceVO    vo = new InvoiceVO();
vo.setNumber(this.getNumber());
vo.setDate(this.getDate());
vo.setTerms(this.getTerms());
vo.setCompany(this.getCompany());
}

public void setValues(InvoiceVO vo)
{
this.setNumber(vo.getNumber());
this.setDate(vo.getDate());
this.setTerms(vo.getTerms());
this.setCompany(vo.getCompany());
}

public Date calcDueDate()
{
    Calendar due = new GregorianCalendar();
    due.setTime(this.getDate());
    due.add(Calendar.DAY_OF_YEAR, this.getTerms().intValue());
    return due.getTIme();
}
}
```

Next, you look at the addition in 2.0 of *container-managed relationship fields* (cmr-fields). These fields enable you to add relationships to other entity beans into your model. You can add any of the following four basic types of relationships, and each one is either unidirectional or bidirectional:

- One-to-one

- One-to-many

- Many-to-one

- Many-to-many

Unidirectional means that navigation flows only one way in the relationship. *Bidirectional* means that both entities know and can navigate to the other entity (or entities) via the relationship.

Message-Driven Beans

I describe in earlier code examples in this chapter the synchronous messaging that session and entity EJBs provide a J2EE application server. The Java Messaging Service provides asynchronous messaging within J2EE. JMS is a *Message-Oriented Middleware* (*MOM*) approach that augments EJBs' request/reply, synchronous messaging. It's like having a post office to guarantee delivery of messages so that senders can go on about their business instead of waiting for a reply from the receiver. In Figure 7-17, I introduce the last bean of this chapter, `InvoiceProcessor`.

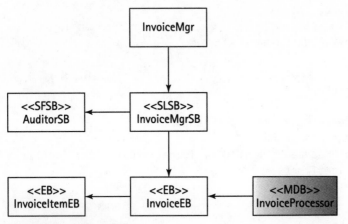

Figure 7-17: MDBs in use

Can't EJBs and JMS get along without message-driven beans (MDBs)? EJBs are very capable at sending JMS messages, but they can't receive JMS messages, mainly because they must remain available to service client requests. Remember that the application server doesn't permit users to create threads within the container. So the old method was to create a Java client to receive JMS messages and make EJB calls, but the client had to live outside the server.

Message-driven beans (MDBs) are the glue that enables asynchronous messages to invoke EJBs. MDBs are very useful, as applications often need to support both synchronous and asynchronous messaging. Your `InvoiceProcessor` MDB receives JMS messages that signify workflow changes for an invoice. To begin your message-driven bean (MDB), you start with the bean class. MDBs don't have remote or local interfaces. Nor do they need home or local-home interfaces. They're not distributed objects. These beans focus entirely on receiving messages from a JMS queue or topic, and that's how clients interact with them — by sending them a JMS message.

iAS 6.5 implements message-driven beans for developer-level support. MDBs in iAS 6.5 aren't intended for production usage. The iAS 6.5 developers guide gives a very good overview of MDBs.

In Listing 7-29, your bean class implements the `javax.ejb.MessageDrivenBean` and `javax.jms.MessageListener` interfaces, and you have a few methods to write. You need the `setMessageDrivenContext()` and no-argument `ejbCreate()` methods. These methods have no requirements, but they provide a place to obtain the context and set up the MDB on creation. All the work gets done in the `onMessage()` method, which passes in the JMS message. Here you can send JMS messages, call EJBs, and call resources.

Listing 7-29: InvoiceProcessorMDB implementation

```java
import java.rmi.*;
import java.util.*;

public class InvoiceProcessorMDB implements MessageDrivenBean
{
    protected MessageDrivenContext        _context        = null;
    private InvoiceEBLocal                 _home          =
null;

    public void setMessageDrivenContext(MessageDrivenContext ctx)
    {
        _context = ctx;
    }

    public void ejbCreate()
    {
        try
        {
            Context jndi = new InitialContext();
            _home = (InvoiceEBHomeLocal)PortableRemoteObject.narrow(
                jndi.lookup("InvoiceEBLocal"));
        }
        catch (Exception e)
        {
            throw new EJBException(e);
        }
    }
```

Continued

Listing 7-29 *(Continued)*

```
public void onMessage(Message msg)
{
    Integer    pk = Integer.parseInt(msg.getText());
    try
    {
    InvoiceEBLocal    inv = _home.findByPrimaryKey(pk);
        inv.setStatus("Sent");
    }
    catch (Exception e)
    {
        //log exceptions
    }
}
}
```

In Listings 7-30 and 7-31, you switch over to your deployment hat and configure the MDB in the deployment descriptor. Your main objective in the descriptor is to configure the JMS queue or topic that the MDB listens for messages on. You can also pool MDBs, which is useful if you're using JMS queues to enable the processing of multiple-queue messages at one time.

Listing 7-30: The standard MDB EJB descriptor

```
ejb-jar.xml:
    <message-driven>
        <ejb-name>InvoiceProcessorMDB</ejb-name>
        <ejb-class>com.invoicemgr.ejb.InvoiceProcessorMDB</ejb-
class>
        <transaction-type>Container</transaction-type>
        <message-selector></message-selector>
        <acknowledge-mode>Auto-acknowledge</acknowledge-mode>
        <message-driven-destination>
            <destination-type>javax.jms.Queue</destination-type>
        </message-driven-destination>
    </message-driven>
```

Listing 7-31: The iAS–specific MDB descriptor

```
<ias-ejb-jar>
  <ias-enterprise-bean>
    <ejb-name> InvoiceProcessorMDB </ejb-name>
    <message-driven-descriptor>
    <jms-destination>
```

```
      <jndi-name>MyMDB</jndi-name>
      <jms-topic-subscription>
        <durable>true</durable>
      </jms-topic-subscription>
    </jms-destination>
    <pool>
       <max-pool-size>100</max-pool-size>
       <min-pool-size>10</min-pool-size>
    </pool>
    </message-driven-descriptor>
  </ias-enterprise-bean>
</ias-ejb-jar>
```

Summary

In this chapter, I take you on a whirlwind tour of EJB development for iAS. The EJB features within the 6.5 version of iAS are mainly of the 1.1 EJB specification, with the exception of message-driven beans (2.0). You progressively build out your sample invoice manager, incorporating services of the declared variety and programmatic flavor. I top off this chapter with a primer of EJB 2.0 features that are present in the 7.0 iAS version.

Part III

Advanced Topics

Chapter 8

IDE Integration

IN THIS CHAPTER

◆ Identifying the day-to-day timesavings that IDE integrations make available

◆ Getting an overview of the IDEs that integrate with iAS

◆ Taking a tour of the Forte for Java IDE

THE IPLANET APPLICATION SERVER enjoys a great reputation on the operations side of the world for its enterprise-class scalability and fault tolerance. Yet, from a developer's perspective, development with iAS and an Integrated Development Environment (IDE) seems somewhat mysterious. In this chapter, you get some exposure to the variety of IDEs that have integrated iPlanet support.

IDEs for iPlanet Application Server

IDEs are long known for simplifying a developer's experience with coding and debugging exercises. As application servers become ubiquitous, IDEs are beginning to ship value-adding plug-ins that supply tight integrations with a variety of common application servers. Plug-ins supply features such as packaging, deployment, and remote debugging. As J2EE developers you're no longer simply in the compile/run/debug paradigm; you're now in the compile/package/deploy/run/debug paradigm (within an application server). This situation is definitely a little more involved than previously.

IDEs can help us cut down on the time, effort, and often error-prone nature of the latter paradigm. In the following sections, I contrast the iAS integration plug-ins that you find in the latest Forte for Java, Visual Cafe, and Together Control Center IDEs.

Forte for Java

Sun Microsystems offers the *Forte for Java IDE*. This IDE is actually a consumer-supportable version of the NetBeans open-source IDE. NetBeans is gaining share in the IDE market because of its rich feature set and attractive price (free). As it's a well-managed open-source project, its adoption of new features, bug fixes and other open-source technologies, such as Ant, are rapid. The NetBeans IDE is designed in such highly modular fashion that it's very extendable. Open-source developers and companies are creating plug-ins (or *modules*, as NetBeans calls them) to help advance the adoption of specifications such as J2EE and virtually any other Java-based framework. Sun Microsystems takes a snapshot of the NetBeans IDE source tree roughly every 90 days as a baseline for the Forte Java IDE.

The Forte for Java IDE product comes in a Community Edition (free) and an Enterprise Edition. At the time of the writing, Forte 4.0 is in beta and a third edition just released: the Mobile Edition. The Enterprise Edition includes Forte modules that enhance the iAS developer experience. Sun incorporates application packaging, deployment and debugging for iAS within this plug-in. I'll take you on a tour of this module in the section "Forte for Java Walkthrough," later in this chapter.

Figure 8-1 provides a good reference for the Forte IDE. The significant windows are present in this figure. The Explore Window navigates your project. The Properties Window enables you to configure settings on elements within your project. The Source editor is obviously where you modify code. And the Output Window displays the results of compiling, deploying, and executing your project (among other things).

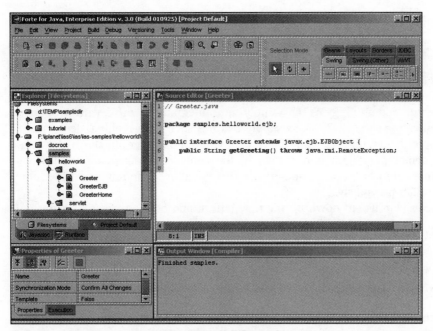

Figure 8-1: The Forte for Java IDE editing an EJB interface

In summary, the Forte for Java IDE offers a well-supported development platform, with plenty of documentation, developer support, and iPlanet value add-ons. On the negative side, because it's a 100-percent Java application, the memory and CPU requirements for the Forte editions aren't minimal. For best results, machines should have 512+ MB of memory and a modern Pentium processor (+500Mhz) or 450Mhz Sun-based platform.

 Those of you who are ahead of the Forte release curve can visit `http://netbeans.org`. You can find a free Community Edition and trial version of Enterprise Edition of Forte for Java at `http://forte.sun.com/ffj/index.html`.

WebGain Visual Cafe

The Visual Cafe (VC) IDE (see Figure 8-2) has a long history in the Java development world. Since the early Java days, Visual Cafe has supplied developers with a pretty solid IDE, compiler, and debugging environment. The advent of J2EE pushed Visual Cafe to incrementally add more developer support for J2EE components, servlets, JSP pages, and EJBs. To cater to the Visual Cafe market share, the iPlanet engineers created a plug-in that enables iAS module creation, packaging, deployment (local and remote), and debugging.

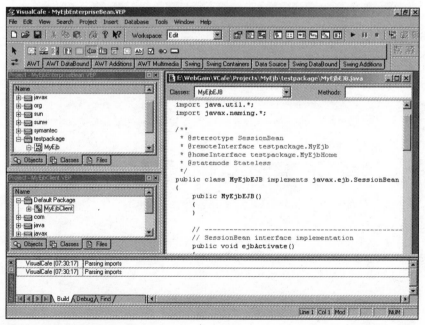

Figure 8-2: Visual Cafe IDE

Visual Cafe iAS tutorials for Session and Entity EJBs are at `http://docs.iplanet.com/docs/manuals/ide/#60`.

A quick summary of the iAS plug-in for Visual Cafe is that the plug-in supplied IDE penetration for iPlanet when Forte for Java didn't have the iAS integration it does today. The Visual Cafe market share with developers is large enough for iPlanet to maintain this plug-in. (But I'd expect iPlanet to build more momentum behind the Forte for Java IDE.)

Together Control Center

Together Control Center (TCC) is a Java-based Model-Build-Deploy development IDE (see Figure 8-3). TCC enables a developer to visually model applications by using Unified Modeling Language (UML) notation while supplying a development environment for code compilation and execution. TCC's clear distinction is that you can model your application code by using prebuilt templates and patterns in a visual way. If you need an EJB, for example, you use an EJB pattern and drop an EJB in your Class Diagram window. Under the covers, the tool's generated the necessary application code for the EJB. Then you can quickly switch over to an integrated code editor and fill in the business functionality for this EJB.

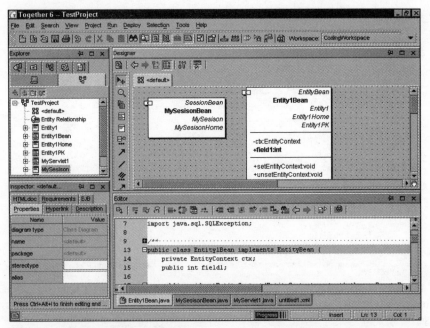

Figure 8-3: Together Control Center

The iAS integration that TogetherSoft offers is a basic package and deploy mechanism for local deployments only. The tool supplies editing of iAS descriptor settings on the deploy process. Overall, the integration with iAS isn't as substantial as Forte or Visual Cafe. The true strengths of Together Control Center lie in its modeling and code-synchronization features.

Forte for Java Walkthrough

In this section, I walk you through packaging and deploying a sample application from your local iAS installation by using the Forte for Java Enterprise Edition 3.0 IDE. From this exercise, you get a feel for the value adds that an IDE plug-in module for iAS can provide.

Although I use Windows 2000 to create this walkthrough, the Forte IDE fundamentals are the same for a Unix install. For best results, make sure that your local KAS process is running, as the Forte plug-in used this process to communicate to the iAS instance. See Chapter 1 for information on controlling your NT/2000 or Unix iAS instance.

You start with the HelloWorld application that ships with iAS. You can find the source for this application in the directory `<IAS HOME>/ias/ias-samples/helloworld`. The HelloWorld application consists of a Web-application module and an EJB module. The Web-application module includes JSP and servlet components (as well as some static content). The EJB module contains a stateless Session EJB component that performs the simple business logic for this application. From the IDE, you first package the respective modules from their components and then assemble the enterprise application and deploy it to a registered iAS instance. After deployment, you can then execute the HelloWorld application from within the Forte IDE.

 I tested this section by using iAS SP4 and the 1.1 version of the Forte plug-in. iAS SP2 and 3 should work as well. At the time of this writing, iAS 6.5 is just released. iPlanet should release an updated version of the plug-in to function with iAS 6.5 in the near future.

Configure the iAS plug-in (module)

Starting the Enterprise Edition of Forte for the first time activates the iAS plug-in (module) setup. The dialog box shown in Figure 8-4 prompts you for the location of your iAS installation. The path information enables the iAS module to access tools and JAR files, which augment the module functionality. After you successfully configure the iAS module, subsequent starts of the Forte tool don't prompt you with the iAS setup dialog box.

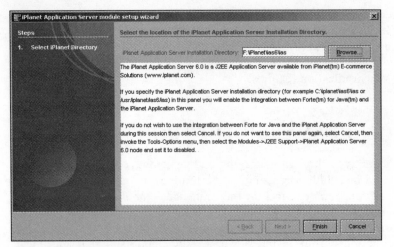

Figure 8-4: First-time startup of the iAS plug-in

You can configure all Forte plug-in modules from the Tools ➪ Options menu (including the iPlanet Application Server module).

After the Forte IDE starts, you can create your HelloWorld project by going to the project manager by choosing Project ➪ Project Manager from the menu bar. From the project manager, you create a new project that you call HelloWorld. After creating the project, you can register your iAS instance. This step enables you to use the registered iAS instance as a deployment and execution target. Figure 8-5 demonstrates the first step of adding a local iAS instance.

In Forte, every object has a set of properties that you can configure via the Properties window. Figure 8-6 shows the properties that are configurable for an iAS instance. The important properties to notice are the Connector URL and password.

Take time to notice the Properties window in Forte. Most of your work in the walkthrough involves configuring various properties for your application.

You can run the iASAT (administration) tool by right-clicking Launch AdminTool on the iAS instance from the Explorer Runtime tab.

After you configure your local iAS instance with Forte, you package your sample application.

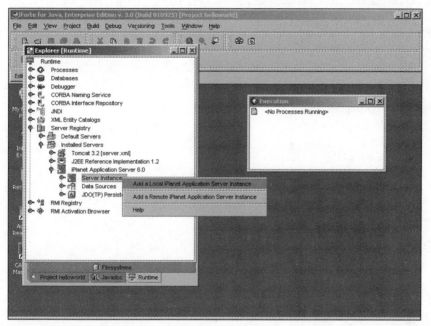

Figure 8-5: Notice the Explorer window and Runtime tab selection.

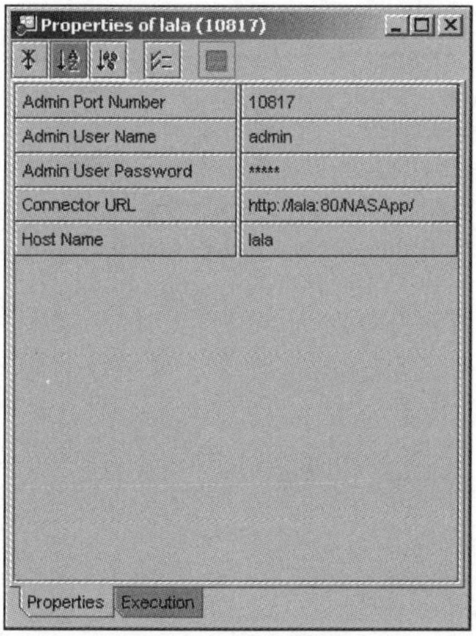

Figure 8-6: Configure the iAS instance settings.

Set up file-system application

Forte works on the premise that you can mount and unmount directory locations as necessary in any project. In your current project, you mount the source directory for the iAS sample application, HelloWorld. Mounting the HelloWorld directory requires you to right-click the Filesystems node in the Explorer window and choose Mount Directory from the pop-up menu. The top portion of Figure 8-7 shows the path to the helloworld source directory (`<IAS HOME>\ias\ias-samples\helloworld\src`).

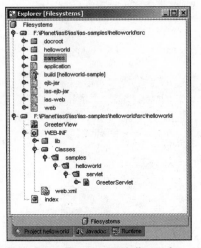

Figure 8-7: The mounted directories

The next mount point that you create is for the Web module in your application. First, create the HelloWorld package within the `src` mount point. The name of this directory is significant, as this directory represents a Web application. As you're executing web components within Forte, URLs are relative to this directory (just as for a real WAR file). Create the HelloWorld directory by right-clicking the `src` mount point and choosing New Package from the pop-up menu. Finally, right-click the newly created mount point and choose Tools → Convert Filesystem from the pop-up menu to complete your Web module creation. Figure 8-7 shows the resulting mount point.

See Chapter 5 for a reference on the structure of a WAR file.

The expanded Web module (HelloWorld) in the lower portion of Figure 8-7 shows the Web components GreeterView JSP at the root of the module and GreeterServlet nesting within its package structure under the WEB-INF/Classes directory. These components, as well as the index HTML, reside within the Web module to represent a well-formed WAR file. You must copy these files from the docroot and samples directories under the src mount point.

Package and assembly

After you set your mount points and no real coding work remains, you can package your Web and EJB modules. First, you construct the EJB component. Then you assemble the EJB module by adding the EJB component. As shown in Figure 8-8, you start by creating a Session Bean.

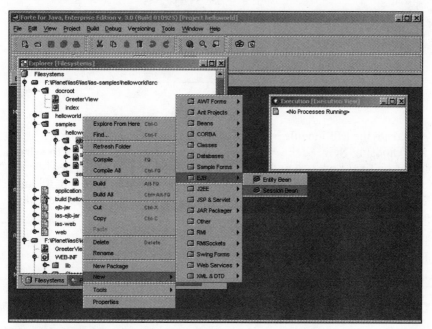

Figure 8-8: Selection of the Session Bean template

Forte includes numerous prebuilt templates that serve as wizards or starting points for components. You can access them by right-clicking any package in your project and choosing New from the pop-up menu.

Figure 8-8 starts an EJB wizard that you use to create a Stateless Session bean called TheGreeter from our existing Greeter Java files. The wizard enables you to select your existing files instead of any generated ones. Figure 8-9 shows the last step in the wizard process. Select the Modify button next to the related Bean class to select an existing source file.

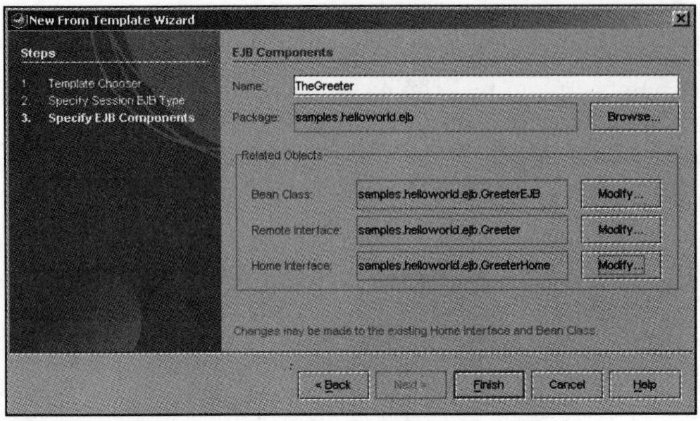

Figure 8-9: Notice the name and the related Objects.

Next you create the EJB module by right-clicking the samples/helloworld/ejb package and choosing New → J2EE → EJB Module from the pop-up menu to select the template. As a final step, you add the TheGreeter component to the newly created EJB module by right-clicking the helloworldEjb (as shown in Figure 8-10) and choosing Add EJB from the pop-up menu. Figure 8-10 shows the progress of your project in the Explorer window.

Figure 8-10: TheGreeter component packaged within helloworldEjb module

Viewing the properties for an EJB in the Properties Window enables you to edit all the deployment descriptor settings (including the iAS specific elements).

After you have your EJB component packaged, you must package the Web-application module. Because the Web module is a mount point as far as Forte is concerned (as I describe in the "Set up file-system application" section), the remaining efforts involve configuring the Web application's deployment descriptor. At a high level, you declare the GreeterServlet component and set up a reference to the TheGreeter EJB component.

Before you can declare the GreeterServlet, you first must help Forte distinguish this servlet from a regular Java class by marking it as a servlet. Right-click the GreeterServlet and choose Tools ⇨ Mark as Serlvet from the pop-up menu to ensure that the Forte recognizes GreeterServlet as a servlet in its subsequent wizards. Refer to Figure 8-7 to see the Explorer window with the GreeterServlet within the Web module. Declaring the GreeterServlet involves modification of the web.xml descriptor. Figure 8-11 shows the properties for the web.xml file. Right-click the web.xml file and choose Properties from the pop-up menu to proceed.

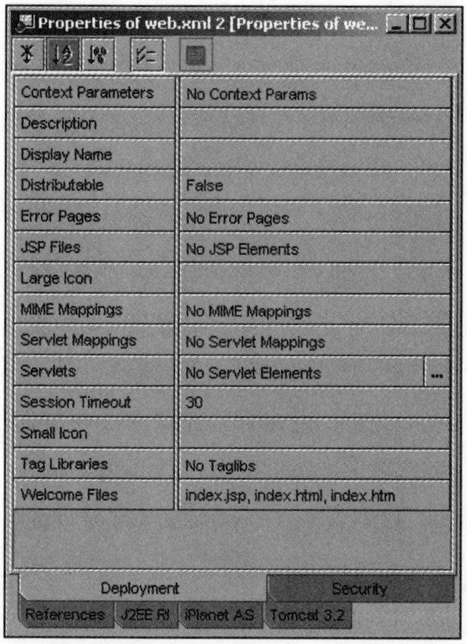

Properties of web.xml 2 [Properties of we...	
Context Parameters	No Context Params
Description	
Display Name	
Distributable	False
Error Pages	No Error Pages
JSP Files	No JSP Elements
Large Icon	
MIME Mappings	No MIME Mappings
Servlet Mappings	No Servlet Mappings
Servlets	No Servlet Elements
Session Timeout	30
Small Icon	
Tag Libraries	No Taglibs
Welcome Files	index.jsp, index.html, index.htm

Deployment | Security
References | J2EE RI | iPlanet AS | Tomcat 3.2

Figure 8-11: The deployment descriptor settings for your HelloWorld Web module

Next, you declare `GreeterServlet` by selecting the `Servlets property` from the web.xml Properties window. Figure 8-12 depicts the results of these steps.

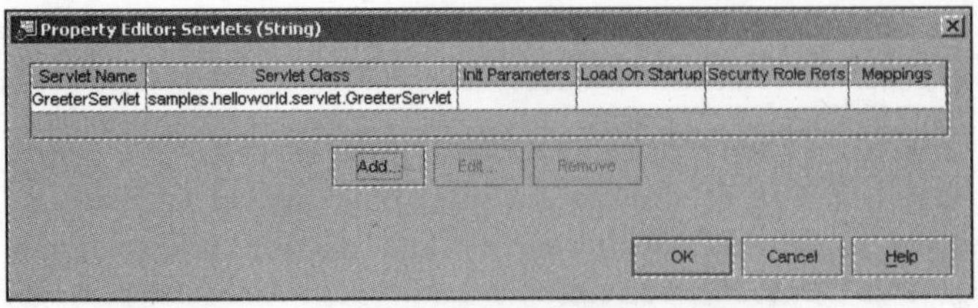

Figure 8-12: Declaring GreeterServlet with a Servlet class

Finally, you declare the EJB reference to your `TheGreeter` EJB component. You do so via the `web.xml` properties. Select the Reference tab of the Properties window and select the EJB References property. Figure 8-13 shows the accurate settings. Click the Browse button for the Referenced EJB Name to select the `TheGreeter` EJB from the `samples/helloworld/ejb` package. Notice that this action populates the remaining text boxes. For completion, select the iPlanet App Server tab and type the iPlanet Internal EJB Lookup JNDI Name `ejb/TheGreeter` in that text box.

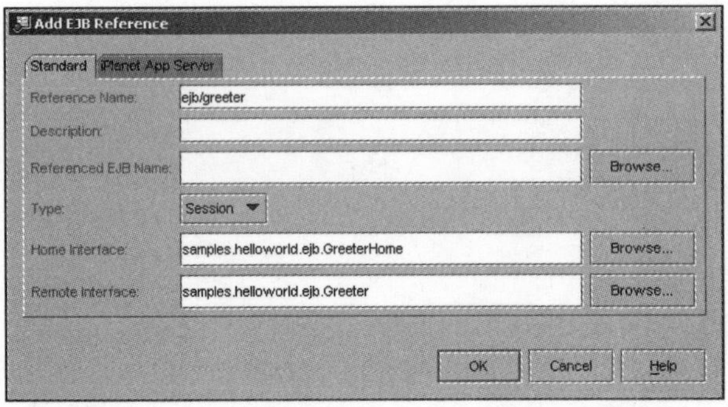

Figure 8-13: EJB reference settings for TheGreeter EJB

The last step remaining is to assemble the HelloWorld Enterprise Application. This involves packaging the War and Ejb[ES1]-Jar archives into an Enterprise Archive. Please reference chapter 5 for more details on this. Forte makes this remarkably simple. Right-click the `src` mount point and choose New → J2EE → Application from the pop-up menu and supply the name helloworld when prompted for the application name. Next, right-click the HelloWorld icon (the purple upward-pointing arrow) and choose Add Module. Figure 8-14 shows the appropriate selections to use for adding your modules.

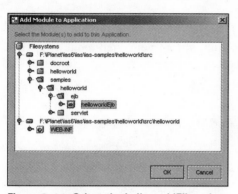

Figure 8-14: Select the helloworldEjb and
WEB-INF modules.

Deployment

The Forte IDE makes deployment very simple. Simply right-click the HelloWorld
application archive that you have created from the previous step and choose
Deploy from the pop-up menu. Figure 8-15 shows the deployment's progress. A
progress indicator will supply you with progress and actions that the module is performing. Under the covers the module is deploying and installing your Enterprise
application archive to iAS.

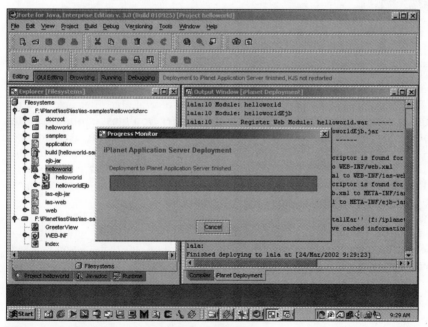

Figure 8-15: Deployment progress with diagnostics

Execute the application

The entry point for your HelloWorld application is from your Web module, in the form of the index HTML page. You use Forte to execute this page. Figure 8-16 shows your starting and end points.

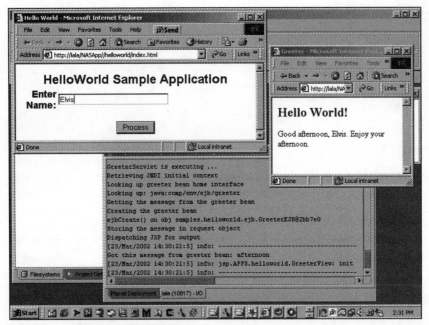

Figure 8–16: Before–and–after picture of your application

Forte has the ability to operate as more than one type of Web container. As depicted in Figure 8-17 we see that TomCat is also available. Because you're launching your application from the iAS Web container, you must configure Forte to use your iAS web container. Figure 8-17 shows the selection of the iAS instance from the WEB-INF Properties dialog box (on the Execution tab), choosing among the available Web containers. To finish, you must set the Context Root to helloworld (on the Properties tab). is[ES2] the URL that you use to launch any pages from your Web module reflects the Context Root setting.

Now you can simply right-click the index HTML page and choose Execute from the pop-up menu. Figure 8-16 demonstrates the application. Supply your name in the Name text box and click Process. In the background of Figure 8-16 you can see the Output window. It shows the output from the KJS process. This information can prove useful for debugging purposes.

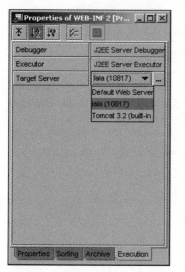

Figure 8-17: Selecting your iAS instance

 TIP   Right-click your iAS instance from the Runtime tab of the Explorer window and choose Server Status from the pop-up menu to issue start and stop commands to your instance.

The objective of this walkthrough is to point out some of the ways that an IDE that you plug into iAS can help aid your day-to-day development cycles. It isn't meant as a tutorial on Forte, because that subject could take up an entire book itself. Following are some of the highlights of Forte integration with iPlanet Application Server:

◆ Simplifies module packaging and application assembly

◆ Streamlines deployment

◆ Provides execution and debugging support

◆ Offers unified control and usage of an iAS instance

As a reader, you have plenty of room to experiment with this example. The wizards that you use to pull in existing code you can also use to create new components. You can do so in a very rapid fashion by using the prebuilt templates that come with Forte.

Summary

IDEs can play an important place in the lives of developers if you use them correctly. One important point to note is that IDEs shouldn't take the place of a canned package or build process such as those that ANT provides. In today's Information Technology world it has become acceptable that common ANT-based build files are to be shared via development, testing, and deployment teams. It's not realistic to have each of these organizations using a developer IDE. An IDE should be treated as one of the tools that a developer can have in his toolbox to aid in day-to-day J2EE development efforts.

Chapter 9

Behind the Scenes of Deployment

IN THIS CHAPTER

◆ Examining how iAS deploys code to the file system

◆ Tracing the execution of the deployment process

◆ Discussing typical deployment strategies

THE J2EE SPECIFICATION very much standardizes the format of an EAR file. But the vendor has almost complete autonomy about how to actually deploy EAR files into the file system of the application server. The person doing deployments (the deployer) views the deployment environment as a "black box" into which he deposits the EAR files.

This chapter explores how iPlanet Application Server's deployment "black box" works. This knowledge can help administrators manage their application servers, aid in debugging deployment problems, and aid in the design of production file systems.

Understanding Deployment Basics

For the purposes of this chapter, I'm using Unix conventions to discuss the file system, because the majority of production iAS systems run on Unix. Specifically, I use colons to separate directories in paths and forward slashes (/) to separate subdirectories. If you're using an NT system, just substitute semicolons for colons and backward slashes (\) for forward slashes.

I also refer to all directories relative to the location of $IAS_ROOT and Web server document root. $IAS_ROOT is the directory that you select during installation for the location of iAS. If you don't know your iAS root, you find a definition for it inside the iasenv.ksh script. For example, if you installed into /opt, then your iAS root might be /opt/ias6 and your Web server document root /opt/server4/docs.

The webserver document root defaults to the docs subdirectory under your webserver root. If you don't know the location of your webserver document root, you find a definition for it in the obj.conf file, starting with the following line:

```
NameTrans fn="document-root" root="your-document-root"
```

Remember that if you have your application server and Web servers running on different machines the webserver document root will reside on an entirely different machine than the $IAS_ROOT.

Modifying the Deployment Environment

The application server expects to control the deployment file system. iAS expects to have the rights to delete, overwrite, and completely control all the files that relate to the applications. You must be very careful, therefore, with any modifications that you make to the deployment environment. Accidentally changing a file permission or file ownership so that iAS can't access it results in serious (and difficult to debug) consequences.

Java Classloaders

When a JVM executes a Java application it loads the application classes on demand for execution. The classloader is the part of the JVM that retrieves Java class files and loads them into memory for execution. The classloader is actually a Java class itself and can be extended to provide additional functionality.

iPlanet Application Server, like all application servers, uses this ability to extend the classloader in order to container services. For example, the dynamic reloading feature of iAS is implemented by using a custom classloader, then checks for newer versions of the class.

Appendix B of the iPlanet Application Server Programmer's Guide goes into detail about the custom classloaders provided by iAS and how the classloaders interact with each other. The most important details to understand from that chapter are summarized in the following list:

◆ Each application gets its own classloader. This isolates each application and gives them their own namespace for Java packages. This prevents identically named classes from different applications from overwriting each other in memory.

◆ The application classloader loads all of its class files directly from class files on the disk, and not from JAR, WAR, or EAR files. The application classloader reads the classes from the unpacked classes under $IAS_ROOT/ias/APPS and not from the compressed versions under $IAS_ROOT/ias/JARS.

◆ Classes included in the system CLASSPATH are available to all applications, but are not dynamically reloaded even if dynamic classloading is enabled.

Understand, too, that the J2EE specification gives vendors complete control over the deployment environment. iPlanet can change the details of the deployment system of iAS at any time. Significant changes were made, for example, to how the classloader interacts with the file system between sp1b and sp2. The following section documents the iAS 6.5 deployment environment, but I can make no guarantees about how the environment may change in the future.

The Deployment File System

Although the J2EE specification encourages developers to regard the application server as a "black box," understanding the internals of the iPlanet Application Server's deployment file system offers many advantages. Developers need to understand the deployment file system so that they can utilize dynamic class reloading and troubleshoot problems in the structure of their WARs and JARs. Administrators need to understand the deployment file system so that they can harden their deployment environment and create scripts aware of the deployment file system.

Notice that the deployment file system is only half the deployment picture. The registry contains all the metadata regarding deployment. This setup limits your ability to directly manipulate the deployment file system. You can't just drop a new servlet into the deployment system, for example, without creating a corresponding entry in the iAS registry.

The following sections discuss each of the deployment file system's directories. I list the contents of each subdirectory as well as the possible uses for that directory to developers and administrators.

The JAR directory

The JAR directory ($IAS_ROOT/ias/JAR) is a subdirectory where iPlanet Application Server stores the JAR, WAR, and EAR files during processing. In iAS versions sp2 and later, the classloader doesn't use the JAR directory to actually load the running classes. It uses the JAR directory only during deployment and undeployment for the intermediate storage of files.

You can use the JAR directory to quickly inspect what applications you've deployed to your system. You can also use the APPS directory for this purpose, but the APPS directory contains more clutter and also doesn't enable you to see the JAR and WAR submodules. Additionally, the undeployment process removes applications that are undeployed from the APPS directory. The JAR, WAR, and EAR files of undeployed applications remain in the JAR directory.

Additionally, because the JAR directory contains the latest version of the deployed modules, it can prove useful in building scripts to manage iAS instances. A script on a test server, for example, may compare the EAR file in the JAR directory to the EAR file on a build server. If the script detects a difference between the two files, the script deploys the new version of the EAR on the QA server.

The deprecated `j2eeappreg` and `webappreg` tools don't use the JAR directory. The JAR directory is up to date only if you use the recommended `iasdeploy` and `deploytool` deployment methods.

The APPS directory

iPlanet Application Server uses the APPS directory (`$IAS_ROOT/ias/APPS`) for all deployed application server content, including class files, JSP files, deployment descriptors, and static content that will be served from the application server tier. The APPS directory itself consists of several system directories (`bin`, `jsp_extensions`, `GXApp`, and `System`), one subdirectory for each deployed EAR, and a `modules` subdirectory for all standalone WAR and JAR modules. iAS doesn't create the modules subdirectory until after the deployment of the first standalone module.

Figure 9-1 shows the directory structure for all the subdirectories under `$IAS_ROOT/ias/APPS`.

System subdirectories

iAS uses the following four system directories under the APPS subdirectory:

◆ `bin`: Currently unused — and should remain empty.

◆ `GXApp`: Used by the proprietary (AppLogic) sample applications. You often remove these directories in production servers to disable the sample applications.

◆ `jsp_extensions`: Used to store the tag library descriptors (TLD) and JARs for the iPlanet JSP `taglib` extensions. (Review Chapter 6 for information about `taglib` extensions.) You don't want to modify the existing TLD and JARs, but you may add your own custom JSP extensions here.

◆ `System`: Used by the application server to house its internal components. You shouldn't modify these files. Some files in this directory are there only to provide backward compatibility with previous versions of iAS.

EAR subdirectories

Each time that you deploy an EAR file to iPlanet Application Server, the server creates a subdirectory under the APPS directory with the same name as the EAR file but without the `.ear` extension. Notice that this process makes the filename of your EAR file significant, because each EAR that you deploy on the server must have a unique filename.

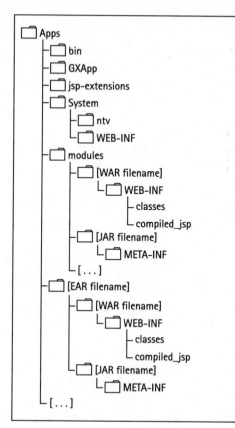

Figure 9-1: APPS subdirectories

The application server then creates additional subdirectories under the EAR file directory for each module, WAR, or JAR within that EAR. Similar to what it does for the EAR directory, the server creates each of these subdirectories with the same name as the filename of the WAR or JAR file but without the extension.

This convention of naming directories requires that each EAR filename is unique. It also requires that WAR and JAR modules within an EAR have unique names within their applications.

First-time iAS developers often place all the Web components in a `myapp.war` Web module and all their EJB components in a `myapp.jar` EJB JAR. This setup causes deployment to fail (without warning), as the Web module and EJB module overwrite each other's subdirectories. To solve this problem, one can name the packages `myapp.war`, `myappEjb.jar`, and `myapp.ear`.

The module subdirectory

iPlanet Application Server uses the module subdirectory under the APPS directory to store all the standalone WAR and EJB modules that you deploy to the server. (iAS creates the module subdirectory only after you deploy the first module.) You can deploy standalone modules to iAS by using the `iasdeploy deploymodule` command.

The module directory contains WAR and JAR subdirectories in the same format as if you deployed them in an EAR file. Module based deployment has the same requirement for filename uniqueness as application based deployment.

WAR subdirectories

The application creates a subdirectory for each WAR file. It creates the subdirectory under the modules directory if you deploy the WAR file as a standalone module by using the `iasdeploy deploymodule` command or under the EAR directory if the WAR file is a submodule of an EAR. The subdirectory for the WAR file contains an unpacked copy of all the files in the WAR. The files unpacked with the same directory structure with which you JAR them. This process typically places the root of the JSPs and static content in the WAR subdirectory and all the classes and metadata in a special `WEB-INF` directory.

`WEB-INF` is special because it's hidden from the user's direct requests. You can use the `http://localhost/NASApp/chapter5/index.html` URL, for example, to download the static `index.html` file in the `$IAS_ROOT/ias/APPS/chapter5/chapter5` directory, but you can't use `http://localhost/NASApp/chapter5/WEB-INF/web.xml` to download the deployment descriptor, because the `WEB-INF` directory is hidden.

The `WEB-INF` directory contains the `web.xml` and `ias-web.xml` deployment descriptors. It also contains a `classes` subdirectory that serves the `root` directory for application classes. The server organizes these classes under the `classes` subdirectory, based on your package structure.

Changing the `web.xml` and `ias-web.xml` deployment descriptors in the deployment directories doesn't change the deployment characteristics of the application. To change an application's deployment descriptors, you need to redeploy the application. (An alternative is to edit the registry, as I describe in Chapter 13, but doing so doesn't update the files in the deployment directories.)

iAS also creates a directory under the WEB-INF directory that it names compiled_jsp, which is for use by the JSP compiler. It actually stores all the JSP compiler files two subdirectory levels deeper, under WEB-INF/compiled_jsp/jsp/APPS, because iAS places all compiled JSPs in a jsp.APPS.*yourappname* package. You can find both the intermediate .java file and the final compiled .class file in this directory.

The compiled_jsp/jsp/APPS directory can prove useful as you're debugging JSPs. The .java files in that directory show you the servlet code that the JSP compiler generates. Your JSP code interlaces in the servlet code as comments so that you can more easily match your original code with the compiler's generated code.

Other directories may also reside under the WEB-INF directory depending on how you build your WAR. You often place prebuilt JAR libraries, for example, in a lib subdirectory if you store them in WAR files. Property files can also go under WEB-INF in a props directory — for example . . .

```
WEB-INF/lib
WEB-INF/props
WEB-INF/classes.
```

JAR subdirectories

The application creates a subdirectory for each EJB JAR file. It creates the subdirectory under the modules directory if you deploy the JAR file as a standalone module by using the iasdeploy deploymodule command or under the EAR directory if the JAR file is a submodule of an EAR.

Just as WAR subdirectories contain an unpacked version of the WAR files, JAR subdirectories contain an unpacked version of the EJB JAR. The JAR contains a META-INF subdirectory, which you use to store the EJB deployment descriptors. The JAR subdirectory is also the root of all the EJB related files, which reside under the JAR subdirectory according to their package structure. (Notice that this is unlike the WAR file, where the root for source files is the WEB-INF/classes directory.) Stubs and skeletons for the EJBs also come with the class files.

Just as you can't edit the Web deployment descriptors in place in the WAR subdirectory, you can't edit EJB deployment descriptors in place in the JAR subdirectory. The server ignores any changes that you make to the files. Redeploy your application or change the registry if you need to alter your deployment characteristics.

Tracing Deployment

The capability to trace the deployment of an application from end to end helps you to understand, troubleshoot, and optimize the deployment process. This section traces the process of deploying an application from a developer's workstation to a production server.

The same general principle applies to deploying applications to an iAS server running on the same workstation. Even if you invoke it locally, the iasdeploy command still connects via TCP/IP to the KAS server just as if it were a remote client. This proxying by the KAS process is useful because it prevents issues with file ownership, as the KAS process acts as a proxy for all deployment actions.

The same process for deploying applications also applies, in a general sense, to deploying modules. The primary difference is that you deploy the class files under the modules directory, and the deployment process creates no registry entry under SOFTWARE\iPlanet\Application Server\6.5\J2EE-Application.

Executing iasdeploy

iasdeploy is the command-line utility that you use to deploy applications, modules, and datasources, as I describe in Chapter 5. The KAS process then acts as a proxy for the deployment, performing the tasks that iasdeploy requests.

iasdeploy takes subcommands to perform all the deployment-related tasks. (Invoking iasdeploy without any parameters creates a list of all the available subcommands.) The most important of these subcommands are deployapp, for deploying applications, and removeapp, for undeploying applications. The deploymodule and removemodule subcommands are also available for deploying standalone WAR and EJB-JAR modules.

Several iasdeploy options also are available. The options enable you to specify the iAS server to deploy to and the authentication credentials that you want to provide to that iAS server. You can provide these options manually by specifying a host, port, user, and password. You can also provide them by using an instance name that you first register in the iPlanet Administration Tool (ksvradmin). You can specify one of your registered servers by using the instance option. If you don't specify any options, iasdeploy uses the first server that you register in ksvradmin, if one is available.

The following are several examples of iasdeploy usage:

◆ iasdeploy deployapp -user admin -password admin -host chico.hungryminds.com -port 10817 chapter9.ear — This command deploys chapter9.ear by using manually specified parameters. This syntax is useful in production scripts where you can't always execute GUI tools such as ksvradmin.

- ◆ `iasdeploy deployapp -instance iAS1 chapter9.ear` — This syntax is much more convenient, leveraging server information that you've already registered in `ksvradmin` with the name `iAS1`.

- ◆ `iasdeploy deployapp chapter9.ear` — This syntax deploys an EAR file by using the default server obtained from the first server registered in `ksvradmin`. This syntax is good for developers who spend most of their time deploying to their local server. If you haven't registered any servers in `ksvradmin`, this command results in a `No servers registered in the registry` error message.

- ◆ `iasdeploy removeapp -instance iAS1` — This command removes the `chapter9` application from the registry and moves the `chapter9` files under `APPS` to the trash directory.

In short, `iasdeploy` provides a unified way of performing application deployment, regardless of whether deployment is local or remote, EAR-based or module-based. The `iasdeploy` command also has the advantage of using the KAS process as a proxy for its actions so that file ownership and file-system security issues aren't a concern.

Deployment authentication

The first task that the KAS process performs when you use the iasdeploy command is to check to make sure that the user has the authority to deploy new applications. To deploy an application, the user must have a matching username/password in the LDAP server and belong to both the `ADMIN` and `DEPLOY` access-control groups.

AUTHORIZING ADDITIONAL DEPLOYMENT USERS

The admin user that the installer creates as you install the server automatically receives `ADMIN` and `DEPLOY` rights. To give additional users deployment rights, you can create the user in the LDAP administration console and then grant that user the `ADMIN` and `DEPLOY` privileges. (You can find more information on creating LDAP users in Chapter 4 of the Admin Server Guide. I provide a link to the guide at the end of this chapter.)

You can give users the `ADMIN` and `DEPLOY` privileges by using the Security tab of the administration tool. Clicking the Security tab displays a list of all Access Control lists. Highlighting the iAS Administration and iAS Deployment items in the list and selecting Modify enables you to grant and remove these privileges from users and LDAP groups.

Another, undocumented way to grant users `ADMIN` and `DEPLOY` rights is via `kreg` and the `nasdomain.gxr` file, which you can find in the `$IAS_ROOT/ias/registry` directory. Edit `nasdomain.gxr` to add your new users under both the `ADMIN` and

DEPLOY entries. Then register the modified file by using the `kreg nasdomain.gxr` command. Listing 9-1 shows a `nasdomain.gxr` file that I modified to add two new users.

Listing 9-1: Modified nasdomain.gxr registry file

```
ACL iAS Administration        | ACL that authorizes Enterprise Administration
admin,ADMIN
newuser1,ADMIN
newuser2,ADMIN


ACL iAS Deployment            | ACL that authorizes application deployment fu
admin,DEPLOY
newuser1,DEPLOY
newuser2,DEPLOY
```

MONITORING DEPLOYMENT AUTHENTICATION

You can monitor administrators logging into the KAS process by watching the KAS log. Successful logins display an `info: ADMIN-008: kas> login of server administrator` message. Login failures display `ADMIN-010: kas> error: invalid administrator password!`, among other messages.

Unfortunately, the KAS log doesn't record the username of users if they successfully authenticate for the purpose of deployment. If you're trying to create an audit log of the users who deploy applications, you must correlate the KAS log with the LDAP server's access log. If you examine your LDAP access log (`$IAS_ROOT/slapd-hostname/logs`) after a deployment, you see the application server perform the following steps:

1. Bind to the application server as the user.

2. Unbind immediately. (The application server is just verifying that the username/password is valid by binding as that user.)

3. Find the administration ACL under the list of ACLs (by using its own LDAP connection).

4. Retrieve the value of the Administration ACL.

5. Find the deployment ACL under the list of ACLs.

6. Retrieve the value of the Deployment ACL.

Listing 9-2 shows an excerpt from the LDAP access log during deployment. Remember that, if you're using your LDAP server for other purposes (personalization, configuration, authorization, or anything else) or if additional activity is taking place on your application server, other LDAP requests may appear interlaced with these deployment queries. I've omitted the timestamps from the listing for brevity; all these queries took place in less than a second.

Listing 9-2: LDAP access log entries during deployment authorization

```
conn=301 op=0 BIND dn="uid=admin,ou=People,o=hungryminds.com" method=128
version=3
conn=301 op=0 RESULT err=0 tag=97 nentries=0 etime=0
conn=301 op=1 UNBIND
conn=301 op=1 fd=55 closed - U1
conn=286 op=167 SRCH base="cn=DB0,cn=ACL,cn=6.5,cn=Application
Server,cn=iPlanet, cn=SOFTWARE,
n=global,cn=iasconfig,cn=iAScluster,o=NetscapeRoot scope=0 filter=
"(objectclass=*)"
conn=286 op=167 RESULT err=0 tag=101 nentries=1 etime=0
conn=286 op=168 SRCH base="cn=iAS
Administration,cn=DB0,cn=ACL,cn=6.5,cn=Application
Server,cn=iPlanet,cn=SOFTWARE,
cn=global,cn=iasconfig,cn=iAScluster,o=NetscapeRoot" scope=0 filter=
"(!(nsvaluecis=*))" conn=286 op=168 RESULT err=0 tag=101 nentries=1 etime=0
conn=286 op=173 SRCH
base="cn=DB0,cn=ACL,cn=6.5,cn=ApplicationServer,cn=iPlanet,cn=SOFTWARE,cn=global
,
cn=iasconfig,cn=iAScluster,o=NetscapeRoot" scope=0 filter="(objectclass=*)"
conn=286 op=173 RESULT err=0 tag=101 nentries=1 etime=0
conn=286 op=174 SRCH base="cn=iAS Deployment,cn=DB0,cn=ACL,cn=6.5,cn=Application
Server,cn=iPlanet,cn=SOFTWARE,cn=global,cn=iasconfig,cn=iAScluster,
o=NetscapeRoot" scope=0 filter="(!(nsvaluecis=*))"
conn=286 op=174 RESULT err=0 tag=101 nentries=1 etime=0
conn=286 op=175 SRCH base="cn=DataString,cn=iAS Deployment,cn=DB0,cn=ACL,cn=6.5,
cn=Application Server,cn=iPlanet,cn=SOFTWARE,cn=global,cn=iasconfig,
cn=iAScluster, o=NetscapeRoot" scope=0 filter="(nsvaluecis=*)"
conn=286 op=175 RESULT err=0 tag=101 nentries=1 etime=0
```

The LDAP access log can be useful in both understanding the LDAP registry system and troubleshooting problems during deployment. If you are ever uncertain about what information is being stored in LDAP, or when that information is accessed, you can always check the raw data found in the LDAP logs to find out the exact details. Similarly, if the application server is having trouble connecting to LDAP, or is failing to find a piece of configuration information, the LDAP log is the first step towards determining the cause of the problem.

File transmission

iasdeploy sends the EAR file to the KAS process by using ordinary TCP/IP communication. Notice that this TCP/IP transmission occurs even if you deploy the file locally. (If you are deploying locally, you can bypass this TCP/IP communication by using j2eeappreg rather than iasdeploy. I do not recommend this, however. j2eeappreg is not only deprecated, but it also skips several deployment steps such as making backup copies.)

Because the iasdeploy command enables users to deploy files remotely by using the KAS process as a proxy, users don't need a user account on an iAS server to deploy applications to it. Similarly, users don't need access to FTP, SMB (the Windows file-sharing protocol), NFS, or other file-transfer protocols. This capability of iasdeploy to transmit files directly is especially useful on hardened production servers where these protocols may be disabled.

After the KAS process receives the file from iasdeploy, it stores it in the $IAS_ROOT/ias/JAR directory. Remember that the KAS uses the JAR directory as a working directory during deployment. If you store your own copies of the EAR files in the JAR directory on a Unix system, the KAS process may run into permission problems as it attempts to overwrite your files because of permission issues.

MONITORING FILE TRANSMISSION

The KAS log indicates when it receives a file from iasdeploy by displaying an ADMIN-015: kas> deployment: file receive message. Although the ADMIN-015 doesn't include the actual filename that it receives, the next step of the registration process reveals the filename of the EAR file that the KAS process is deploying.

Submodules extraction

After the KAS process receives the EAR file from iasdeploy, it executes the j2eeappreg command on the newly received file. j2eeappreg is the utility that performs the work of application deployment.

j2eeappreg extracts the submodules (WARs and EJB JARs) from the EAR file and also places them in the JAR directory. It then takes the contents of those submodules and explodes them under the APPS directory, as I describe in the section "The Deployment File System," earlier in this chapter, where I discuss the deployment file system.

An important point to notice is that deploying an application doesn't remove any previous versions of an application from the file system. So if you delete a class or other file from your application, you should undeploy your application before redeploying it. Doing so clears your file system of the unwanted files and also removes any old descriptor entries in the registry.

MONITORING SUBMODULE EXTRACTION

j2eeappreg places messages in the KAS log to record its activities. One easy message to observe is the

```
info: ADMIN-159: kas> deployment action ''J2EEInstallEar''
```

message that logs after you invoke j2eeappreg. The ADMIN-159 message also logs the name of the EAR file that the server is registering.

This ADMIN-159 message logs any time that you invoke j2eeappreg, regardless of whether j2eeappreg is in deploy mode or undeploy mode. One way to determine whether an ADMIN-159 message is a deployapp or a removeapp is to examine the line immediately preceding the ADMIN-159 message. If the previous message is an ADMIN-015: kas> deployment: file receive message, a new file was received for deployment, and the current action is a deployapp. If you find no file receive message, the current action is a removeapp.

Registry updates

j2eeappreg also performs the work of updating the iAS registry while it deploys the contents of the EAR file to the file system. The five main areas of the registry that update during application deployment are as follows:

◆ The server updates SOFTWARE\iPlanet\Application Server\6.5\CCSO\ HTTPAPI\ServletPatternTrans to include any new servlet mappings.

◆ The sever adds new EJB components to the SOFTWARE\iPlanet\ Application Server\6.5\EJB-Components registry key. Notice that this fact implies that you have a global namespace for EJBs. You must uniquely name EJBs across all iAS instances by using the same registry.

◆ The server adds the application information to the SOFTWARE\iPlanet\ Application Server\6.5\J2EE-Application key, including the information in the application.xml deployment descriptor.

◆ The server store submodule information in the SOFTWARE\iPlanet\ Application Server\6.5\J2EE-Module key.

◆ The server adds information about individual components to the GUID database (SOFTWARE\iPlanet\Application Server\ClassDef, SOFTWARE\ iPlanet\Application Server\ClassImp, and SOFTWARE\iPlanet\ Application Server\NameTrans), as follows:

- NameTrans enables the server to translate requests for components into GUIDs.

- ClassImp stores information about the implementation of components, such as which module they belong to, where you can find their component class files, and what type of component they are.

- ClassDef stores the component metadata, including the information in the deployment descriptors specific to that component. (The ClassDef key also includes information about how the component is partitioned in the cluster.)

For more information about the registry, and how the registry stores application information, see Chapter 13.

The registry updates during application deployment can place a significant load on the LDAP server. Even more significant than the CPU load on the LDAP server is the amount of temporary disk space that the LDAP server uses to store its checkpoint logs. Depending on the size of your application, the directory server may use hundreds of megabytes of temporary storage during deployments and undeployments.

The LDAP server defaults to executing a checkpoint every 60 seconds. The checkpoint flushes the checkpoint logs, releasing the temporary storage. Reducing the amount of time between checkpoints reduces the amount of space that the checkpoint logs use.

If you're using your LDAP server only for storing your iAS configuration, you may want to reduce the checkpoint interval. The increase in overhead to process the additional checkpoints is usually negligible, and the reduction in checkpoint log size may prove helpful.

Change the checkpoint interval to 10 seconds by changing the `nsslapd-db-checkpoint-interval` setting in the `$IAS_ROOT/ias6/slapd-`*servername*`/config/dse.ldif` configuration file. (The directory server must be offline to make this change.)

You can find more information on changing the checkpoint interval and about other directory tuning parameters in the Directory Server Admin Guide. A link to the online documentation appears at the end of this chapter.

Understanding how the registry stores component metadata enables you to make manual changes to that information by using the registry editor. It also gives you a better capability to troubleshoot deployment problems. If two components have the same GUID, for example, they appear to deploy successfully. But they don't execute correctly because the second component overwrites the `ClassDef` and `ClassImp` entries of the first component. Inspecting these entries manually, however, quickly reveals the duplicate GUID problem.

If you are looking for information on a specific component, you can look up its GUID from your deployment descriptors, or under the J2EE-Modules section of the registry. (EJBs will be under an `ejbs` subkey and servlets/JSPs will be under a `servlets` subkey.) You can then use the GUID to look up the registry for that component under the `ClassDef` and `ClassImp` keys.

MONITORING REGISTRY UPDATES

The LDAP access log shows all updates that the server makes to the central LDAP portion of the registry. Searching for `ClassDef` or `NameTrans` in the access logs shows each component's updates.

The `reg.dat` file (on Unix) or the NT registry shows any changes that you make to the local portion of the registry. To monitor the changes that you make to the registry, you can make a backup of the local registry before deployment and then compare it with the local registry after deployment. The local directory stores the `ClassImp` information, which changes with each deployment.

JSP compilation

As I discuss in Chapter 6, JSPs are a combination of HTML and Java code that iAS compiles into servlets on demand at run time. iPlanet Application Server doesn't perform this compilation until the first request for that JSP. So, even after `iasdeploy` finishes execution, the application doesn't completely compile until user invokes all the JSPs and converts them into servlets.

JSP compilation is a two-phase process: First, iAS compiles the JSP file into pure Java code by using the Jasper JSP compiler. This compiler converts the JSP file that you place in the `root` directory of the deployed Web module into a `.java` file that it locates in the `WEB-INF/compiled_jsp/jsp/APPS/web-module` subdirectory of that module's `root`. Second, iAS compiles this `.java` file into a `.class` file by using the JDK Java compiler.

JSP Compiler Security Concerns

Occasionally, operations groups object to the fact that the JSP compiler compiles JSPs on demand because of a corporate policy about having compilers on hardened production boxes. (The value of such a policy is questionable.) Accommodating this type of policy is possible if you use the command-line JSP compiler to precompile all of the JSP files.

This approach makes deployment considerably more difficult, however, as you must precompile the JSP files on a different server. You must then manually copy the compiled `.java` and `.class` files to the `compiled_jsp` directory of the production server.

You can then disable the JSP compiler and Java compiler on the application server by removing the `jspc` and `javac` programs. This configuration isn't an officially supported iAS configuration, however, as it's an error-prone deployment process that involves intentionally breaking the JSP compilation functionality of the server.

BACKWARDS JSP COMPILER COMPATIBILITY

Versions of iPlanet Application Server prior to sp3 used an internal JSP compiler rather than the standalone Jasper compiler. The Jasper compiler enforces strict JSP syntax and also generates Java code that differs slightly from that of the internal JSP compiler.

If migrating from the internal compiler to the Jasper compiler is causing difficulty, you can direct iPlanet Application Server to use the older JSP compiler. You can enable the internal JSP compiler by passing the `DIAS_JSPSTRICT=false` argument to the KJS engine. You can find information about passing this argument and information about the differences between Jasper and the internal compiler in the iASsp3 release notes.

MONITORING JSP COMPILATION

The JSP compiler doesn't generate any log files and executes on demand as individual JSPs are requested. You can inspect the `compiled_jsp` directory, however, to determine which JSPs have compiled and to debug the generated Java code.

Inspecting the Java files that generate in the `compiled_jsp` can prove very useful as you're debugging JSPs. Some IDEs can use the Java source files to enable you to step through the generated servlet code. Even without an IDE, the generated comments can also prove very helpful in tracing JSP execution. The JSP compiler includes line numbers of the original JSP source as comments in the generated Java, making the process of correlating the generated Java with the JSP sourceeasier.

Listing 4-3, for example, shows an excerpt from the `TestJSP.jsp` JSP in the `chapter9` sample application. Listing 4-4 shows the Java code that the Jasper JSP compiler generates from the JSP excerpt.

Listing 9–3: Excerpt from the source of TestJSP.jsp

```
<p>Today's date is : <%= myDate %></p>
<p>The day of the week is :
<% SimpleDateFormat fmt = new SimpleDateFormat("EEEEEEEE");
   out.println(fmt.format(myDate)); %></p>
</body></html>
```

Listing 9–4: Excerpt from the servlet Java code generated from TestJSP.jsp

```
        // HTML // begin [file="/export/home/apps/ias1/ias/APPS/chapter9/cha
pter9/TestJSP.jsp";from=(11,34);to=(13,0)]
            out.write("</p>\r\n<p>The day of the week is : \r\n");
        // end
        // begin [file="/export/home/apps/ias1/ias/APPS/chapter9/chapter9/Te
stJSP.jsp";from=(13,2);to=(14,36)]
            SimpleDateFormat fmt = new SimpleDateFormat("EEEEEEEE");
              out.println(fmt.format(myDate));
```

```
            // end
            // HTML // begin [file="/export/home/apps/ias1/ias/APPS/chapter9/cha
pter9/TestJSP.jsp";from=(14,38);to=(18,0)]
                out.write("</p>\r\n</body></html>\r\n\r\n\r\n");
```

Notice that the generated Java code includes comments that correlate the servlet code with the corresponding JSP code. The first comment in the Java code indicates that the following `println` statement was generated from line 11, character 34, through line 13, character 0, of the JSP source. This excerpt also shows how the Jasper compiler converts ordinary HTML into `println` statements and embeds the JSP scriptlets in between those statements.

Undeployment

The `removeapp` and `removemodule` subcommands of `iasdeploy` enable you to remove applications and modules from the application server. These commands reverse the deployment process , removing files from the APPS directory and deleting corresponding entries from the registry.

During undeployment, the application's file system under APPS moves to a timestamped directory under `$IAS_ROOT/ias/trash`, instead of being deleted. This directory enables you to recover any files that you accidentally remove during undeployment. Notice that the JAR files remain in the `$IAS_ROOT/ias/JAR` directory. This feature enables you to easily redeploy the application by invoking `iasdeploy` on the leftover EAR file.

MONITORING UNDEPLOYMENT

You can observe the undeployment steps by following the inverse of the steps that you use to monitor deployment. You can monitor the filesystem and LDAP logs, for example, to watch the undeploy process remove the application files and registry entries.

Summary of Deployment

The `iasdeploy` command performs the following steps after you invoke it to register an EAR file:

1. Connects to the KAS process.

2. Presents the user's authentication credentials.

3. Transmits the EAR file to the application server.

4. Invokes the `j2eeappreg` registration tool on the application server (via KAS).

The KAS process is responsible for the following deployment steps:

1. Saving the EAR file in the JAR directory.

2. UnJARing the submodules into the JAR directory.

3. UnJARing the contents of the submodules into their own subdirectories of the APPS file system (via `j2eeappreg`).

4. Registering the deployment descriptors and modules into the registry (via `j2eeappreg`).

5. Registering the individual components into the registry (via `j2eeappreg`).

The application server has the following deployment-related responsibilities:

1. Checking the timestamp of class files to determine whether they need to dynamically reload them. (If dynamic classloading is enabled.) (I discuss dynamic classloading further in the "Hot deployment" section later in this chapter.)

2. Compiling JSPs on demand.

Deployment Strategies

As part of your deployment processes you need to make several fundamental philosophical decisions about your deployment architecture. One important decision is how to handle your application's external dependencies. I discuss the issues regarding this decision below in "The Philosophy of Self-Contained Packaging."

Another important deployment decision is about how to handle static content. Deploying static content in your EAR file is a waste of server resources. However, removing the static content from the EAR increases the external dependencies of your application.

The Philosophy of Self-Contained Packaging

Chapter 8.1.3 of the J2EE specification indicates that the application EAR file shouldn't depend on the existence of any packages other than those that the J2EE specification mandates. The goal of this recommendation is to ensure that the EAR files are easily portable. In an ideal world, deployment of an application is as simple as a one-line command against the EAR file. A common practice, however, is for EAR files to have external dependencies. Even in the best cases, EAR files are often dependent on external resources such as datasources and external drivers. And in many cases, application packagers intentionally make their EAR files dependent on reusable utility packages that they know are present on the target server. (See the section "Deploying reusable code," later in this chapter, for more discussion about the advantages and disadvantages of this practice.)

Self-contained packaging is an admirable goal but often isn't realistically achievable in the enterprise environment. In planning your deployment environment, you must realize that self-contained packaging isn't a reality yet. Fully document the resources available to your server's deployment. This process includes documenting the following information for your application packagers:

◆ All the datasources available on the machine, including the JNDI information necessary to access those datasources.

◆ All the EJBs that are deployed as common components, including the JNDI information for those beans.

◆ Any Java packages that you've added to the server CLASSPATH either by modifying $IAS_ROOT/ias/env/iasenv.sh (on UNIX) or the SOFTWARE/ iPlanet/Application Server/6.5/Java/Classpath registry key (on Windows).

◆ The IP and port numbers of all the KXS processes in your iAS clusters. (This information is a requirement for specifying the clustering information in the Web component's deployment descriptors.)

◆ Information about the LDAP users and groups that you can expect to exist in the LDAP directory. (This information is a requirement for mapping application roles to LDAP groups and users.)

◆ Any other information about resources available to the server, such as installed connectors or JMS providers.

With these caveats in mind, you should still try to enforce the spirit of the J2EE recommendations about self-contained packaging. Resources that are application-specific you should package with the application. Resources that are server or cluster wide you should install at the server level.

Deploying static content

Many of the samples that I include in this book and that come with iPlanet Application Server use the application server to serve static content. The index. html file that I include in the chapter9 sample, for example, you deploy and serve from the application server.

You access the index.html file by the http://webserver/NASApp/chapter9/ index.html URL. The Web server detects the NASApp token and forwards the request to the application server. The application server then uses a system servlet, StaticServlet, to return the contents of the HTML file.

DISADVANTAGES OF USING IAS FOR STATIC CONTENT

This process is very wasteful. If you serve the `index.html` from the application server:

- ◆ The webconnector examines the request for a servlet mapping.

- ◆ The webconnector load-balances the request according to application partition rules and its performance tracking information.

- ◆ The webconnector parses and forwards the request to the application server's KXS process.

- ◆ The KXS process forwards the request to a KJS engine.

- ◆ The StaticServlet servlet in the KJS engine processes the request and serves the static file.

In contrast, if you copy the `index.html` to the Web server's file system, the Web server can directly serve that file. This approach eliminates the entire round trip to the application server and also gives the Web server the opportunity to cache the file in memory. The web sever is also much more efficient about using file caching than the StaticServlet in iAS. Serving static content from a Web server is often orders of magnitude faster than returning static content from the application-server tier. Serving static content from the Web-server tier also requires far fewer system resources (by orders of magnitude) than does serving static files from the application-server tier.

For many applications, deploying static content to the Web-server tier can significantly affect the performance of the application. It reduces not only latency by placing content closer to the user, but also throughput by reserving application-server resources for dynamic requests.

ADVANTAGES OF USING IAS FOR STATIC CONTENT

The biggest advantage of deploying static content to the application-server tier is simplicity. By packaging the static files in your WAR files, you reduce the number of steps necessary for application deployment. Similarly, bundling your dynamic and static content together reduces the likelihood of the dynamic and static content getting out of synchronization.

Including the static content in the application server also enables you to take advantage of the J2EE declarative-security functionality. This process enables you to use the same security policies on your static content that you do for your dynamic content. But if you need to protect your HTML by using declarative security, you still may not need to protect all static content. Images and stylesheets, for example, you don't often need to secure.

RECOMMENDATIONS FOR STATIC CONTENT

Ideally, you should design your applications such that either the application-server tier or the Web-server tier can serve the static content. Designing your applications to be this flexible can prove challenging, however, because it prevents you from using relative links from static content to dynamic content. (This problem occurs because the static content URLs may or may not include the NASApp token.) You'd need, therefore, to hardcode the NASApp token in the static content. Doing so would reduce the portability of the application, however, because the URL would be dependent on the value of the token.

If this alternative isn't a reasonable one for your application, you must make a choice about the location of static content. Deploying as much static content as possible to the Web-server tier is the preferable solution for enterprise applications.

If you're using Ant to deploy your application via the iAS extensions to Ant, you can use the NetComponents extension to Ant to enable you to automatically FTP static content to a Web server during application deployment. This approach makes deploying static content as simple as deploying an EAR file. It does, however, break the paradigm of self-contained packaging.

Deploying reusable code

Development frameworks such as Struts, Turbine, and Cocoon are becoming more popular as the J2EE environment itself becomes more pervasive. Using a development framework or other prebuilt components reduces the amount of time that you spend developing utility code and enables developers to focus on custom business logic. As the J2EE market matures, these prebuilt components are sure to become even more prevalent.

Even if enterprises don't use a third-party framework, such as those that I list in the preceding paragraph, they often develop their own internal frameworks of common Java components. These internal frameworks enable enterprises to develop a standard set of business-logic components that they customize for their enterprises. Internally developed components may, for example, provide catalog searching, pricing services, or backend system connectivity. These common components may be EJB modules, or they may be ordinary Java classes.

If your organization elects to standardize on a set of common Java components, it may prove beneficial to incorporate these standard components into the CLASSPATH of the application server.

ADVANTAGES TO ADDING COMMON COMPONENTS TO THE SERVER CLASSPATH

♦ **Reduces the size of EAR files:** If the server CLASSPATH doesn't include the common components, each module must include the common components.

♦ **Simplifies the process of upgrading the common components:** If you store the common components in a shared location and then include them in the server CLASSPATH, you can upgrade them simply by updating the shared location. If you include the common components in each application, you must redeploy each application to upgrade the common components.

◆ **Encourages the adoption of the common components:** Preinstalling the common components on the server helps validate the adoption of the component standards. It also enables developers to use them more easily, because it removes the work of packaging the common components.

DISADVANTAGES TO ADDING COMMON COMPONENTS TO THE SERVER CLASSPATH

◆ **Violates the philosophy of self-contained packaging:** Requiring the server CLASSPATH to contain Java code in addition to the EAR file is contrary to the general philosophy of self-contained packaging.

◆ **Increases the effect of upgrading common components:** Because all applications share a common installation of the common components, the effect of changing those common components becomes more significant. If one application needs to upgrade the common components of one application to use new functionality, for example, you then need to retest all applications with the new version of the common components.

◆ **Increases the complexity of installing new server instances:** Installing common components to the CLASSPATH of the server requires manual installation of the components on each newly installed server. Because the exact CLASSPATH order and component versioning can prove critical, you need to strictly enforce this installation procedure.

◆ **Negatively affects other applications:** If many applications are sharing one common set of components and one application requires an upgrade, this upgrade can negatively affect the other applications, causing many inconsistencies and problems.

CLASSPATH MODIFICATION INSTRUCTIONS

You modify the iAS server's CLASSPATH by editing the iasenv.ksh script in the $IAS_ROOT/ias/env directory (on UNIX) or by modifying the SOFTWARE/iPlanet/ Application Server/6.5/Java/Classpath registry key (on Windows). To add your common components on UNIX, you should do the following:

◆ **Create a directory to house the common components:** $IAS_ROOT/ ias/common is a good location for this directory, but you can use any directory that the application-server processes can access.

◆ **Create a new environment variable within the iasenv.ksh script to list all the necessary additions to the CLASSPATH:** A good idea is to package each component as a JAR file so that you can easily identify and upgrade component versions.

◆ **Prepend the new environment variable to the** `CLASSPATH` **that the**
   `iasenv.ksh` **script defines:** Creating a new environment variable instead
   of appending the component JARs to the `CLASSPATH` enables you to easily
   identify the purpose of the added JAR files and distinguish them from the
   default `CLASSPATH`.

Adding common components on Windows is very similar except that the
CLASSPATH is modified by editing the `SOFTWARE/iPlanet/Application Server/`
`6.5/Java/Classpath` registry key rather than `iasenv.ksh`.

Hot deployment

Hot deployment, also known as *dynamic class reloading,* is an iPlanet Application
Server feature that enables faster development cycles. If you enable hot deployment, the application server automatically detects new compiled class files and
reloads them as necessary. This feature enables developers to test application
changes without running a complete packaging and deployment cycle or restarting
the application server.

 If the deployment descriptors change, you must redeploy the application by
using `iasdeploy` so that you can register the new deployment descriptors.

If you enable dynamic class reloading, you can dynamically reload Web components and EJB implementations by replacing the existing class files with the
updated versions of the class. The application server notices the change in the file's
time/date stamp and loads the new version of the `.class` file. Dynamic class
reloading is disabled by default. You can enable dynamic class reloading by
setting the registry value `SOFTWARE/iPlanet/Application Server/6.5/CCSO/`
`SYSTEM_JAVA/Versioning/Disable` to 0.

You shouldn't use dynamic classloading in a production environment. Active
sessions can be lost if a class dynamically reloads. And production environments
generally don't want the underlying class files to get out of sync with the EAR file
that you deploy.

You should also avoid hot deployment during production because it could cause
the user experience to change suddenly in the middle of a session. Hot deployment
isn't a suitable technology with which to build a continuous uptime infrastructure.
You can find the best practices for continuous uptime infrastructures in Chapter 18.

The `chapter9` sample includes a hot-deploy Ant target in its `build.xml` file. The
`hot_deploy` target copies the class files directly to the `APPS` directory of the local
application server instead of using `iasdeploy`. Using the `hot_deploy` build target
requires that you first perform the following tasks:

◆ Modify the `application server` property in the `build.xml` to point to the APPS directory of the locally installed application server.

◆ Modify the permissions in the APPS directory to enable the current user to copy the files. (This course is necessary only if the build script is running as a different user than the application server on a Unix platform.)

◆ Deploy the application by using `iasdeploy` at least once to register the deployment descriptors and create the `chapter9` directory structure under APPS.

The hot-deploy target is shown in Listing 9-5. The target copies the contents of the `docroot` to the `root` of the Web application, the servlet classes to the WEB-INF/ `classes` subdirectory, and the EJB implementations to the `root` of the JAR module.

Listing 9-5: Hot deploy target of chapter9 build.xml sample

```
<target name="hot_deploy" depends="compile">
    <copy todir="${application server.docroot}">
        <fileset dir="${src.docroot}" excludes="cvs,annotation"/>
    </copy>
    <copy todir="${application server.webroot}">
        <fileset dir="${build.classesdir}/${war.pkgprefix}/web"
            excludes="cvs,annotation"/>
    </copy>
    <copy todir="${application server.ejbroot}">
        <fileset dir="${build.classesdir}/${war.pkgprefix}/ejb"
            includes="*EJB.class"  excludes="cvs,annotation"/>
    </copy>
</target>
```

Notice that the build target is very simplistic. It differentiates EJB implementations from, for example, remote and home interfaces only via a file-naming convention. The target isn't meant as a comprehensive deployment option but only as a quick way to test straightforward class updates.

Summary

This chapter gives you an inside look into the iPlanet Application Server deployment environment. It examines the organization of the deployment file system, how the deployment tools work, and some basic strategies for optimizing deployment.

Application packaging and deployment is a relatively new concept to J2EE. Understanding the deployment implications of application packaging can help you optimize operational procedures and application performance. A solid understanding of the deployment environment also helps administrators troubleshoot problems that deploying applications introduces.

Enterprise applications remain in deployment for years after the original development team moves on. Creating a repeatable, well-understood deployment process, therefore, is one of the most important practices for ensuring the long-term success of enterprise applications. Self-contained packaging is one attempt to try to ensure this repeatable process, but a thorough understanding of the server environment is also critical for deployment success.

The following links provide more information on the topics that I cover in this chapter:

iPlanet Application Server Documentation

♦ `iasdeploy` Instructions (iASsp2 release notes): `http://docs.iplanet. com/docs/manuals/ias/60/sp2/releasenotes/ias60sp2_rn. htm#iasdeploy`

♦ Administrating Access Control Lists in `iPlanet Application Server Administration Tool` (Chapter 5 of the iAS Administrator's Guide): `http://docs.iplanet.com/docs/manuals/ias/60/sp3/admin/ adsecuri.htm#13370`

♦ Discussion of Third-Party Components and Application Packaging (`developer.iplanet.com` article on J2EE Packaging): `http:// developer.iplanet.com/docs/articles/packaging/packaging. jsp#Modularizing_J2EE_Applications`

Other Documentation

♦ Creating Users in the LDAP Directory by Using the Admin Console (Chapter 4 of the Admin Server Guide): `http://docs.iplanet.com/ docs/manuals/console/41/html/4_users.htm#1010174`

♦ IBM Developerworks Article on Classloaders : `www-105.ibm.com/ developerworks/education.nsf/java-onlinecourse-bytitle/ 06B49359139A1AD186256A310049AC9B?OpenDocument`

♦ Changing the Checkpoint Interval of the LDAP Server (Chapter 17 of the Directory Server Admin Guide): `http://docs.iplanet.com/docs/ manuals/directory/41/admin/config.htm#1060806`

Third-Party Product Documentation

◆ Ant Extensions for iPlanet Application Server (ICSynergy iPlanet Ant extensions): `www.icsynergy.com/downloads/iplanetAnt/ antExtDocs.html`

◆ Using FTP within Ant (NetComponents Ant extension): `www.savarese. org/oro/software/NetComponents.html`

Chapter 10

Understanding iAS Clustering

IN THIS CHAPTER

◆ Load-balancing iAS applications

◆ Using DSYNC to distribute session and state

◆ Understanding DSYNC alternatives

IPLANET APPLICATION SERVER'S load-balancing and clustering features are arguably its most powerful value-add features. This chapter explains how the load-balancing and DSYNC features work and how and when to utilize them.

Defining iAS Clustering

The term *clustering* has a very specific meaning when discussing iPlanet Application Server. iAS clustering is not related to SunCluster, or any other hardware clustering solution. *Clustering* provides us with the capability to have applications distributed across multiple JVM engines, multiple iAS instances, and multiple servers all sharing access to the same application data.

This application data store is named DSYNC. DSYNC stores the application information (primarily `HttpSession` and `ServletContext` attributes) in a highly available, in-memory database that will remain intact even if a server is shut down or suffers catastrophic failure. This resilient DSYNC data store, in combination with adaptive load balancing, prevents users from being affected by server problems. If a process fails or a server crashes, the user's session will be preserved and the user's requests will be able to be handled by another process or server.

Load-Balancing iAS Applications

Clustering isn't useful, therefore, without the capability to distribute the requests for our application across these multiple JVMs and instances.

iPlanet Application Server actually provides several features that relate to load balancing. iAS provides intraserver load balancing so that the KXS and CXS engines can distribute incoming requests to one of the instance's KJS engines. It also provides interserver load balancing so that the Web connectors and KXS can distribute incoming requests between server instances. iAS also offers application-partitioning and sticky load-balancing capabilities that can modify the behavior of the load-balancing engines. (Sticky load balancing is explained in a later section, "Sticky Load Balancing".)

Figure 10-1 illustrates the four parts involved in load balancing an incoming Web request. I explain each of the steps in the diagram in the following sections.

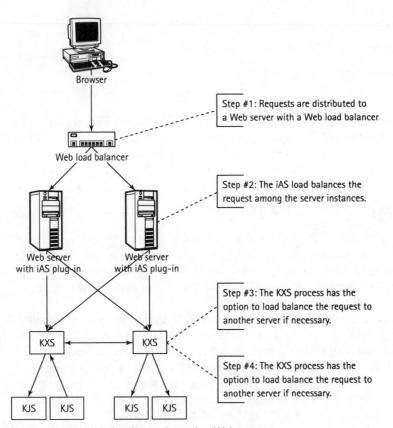

Figure 10-1: Load balancing an incoming Web request

Web server load balancing (Step 1)

Before iPlanet Application Server even receives an incoming HTTP request, the request is typically load balanced by an external load balancer across a farm of Web servers. A variety of hardware and software solutions are available to perform this load-balancing task. Common Web load balancers include Cisco's LocalDirector, Cisco's Arrowpoint, F5 Lab's BigIP, and Resonate's Central Dispatch. All these products distribute incoming requests across multiple Web servers.

These load balancers offer a variety of tools to enable you to manage the distribution of requests. These load balancers may use multiple methodologies for distributing requests and may also automatically detect and route requests around failed Web servers.

In using an iPlanet Application Server cluster, however, an important point to remember is that the Web load balancer does *not* need to perform sticky load balancing of incoming requests. Any iAS Web server in the cluster is capable of serving any request. (See the section "Sticky load balancing," later in this chapter, for more information about session stickiness.)

Advanced load-balancing techniques at the Web load-balancer level typically isn't very effective either, because the application-server tier handles most of the work-processing requests. Typically, the best course is to configure Web load balancers to distribute incoming requests by using a simple round-robin methodology.

I present an exception to this suggestion for simple Web load balancing in Chapter 18 in discussing configurations that use more than one cluster. In this case, the Web load balancer must use sticky load balancing to distribute requests to the correct cluster.

Interserver Load Balancing (Steps 2 and 3)

You configure the interserver load-balancing method on the Load Balancing section of the ksvradmin tool. The load-balancing method that you select on this section determines how Web requests load balance across the iAS instances.

The various methods of load balancing determine whether iAS bases the load-balancing decision on information that the Web connector collects or information that the iAS servers provide. Regardless of which method you select, both the Web connector and the iAS server are capable of distributing requests. At Step 2 in the diagram, the Web connector determines which server instance is best capable of handling the request and forwards the request to that server instance's KXS process. At Step 3, the KXS process receives the request and may elect to forward the request again if it's too busy to handle the request effectively.

This step of transferring the request from one server to another is called *hopping* the request. You can limit the number of hops by adjusting the Maximum Hops value on the Advanced tab of the ksvradmin load-balancing section. Limiting the maximum number of hops so that requests that users make on a busy cluster don't repeatedly pass from server to server is a good idea.

iPlanet Application Server can utilize two major load-balancing methodologies to determine how system processes route requests between server instances. The first methodology is for the Web connector to independently make the decision about where to route requests, basing its decision on its own information. In the second methodology, server-based load balancing, the Web connector is still responsible for routing the incoming requests, but it bases the load-balancing decisions on information that the KXS processes at the application-server tier provide.

 iPlanet Application Server handles RMI/IIOP requests much differently than Web requests. Unlike Web requests, RMI/IIOP requests directly specify the TCP/IP address and port of the CXS process that handle that request. RMI/IIOP requests, therefore, bypass steps 1-3 of Figure 10-1 and aren't load balanced until after the request is already at the application-server tier.

If iAS needs to distribute RMI/IIOP requests across multiple CXS processes, the RMI/IIOP client code must manually distribute the requests.

WEB CONNECTOR LOAD BALANCING

Three web-connector-based load-balancing methodologies are available: Round-robin, per server response time, and per component response time. These methodologies determine the decision criteria that the Web connector collects to determine the best server to handle requests.

ROUND ROBIN   In utilizing round-robin load balancing, the Web connector doesn't retain any information about the relative responsiveness of the available iAS servers. The Web connector distributes incoming requests based on a preconfigured round-robin or weighted round-robin pattern. (Although application stickiness and application partition rules are still followed, as I describe below.)

By default, round-robin load balancing uses equal weights for all known servers. Each Web connector distributes its requests between all available servers equally and consecutively (again, assuming no application partitioning or sticky load balancing).

To set up weighted round-robin load balancing, you must configure the server weights in the iAS registry by using the `kregeidt` registry tool. Weighted round-robin load balancing is useful if your iAS servers are significantly different in processing power. If, for example, you have two iAS servers — one with two CPUs and one with four CPUs — you may want to configure weighted round-robin load balancing. You can configure the first server with a weight of one and the second server with a weight of two. The first server then receives one third of all requests and the second server two-thirds of the requests, giving each server a workload proportionate to its processing capacity.

The following steps are necessary to set up weighted load balancing:

1. Set the `SOFTWARE\iPlanet\Application Server\6.0\CCSO\Loadb\RoundRobin` registry value to 1 to enable round-robin load balancing.

2. Add a registry value for each server under the registry key `SOFTWARE\iPlanet\Application Server\6.0\CCSO\Loadb\ServerWeights`. Set the name to the IP and port of the server's KXS process, with a colon delimiting the IP and port. Set the value to the desired server weight and set the type to Integer. To create a server weight of 2 for an iAS server running on IP 192.168.1.3 using the default KXS port of 10818, for example, you create a registry value with a name of 192.168.1.3:10818, with a value of 2 and a type of Integer.

3. You must restart all iAS servers and Web connectors after you save the registry settings to enact these changes.

I generally don't recommend round-robin for production systems. Although round-robin does have the advantage of requiring the least Web connector resources of all load-balancing methods, other load-balancing mechanisms are more effective at distributing incoming requests. You sometimes use round-robin during development, however, as it makes testing clustered deployments more predictable and repeatable.

PER SERVER RESPONSE TIME   In the per-server-response-time load-balancing methodology, the Web connector tracks the time that each server takes to respond to Web requests. The Web connector then sends a larger percentage of its requests to servers that respond to requests more quickly.

This feature enables the Web connector to react to a server that's overloaded with requests. As a server becomes saturated with requests, its response time slows down. The Web connector then reacts to this slowdown by reducing the percentage of requests that it forwards to that server until its response time returns to normal.

The per-server-response-time methodology provides a simple but effective method of distributing incoming requests. It requires only a small amount of calculation on the part of the Web connector, but enables the incoming requests to automatically adapt to the current conditions of the application-server tier.

The per-server-response-time methodology does, however, have a few weaknesses. It works best if each Web component is roughly equal in difficulty for the appserver to process.

If certain components require significantly more resources to process, this fact can distort the results that the Web connector's measuring. Consider, for example, an application that you use to analyze sales data. The user makes several requests to log on to the application and pick which data to analyze. These requests are easy for iAS to process and result in rapid response times. But if the user makes the request to actually process the sales data, the results can take a long time to generate, causing a very long response time. This long response causes the Web connector to avoid sending any more requests to the instance that processes the analysis request, because it mistakenly believes that server to be overloaded. Even if the server has plenty of remaining processing capacity, the amount of time that processing the analysis request takes causes the Web connector to avoid sending additional requests to that server.

This example also highlights the fact that the Web connector is responding to the total response of the iAS server, regardless of where the processing occurs. The Web connector reacts to a long response time even if the majority of the processing is occurring in a database or backend system. The iAS server may sit idle while waiting for the backend system to return a result set, but because the application server is taking a long time to return the results to the Web connector, the application server starts receiving fewer requests because the Web connector starts routing its requests to other servers in the cluster.

Because of these factors, you're best off using per server response time if each application component requires roughly equivalent processing power. Where server response time is a good indicator of overall server load, it can prove a very effective method of distributing requests.

PER COMPONENT RESPONSE TIME   The per-component-response-time methodology tracks the response time for each individual component. This method avoids the issue that the server-response-time methodology encounters if some components take significantly longer to process.

If an analysis component takes longer to process than the other components, for example, the Web connector automatically compensates for the extra time that component takes to process in considering which servers currently have the best response time. The component response time adds some additional overhead tracking of the individual components, but it can make load balancing more accurate (and, therefore, effective) if components have varying degrees of processing complexity.

The per component response time is the default load-balancing methodology and is often the most effective technique. If you're in doubt of the best load-balancing methodology to use, component response time is a good starting methodology and a good baseline for comparison.

SERVER-BASED LOAD BALANCING

The *server-based load-balancing methodology* (also known as the *user-defined criteria methodology*), takes an entirely different approach to determining the best server to process an incoming request. Instead of the Web connector guessing the current capacity of a server by its responsiveness, the Web connector actively retrieves information from the application-server cluster about the status of the iAS servers.

In utilizing the server-based load-balancing methodology, the iAS servers periodically transmit information about their status. The Web connectors are still responsible for making the decision for where to route each request, but they have much more detailed information available to make that decision. A Web connector may, for example, choose to route a request based on which server has a result cache for a given component. (Result caching is an HTML result caching technology used by iAS to increase performance. For more information on result caching, see the caching sample provided with iAS.)

After selecting server-based load balancing in the `ksvradmin` tool, you get several screens of slider controls, where you can configure the relative importance the Web connector is to give each criteria. You have two types of criteria: *server criteria* and *component criteria*. The server criteria are as follows:

- ◆ CPU time available

- ◆ Amount of disk I/O

- ◆ Amount of memory paging

- ◆ Length of request queue

In deciding how to route a request, a Web connector combines the server criteria with criteria that it measures for each component. The criteria that it measures component by component are as follows:

- ◆ Average response time (for all components)

- ◆ The existence of a results cache

- ◆ Average response time (for a specific component)

- ◆ Last execution time (recently executed components may have cached data)

- ◆ Total number of executions

So in tuning load-balancing criteria (via the slider controls) for an application that performs CPU-intensive calculations, you may decide to weigh CPU time available and available results cache. This type of setting enables the application to route requests based on the important criteria while ignoring data that's not as meaningful, such as average response time.

Server-based load balancing is a very powerful tool that can enable effective load balancing of applications that are otherwise difficult to tune. The overhead that you spend in tracking and transmitting this information, however, isn't justified for all applications. If the Web connector can accurately determine the approximate server load based on the response time of the server, Web–connector-based load balancing is the most effective technique. If, however, more information is necessary to make an educated load-balancing decision, a server-based load-balancing methodology may prove more effective.

Intraserver load balancing (Step 4)

The KXS and CXS are the two processes responsible for distributing the requests that an iAS instance receives. The KXS is responsible for distributing requests that Web connectors forward, and the CXS is responsible for distributing requests that it receives directly via RMI/IIOP.

Both the KXS and CXS use a simple round-robin method of distributing requests to the KJS engines that belong to that instance. (Sticky load balancing is an exception to this rule, as I discuss in the section "Sticky Load Balancing," later in the chapter.)

This simple method is the most efficient method of distributing requests among the KJS engines. Because the KJS engines share their resources (CPU, memory, file system I/O), more sophisticated methods of distributing requests result in unnecessary overhead. No matter what load-balancing mechanism you select for it, intraserver load balancing always uses a round-robin methodology.

Application partitioning

Up until this point, all our discussions about load balancing assume that all applications are available on all servers. This situation, however, isn't necessarily true. You may elect to deploy applications only on some servers. You may, for example, want to use a dedicated server to serve one application. You'd still want that server to participate in a larger cluster so that the application can failover in case of server failure. But by creating a dedicated server for that application, you ensure a certain degree of quality of service for that application, because no other application can use the resources of that server. Additionally, by using tools such as Solaris Resource Manager, you can even guarantee the availability of system resources for that server.

This capability to restrict which servers are eligible to process a specific application is known as *application partitioning.* In iPlanet Application Server, application partitioning happens automatically.

Figure 10-2 shows an example of an iPlanet Application Server cluster that uses application partitioning.

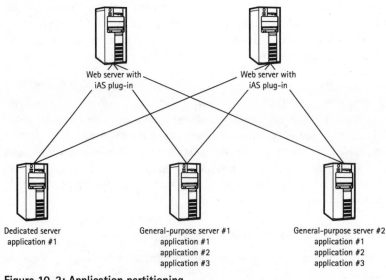

Figure 10-2: Application partitioning

Because I cluster all the servers together in this diagram, they all can utilize each other for the purposes of DSYNC failover as described below. But if users flood application #2 with requests, the loads are still restricted to servers #2 and #3, preventing the traffic from affecting server #1. Requests for application #1 continue processing quickly, as the Web connectors route most of the requests for application #1 to server #1 if servers #2 and #3 are busy.

You can also utilize application partitioning on a per-component basis. Imagine, for example, that your application must interact with a native library that exists on only one of the servers in the iAS cluster. The iAS application can use a JNI interface to communicate with that library, and you can partition the components that use that JNI interface to run only on the server where the native library resides.

TIP

Although application partitioning is a useful tool, it's not a good load-balancing strategy. You can use application partitioning to distribute requests across multiple servers, but leaving iAS to automatically distribute the requests in response to application load is more effective.

Theoretically, creating a dedicated server to serve each component would aid performance by requiring fewer classes in memory on each server. In practice, however, the overhead of transmitting the session information and the reduced capability of iAS to perform load balancing significantly outweigh any benefits that derive from reducing the number of classes in memory.

iPlanet Application Server automatically partitions applications, basing its decision on where you deploy them. (Specifically, iAS routes request only to servers deploying the requested component.) You can also conceivably partition an application by disabling components in the `ksvradmin` Applications panel.

Sticky load balancing

Sticky load balancing, sometimes known as *session affinity* in other products, is the capability to have the same server and the same JVM process all of a user's requests. The first time that a user accesses an iAS-enabled Web server, his request load balances normally. But on subsequent requests, that user's requests for all requests return to the same server and JVM that processed his initial request.

iPlanet Application Server implements sticky load balancing by returning a cookie that it encodes with the IP and port of both the KXS and KJS processes that it uses to process the initial request. (If the user doesn't enable cookies in his browser, iAS utilizes hidden fields and URL rewriting to provide the same functionality as cookies.) As the user's browser makes its subsequent requests, it returns the cookie to the Web connector. The Web connector then uses the KXS information encoded in the cookie to determine how to route the request. Similarly, the KXS uses the information encoded in the cookie to route the request to the original KJS.

Deployers actually enable sticky load balancing on a per-component basis by changing the sticky element of the `ias-web.xml` deployment descriptor. After a sticky component is requested, however, all subsequent requests are sticky, even for requests for nonsticky components.

After a sticky component is requested, the sticky cookie returns to the user. You can use this ability to specify stickiness on a per component basis to prevent the load balancer from using stickiness until necessary.

If the original KJS no longer exists or isn't capable of handling a request because of application partitioning, iAS automatically routes the request to a new KJS. In other words, iAS never permits a request to fail because of sticky load balancing. If a server is shut down, for example, all the user sessions "stuck" to that server are load balanced to other servers.

Developers sometimes use sticky load balancing to avoid some of the complications of clustered applications. If, for example, the developer stores some of the user's application state in the file system of the application server, sticky load balancing ensures that the user's request returns to the same file system with each request. (This approach requires caution, however, because if the server shuts down or fails, the user's session fails over to a new server.)

System administrators also benefit from sticky load balancing, because they can use sticky load balancing to help performance-tune an application. Using sticky load balancing enables the server to access the session information faster than is possible without stickiness, either by enabling iAS to store the session information directly in the JVM (lite sessions) or by increasing the effectiveness of the distributed session manager cache (DSYNC).

 Enable stickiness load balancing in your applications. Although stickiness limits load balancing somewhat, the performance boost from sticky load balancing is measurable.

Troubleshooting load balancing

The most common problem that you face in configuring load balancing is making sure that the load-balancing feature is actually on for that component. You can deploy application components as *Local*, *Distributed*, or *Global*. You can inspect the deployment method in the `ksvradmin` tool in the Applications panel.

Local deployment means that you disable load balancing. Requests for that component always forward to the default KXS that you specify during the installation of the Web connector. Accidental deployment of applications as Local is the most common cause of load-balancing problems.

Distributed deployment is the typical mode of deployment, where the registry contains a list of all servers that are eligible to run a particular component. The GDS subkey of each component's entry in the ClassDef section of the registry stores the list of eligible servers.

Global deployment indicates that a component can run on all available servers. You can't use deployment descriptors to deploy applications globally; you must modify them in the ksvradmin tool after deployment to Global status. A global component displays the value of 255.255.255.255 in the GDS subkey instead of a list of eligible servers.

Chapter 14 includes instructions for enabling detailing logging for server-based load balancing.

DSYNC Clustering

DSYNC is the name of the iPlanet Application Server technology that enables iAS to share information between clustered servers. One of its most important uses is the distribution of HttpSession information. This feature enables programmers to maintain a user's conversational state in the HttpSession even if a user's requests load balance across multiple servers.

I present information on DSYNC from a system administrator's point of view, including how to configure DSYNC, in Chapter 11.

The only requirement for Java developers is that they make sure that any objects that they store in HttpSession and ServletContext attributes implement the Serializable interface. This setup enables DSYNC to serialize the session for transmission across the network.

Other than the Serializable requirement, Java developers interact with the HttpSession and ServletContext APIs just as if they're programming for a single JVM deployment environment. When ready to deploy, setting the impl subelement in the session section of the ias-web.xml deployment descriptor enables the DSYNC engine. iAS ensures that, no matter what JVM handles a user's request, the HttpSession and ServletContext attributes are available.

TIP Accidentally storing nonserializable objects in the HttpSession is a common cause of lost session information. If you're experiencing session loss, search your KJS logs for SERVLET-put_nonserial errors that indicate the inadvertent use of nonserializable objects.

The DSYNC engine can also provide transparent failover of stateful session beans. You need no special API to enable failover. (Because the EJB specification requires that all nontransient stateful session bean states are serializable after the ejbPassivate callback, iAS doesn't need to make any additional serialization requirements.) The deployment descriptor and an additional ejbc flag (fo) specify whether a bean is enabled for failover. Setting a bean's failoverrequired element to a value of 1 causes the server to save that bean's state into the DSYNC data store periodically. This feature enables the server to recover the bean's state should the original server fail or shut down.

Because stateful session beans typically contain a reasonably large amount of state, the overhead of propagating this state can significantly affect the performance of applications. You should enable failover only for beans with nonrecoverable and critical states.

TIP Although stateless session beans don't require a special API to function, an API is available to help minimize the performance effect of session bean failover.

iAS defines a com.netscape.server.ejb.IEBFoStateModification interface that contains two methods: isDirty and setDirty. If a stateful session bean implements this interface, the container saves the bean state only if the isDirty method returns true. (At which point it then resets the dirty flag by using the setDirty method.)

Using this API enables developers to prevent the container from needing to back up the bean's state if no changes were made since the last backup.

Because the deployment descriptors and not the Java code specify the failover properties of HttpSession and stateful session beans, you can change the failover properties at deployment time. This capability enables you to make adjustments to the failover characteristics at deploy time. As maintenance windows and uptime requirements change, system administrators can adjust the failover properties of applications without needing to redeploy or repackage applications.

An important point to notice is that clustering relates only indirectly to load balancing. You can load balance users across unclustered servers, and you can disable load balancing but enable clustering. (This setup enables failover within the JVMs of the single server.) Clustering and load balancing relate only indirectly, however, because if you enable load balancing without clustering, you must utilize some alternative method of maintaining HttpSession integrity. I consider these alternatives in the following section.

DSYNC Alternatives

Nearly all Web applications need some method for storing conversational state about a user's session. The most common method for storing this conversational state in server-side Java applications is to store attributes in the HttpSession. In the preceding section "DSYNC Clustering," you learn how to utilize iPlanet Application Server's DSYNC session manager to distribute the HttpSession across a cluster.

The DSYNC session manager is a powerful feature that iAS offers. It's fast, supports failover, and is simple to use. DSYNC does, however, have the following disadvantages:

♦ DSYNC requires that objects that you store in the session are serializable. If you need to store objects that are difficult to serialize, using DSYNC also is difficult.

♦ Although fast, DSYNC does replicate all session data to support failover. This duplication can cause a measurable amount of overhead. If failover isn't necessary, this replication overhead also is unnecessary.

♦ DSYNC stores all session information in the memory of the KXS process. If you store a large amount of data per user in HttpSession by using DSYNC, memory utilization becomes excessive.

If one of these limitations prevents you from implementing DSYNC using an alternative method for managing conversational user state is sometimes advantageous. (If possible, you should defer the decision about whether to use DSYNC until a performance testing phase. Deferring the decision allows you to quantifiably measure the effects of DSYNC rather than guess about the impact.) The rest of this chapter explores some of the alternatives to DSYNC and the situations in which they prove beneficial.

Lite sessions

iPlanet Application Server provides an alternative HttpSession session manager known as the *lite session manager*. You enable it by setting the value of the impl subelement of the session XML element in the ias-web.xml deployment descriptor equal to lite. Notice that since the setting is in the application deployment descriptor you can select the lite session manager on an application-by-application basis. You can even use the DSYNC and lite session managers simultaneously on the same server.

The lite session manager is a lightweight session manager that stores the `HttpSession` attributes directly in the JVM without any failover capabilities. This feature makes the lite session manager very fast because it doesn't have the failover overhead of DSYNC. And because the server never transmits the session information over the network, the lite session manager doesn't require that session objects are serializable.

Because the lite session manager stores session information in a single JVM, the same JVM must process all of a user's requests. (You can isolate a user's requests either by enabling sticky load balancing or by partitioning the application to a server with a single JVM.) If that JVM fails, the user's session doesn't have a backup and is lost.

The lite session manager has the following advantages:

◆ It's extremely fast because it has no serialization, network lag, or replication overhead.

◆ It doesn't require serializable session objects.

◆ It uses the `HttpSession` API and, therefore, is transparent to the developer.

◆ It enables you to easily switch to the DSYNC session manager if requirements change.

The lite session manager is very simplistic, however, and the following significant disadvantages apply:

◆ It offers no failover capabilities. If a JVM fails or stops, you lose session information.

◆ It stores sessions in memory and, therefore, physical memory limits the session repository.

◆ It doesn't distribute session information and, therefore, you must introduce sticky load balancing if you intend to use more than one JVM to service the application.

◆ It very commonly gives you a bunch of nonserializable errors after moving from `dev` `env` to an `env` with DSYNC enabled.

The lite session manager is your best solution if failover isn't a requirement. In situations where only a single server instance is in use, DSYNC causes needless overhead in comparison to lite sessions. Lite sessions can also prove an easy solution if nonserializable objects are unavoidable. (The lack of failover is unavoidable if you can't serialize sessions effectively.)

Alternative state repositories

The Web tier isn't the only place where you can store user state. If the size of data is small, for example, the session data can return as a cookie or hidden field to the user's browser. Or you can store session information in a stateful session bean. (Although you'd need to store the handle to the bean in `HttpSession` or in a cookie or hidden field.)

These alternative storage locations generally aren't as efficient as `HttpSession` or as easy to implement. They do provide alternatives, however, that can help in some unusual situations. Using a persistent cookie, for example, enables the storage of state without a timeout. A persistent cookie remains even after a user restarts his browser.

Storing conversational state in a stateful session bean enables non-Web clients to access conversational state. It also enables you to store a larger volume of information, because stateful session beans can passivate themselves to disk in between access. Stateful session beans have significantly more access overhead, however, so scalability is reduced dramatically in comparison to DSYNC.

Alternative session state repositories are generally not as scalable or convenient as using an `HttpSession`-based mechanism. Alternative repositories can offer functionality that's difficult to implement with `HttpSession`, however, so they can provide an interesting supplement to the functionality that DSYNC offers.

Custom solutions

Some enterprises elect to develop their own conversational-state storage mechanism. You have many reasons to implement a custom solution for conversational state, including the following:

◆ The need to store more state information than can fit in physical memory. (These types of custom solutions normally use a RDBMS as a data store.)

◆ The need to access conversational state from multiple applications.

◆ A desire to abstract or control the state repository. `HttpSession` enables you to place arbitrary objects in attributes. By forcing developers to use custom business methods to store and retrieve conversational state, you can exercise more control over the state repository.

A custom solution can distribute the storage of the state across multiple repositories — for example, a combination of persistent cookies, DSYNC, and the local file system, based on the size of the session data and persistence requirements.

Developing your own custom solution for conversational storage is obviously less convenient than using one of the built-in session managers. If the application requirements aren't a good fit with the built-in session managers, however, a custom solution may prove your only solution.

Summary

DSYNC is one of iPlanet Application Server's most powerful features, but DSYNC is also one of the least understood features. Implementing DSYNC clustering poorly leads to frustration for both developers and operations. The information presented in this chapter can help you understand what happens behind the scenes with DSYNC: information that can be invaluable when deciding how and when to use clustering.

For more information on the topics covered in this chapter, check the following:

◆ iAS Administrator's Guide on Balancing User-Request Loads: `http://docs.iplanet.com/docs/manuals/ias/60/sp3/admin/adldbal.htm#11284`

◆ iAS Clustering forum: `softwareforum.sun.com` (under Application Server – Clustering)

Chapter 11

Failover

IN THIS CHAPTER

- ◆ Building an architecture to meet your application's high availability requirements

- ◆ Using only the failover features necessary to meet your business requirements, thereby optimizing your application performance

- ◆ Troubleshooting any problems that your application experiences as a result of running in a clustered environment

- ◆ Tuning and maintaining your application servers in a clustered environment

HIGH AVAILABILITY is a common business requirement for enterprise applications. iPlanet Application Server provides several failover features unique to the application server marketplace that make developing applications to meet these high-availability requirements easier. iPlanet Chapter 10 discusses how to use clusters to provide this high availability and the effects of clusters on the programming APIs. This chapter discusses clustering from the administrator's point of view and the details of how iAS supports failover behind the scenes.

In this chapter, I discuss DSYNC from the system administrator's point of view. (For information about DSYNC from the programmer's point of view, review Chapter 10.) I examine how DSYNC works behind the scenes, how to verify that your cluster can failover correctly, and how to troubleshoot problems that relate to failover. I also examine a case study for building a highly available iAS architecture, examining the server logs as a cluster responds to failover events.

This chapter assumes that you configure your cluster to have one DSYNC backup. You can change the number of backups by using the Admin Tool on the Cluster tab of the General settings. Setting this number of backups to anything other than one is generally inadvisable. (One backup is the default for any cluster of two or more servers.)

Less than one backup prevents DSYNC from being highly available. A failure in the DSYNC Primary causes the loss of all DSYNC data. If failover isn't necessary, you're better off using lite sessions instead of configuring zero DSYNC backups. (More information on lite sessions can be found in Chapter 10.)

Using more than one DSYNC backup is of limited usefulness because it offers an advantage only if both the DSYNC Primary and DSYNC Backup fail in rapid succession before you can create a new backup. This extremely rare situation generally isn't worth the performance penalty that doubling the amount of backup replication causes.

Primaries, Backups, and Alternates

DSYNC is an iPlanet term that you use for the replicated in-memory hierarchical database that iPlanet Application Server uses to share information between the KJS engines. Developers never access DSYNC directly, but it serves as the backend data store for HttpSession, ServletContext, ISession, and other objects that you need to access from disparate KJS engines. DSYNC is the component of iAS that enables developers to use these standardized API's while still providing behind-the-scenes data replication and failover.

The KXS process of the first iAS machine that starts in the cluster automatically creates the DSYNC database. After starting, the KXS automatically discovers that it's the only server running and initializes itself as the *DSYNC Primary*. As the Primary, it's the authoritative source for all DSYNC information.

After the second DSYNC-enabled server in the cluster starts, the DSYNC Primary detects it joining the cluster and automatically replicates its DSYNC database to the new server, making the new server the *DSYNC Backup*. The Backup's function is to take over the role of Primary should the Primary fail or shut down.

Any additional servers that start in the cluster become *DSYNC Alternates*. (Assuming that you have kept the default of one DSYNC Backup per cluster.) Alternates don't perform any DSYNC functions other than waiting for possible future promotion to Backup status.

You can designate a server so that it can never become a DSYNC Primary or DSYNC Backup. Servers that you designated this way are known as *DSYNC Locals*. They can act as DSYNC clients but can never store the DSYNC database.

Designating servers as DSYNC Locals is generally inadvisable. I recommend using this feature only if you have one extremely underpowered server and, therefore, it's completely unsuitable as a DSYNC Primary.

The key concept to remember is that (with the exception of DSYNC Locals) the configurations of all the servers are identical. Which server starts first determines the Primary server and not any special configuration.

Because the DSYNC Primary functions identically to all the other servers in the cluster, the only way to determine which server is currently the Primary is to examine the log files.

Figure 11-1 shows a three-server cluster with two KJS engines per server. The first server to start is the Primary; the second server is a Backup; and the third server is an Alternate. All the KJS engines are DSYNC clients that connect to the DSYNC Primary. The DSYNC Primary also maintains a connection to the DSYNC Backup so that it can replicate the changes that you make to its database.

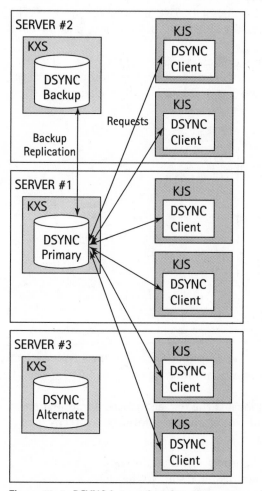

Figure 11-1: DSYNC interactions in a three-server cluster

For day-to-day operations, you should never concern yourself with which server is currently the DSYNC Primary and which server is currently the DSYNC Backup. But understanding the concept of Primaries and Backups is important for understanding the nature of iAS failover. Additionally, the ability to follow the promotion and election of Primaries and Backups enables you to troubleshoot and verify your cluster's failover capabilities.

Behind the Scenes of DSYNC

Understanding how DSYNC works enables you to better troubleshoot and tune your cluster configuration. DSYNC is one of the most powerful features of iPlanet Application Server, and utilizing it effectively is important in building applications that are both highly available and highly scalable.

Each DSYNC client contains a local cache of DSYNC information. The DSYNC Primary retains the authoritative sources for all DSYNC information, plus a record of who currently has cached information.

The DSYNC client in the KJS process optimizes reads so that it uses the local cache whenever possible. Reads, therefore, are fast and network traffic and load on the DSYNC Primary are minimized. Figure 11-2 shows a DSYNC client requesting information from a DSYNC Primary.

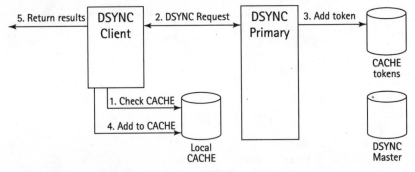

Figure 11–2: Reading information from DSYNC

Figure 11-2 illustrates the following five steps performed by the DSYNC client and server in response to a request for session information:

- ◆ *Check Cache:* Client checks its local cache for the requested information. If it finds the information locally, it returns the information directly, and no further steps are necessary.

- ◆ *DSYNC Request:* The DSYNC client requests the information from the DSYNC Primary. The Primary returns the results to the client.

- ◆ *Create Read Token:* The DSYNC server notes that the client has a cached copy of the requested information by giving that client a read token.

- ◆ *Add to Cache:* The client adds the requested information to its local cache for possible future use.

- ◆ *Return Results:* The client returns the information to the requester.

Because of the local cache created by this process, DSYNC writes must therefore invalidate all the local caches as well as update the Primary and Backup databases. (The Backup must remain identical to the Primary in case of a Primary failure.) Figure 11-3 shows a DSYNC client updating information in a DSYNC Primary.

- ◆ *Send Update:* The client sends the update to the DSYNC Primary.

- ◆ *Invalidate Caches:* The Primary checks its list of DSYNC clients currently caching that piece of information and sends those clients an instruction to discard their current cached information as invalid.

- ◆ *Update Master:* The Primary updates its store of information.

- ◆ *Update Backup:* The Primary sends the update to the DSYNC Backup so that the DSYNC Backup is kept up to date in case of failover.

- ◆ *Add Token:* The Primary notes that the client sending the update retains a cached copy of the new information by issuing the client a read token.

- ◆ *Add to Cache:* The client retains a copy of the new information in its local cache.

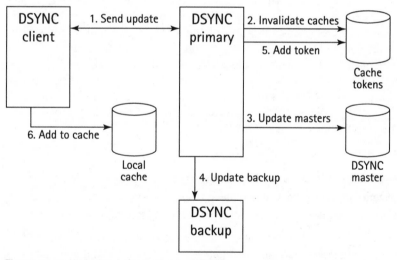

Figure 11-3: Updating information in DSYNC

An important point to notice is that DSYNC isn't a transactional system. Updates occur asynchronously. Updates take a small but finite amount of time to propagate through the DSYNC system. A transactional locking system would introduce too much overhead and delay to a system where you assume little contention for the same information to exist.

Another important observation is that DSYNC caches and tracks each piece of information individually. This feature helps minimize network overhead and improves the effectiveness of the cache. But it can prove to be a disadvantage if DSYNC is storing a large quantity of related but small entries separately.

Knowing this DSYNC mechanism also reveals an advantage to sticky load balancing. Because sticky load balancing causes sessions to have an affinity for a specific KJS, that KJS's process naturally develops a cache for that session's HttpSession information. Sticky load balancing can help increase the efficiency of DSYNC by increasing the efficiency of the DSYNC caching mechanism.

Thus, understanding the DSYNC mechanism can help you optimize your application's performance. You can accomplish this task by minimizing the number of DSYNC entries, such as HttpSession attributes, that DSYNC needs to track by grouping them into serializable objects. Consider, too, using sticky sessions to optimize the DSYNC cache.

Recovery from a Failure

The various engines of iPlanet Application Server maintain a web of TCP/IP connections over which they send periodic heartbeat information. The engines detect failures by noticing the loss of one of those heartbeat connections. A hardware failure, a core dump in the KJS, a termination of the KJS, or a system administrator killing the process could cause these failures. Anything that could cause a KXS or KJS to stop responding to heartbeat requests you can consider a "failure."

Each iPlanet Application Server process has a corresponding watchdog process. The KXS processes monitor the KJS processes. The KAS processes monitor the KXS process. And a small watchdog process monitors the KAS. Should any process fail, its watchdog process restarts it automatically.

 Restarting a process doesn't fix all problems. Systemic problems, such as a file-system crash, the incapability to connect to a configuration directory, and registry corruption all are examples of errors that process restarts can't resolve.

Systems that must remain highly available should avoid all single points of failure, including redundant configuration directories, to avoid these unrecoverable errors.

Non-DSYNC Failures

For processes that don't store any DSYNC data (KAS processes, DSYNC Alternates, and DSYNC Locals), this restart of the process is all that's necessary to restore functionality. The processes enter warnings into the logs, noting these failures, but the DSYNC needs to take no action to recover data.

Notice that the Web connector keeps track of which KXS processes fail. Web connectors react to a KXS failure by halting additional requests to the failed KXS until the KXS process is restored.

 TIP After the Web connector detects a failure in a KXS process, it attempts to reconnect to that KXS periodically. The following registry key defines (in seconds) the interval between retries: `SOFTWARE\iPlanet\Application Sever\6.0\CCSO\LOADB\ConnectRetry`.

Recovering from the loss of a DSYNC client

Restarting a KJS engine doesn't cause the loss of any DSYNC information, because KJS engines are only DSYNC clients. Information that you store in lite session stores and within normal Java variables, however, is lost permanently. The local DSYNC cache is also lost, but the local DSYNC client rebuilds the cache as necessary, basing the rebuild on incoming requests.

Recovering from the loss of a DSYNC Alternate or Local

If a KXS process containing a DSYNC Alternate fails, no special action is necessary. The KXS process restarts and rejoins the cluster as an Alternate again after it initializes. Alternates don't store DSYNC information, so no interruption to the DSYNC data store occurs.

Recovering from the loss of a DSYNC Backup

If a KXS process containing a DSYNC Backup fails, the Primary notices that failure. The DSYNC Primary responds by promoting one of the available Alternates to become a new Backup. If no Alternates are currently available, the Primary waits until a new Alternate becomes available. If more than one Alternate is available, the Primary chooses the Alternate with the highest server priority. (You can configure server priority on the Clusters tab of the General settings of the Admin tool. Use the Increase and Decrease buttons to adjust the list so that the server with the highest priority appears at the top in the list of servers.)

After the DSYNC Primary promotes a new server to Backup status, it asynchronously replicates the current DSYNC database to that new Backup. It must replicate the database asynchronously because the process can take several minutes, and the cluster must continue to service requests during this replication period. If the Primary fails during this replication to the new Backup, however, the Backup gets an incomplete copy of the DSYNC database and you may lose some data.

In performing system maintenance that involves shutting down the DSYNC Primaries and Backups, therefore, make sure that you leave enough time after the shutdown to enable the Primary to complete the replication before you make the next shutdown. (Fifteen minutes is a good rule of thumb for a moderately busy site.)

Recovering from the loss of a DSYNC Primary

The loss of a DSYNC Primary means that the authoritative source for all DSYNC requests across the entire cluster is gone. The DSYNC Backup notices this loss, however, and immediately steps in to take over this role of authoritative data source. It promotes itself to Primary and sends a message to all the DSYNC clients that they should now recognize it as the new Primary and authoritative data source.

The new Primary then elects a new DSYNC Backup from the available DSYNC Alternates. If no Alternates are currently available, the Primary waits until a new Alternate becomes available. If more than one Alternate is available, the new Primary chooses the Alternate with the highest server priority. In this way, the cluster maintains its high availability even after the original Primary fails.

The same asynchronous replication of data to a new DSYNC Backup server occurs after the failure of a Backup. Make sure that you give the new Primary enough time to replicate its data to the new Backup; otherwise, data loss may occur.

Routing around failed servers

The Web connectors also have a heartbeat mechanism. However, in addition to using the TCP/IP connection to check the status of the KXS process, the Web connectors also use UDP to ping the KXS. Using UDP enables the Web connectors to detect failures more quickly, since the Web connectors do not have to wait for the TCP/IP timeout to expire.

UDP is sometimes discouraged by firewall administrators. For more information about the exact ports and requirements of the Web connector's UDP ping, consult Chapter 17. Chapter 17 also gives instructions for disabling this feature if your firewall administrators will not allow UDP.

Once the webconnector detects a failed KXS process (either by TCP/IP timeout or by UDP ping) the webconnector will stop routing requests to that server. If there are other servers in can load balance to, it will do so. If there are no other servers available, the webconnector will return a "service not available" error page. The webconnector will attempt to reconnect to the KXS periodically. The amount of time between retries is defined in the `\SOFTWARE\iPlanet\Application Server\6.5\CCSO\LOADB\ConnectRetry` registry key.

Abnormal Clusters and Recovery

Under normal conditions, an iAS cluster has one — and only one — Primary DSYNC server. Each DSYNC client agrees on which server is the Primary, and they send all DSYNC requests and updates to that single Primary. Under unusual conditions, however, mistakes can happen.

These conditions are known as *abnormal clusters* and the cluster typically recovers from them automatically. You need to understand abnormal clusters, however, to prevent them from occurring, and you also need to understand the automatic resolution process for abnormal clusters.

Split-brain clusters

The most common abnormal is the *split-brain cluster*, where more than one Primary DSYNC server exists. The most common cause of a split-brain cluster is a temporary network failure. The network failure prevents the DSYNC Backup from receiving a heartbeat from the Primary, and the DSYNC Backup promotes itself to Primary. After restoration of the network, both servers consider themselves the Primary.

The DSYNC clients that received the message from the Backup that it was promoting itself recognize the "new" Primary as *the* Primary. DSYNC clients that didn't receive the message still perceive the original Primary as the correct Primary.

This situation causes obvious problems because updates and requests don't always go to the same DSYNC database. Changes that you may make to the new Primary don't propagate to the original Primary, and vice versa. The cluster experiences a loss of data integrity until either you or the cluster resolve the split-brain condition. Normally, the cluster will resolve this type of condition automatically, as described below in "Automatic Recovery from abnormal clusters." If you have disabled automatic recovery, you can recover from a split-brain condition by manually shutting down and restarting one of the Primary DSYNC servers.

No-brain clusters

A much rarer condition is the *no-brain* cluster, where none of the servers recognize themselves as a Backup or Primary. You generally see this condition only in the case of rapid multiple failures, where you lose both the Primary and Backup. Some of the DSYNC clients may still believe that they connect to a DSYNC Primary, but no server is actually willing to accept updates or requests for DSYNC information.

This situation indicates a loss of DSYNC data. Additionally, DSYNC clients can't store new DSYNC data until the cluster agrees on the identity of the DSYNC Primary.

Automatic recovery from abnormal clusters

On the Cluster tab of the General settings of the Admin tool you find a Restart in Case of Abnormal Cluster check box. If you select this setting (so that a check mark appears in the check box), the cluster automatically attempts to recover from abnormal clusters. (This feature is on by default, and you have no reason to turn it off unless you don't plan on using DSYNC.)

In the case of a split-brain cluster, the cluster forces the DSYNC Primary with the lower server priority to restart. After that server restarts, it recognizes the other Primary's existence and becomes a DSYNC Alternate or DSYNC Backup. The remaining DSYNC Primary also sends a message to all DSYNC clients that it's the Primary and to direct all updates and requests to it. The only data at risk are updates that you may make during the split-brain period to the Primary that the cluster forces to restart.

In the case of a no-brain cluster, the cluster forces the DSYNC with the highest server priority to take over as DSYNC Primary. That server then creates a new DSYNC database and appoints a DSYNC Backup.

Manual inspection of cluster status

The Admin tool enables you to make each process report on its DSYNC cluster status. Selecting the Dump Cluster Info button on the DSYNC tab of the Logging settings of the Admin tool causes each process to print a brief log of its cluster status.

The KXS creates each log in the log directory of the server, giving the log the name `iasdsync-cluster -xxxxx.log`, where *xxxxx* is the port number of the reporting process. Listing 11-1 is an example of a DSYNC cluster's status log from a normal DSYNC Backup.

Listing 11-1: DSYNC Backup iasdsync cluster log

```
[Sun Jul  8 12:44:33 2001]
***************************
*    DSync Cluster State
***************************
Host: 0xc0a80103
Port: 10818
Role: SyncBackup
Current Engine's order #: 0
SyncPrimary: 0xc0a80104:10818
Is connected to primary? YES
Changing primary? NO
Max number of SyncBackup#=1
SyncBackup[1]: 0xc0a80103:10818
SyncLocal[1]: 0xc0a80104:10820
SyncLocal[2]: 0xc0a80104:10822
SyncLocal[3]: 0xc0a80103:10820
SyncLocal[4]: 0xc0a80103:10822
```

The DSYNC log contains its Host IP (in hex), its port, what it believes its DSYNC role is, which server it believes is the Primary, how many backups should exist, and the list of other DSYNC servers and clients that it's aware of. Cross-referencing this information with the other process logs allows you to easily spot any discrepancies. Everyone should agree on who the Primary is, and the Primary should be aware of everyone in the cluster.

A DSYNC client has a much simpler report, because it needs to know less information about the cluster. The client's report contains which servers it believes are the Primary and Backup along with basic information about its IP and port. Listing 11-2 is a cluster status log from a normal DSYNC client in the same cluster.

Listing 11-2: DSYNC client iasdsync cluster log

```
 [Sun Jul  8 12:44:33 2001]
**************************
*    DSync Cluster State
**************************
Host: 0xc0a80103
Port: 10820
Role: SyncLocal
SyncPrimary: 0xc0a80104:10818
Is connected to primary? YES
Changing primary? NO
Max number of SyncBackup#=1
SyncBackup[1]: 0xc0a80103:10818
```

Failover Case Study

In the following case study, you observe the failover in the cluster shown in Figure 11-1. You observe the log files as you start the cluster and cause various failover scenarios to occur. For brevity's sake, I've removed the timestamps and non-DSYNC messages of all the log files that I include here as examples.

Starting the Primary

You begin by starting the first server. Because it's the first server in the cluster, it becomes the Primary and initializes the DSYNC database. If you examine the KXS log, you see the messages in Listing 11-3.

Listing 11-3: Primary's DSYNC log messages on startup

```
info: DSYNC-039: We (0xc0a80103:10818), are coming up as a Primary and max # of
hot backup(s)=1
info: DSYNC-078: The Sync Local, (0xc0a80103:10820), joined our
cluster
info: DSYNC-078: The Sync Local, (0xc0a80103:10822), joined our cluster
```

These three messages correspond to the start of the KXS as a Primary and the two KJS engines connecting to that Primary as clients.

Starting the Backup

After waiting for the Primary server to fully start, you next start the second server. The Primary notices it joining the cluster and immediately promotes it to Backup.

The messages in Listing 11-4 appear in the Primary's KXS log, showing the new Backup and two KJS clients joining the cluster.

Listing 11-4: Primary's DSYNC log messages on Backup startup

```
info: DSYNC-078: The Sync Backup, (0xc0a80104:10818), joined our cluster
info: DSYNC-078: The Sync Local, (0xc0a80104:10820), joined our cluster
info: DSYNC-078: The Sync Local, (0xc0a80104:10822), joined our cluster
```

The two messages in Listing 11-5 appear in the Backup's KXS log, indicating its successful startup and promotion to Backup status.

Listing 11-5: Backup's DSYNC log messages on startup

```
info: DSYNC-040: We (0xc0a80104:10818), are coming up as a Sync.
Alternate and max # of hot backup(s)=1
info: DSYNC-037: We (0xc0a80104:10818), have been nominated as a
backup by 0xc0a80103:10818
```

Starting the Alternate

The final step of initializing the cluster is starting the third server. Because both a DSYNC Primary and Backup already are running, the new server becomes a DSYNC Alternate. The Primary observes the Alternate and its KJS engines joining the cluster, but it needs to take no special DSYNC actions. Listing 11-6 shows the log messages that appear on the Alternate's startup.

Listing 11-6: Primary's DSYNC log messages on Alternate startup

```
info: DSYNC-077: The Sync Alternate, (0xc0a80105:10818), joined our cluster
info: DSYNC-078: The Sync Local, (0xc0a80105:10820), joined our cluster
info: DSYNC-078: The Sync Local, (0xc0a80105:10822), joined our cluster
```

Killing the Alternate

Killing the Alternate shows the effects of killing a non-DSYNC server. (The results of killing a KJS process are similar.) A series of error messages appear, indicating the loss of a heartbeat. A few seconds pass as the process automatically restarts, and then the Primary records the new Alternate rejoining the cluster. The Alternate also restarts its children KJS engines as part of its re-initialization, so these engines are also observed as leaving and then re-entering the cluster.

Listing 11-7 is an excerpt from the Primary DSYNC server observing the loss of the Alternate.

Listing 11-7: Primary's DSYNC log messages during Alternate failure

```
warning: DSYNC-043: We (0xc0a80103:10818),lost connection to the
Sync Alternate, (0xc0a80105:10818)
info: DSYNC-077: The Sync Alternate, (0xc0a80105:10818), joined our
cluster
warning: DSYNC-044: We (0xc0a80103:10818),lost connection to the
Sync Local, (0xc0a80105:10820)
info: DSYNC-078: The Sync Local, (0xc0a80105:10820), joined our
cluster
warning: DSYNC-044: We (0xc0a80103:10818),lost connection to the
Sync Local, (0xc0a80105:10822)
info: DSYNC-078: The Sync Local, (0xc0a80105:10822), joined our
cluster
```

Killing the Primary

Killing the Primary demonstrates the actual failover of a DSYNC database. The Backup log shows the Backup noticing the failure, promoting itself to Primary (see Listing 11-8) and promoting the Alternate to a new Backup. A few seconds later, you observe the old Primary and its children rejoining the cluster. The old Primary now serves as an Alternate.

Listing 11-8: Backup's DSYNC log messages as it promotes itself to become the new Primary

```
warning: DSYNC-045: We (0xc0a80104:10818), lost connection to the
Sync Primary, (0xc0a80103:10818)
info: DSYNC-041: We (0xc0a80104:10818), are taking over as Primary
and we have 1 backup(s)
info: DSYNC-077: The Sync Alternate, (0xc0a80103:10818), joined our
cluster
info: DSYNC-078: The Sync Local, (0xc0a80103:10820), joined our
cluster
info: DSYNC-078: The Sync Local, (0xc0a80103:10822), joined our
cluster
```

The Alternate's KXS log (Listing 11-9) shows its promotion to Primary, as well as its notification of the new Primary server.

Listing 11-9: Alternate's DSYNC log messages as it's promoted to become the new Backup

```
warning: DSYNC-045: We (0xc0a80105:10818), lost connection to the
Primary
info: DSYNC-037: We (0xc0a80105:10818), have been nominated as a
backup by (0xc0a80104:10818)
info: DSYNC-038: We (0xc0a80105:10818), have been told that the new
Primary is (0xc0a80104:10818)
```

The old Primary's log also contains an interesting message. As it restarts, it tries to resume its role as Primary but discovers that the Backup's already promoted itself to take over the Primary role. It yields to the new Primary, therefore, and takes a role of Alternate (see Listing 11-10).

Listing 11-10: Primary's DSYNC log messages as it yields to the newly promoted Primary

```
info: DSYNC-039: We (0xc0a80103:10818), are coming up as a Primary
and max # of hot backup(s)=1
warning: DSYNC-009: RegisterServer: yielding to another Primary
```

Killing the Backup

Killing the Backup results in the promotion of a new Backup. It also demonstrates that the server can survive multiple failures as long as the Backup gets sufficient time to promote itself.

After killing the Backup server (server #3), you see in the following log message from the Alternate (Listing 11-11) that the Alternate (server #1) is promoting itself to take over the role of Backup.

Listing 11-11: Alternate's DSYNC log message as it's promoted to become the new Backup

```
info: DSYNC-037: We (0xc0a80103:10818), have been nominated as a
backup by (0xc0a80104:10818)
```

Notice that, this time, no "lost connection" message appears, because the connection to the Primary wasn't lost, and the Alternate doesn't maintain a direct connection to the lost Backup.

The Primary also notes the loss of its Backup with the log message that you see in Listing 11-12.

Listing 11-12: Primary's DSYNC log message as it loses connection to Backup

```
warning: DSYNC-42: We (0xc0a80104:10818), lost connection to the hot
backup, 0xc0a80105:10818
```

Summarizing the Case Study

After multiple failures to the cluster, the identity of the Primary and Backup change multiple times without loss of data or functionality in the cluster. Each server is capable of serving in any of the three roles: Primary, Backup, or Alternate.

From the point of view of administrator, which server is the Primary is unimportant, as the administrator can access the DSYNC Primary transparently from any client. Additionally, the cluster's failover mechanism always makes sure that one hot backup of the DSYNC information exists at all times so that the cluster can recover from the loss of the DSYNC Primary.

Summary

Failover is an important element of increasing application availability. The clustering features of iAS provide a strong platform for providing application failover with no impact on end users. The information in this chapter enables you to utilize these failover features wisely. We reviewed the concepts of DSYNC Primaries and Backups and how they relate to failover. We also discussed the ways that clustering can go wrong, such as split brain and no-brain situations, and how to avoid these situations.

Chapter 12

Introducing SOAP

IN THIS CHAPTER

- ◆ Understanding the purpose and goals of the SOAP specification

- ◆ Learning the basic architecture of a SOAP service

- ◆ Discussing the advantages of using SOAP in conjunction with iAS

THE ACRONYM *SOAP* stands for *Simple Object Access Protocol*. SOAP is a protocol for remote-method invocation that uses an XML syntax to describe requests and responses. This chapter introduces the basic concepts of SOAP and the details of how SOAP integrates with iAS. This chapter, however, isn't a tutorial on how to use SOAP in general. SOAP is an extremely versatile technology, and I can't present a reasonable summary in one chapter of this book. If you already have experience in writing and using SOAP services, this chapter gives you some tips and tricks to applying that knowledge to iPlanet Application Server. If you're not yet familiar with SOAP, this chapter should whet your appetite to the value that SOAP can bring to your Web applications and give you a high-level understanding of how you can use iAS to host and access SOAP services. After reading this chapter an excellent next step is to deploy and examine the SOAP sample bundled with iAS.

Fundamentals of SOAP

SOAP is an XML-based method of exchanging information that includes specifications for enveloping messages, serializing data types, and giving instructions for processing remote method invocations. Although SOAP has other purposes, it's most common use is to make RPCs (remote-procedure calls) by using HTTP as a transport mechanism.

A remote-procedure call (also known as remote-method invocation when using object-oriented terminology) is exactly what it sounds like: a client calling a procedure (or method) on a remote server. The role of SOAP and other RPC mechanisms is to provide the communication layer between client and server. In short, the role of an RPC mechanism is to make procedures and objects residing on a remote machine function as if they were running on the local machine.

If you utilize SOAP as an HTTP-based RPC mechanism, a SOAP client application constructs a SOAP XML message that contains all the input parameters to the remote method. It then transmits the message to a SOAP server, which interprets the message and performs the requested action. The SOAP server then returns a SOAP message containing the results of the action. People often use SOAP for stateless transactions, but it does support the use of cookies as a method of maintaining state over a series of SOAP interactions.

A large part of SOAP's value, however, is its capability to function cross-platform. A SOAP client can make remote procedure calls on a SOAP server, regardless of how you implement that method on the SOAP server. SOAP would, for example, enable an iAS application to seamlessly invoke methods on a DCOM-based application running on the Microsoft Transaction Server (assuming, of course, that a SOAP RPC router is running on the Microsoft server). The iAS application doesn't need to know anything about what the SOAP service is implementing and can remain completely ignorant about the platform or language with which the SOAP service has been implemented.

 I cover the naming services that relate to SOAP in Chapter 16. These naming services enable SOAP clients to explore what SOAP services are available and how to connect to them.

Wide industry support exists for using SOAP, including major efforts from IBM, Sun Microsystems, Microsoft, and the Apache Software Foundation. Although SOAP is a relatively new technology, this wide industry support and its capability to facilitate integration across these diverse platforms has led to its swift adoption.

iAS as a SOAP client

Although SOAP is an emerging protocol, SOAP 1.1 already provides several implementations. iPlanet doesn't have its own SOAP implementation, but iPlanet does test and support the use of the Apache SOAP 2.2 implementation with iPlanet Application Server. (Notice that the 2.2 version number refers to the implementation version and not the SOAP version. Apache SOAP 2.2 supports version 1.1 of the SOAP protocol.)

The Apache SOAP Java libraries enable developers to automatically generate and transmit RPC requests via SOAP messages. These Java libraries enable developers to focus on developing functionality and not on building XML messages by hand or processing them by hand by using an XML parser.

In using iAS as a SOAP client, SOAP acts as just another backend system. But instead of using JDBC or JCA to access the backend, you construct your SOAP requests by using the Apache SOAP API. Because SOAP is platform and language neutral, the SOAP client doesn't need to know anything about how the service provider actually determines the results. The client needs to know only the URL of the SOAP provider and the format of the message that the provider expects.

Figure 12-1 shows the basic architecture of an iAS application acting as a SOAP client. The browser or standalone Java application connects to the iPlanet

Application Server application by making an HTTP or RMI/IIOP request. The application then constructs a SOAP message by using the Apache SOAP API and sends it to a SOAP service provider. The SOAP service provider returns a SOAP response, which the application reads by using the Apache SOAP API.

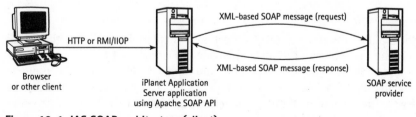

Figure 12-1: iAS SOAP architecture (client)

Understanding the XML messaging that the Apache API is generating behind the scenes is important, however, if you want to design effective SOAP solutions and also to help in debugging SOAP transactions. Apache SOAP, for example, includes a TCP/IP proxy that enables you to monitor the actual on-the-wire communications. To understand the output of this tool, an understanding of the underlying XML message format is necessary.

Listing 12-1 is a code sample from the SOAP sample that comes with iPlanet Application Server. It demonstrates the basics of using the Apache SOAP API to call a SOAP service.

Listing 12-1: iAS SOAP HelloWorld sample (excerpt)

```
String name = argv[1];
Call call = new Call();
call.setTargetObjectURI("urn:Greeter");
call.setMethodName("getGreeting");
call.setEncodingStyleURI(Constants.NS_URI_SOAP_ENC);
// Invoke the call.
Response resp;
try {
   resp = call.invoke(url, "");
}
catch (SOAPException e) {
   System.err.println("Caught SOAPException (" +
      e.getFaultCode() + "): " + e.getMessage());
   return;
}
// Check the response.
if (!resp.generatedFault()) {
   Parameter ret = resp.getReturnValue();
```

Continued

Listing 12-1 *(continued)*

```
    Object val = ret.getValue();
    System.out.println("Hello World sample with Soap.");
    System.out.println("Good " + val + " " + name +
        ". Have a great " + val + ".");
}
```

The Apache API provides the `Call` object as a method for building the SOAP message necessary to make an RPC call. The code in Listing 12-1 uses several methods (`setTargetObjectURI`, `setMethodName`, and `setEncodingStyleURI`) to create the envelope for the SOAP request and then calls the `invoke` method to send the SOAP message. The `invoke` method's parameter specifies the SOAP service provider to which you plan to send the request. If the client is more sophisticated (such as the `Cart` sample that comes with iAS) it may also add parameters to the request by using the `setParams` method or enable session cookies by using the `setMaintainSession` method.

After making the request, the sample client examines the response for the return values. (It also does some error checking that the preceding excerpt doesn't include.) It extracts the return value by using the `getValue` method and returns it to the user.

This `HelloWorld` application is obviously a very simple example of creating a SOAP client, but it does show how the Apache SOAP API enables the creation of applications that use SOAP RPC calls without needing to manually create or send the SOAP XML messages. The Apache SOAP implementation handles the process of creating and parsing the XML messages behind the scenes. The HTTP transport protocol also remains abstracted from the user, other than the need to know the URL of the SOAP RPC router where the request goes.

Many development tools also include wizards and tools for interacting with SOAP services. Sun's Forte for Java IDE (on the enclosed CD) includes SOAP support in the Web Services module. The Web Services module comes with the Enterprise Edition upgrade pack that you can download from the Forte for Java Update Wizard.

iAS as a SOAP service provider

The server component of the Apache SOAP implementation is an RPC router that enables iAS to receive SOAP-based RPC requests. The RPC router receives the incoming requests and decides how to respond to them, basing its decision on a deployment descriptor for the requested SOAP service. The deployment descriptor can tell the RPC router to execute an ordinary Java class, an Enterprise Java Bean, or a BSF (Bean Scripting Framework) script to generate the SOAP response.

Thus the RPC router acts as a proxy for the incoming SOAP requests, as shown in Figure 12-2. The Apache RPC router receives SOAP messages and then executes code on the application server to generate the SOAP response. The RPC router is responsible for constructing the SOAP response, basing that response on the return values of the executed code.

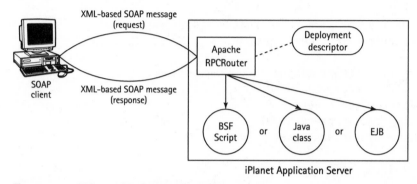

Figure 12-2: iAS as a SOAP service provider

The deployment descriptor is the critical part of SOAP-enabling iAS code. You can either generate the deployment descriptors automatically, by using the Web-based administration tool that's a part of the Apache RPC router, or you can create an XML deployment descriptor by hand and deploy it from the command line. The deployment descriptor defines the following attributes:

◆ The URN (Universal Resource Name) of the service

◆ The scope of the request

◆ The list of exposed methods

◆ The provider type (EJB, Java class, or script)

◆ Information about the provider (the implementation class for EJBs and Java classes or the script or filename for a script)

◆ The type mappings (classes that the RPC router uses to serialize and deserialize any nonstandard classes that you need to pass in the SOAP message)

Taking a look at the deployment descriptor and implementation class of the HelloWorld sample that comes with iAS shows how simple adding SOAP support to an existing application is. Listing 12-2 shows the Java class that the RPC router calls to support the getGreeting SOAP method.

Listing 12-2: GreeterService.java (excerpt)

```java
public class GreeterService extends Object
{
    public GreeterService() {
    // initialize the service
    }
    /**
     * Internally calls the <code>getGreeting</code> method of
     * Greeter stateless session bean.
     */
    public String getGreeting() throws Exception {
        javax.ejb.Handle beanHandle;
        Greeter myGreeterBean;
        GreeterHome myGreeterHome;
        Greeter myGreeterRemote;

        InitialContext initial = null;
        Hashtable env = new java.util.Hashtable(1);
        System.out.println("\nGreeterServlet is executing ...");
        System.out.println("Retrieving JNDI initial context");

        try {
            initial = new javax.naming.InitialContext();
        }
        catch (Exception e) {
            System.out.println("Exception creating InitialContext: "
                + e.toString());
            return null;
        }

        System.out.println("Looking up greeter bean home interface");
        String JNDIName = "ejb/TheGreeter";
        System.out.println("Looking up: " + JNDIName);
        Object objref = initial.lookup(JNDIName);
        myGreeterHome = (GreeterHome)PortableRemoteObject.narrow(
            objref, GreeterHome.class);
        System.out.println("Creating the greeter bean");
        myGreeterRemote = myGreeterHome.create();

        System.out.println(
            "Getting the message from the greeter bean");
        String theMessage = myGreeterRemote.getGreeting();

        System.out.println("Got this message from greeter bean: " +
```

```
theMessage);
    return theMessage;
  }
}
```

The preceding code instantiates the `TheGreeter` EJB and invokes the `getGreeting` business method. It then returns the `String` that the `getGreeting` method returns. The majority of the code is logging a message that tracks the progress of the class. (The deployment descriptor can directly invoke the EJB, but this wrapper class provides the additional logging messages.)

The corresponding deployment descriptor is shown in Listing 12-3.

Listing 12-3: DeploymentDescriptor.xml

```
<isd:service xmlns:isd="http://xml.apache.org/xml-soap/deployment"
   id="urn:Greeter">
  <isd:provider type="java" scope="Request" methods="getGreeting">
     <isd:java class="samples.soap.helloworld.GreeterService"
        static="false"/>
  </isd:provider>
  <isd:mappings>
  </isd:mappings>
</isd:service>
```

This simple deployment descriptor links incoming requests for the `getGreeting` method of the `urn:Greeter` service to the Java class of `samples.soap.helloworld.GreeterService`. No custom mappings are necessary, as you can see by the empty `<isd:mappings>` tag pair.

The `HelloWorld` sample gives us a simple introduction on how to SOAP-enable an existing EJB. It shows us how the Apache RPCRouter enables iPlanet Application Server to receive, parse, and respond to SOAP messages. You can find more complex SOAP examples in the `Cart` sample that comes with iAS and in the Apache SOAP documentation.

Benefits of SOAP on iAS

Now that you understand the basics of SOAP, you can consider the benefits of SOAP that are specific to iPlanet Application Server. Although iPlanet uses a third-party SOAP implementation from the Apache Foundation, utilizing SOAP on iAS as compared to using RMI/IIOP, offers some unique advantages. (In fact, some may consider using a third-party SOAP implementation an advantage itself, because it prevents developers from needing to learn a proprietary API to work with SOAP.)

Cross-platform integration

SOAP offers many inherent advantages over RMI/IIOP. I've already enumerated some of them in the preceding sections, including SOAP's capability to perform cross-platform and language-neutral requests. The third-party nature of the SOAP specification ensures the continued capability of SOAP to cross these barriers even as competition increases between J2EE and other platforms, such as Microsoft's .NET.

Because iPlanet Application Server is currently the third-most popular J2EE application server, this cross-platform capability is especially important. iPlanet Application Server's market share often requires it to integrate not only with legacy applications, but also with other J2EE application servers. Performing this integration is much easier with SOAP than with RMI, as the following list describes:

♦ *SOAP doesn't require any proprietary client-side code.* Most J2EE application servers either require proprietary RMI extensions (such as BEA Weblogic's T3 protocol) or support only a specific ORB (such as iAS).

♦ *SOAP is more firewall-friendly than IIOP.* SOAP typically operates over HTTP, which the configurations of most firewalls already permit. IIOP doesn't operate over a well-known port, and each J2EE application server requires opening a different port (or range of ports).

♦ *SOAP requires opening up firewalls only to the Web server.* The fact that RMI/IIOP access to the application server requires that the client application can open a TCP/IP directly to the application-server tier violates the typical n-tier network security models.

Chapter 17 shows typical firewall configurations for production iPlanet Application Server deployments. Examine Figure 17-1 to see why opening a TCP/IP directly from a client application to the iAS cluster is disadvantageous.

Fault tolerance

iPlanet Application Server's history is as a Web-application server. Its capability to respond to HTTP requests is highly optimized and based on Kivasoft code that's undergone five years of production use and the resultant "battle hardening." The iAS request path is extremely fault tolerant, enabling web requests to distribute requests across multiple fault-tolerant Web servers and multiple fault-tolerant application servers.

In contrast, iPlanet Application Server has supported RMI/IIOP only since the 6.0 release in February 2000. The RMI/IIOP request path requires that the client application directly establish the connection by using a CXS process listening on a specific TCP/IP port. RMI requests fail if the CXS process or underlying server fails, unless the client application is hand-coded to failover to another CXS process.

Because SOAP uses HTTP as its transport protocol in making RPC requests, SOAP can take advantage of iAS's strong HTTP request path. On the other hand, RMI requests must use the CXS-based IIOP request path.

Performance and scalability

In addition to being more fault tolerant, the HTTP request path of iAS is also much faster than the RMI/IIOP request path. This performance difference isn't an issue with the protocols themselves, but merely an issue of the iAS implementations. The CXS process isn't as efficient at routing RMI/IIOP requests as the KXS is at routing HTTP requests.

Of course, these performance characteristics may change in future versions of iAS. But the current architecture is more efficient at handling HTTP requests than it is at IIOP requests. SOAP RPC calls (which use HTTP as a transport layer), therefore, offer better performances than do RMI RPC calls (which use IIOP as a transport layer).

iAS and SunONE Web services

Sun's announced its support of SOAP as part of its SunONE Web services initiative. As Sun continues to release SunONE servers, development tools, and prebuilt services, you can expect them to integrate with the iPlanet Application Server. You can expect the next generation iPlanet Directory Server, for example, to act as a UDDI repository for iAS Web services and the next generation Forte for Java IDE to use wizards to generate SOAP-based Web services that run on iAS.

SunONE is the core of Sun's software direction, and SOAP-based Web services are critical to SunONE. Building your enterprise's Web services can enable you to better take advantage of the forthcoming SunONE tools and services.

Summary

Web services is the latest fad in the IT industry. Like most IT fads, Web services is a combination of real value and hype. This chapter helps you understand the real value of Web services and gives you an idea of the weaknesses of Web services. This chapter also describes, on a general level, how iPlanet Application Server can act as a supplier and consumer of Web services.

Apache SOAP documentation

- ◆ Apache SOAP Implementation: `http://xml.apache.org/soap/`

- ◆ API Documentation for Apache SOAP:
  `http://xml.apache.org/soap/docs/apiDocs/index.html`

General SOAP documentation

◆ Sun Dot-Com Builder's Overview and Assessment of SOAP: `http://dcb.sun.com/practices/webservices/overviews/overview_soap.jsp`

◆ W3C Note for the Creation of SOAP Working Group (SOAP 1.1): `www.w3.org/TR/SOAP/`

◆ Soapware, a Directory of SOAP Utilities and Documentation: `www.soapware.org/`

Sun and iPlanet SOAP information

◆ iPlanet SOAP Sample Documentation: `http://developer.iplanet.com/appserver/samples/soap/docs/index.html`

◆ SunONE Web Services: `www.sun.com/software/sunone/`

◆ Building Web Services with Forte for Java: `www.sun.com/forte/ffj/resources/documentation/websrvcs.pdf`

Other information

◆ Bean Scripting Framework: `www-124.ibm.com/developerworks/projects/bsf`

◆ Microsoft .NET Web Services (including SOAP): `www.gotdotnet.com/team/XMLwebservices/default.aspx`

Chapter 13

The iAS Registry

IN THIS CHAPTER

- ◆ Navigating the registry and its contents
- ◆ Understanding the dependencies of an iAS instance on the registry
- ◆ Performing common registry modifications

THE IPLANET APPLICATION SERVER (iAS) REGISTRY is a core runtime component that maintains virtually all configuration information for your iAS instance. In this chapter, you examine the infrastructure supporting the registry, the entries that a typical J2EE application creates within the registry, and the tools that you use to maintain the contents of the registry.

Registry Overview

In general terms, the *registry* is just a collection of information. Many software products that you use daily contain a registry. The Windows operating system, for example, contains a registry. This registry is a primary source of configuration information that is used to support your OS and its applications. Within an iAS instance, a registry is used in a very similar fashion. All core application-server and application-related settings are represented as entries within the iPlanet registry. The registry is optimized for quick reads and mainly static data. Thus the application server reads the majority of the configuration settings into memory on startup. This information ranges from TCP/IP ports and addresses to J2EE deployment descriptor settings.

Logically, the iAS registry is a structured hierarchy of keys and values, which are organized by the type of information that they represent. For example, the EJB-Components key contains a list of *values* representing deployed EJB components. To best visualize the treelike structure of the registry, run the iAS `kregedit` tool, as shown in Figure 13-1. You find the `kregedit` tool in the `<IAS_HOME>/bin` directory.

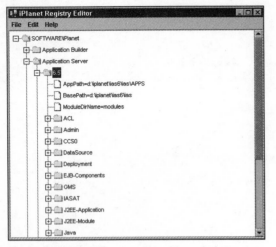

Figure 13-1: The iPlanet registry hierarchal structure

The physical iAS registry

Physically, the iAS registry is stored in two portions: one portion local and the other in a directory server instance. The local portion of the registry is stored either as a text file in Unix installations or as a subset of the Windows registry in NT/2000 installations. The portion that resides in the directory server (LDAP) instance is known as the *configuration directory*, whereas the local portion is known as the *local registry*.

The rationale for partitioning the registry into a local registry and a configuration directory is accessibility. As the application server starts, it reads the local registry. This portion of the registry contains information about where to find the configuration directory and how the keys within it map, as I discuss in the following paragraphs. The purpose of the local registry's content is to provide specific configuration settings for the iAS instance, while the configuration directory can host information that amongst multiple iAS instances can share (perhaps within a cluster).

The majority of the entries in the local portion of the registry relate to configuration, such as the TCP/IP settings for the iAS processes, where to find the configuration directory and its keys, database connections, and logging levels. The entries in the configuration directory relate mainly to the application. This division of entries is to facilitate the sharing of component information that can shared within a cluster. You get to navigate the registry and the entries in the section "Navigate a Deployed Application," later in this chapter.

The configuration directory server stores 20+ keys, and the local registry stores this mapping information in the GDS\Subtreemaps directory (which you can view from the kregedit tool). Any module accessing a mapped GDS subtree, therefore, transparently accesses the LDAP back end.

Unix-based iAS installations store the local portion of the registry in the file system, in the file `<IAS_HOME>/ias/registry/reg.dat`. Windows-based installs use a subset of the Windows registry.

iAS registry topology

The preceding section establishes the physical registry's makeup, and this section illustrates a few registry topologies that you commonly encounter in iAS installations.

Figure 13-2 is synonymous with most developer-oriented installations, where you install all software supporting a development instance on one machine, including the Web server and the iAS instance.

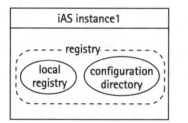

Figure 13–2: Typical iAS instance with registry

Figure 13-3 depicts a cluster where the configuration directory physically resides on a separate server. Notice that each iAS instance has its own local registry. This figure should clearly show you that each machine has unique settings that only it should know about.

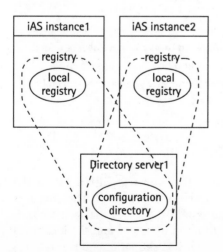

Figure 13–3: Remote configuration directory

The next common topology that you often see, as shown in Figure 13-4, is to put the Web server on one physical machine and the iAS instance on another. The key detail to notice here is that the Web connector also has its own registry. You see an example where this setup has some significance in the section "Some Common iAS Registry Edits," later in this chapter.

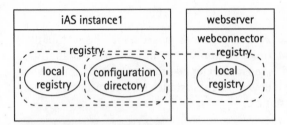

Figure 13–4: Local registry on Web–connector box

You now know that the registry supplies a unified view of configuration information that is stored in multiple physical locations. The leading question now is how you interact with these entries. In the following section, I review the tools at your disposal for registry manipulation.

iAS Registry Editing Tools

With any typical iAS installation, you have various graphical and command-line tools at your disposal to help facilitate registry manipulation. As I discuss in the preceding sections, the registry contains both application-server and application-configuration entries. So you should find no surprise in the fact that you have at your disposal tools that help address both types of entries.

 Misuse or misunderstanding of the following tools can have severe effects on the stability of your application server and possibly your system. Please refer to Chapter 21 for procedures on ensuring that you have a recoverable iAS instance.

kregedit

The most common general-purpose registry tool that you use within iAS is the iPlanet Registry Editor, a.k.a. `kregedit` (as I outline in Table 13-1). This tool is a Java Swing (GUI) -based application that transparently enables the maintenance and navigation of entries from both the configuration directory and the local registry for the given iAS instance. The `kregedit` tool is as shown in Figure 13-1.

TABLE 13-1 KREGEDIT OVERVIEW

How to run	From `<IAS_HOME>/ias/bin/kregedit`.
Can tool run remotely?	No. You must run it on same server as local registry.
GUI-based?	Yes.
Edits both configuration directory and local registry?	Yes.
Edits more than one iAS instance?	Partially yes. Entries that you store in the configuration directory can share among multiple iAS instances (cluster). This tool can modify these.
Strength	Can edit all registry entries. Contains entries unavailable for edit from administration tool (iASAT).
Limitations	On Unix, you must install an X-Windows server to run this GUI-based tool. Many production environments don't install an X-Windows server.
	Can't run it remotely. User must have an account on server to run this tool.
	The application server(s) don't dynamically pick up changed settings. If you change settings via the `kregedit` tool, you need to restart the application server for it to pick up the changes.

Never use the Windows tools `regedit` or `regedt32` in place of `kregedit`. `kregedit` performs edits that can take place in the local registry and/or the configuration directory.

iPlanet Application Server Administration Tool (iASAT)

The iPlanet Application Server Administration Tool (iASAT) is a Java Swing-based application that you can use to administer one or more iAS instances. iASAT is launched from the command line via ksvradmin. The primary iASAT tool strengths are a sophisticated interface for manipulating local and configuration directory settings and remote accessibility to administration features for one or more iAS instances. In Table 13-2, you can get an overview of the iASAT. Figure 13-5 shows a basic GUI view of iASAT.

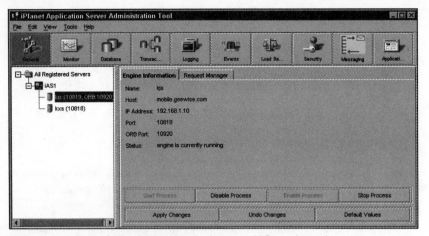

Figure 13-5: The iASAT console with the instance iAS1 registered

TABLE 13-2 iASAT OVERVIEW

How to run	On Unix, from `<IAS_HOME>/ias/bin/ksvradmin`.
	On NT, from the program files->iPlanet Application Server-> iAS Administration Toolmenu or the command line.
Can tool run remotely?	Yes.
GUI-based?	Yes.
Edits both configuration directory and local registry?	Partially yes. Covers typical administration settings — for example, database settings, JMS queues, and application-component settings.
Edits more than one iAS instance?	Yes, with the above restriction.
Strengths	Rich UI (much friendlier than `kregedit`). iASAT is a GUI that's streamlined for many typical administration tasks — for example, creating clusters, adjusting logging levels, and monitoring iAS instances.
	Requires login for access to administer the application servers.
	The application servers dynamically pick up most changes as soon as you apply them.

Limitations

Needs `kregedit` for certain entries — for example, in setting up specific Web-connector-based load balancing (weighted round robin).

On Unix, you must install an X-Windows server to run this GUI-based tool. Many production environments don't install an X-Windows server.

kreg

At times, creating and restoring snapshots of the registry is useful. While practicing correct restore practices, for example, you may back up the registry before deploying a new application. Depending on the outcome, you can restore the registry to its previous state by reloading the snapshot. The `kreg` tool (which I describe in Table 13-3) is useful in this backup and restore capacity. `kreg` has a historical presence from previous iPlanet Application Server versions, all the way back to 2.*x* days. You also use it to deploy legacy AppLogic-based applications. In Table 13-3 you can review the kreg tool.

 `kreg` doesn't show -save and -load options as you use in the following examples. This is an undocumented feature.

You can use `kreg` with -save or -load options, as follows:

```
kreg -save back.txt "\SOFTWARE\iPlanet\Application Server\ClassDef"
kreg -load back.txt
```

TABLE 13-3 KREG OVERVIEW

How to run	From `<IAS_HOME>/ias/bin/kreg`.
Can tool run remotely?	No.
GUI-based?	No.
Edits both configuration directory and local registry?	Yes. Can back up and restore any subtree within the registry.

Continued

TABLE 13-3 *(Continued)*

Edits more than iAS one instance?	Partially yes. Entries that you store in the configuration directory can be shared among multiple iAS instances (cluster). This tool can modify these.
Strengths	Can back up and restore.
Limitations	As a registry user, you must know in advance the subtree that you want to back up.
	The Unix version requires additional steps to implement correctly. Run the `.kreg` process in Unix instead of the `kreg` script. You must set up the environment to run the `.kreg` process. Sourcing the `kreg` script and killing it by pressing Ctrl+C after you get a prompt for the AppLogic/Module name sets up the environment as necessary. To source the `kreg` script run: `". kreg"`.

iasdeploy

You can use the `iasdeploy` command-line tool to deploy, redeploy and undeploy J2EE applications and modules (among other auxiliary features). The byproduct of deployment is the creation of application-related entries within the registry. You store application entries primary within the configuration directory. Creating application component entries within the configuration directory makes for easy work in placing a component into a clustered environment. Table 13-4 reviews the feature of the iasdeploy.

TABLE 13-4 IASDEPLOY OVERVIEW

How to run	From `<IAS_HOME>/ias/bin/iasdeploy`.
Can tool run remotely?	Yes.
GUI-based?	No.
Edits both configuration directory and local registry?	Partially yes. Creates and removes only application-related (EAR, WAR orJAR) entries, in both, based on your deployment descriptors. (See Chapter 9 for deployment descriptors and deployment overview.) iasdeploy also deploys resource files which are only stored locally.

Edits more than one iAS instance?	Partially yes. Deployment descriptor and iAS specific entries that you store in the configuration directory [?] can share among multiple iAS instances (cluster).
Strengths	It's simple.
	Secure login for remote deployment of applications.
	This tool can be scripted into build tools like ANT or `make`.

LDAP tools

I list the LDAP tools `ldapdelete`, `ldapmodify`, and `ldapsearch` for completeness, because you store a portion of the registry in the configuration directory instance. The name of each tool reveals its purpose.

> You can find documentation on `ldapdelete`, `ldapmodify`, and `ldapsearch` at `http://docs.iplanet.com/docs/manuals/ias/65/reg/65regist.htm#129798`.

Navigate a Deployed Application

As an iAS user, getting familiar with the contents of the registry aids you in your day-to-day interactions with iAS. Typically, one of the first needs that you may have for the registry (other than changing your license key) is to investigate a deployed J2EE application or module. In this section, I assume that you just ran the `iasdeploy` tool on the Helloworld application (one of the iAS sample applications). I pick things up from running `kregedit`.

After the iPlanet Registry Editor launches, navigate to the J2EE-Application *key*, as shown in Figure 13-6. You can find this key under `SOFTWARE\iPlanet\ Application Server\6.0\J2EE-Application`.

Notice that you can quickly see the modules that comprise this application and their types (WAR or JAR) by expanding the module *key*.

Next, navigate to the J2EE-Module *key* (see Figure 13-6). On expanding the J2EE-Module *key*, you can identify the helloworld and helloworldEjb modules. You can now expand either module to see what components are deployed. For the helloworld module, which is a WAR module, you can expand the servlets *key* to see what Web components you've deployed. Similarly, for the helloworldEjb module, you can expand the `ejbs` *key* to see what EJB components you've deployed.

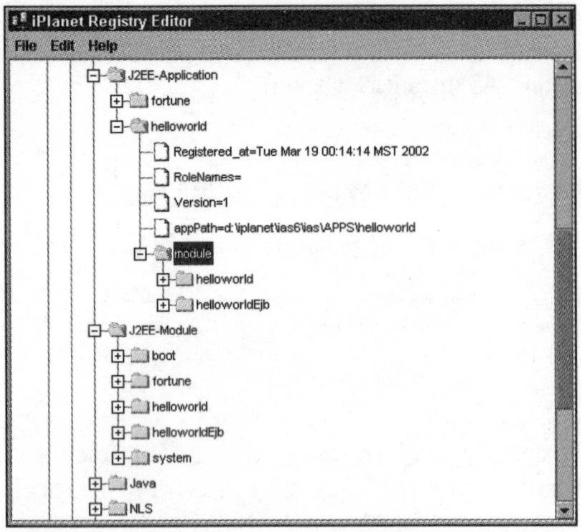

Figure 13-6: The J2EE-application HelloWorld, modules helloworld and helloworldEjb

From these simple steps, you can figure out an application's modules and components. One more step remains: accessing the descriptor settings for each module and its components. By simply expanding the `helloworld` module again (under the J2EE-Module key), you can see many of the WAR file's descriptor settings (see Figure 13-7).

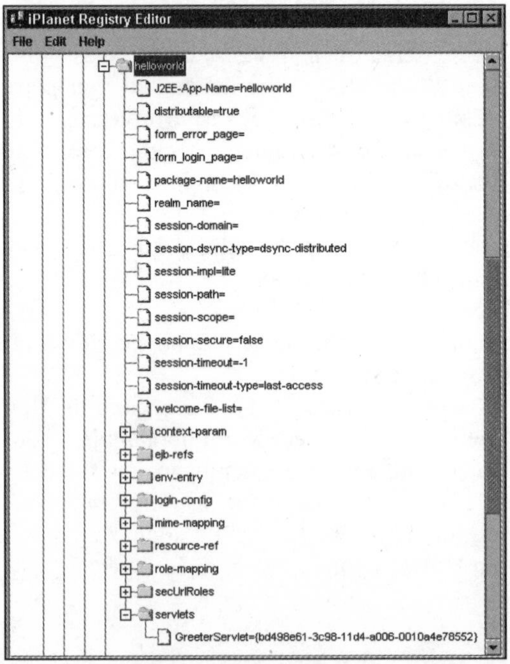

Figure 13-7: Web application's descriptor settings

These settings are at the Web-application level and don't contain descriptor settings at the Web-component level (JSP or servlet). To get the Web component's descriptor settings, you need to note the servlet name and GUID under the servlets *key*. In this case, the GUID looks as follows (as shown in Figure 13-7):

```
GreeterServlet={bd498e61-3c98-11d4-a006-0010a4e78552}
```

A *GUID* (globally unique identifier) is a 128-bit number that iAS uses internally to uniquely identify components. GUIDs are guaranteed unique across time and space. iAS uses GUIDs to avoid internal naming clashes for components that you deploy within an application server.

Expanding the `SOFTWARE\iPlanet\Application Server\ClassDef` *key*, you have a listing of all the components by their internal GUID names. Notice that the expansion of this key takes a moment, because `kregedit` is reading these entries from LDAP (the configuration directory). Figure 13-8 shows success in locating the `GreeterServlet`.

```
iPlanet Registry Editor
File  Edit  Help
    {b66ab8a0-568b-171e-da88-080020a16896}
    {bd498e61-3c98-11d4-a006-0010a4e78552}
        J2eeAppName=helloworld
        J2eeModuleName=helloworld
        SecurityFlags=0
        load-on-startup=0
        number-of-singles=10
        servlet-class=samples.helloworld.servlet.GreeterServlet
        servlet-name=GreeterServlet
        validation-required=false
        GDS
        SecurityRoleRef
        ias-params
        init-param
    {d5fd15d0-a156-11d5-b5a3-00047631c810}
    {dfc2de60-7fbc-11d5-b4b6-00047631c7dd}
    {ea1c3ae0-a156-11d5-b5a3-00047631c810}
    {ed44fa16-eaaa-42e9-b899-fd4b4b9a97bc}
    {f4379ccc-e3de-185a-ffe0-08002089d1a0}
    {fdbdf9b7-ff4f-1687-f1f0-080020a16896}
    {fdbdfa78-ff4f-1687-f1f0-080020a16896}
```

Figure 13-8: Web component's descriptor setting under ClassDef

To set the application server CLASSPATH on a Windows installation, use the SOFTWARE\iPlanet\Application Server\6.0\Java\ClassPath value. On a Unix install, this entry doesn't exist. Set the CLASSPATH in the <IAS_HOME>/ias/env/iasenv.ksh file instead.

Some Common iAS Registry Edits

The iAS registry contains too many entries to explain in this book. Instead, in this section, I review a few commonplace registry edits. I'm assuming that you've run the kregedit tool to perform these edits. Notice that all values in the registry present an Edit dialog box after you double-click them:

The iPlanet registry always presents something of a mystery — one in which not all the contents of the registry are fully disclosed. As of the writing of this chapter, iPlanet has published a registry-entry guide at http://docs. iplanet.com/docs/manuals/ias/65/reg/contents.htm.

◆ Change License Key — If your iAS license key expires, you notice that your kxs process doesn't start anymore. To validate this process, type **kxs** in a DOS or Unix terminal window and a license message appears. Supply a new license key in the following value to get up and going:

```
SOFTWARE\iPlanet\Application Server\6.0\CCS0\ENG\Key
```

◆ Modify the CLASSPATH — iAS ships with many common JAR and ZIP files (XML parsers and core J2EE SDKS) in its CLASSPATH; yet there are times when you need to augment the CLASSPATH. Make sure that you restart your iAS instance after modifying the CLASSPATH.

Windows NT/2000

```
SOFTWARE\iPlanet\Application Server\6.0\CCS0\java\ClassPath
```

In Unix, you modify the CLASSATH setting in the <IAS_HOME>/env/ iasenv.ksh script. I suggest that you create a variable in the script to store your specific settings and simply add your variable to the end of the CLASS-PATH variable definition in the section "# Union of all CLASSPATHS" of the iasenv.sh script.

◆ Pass arguments to the JVM: — At times, you need to pass arguments to your applications in the form of JVM arguments or to change the JVM settings (for example, memory size).

Windows NT/2000

```
SOFTWARE\iPlanet\Application Server\6.0\CCSO\java\JavaArgs
```

In Unix, you modify this setting in the `<IAS_HOME>/env/iasenv.ksh` script. I suggest that you create an variable in the script to store your specific JVM argument settings and simply add your variable to the `JAVA_ARGS` variable definition in the `"kjs"` section of the iasenv.sh script.

◆ `kxs` request logging — As I discuss in Chapter 3, the `kxs` process dispatches requests out to the `kjs` engines. Logging statistics such as GUID, dispatched `kjs` engine, and round-trip time can prove useful information for developers and operations folks. Change this value from 0 to 1.

```
SOFTWARE\iPlanet\Application Server\6.0\CCSO\REQ\Debug
```

◆ Change `NASApp` URL keyword — By default, Web applications that you deploy to iAS have the keyword `NASApp` in the URL that you use to invoke Web components. Your operations folks more than likely want to change this keyword to a more vender-neutral name. Modify the value `NASApp` to your new keyword in the following entries:

```
SOFTWARE\iPlanet\Application Server
\6.0\CCSO\HTTPAPI\SSPL_APP_PREFIX
```

Windows NT

```
SOFTWARE\iPlanet\Application Server
\6.0\CCSO\HTTPAPI\SSPL_APP_PREFIX\<no key>
```

Unix

```
SOFTWARE\iPlanet\Application Server
\6.0\CCSO\HTTPAPI\SSPL_APP_PREFIX\<Default>
```

◆ Connection pool logging — Logging database connection acquiring and releasing can prove a very important logging feature in applying load to your application. Validating matching acquire/release messages can confirm that your application isn't leaking database connections.

For iAS type database drivers (not third-party drivers), adjust the value from 0 to 1. Notice that <*driver type*> is ORACLE_OCI if you're using Oracle.

```
SOFTWARE\iPlanet\Application Server
\6.0\CCSO\DAE2\<driver type>\CacheDebugMsgs
```

◆ Turn on Versioning — Enabling the JVM to dynamically reload your Java CLASS files and JSPs can save development time. Instead of restarting the iAS instance (or kjs engine), modifying the following value enables reloading. (I don't recommend this setting in nondevelopment environments.) Change the value in the following line from 1 to 0.

```
SOFTWARE\iPlanet\Application
Server\6.0\CCSO\Versioning\Disable
```

Summary

After reviewing this chapter, you can see that the strength of the iPlanet Registry is simply the unification of configuration information. In nearly all situations, you needn't bother hand-editing disparate configuration files to alter your application-server configuration. The registry supplies a single point of maintenance for both application-server and application-component-related information. As a developer, you needn't worry about deployments (which alter the registry) beyond using the simple command-line tool iasdeploy. As an administrator, you have local and secure remote control over virtually all the settings for an application server by using the kregedit and ksvradmin tools.

Chapter 14

Log Files

IPLANET APPLICATION SERVER produces a large number of log files to enable you to monitor and debug the server. This chapter enumerates all the iAS log files and discusses methods for getting the most information from them.

Web Server Logs

In tracing the execution of a request, the first logs to check are the Web-server logs. The Web-server logs are critical for both monitoring and debugging your iAS applications. The Web server is the access point to your application (excepting RMI clients) and, therefore, has a wealth of information about your application available to it.

Because the overwhelming majority of iPlanet Application Server users utilize iPlanet Web Server, this chapter focuses on the iPlanet Web Server logs. The same concepts apply to the log files of Microsoft Internet Information Server and Apache HTTP Server, but IIS and Apache format and locate their logs differently.

Access logs

iAS doesn't actually generate the Web-server access log, but this log is nonetheless critical for debugging and monitoring iAS. The access log contains one line for each HTTP request that anyone's made of that Web server. You can customize the access log to include a wide variety of information, but the log includes the following information by default:

◆ The IP of the requester (or hostname if reverse DNS is enabled)

◆ The timestamp of the request

◆ The URL requested

◆ The request code returned

◆ The content length returned

The referrer and user-agent HTTP headers are two additional pieces of information that system administrators often add to the log files to facilitate tracking more information about how users interact with the Web server.

By default, you can find the access log under the `logs` directory of the HTTP server instance directory. If you name your Web server instance `chico`, for example, the default location for the access log is `/usr/netscape/server4/https-chico/logs/access` (or `c:\Netscape\Server4\https-chico\logs\access` on Windows).

Following are a few sample lines from an access log:

```
192.168.1.3 - - [16/Aug/2001:13:34:16 -0400] "GET
/NASApp/fortune/fortune HTTP/1.1" 200 -
192.168.1.3 - - [16/Aug/2001:13:35:15 -0400] "GET /index.html
HTTP/1.1" 200 2431
192.168.1.3 - - [16/Aug/2001:13:35:36 -0400] "GET
/NASApp/chapter9/index.html HTTP/1.1" 200 -
192.168.1.3 - - [16/Aug/2001:13:35:23 -0400] "GET
/NASApp/fortune/fortune HTTP/1.1" 200 -
192.168.1.3 - - [16/Aug/2001:13:35:57 -0400] "GET
/NASApp/chapter9/TestEJB HTTP/1.1" 200 -
```

These lines show some basic requests for static objects on the Web server (`/index.html`) as well as servlets on the application server (`/NASApp/fortune/fortune`, `/NASApp/chapter9/index.html`, `/NASApp/chapter9/TestEJB`), all on August 16 and from a browser with the IP of 192.168.1.3.

To change your logging preferences or the location where you keep the log files, go to the Log Preferences side tab of the Status tab of the Web server's administration screen. (For more information about Web-server administration or how to get to the Web-server administration screen, consult the Web-server documentation. I provide a link to the online documentation at the end of this chapter.)

The access log is a critical log because it enables the easy analysis of application usage. You can perform a simple analysis by using simple Unix commands. The command `grep -c NASApp access`, for example, returns the total number of application-server requests, and `grep -c 02/Nov/2001.*NASApp/fortune/fortune access` returns the number of times that someone accessed the sample `fortune` servlet on November 2.

Many software packages (both commercial and open source) are available to enable you to perform a more sophisticated analysis of Web-server access logs. These more sophisticated analysis tools can generate charts and graphs, basing them on your application's usage, and help you monitor how users utilize your application. The better that you understand your users' usage patterns, the better prepared you are to tune your application. Graphing the historical usage patterns of your application can also help you predict future usage and, therefore, future hardware requirements.

In summary, the Web-server access log is a simple but effective tool for analyzing application usage and verifying basic connectivity between the browser and the Web server.

Web-connector logs

The Web-connector log is the other log file on the Web-server tier. By default, the Web connector places its log entries into the errors log of the Web server (which you find in the same directory as the access log). You can change the location of the Web-connector log by setting the IAS_PLUGIN_LOG_FILE environment variable.

TIP   Although the errors log may not seem an intuitive place to store Web-connector log messages, it does enable you to take advantage of the log rotation features of the Web-server. It also enables easy correlation with the other Web-server messages. Unless you have a compelling reason to do otherwise, you're probably best off permitting the Web connector to use the errors log.

Each line of the Web-connector log has the following information, separated by colons:

◆ The timestamp

◆ The severity assigned to the log message (info/warning/failure)

◆ The process id of the Web-server process (in parentheses)

◆ The Web-connector component generating the log message

◆ The body of the actual log message

This log format enables easy analysis, because you can easily grep each component of the log message.

You can filter the contents of the Web-connector log file by severity by using the ksvradmin administration tool. On the Logging tab of the tool, in the General area, you find a Message Type drop-down list box. This drop-down list box enables you to limit logging messages to include only Errors or Errors and Warnings. Reducing the amount of logging can slightly improve the performance of the Web-server tier. A reduced amount of logging messages obviously also reduces the amount of disk space necessary for the logs.

You can only modify the logging level of the webconnector using the administration tool if your webconnector is on the same machine as your application server. To modify the logging level on a standalone webconnector, you can modify the \SOFTWARE\iPlanet\Application Server\6.5\CCS0\ LOGGING\Mode registry key. Setting the key to a value of 0 enables all logging messages. A setting of 1 enables only messages with error and warning severities. A setting of 2 allows only error messages.

Several flags in the iAS registry can force special logging modes that give you a finer grained control of logging. If you set the \SOFTWARE\iPlanet\Application Server\6.0\CCS0\HTTPAPI\NASRespTime registry value to 1, for example, the Web connector records the amount of time (in milliseconds) that iAS takes to respond to each request. The following log entry, for example, shows the results of a client requesting the AppInfo servlet that you create in Chapter 4:

```
[16/Nov/2001:15:37:40] info (28241): FilterLite::ExecuteApplogicRequest()
reports: NAS response time for </NASApp/chapter4/AppInfo> is 109 msec
```

The NASRespTime measures the amount of time that the Web connector waits for the application server to return the complete response. It includes the network latency between the web-server and application-server tiers, but it doesn't include any of the latency that the Web connector itself introduces. This metric, therefore, is a good determination of the health of the application-server tier and of the relative difficulty of processing specific components.

Because the NASRespTime doesn't include the latency of the Web connector-tier itself, however, the NASRespTime flag doesn't accurately represent the end-user experience. The \SOFTWARE\iPlanet\Application Server\6.0\CCS0\HTTPAPI\ NASRespTime flag makes a performance measurement that measures the latency of the Web connector. This measurement is the amount of time that the plug-in takes to resolve any servlet mapping and to load balance the request. The following log entry shows that this overhead can be extremely small if the Web connector isn't under load:

```
[16/Nov/2001:15:37:27] info (28241): reports: Time elapsed for
</NASApp/chapter4/AppInfo> is 0 msec
```

Using these performance logging flags in conjunction with an external performance measurement tool (such as Mercury LoadRunner or Radview's WebLoad) enables you to determine not only the total response time, but also how the iAS spends the time.

You can also set a \SOFTWARE\iPlanet\Application Server\6.0\CCS0\ HTTPAPI\DebugMode flag. This flag adds an extremely large amount of information to the Web-connector log, including a packet-by-packet accounting of information passing between the Web connector and the application server. Because of this large volume of information, keeping the DebugMode flag set during production use isn't practical. The DebugMode flag can prove useful in diagnosing certain problems, such as verifying that the Web connector is correctly interpreting servlet mappings, but you shouldn't set it for extended periods of time.

Application Server Logs

iPlanet Application Server maintains many logs at the application-server tier to help you monitor and diagnose iPlanet Application Server. In general, you have one log for every process that's running at the application-server tier, a series of console logs, plus a few additional special-purpose logs. You configure all the application-server tier logs on the Logging tab of the ksvradmin administration tool.

This section focuses on the core application-server logs that you enable by selecting the Log to File or Log to Database check boxes in the Logging section of the administration tool. I discuss the console and special logs in the following sections. The core application-server logs are the best tool for long-term monitoring of the application server. You can adjust the verbosity of the logs from a very concise level appropriate for stable production boxes to a high level of detail for debugging and development. iAS also includes built-in log-rotation capabilities, which enable you to maintain logs on production boxes without the need for any server downtime.

Server log contents

The application-server logs are the destination for all normal iAS status messages. Each status message has one of three status levels: *informational*, *warning*, or *error* (also called *failure messages*). By adjusting the Message Type drop-down list box on the ksvradmin Logging tab, you can filter the application-server logs. During debugging, you may want to set the All Messages option, which results in no filtering. On a production server you may want to select Errors and Warnings or Errors to filter the messages down to those that may require operator intervention.

I discuss some of the specific log messages in other chapters (such as the DSYNC messages that I examine in Chapter 11). The majority of iAS log messages use the following format: timestamp, severity, error code, and error description, with a colon delimiting each component. Error codes consist of a component code, a hyphen, and then a numeric or alphabetic code, as you see in the following example of a log message:

```
[22/Mar/2002 8:23:04:1] warning: DSYNC-043: We (0xc0a80103:10818),lost
connection to the Sync Alternate, (0xc0a80105:10818)
```

This log message indicates that contact with another server in the cluster was lost, most likely because of a failure in the other server. It receives a severity classification as a warning because it negatively affects the server cluster but is handled automatically and doesn't require operator intervention.

The error code is DSYNC-043. The DSYNC component code indicates that the message relates to the DSYNC distributed session manager, and the 043 error number identifies the specific condition of losing contact with an Alternate (and not losing contact with a Primary or Backup.) The error code is especially useful for analyzing logs, as you can easily search a log file for DSYNC-, resulting in all log messages relating to distributed sessions; warning: DSYNC-, resulting in all important changes in DSYNC state; or DSYNC-043, resulting in all "lost-contact" messages.

 Lost contact with Local is DSYNC-044; lost contact with Primary is DSYNC-045; and lost contact with Backup is DSYNC-042.

If you send log messages to a file, the application-server uses a file with the filename that you specify in the Logging tab (the default is logs/ias), followed by a period and the port number of the process creating the log message. The KJS process, for example, operates on port 10818 by default, so the default KJS log file is logs/ias.10818. You can find information on log rotation and logging to alternative destinations in the sections "Rotating logs" and "Alternative Log Destinations," later in this chapter.

The following sections provide a partial list of some of the component codes and error codes.

BINDER COMPONENT MESSAGES

The BINDER component translates component requests into actual class files on the file system. BINDER log messages typically relate to issues resolving the registry (which the server uses to translate component requests) and OS-related issues that involve accessing the class files on the file system.

- ◆ BINDER-OS messages — Occur when iAS receives an unexpected operating-system error. This error can result from any number of conditions, including a full file system, the lack of expected libraries or OS patches, or a missing iAS file.

  The BINDER-OS message should include more detail about the exact OS error. You should use this message to give you debugging clues. A missing library on Solaris may require a change in the LD_LIBRARY_PATH. An out of space message is probably indicative of a full file system or a file permissions problem. The following list describes some possible BINDER-OS messages:

◆ BINDER-004: GXBindWorker: invalid key defs — Indicates that the server couldn't find a GUID in the ClassDef section of the registry. A corrupted registry, an incorrectly registered application, or an attempt to call a nonexistent GUID manually can cause this error.

You can resolve this problem by restoring the registry (if it's corrupted) and correctly registering the application. The BINDER-004 message reports the problematic GUID, so you can search the ias-web.xml and ias-ejb-jar.xml for a matching GUID. This log message enables an administrator to identify the broken application and component.

◆ BINDER-007: GXBindWorker: error resolving library ... — Typically indicates that the iAS classloader couldn't find a class on disk where the registry indicates that you can find it. The incomplete undeployment of an old application or a file-permissions issue can cause this condition.

If the component shouldn't exist, you should update the registry by undeploying the application. If the component should exist, you can update the file system either manually or by undeploying and redeploying the application. You can resolve file-permissions issues by using the respective OS commands.

CONN COMPONENT MESSAGES

The CONN (connection) component logs messages relate to failures in communication between iAS processes. CONN messages often precede messages from the functional components that are trying to communicate. DSYNC messages that indicate lost contact between DSYNC servers (such as DSYNC-042), for example, generally follow CONN-003 messages that indicate the loss of socket-level communication. The following list describes some common CONN component messages:

◆ CONN-OS: *VARIOUS MESSAGES* — These messages indicate that iAS encountered an operating-system-level message in the communication module. The message text includes the actual operating-system error. To resolve the CONN-OS problem, you must resolve the underlying operating-system error. If Solaris is running out of file descriptors, for example, you can increase the limit by adjusting the rlim_fd_cur and rlim_fd_max parameters in the /etc/system kernel configuration file.

◆ CONN-002: socket send error ... — This error is very similar to the following CONN-003 but is less common (and more indicative of a real problem).

◆ CONN-003: socket receive error — The CONN-003 error indicates a failure in the communication protocol between iAS processes. iAS maintains its own heartbeat ping so that it maintains a sensitive monitor of the connectivity between processes. (The heartbeat ping reacts much more quickly than an operating-system socket timeout.)

CONN-003 errors most often result from a process shutting down or failing. This failure causes the other components with which that process was in communication to notice its absence, first with CONN-003 messages marking the failed communication and then with DSYNC messages that record the high-level implication of the loss of communication (such as the promotion of a Backup).

DSYNC COMPONENT MESSAGES

The DSYNC component manages the high availability of the session information. DSYNC messages enable you to track the state of each of the various processes (Primary, Backup, Alternate, or Local). The DSYNC messages also alert you to any irregularities in the state of the session-management system. Following are some common DSYNC messages:

Chapter 11 reviews several of the DSYNC messages in depth and includes walkthroughs of the various failover scenarios and the DSYNC log messages that they generate.

◆ DSYNC-002: MakeConn failed in ... — Indicates a failure in opening a socket connection between DSYNC components. The most likely cause is a network failure, but a down or extremely busy DSYNC engine on the other end of the request can also cause this message.

If the cause of the problem is a networking or down DSYNC issue, you can resolve the problem by fixing the underlying problem. If the underlying problem is an overloaded DSYNC engine, for example, you can resolve the problem by creating an additional iAS instance or cluster to reduce the load on the DSYNC engine. Or, if possible, reducing the load on the DSYNC engine by reducing the number or size of the session information.

◆ DSYNC-029: Primary died and no backups are configured ... — Indicates that contact was lost with the authoritative source for DSYNC information, and no Backup is there to failover to. This message can log during normal shutdown, as the various engines shut down, but you shouldn't observe it during normal operation.

Receiving this message indicates that the process (either KJS or KXS) can no longer operate in DSYNC mode. If you receive it unexpectedly, therefore, it indicates an abnormal cluster configuration. Check your DSYNC configuration to ensure that all the various KXS servers are operating in the DSYNC mode in which you expect them to operate and that you have no network-connectivity failures between those servers.

◆ DSYNC-037: We have been nominated as a backup ... — Indicates the normal promotion of a DSYNC Alternate to DSYNC Backup status.

◆ DSYNC-038: We are told that the new Primary is ... — Indicates that a Backup has promoted itself to Primary status. If all servers don't log this message correctly, a "split-brain" scenario may exist.

The cluster should automatically resolve split-brain scenarios and, if enabled, resolve them by restarting the servers that don't recognize the correct Primary. Otherwise, you can manually restart the servers that don't log the DSYNC-038 message correctly.

◆ DSYNC-040: We are coming up as a SYNC alternate ... — Indicates that an iAS server is starting up in DSYNC Alternate mode (and, therefore, recognizes another Primary). If the cluster is in need of a Backup, this message may precede a DSYNC-037 message indicating promotion to DSYNC Backup.

◆ DSYNC-041: We are taking over as the Primary ... — Indicates that a DSYNC Backup is taking over the responsibilities of DSYNC Primary. (The DSYNC-041 message should follow a DSYNC-045 message marking the loss of connection to the previous DSYNC Primary.)

◆ DSYNC-042: We lost connection to the hot backup ... — Indicates that the Primary has lost connection to the hot Backup, most likely because of a shutdown, a failure, or loss of connectivity. If any DSYNC Alternates are in the cluster, the Primary should promote them to Backup status. (And the new backup should log that promotion with a DSYNC-037 message.)

◆ DSYNC-044: We lost connection to the Sync Local — Indicates the loss of connection with a KJS process or KXS process operating in Local mode. You often see this message during the normal shutdown of a server as a DSYNC Primary notices the KJS engines that are leaving the cluster.

◆ DSYNC-045: We lost connection to the Sync Primary — Indicates the loss of connection with a DSYNC Primary. This message is normal, assuming that the Primary actually shuts down, fails, or is removed from the network. Assuming that a DSYNC Backup exists, it should respond with a DSYNC-041 message marking its promotion to DSYNC Primary. Every other KXS and KJS should then log their recognition of this promotion by sending a DSYNC-038 message.

◆ DSYNC-053: Failover manager could not direct a message — Similar in nature to a DSYNC-002 message, a DSYNC-053 indicates a communication error between DSYNC engines. This message can result from a temporary situation during failover conditions or extreme loads or as a result of a bad cluster configuration.

◆ If you receive this message repeatedly, investigate the state of each of the DSYNC engines, ensuring that they're operating in the expected mode. Restarting the DSYNC engines can also help restore the DSYNC engines to a known state.

◆ DSYNC-055: Failed during sending message ... — Very similar to a DSYNC-053 message, a DSYNC-055 is a more general case of a communication error between DSYNC engines. A DSYNC-055 message, however, has only a warning status.

LOADB COMPONENT MESSAGES

The LOADB (load balancer) component logs the intraserver load-balancing process. It logs problems that occur in collecting and distributing load-balancing information (for server-based load balancing) as well as problems in directing component requests. The following list describes some of these messages:

◆ LOADB-008: Could not find server to execute ... — Indicates that a server received a request that it can't process because of application-partitioning requests. If server B receives a request for a component that exists only on server A, for example, it ordinarily forwards the request to server A automatically. But if server A is unavailable, server B can't process the request and reports a LOADB-008 message.

Sometimes this result is desirable because of server configurations or Quality of Service issues (for example, if you must reserve server B for high-priority components). If you want, however, you can avoid this error by deploying the component on more servers and then marking the component as *distributed* or *global*. This course enables the component to load balance across additional servers.

◆ LOADB-022: local AppLogic definition overrides others — This message logs if both the local registry and central registry have information for a given component. (The local definition supercedes the central definition.)

This message is generally innocuous and you can safely ignore it. Theoretically, it could indicate an inconsistent cluster state but is generally just redundant data. If an inconsistent cluster state causes it, BINDER errors typically accompany the LOADB-022 as the server utilizes the inconsistent registry data.

◆ LOADB-040: Data collection frequency ... — This error results from inconsistent monitoring intervals in using server-based load balancing. Make sure that all the intervals on the list in the Advanced Settings area of the Advanced Settings of Your Load Balancing tab of ksvradmin are multiples of the Base Broadcast/Update Interval. This error applies only if you're using server-based load balancing.

MISCELLANEOUS COMPONENT MESSAGES

The following is a list of some common miscellaneous component messages:

◆ `APPEVENT-031: Received error 0x80350005 from main engine (0xd00c3a45, 10818) for event EventServer` — The KJS log records this error whenever the KJS makes a request of the KXS that relates to the `IAppEvent` interface and the KXS encounters an error. The KXS log logs the details of the actual error encounter.

To resolve this error, consult the KXS log and fix the root cause of the event-handling difficulty.

◆ `ODBC-002: LIBRARY entry not specified for ODBC driver` — The ODBC driver is missing or misconfigured. Check the settings for ODBC in the iPlanet Type JDBC drivers control of the Database tab of `ksvradmin`.

◆ `SERVER-0S: Address already in use .. / SERVER-015: bind failed. Check if another server is using port ...` — Either of these server messages (or both) can result from iAS attempting to utilize a TCP/IP port that's already in use. This situation can result from the following causes:

   ■ *Conflict with another application.* Although iAS uses nontraditional ports, another process on your box may possibly be using a port you allocate to iAS. In this case, reconfigure either iAS or the other application to use another port.

   ■ *Conflict with another iAS instance.* If you run two iAS instances on the same physical server, make sure that you install each instance on different ports. (iAS binds to all IPs, so using multiple IP addresses doesn't separate two instances of iAS.)

   ■ *An incorrectly closed port.* If you must shut down iAS ungracefully (`kill -9` on Solaris), the ports may remain open in a `TIME_WAIT` state after iAS shuts down. If you restart iAS before the operating system reclaims the ports, iAS can't reopen them. To resolve this situation, either reboot the system or (preferably) wait for the operating system to time out the sockets (a few minutes).

◆ `UTIL-013: GXGUID: NameTrans lookup failed ()` — This error results from a missing GUID in the `NameTrans` section of the registry. A corrupt registry, a missing component, or more commonly, a misspelled component name can cause this error.

To resolve this error, verify the component (servlet, JSP, EJB) names that you're utilizing and check the `NameTrans` folder of your registry. Redeploying your application and/or restoring your registry from backup are possible avenues to fix a problem with the registry itself.

Add custom log content

Your application can add entries into the iAS server log files by using the log(String) or log(String, Throwable) method. (These methods exist in both ServletContext and GenericServlet so that you can access them easily.) Custom log messages log as "info" messages, enclosed by lines of dashes and preceded by the name of the component.

Suppose, for example, that you add the following line of code to the AppInfo servlet in most of the chapter samples:

```
log("test logging");
```

You get the following entries in your ias.10818 log file:

```
[16/Nov/2001 05:55:08:6] info: ---------------------------------------
[16/Nov/2001 05:55:08:6] info: AppInfo: test logging
[16/Nov/2001 05:55:08:6] info: ---------------------------------------
```

Adding custom log messages to the KJS log files adds a lot of excess volume to these log files because of the extra dash delimiters. Additionally, custom messages log only if you set the logging filter to All Messages. This setting also adds considerably to the amount of log files that iAS generates.

The limitations of iAS's internal logging features are one of the reasons that I list alternative logging packages in Appendix B.

Log rotation

You can configure iPlanet Application Server to automatically rotate its file-based logs. Simply set the Enable File Rotation drop-down list box of the logging tab to Yes and select the desired rotation interval in the adjacent drop-down list box.

At every rotation interval, iAS renames the existing log files to add another filename suffix marking the date and time of the rotation. Logging then continues in a new file of the same filename. iAS renames the default KJS log file ias.10818, for example, to ias.10818.011106_000000 and creates a new ias.10818 file.

Alternative log destinations

iAS can also send logs to relational databases (RDBMSs) or to the Windows event log. These alternative destinations offer some advantages but aren't as commonly used as normal flat files. These alternative log destinations can either replace the flat file logs, or you can create them as additional destinations for logging messages.

LOG TO A RELATIONAL DATABASE

Relational database log files are useful in that you can consolidate the log messages of several servers in one database table. Additionally, you can utilize standard RDBMS reporting tools to analyze and present the information in the database log destination.

On the other hand, database log files require significantly more processing power on the part of the iAS server. Additionally, the database logs depend on the capability of the application server to connect to the database. If a connectivity problem exists between the application server and the database, iAS can't log the error messages relating to the connectivity problem.

These difficulties make utilizing relational database logs fairly uncommon. To enable them, you must perform the following tasks:

◆ Create the destination database table in your relational database of choice. (You can find scripts to assist in the creation of the database table in `$IAS_ROOT/ias/ias-samples/dblog/src/schema`. You find versions of the table-creation script for several major relational databases.)

◆ Create a datasource for the destination database, if one doesn't already exist.

◆ Specify the datasource, table name, username, and password on the Logging tab of `ksvradmin` for the iAS instance that you want.

◆ Click the Log to Database check box on the Logging tab of `ksvradmin`.

LOGGING TO THE WINDOWS EVENT LOG

The capability of iAS to send log messages to the Windows Event Log can prove very useful if you've already developed an infrastructure to monitor and collect information in the Event Log. You can review the Windows Event Log remotely and set Windows to automatically rotate themselves based on either space consumed or a fixed time interval. You view the Event Log by using the Event Viewer, which can automatically sort and filter log messages as you want. Additionally, because all the iAS processes on a single server send their messages to the same Windows Event Log, utilizing this logging method enables you to view a somewhat centralized view of the server status.

The primary drawback of using the Windows Event Log is that it's a proprietary format that's available only on the Windows platform. Because of this proprietary nature, creating custom tools to monitor and analyze the log is more difficult than other more open log formats. And any tools or infrastructure that you create to monitor the Event Log aren't portable to the Unix platform. Another disadvantage of utilizing the Windows Event Log is that only error messages go to the Event Log, regardless of what level of logging you enable in `ksvradmin`.

Sending your application-server log messages to the Windows Event Log is as simple as selecting the Log Errors to WinNT Event Log check box on the Logging tab of `kvradmin`. (This check box works regardless of whether you're using Windows NT or Windows 2000.)

Console Logs

In some ways, console logs are just another log destination, similar to a relational database to which you send logs or the Windows Event Log. But console logs exhibit some special properties that mandate treating them separately.

Because of their additional content, console logs are especially helpful to developers and in debugging applications. As an additional appeal to their development and debugging functions, console logs also are easy to monitor interactively in both Windows and Unix (unlike database logs and the Event Log).

On the other hand, the interactive and verbose nature of console logs makes them less appealing for long-term monitoring and administration. Understanding the advantages of console logs and the difference between console and file logs is important to the process of selecting a logging methodology appropriate to the current task.

Console logs on the Windows platform

The console log functions very differently on Windows than on Unix platforms. You can display the console log on Windows by enabling console logs in the `ksvradmin` tool and then selecting the Allow to Interact with Desktop check box for the iPlanet Application Server service. (This check box is on the menu that appears after you click the Advanced button on the iPlanet Application Server in the Service Manager Control Panel.)

After you select this check box, iPlanet Application Server opens the console logs on the desktop the next time that you restart it. Several new windows appear on the desktop of the current user: one for each process of the application server. These windows contain the output of the console logs and provide a good way to interactively monitor the state of the application-server processes. Although you can adjust the size of the window buffer in the Window properties accessible from the title bar of the window, you can't save the console log on the Windows platform.

Console logs on the Unix platform

On Unix platforms, you save the console logs (if you enable them) in files that iAS names after the processes that create them. The KXS log, for example, receives the name `kxs_0 &&&FIXME`. Notice that the server can't automatically rotate console logs, unlike iAS's other file-based logs.

Console log contents

Several subtle differences exist between contents of the console logs and the file logs. One difference is that Java `System.out()` statements send their output to the console logs but not to the actual iAS logs. Many developers, therefore, use `System.out()` statements to send debugging information to the log files. (Many of the examples in this book use `System.out()` statements to record information in the console logs.)

Special Log Files

In addition to the log files that each iAS Process creates (console, file, database, and so on), you have several special purpose log files that you can use to monitor specific components.

HTTP logs

In passing requests to the iPlanet Application Server tier, the Web connector passes along much of the HTTP header information. iAS can optionally send this information about the HTTP requests to a relational database table.

To enable HTTP logging, you must manually create the appropriate database table by using one of the scripts that you find in `$IAS_ROOT/ias/ias-samples/dblog/src/schema`. After you create the tables, you can enable HTTP logs in much the same way that you can enable iAS relational logging. Select the HTTP tab of the Logging area of `ksvradmin` and add the table name, datasource, database, username, and password in the appropriate text boxes. At this point, selecting the Enable HTTP log check box sends the following HTTP information into the database table that you created:

- ◆ Timestamp
- ◆ Content length
- ◆ Content type
- ◆ `http_accept` (the content types acceptable to the browser)
- ◆ `http_connection` (`keepalive` or not)
- ◆ `http_host` (client host)
- ◆ `http_referer` (referring link, if any)
- ◆ `http_user_agent` (browser type)
- ◆ `path_info` (URI of request)

- ◆ remote_addr **(IP of client)**
- ◆ request_method **(GET/POST)**
- ◆ server_protocol **(HTTP version)**

HTTP Logging can prove useful in certain specialized situations to consolidate usage information for an entire iAS cluster, but you generally don't use it in production systems. The Web server can more efficiently collect the HTTP log information than iAS. Additionally, third-party log-analysis tools can more easily parse HTTP logs as flat files.

DSYNC logs

The DSYNC logging options exist for troubleshooting only. iAS writes the DSYNC log messages only in an on-demand basis if you click the Dump Cluster Info or Dump Node Info buttons on the DSYNC tab of the Logging settings of the iPlanet Application Server Administration Tool. Learning about the DSYNC logs can prove very instructive regarding the internal workings of the DSYNC engine.

The section "Behind the Scenes of DSYNC," in Chapter 11, explains the details of DSYNC. Understanding the inner workings and terminology of DSYNC is helpful in reading the DSYNC logs.

Dumping the node information causes each DSYNC client and server to dump its stored and cached information. Listing 14-1, for example, provides a sample of the information that a KXS may produce by dumping its node information.

This listing is from a very recently started server with only a single session stored in DSYNC. A full production system would result in each client and server reporting on thousands of nodes.

Listing 14-1: iasdync-node-10818.log

```
****************************
*      DSync Token State
****************************
[1]    ID: /
       Status: with Read Token
       Scope: GLOBAL
       Cached engine[1]: this engine
       Cached engine[2]: 0xc0a80103:10820
```

```
                 Workset engine[1]: this engine
                 Child[0]:gxsess_appname_list
                 Child[1]:ias_application_states
                 Child[2]:EBFoRootNode
                 Child[3]:gxsessroot
[2]              ID: /gxsessroot/
                 Status: with Read Token
                 Scope: GLOBAL
                 Cached engine[1]: 0xc0a80103:10820
                 Cached engine[2]: this engine
                 Workset engine[1]: this engine
                 Child[0]:b10739d00c93c172
[3]              ID: /gxsess_appname_list
                 Status: without Read or Write Token
                 Scope: GLOBAL
                 Cached engine[1]: 0xc0a80103:10820
                 Workset engine[1]: 0xc0a80103:10820
                 Writer engine: 0xc0a80103:10820
[4]              ID: /ias_application_states/chapter4
                 Status: without Read or Write Token
                 Scope: GLOBAL
                 Cached engine[1]: 0xc0a80103:10820
                 Workset engine[1]: 0xc0a80103:10820
                 Writer engine: 0xc0a80103:10820
[3]              ID: /gxsess_appname_list
                 Status: without Read or Write Token
                 Scope: GLOBAL
                 Cached engine[1]: 0xc0a80103:10820
                 Workset engine[1]: 0xc0a80103:10820
                 Writer engine: 0xc0a80103:10820
[4]              ID: /ias_application_states/chapter4
                 Status: without Read or Write Token
                 Scope: GLOBAL
                 Cached engine[1]: 0xc0a80103:10820
                 Workset engine[1]: 0xc0a80103:10820
                 Writer engine: 0xc0a80103:10820
[5]              ID: /ias_application_states
                 Status: with Read Token
                 Scope: GLOBAL
                 Cached engine[1]: 0xc0a80103:10820
                 Cached engine[2]: this engine
                 Workset engine[1]: this engine
                 Child[0]:chapter4
[6]              ID: /gxsessroot//b10739d00c93c172
```

Continued

Listing 14-1 *(Continued)*

```
          Status: without Read or Write Token
          Scope: GLOBAL
          Timeout:TIMEOUT_DEFAULT,        53991 seconds till expiration
          Cached engine[1]: 0xc0a80103:10820
          Workset engine[1]: 0xc0a80103:10820
          Writer engine: 0xc0a80103:10820
          Attribute[GX_CB_KEY_DISABLE]:1
          Attribute[safecounter]:2
          Attribute[GX_CB_KEY_PORT]:10820
          Attribute[GX_CB_KEY_HOST]:-1062731517
          Attribute[GX_SESSION_CB_AE_KEY]:SessionInvalidator
[7]       ID: /EBFoRootNode
          Status: without Read or Write Token
          Scope: GLOBAL
          Cached engine[1]: 0xc0a80103:10820
          Workset engine[1]: 0xc0a80103:10820
          Writer engine: 0xc0a80103:10820
[8]       ID: /gxsessroot
          Status: with Read Token
          Scope: GLOBAL
          Cached engine[1]: 0xc0a80103:10820
          Cached engine[2]: this engine
          Workset engine[1]: this engine
          Child[0]:


****************************
*       Timeout Manager State
****************************
Entry[0]: ID=/gxsessroot//b10739d00c93c172, 53991 seconds till expiration
```

Examining this log reveals several interesting things about the DSYNC engine, as the following list describes:

◆ iAS stores information in DSYNC hierarchically. The root / has four children, gxsess_appname_list, ias_application_states, EBFoRootNode, and gxsessroot, as the value that a Child[] array stores indicates. These child nodes are also capable of having child nodes, such as the /gxsessroot node under which DSYNC stores all the sessions.

◆ Each DSYNC node contains a list of the engines that have a cache of the node and also a list of which engines have write tokens available. You can see, for example, that the KJS with the IP address of 0xc0a80103:10820

caches the node containing the only session (/gxsessroot//
b10739d00c93c172). You can also see that the same KJS (0xc0a80103:
10820) is the writer engine meaning that that KJS has the current write
token for that node.

♦ Each node has a scope of distribution. In this log file, all nodes are global,
meaning that all DSYNC engines share them. If you were to deploy an
application by using the dsync-local session option, however, you could
see DSYNC nodes with local scope. Only the local server would distribute
these nodes.

♦ Some nodes are set to expire. Session nodes are set to expire after a certain amount of time. The Timeout Manager section shows a summary of
the current timeouts. Other nodes, such as the application state, don't
timeout.

♦ Information that you store in HttpSession attributes stored as attributes
on DSYNC nodes. Node 6 (/gxsessroot//b10739d00c93c172) has the
attribute safecounter, which the Chapter4 sample application uses to
demonstrate the use of HttpSession to store a counter value.

An interesting thing to notice is that this feature gives you a way (albeit an inefficient one) to count the current number of active sessions. Running a grep -c
"ID: /gxsessionroot// on the DSYNC log file that the Primary DSYNC engine
generates gives you a count of the number of currently valid sessions.

The log file that a DSYNC client generates is similar, although the client has considerably less information. A client doesn't have timeout information, for example,
or the information about which nodes which DSYNC engines are caching. The
client does, however, know which nodes it's cached and for which nodes it has the
write token. Listing 14-2 shows the information from a DSYNC client in the same
cluster as the DSYNC server in Listing 14-1.

Listing 14-2: iasdsync-node-10820.log

```
***************************
*      DSync Token State
***************************
[1]    ID: /
       Status: with Read Token
       Scope: GLOBAL
       Child[0]:gxsess_appname_list
       Child[1]:ias_application_states
       Child[2]:EBFoRootNode
       Child[3]:gxsessroot
[2]    ID: /gxsessroot/
       Status: with Read Token
```

Continued

Listing 14–2 *(Continued)*

```
         Scope: GLOBAL
         Child[0]:b10739d00c93c172
[3]      ID: /gxsess_appname_list
         Status: with Write Token
         Scope: GLOBAL
         Attribute[]:0
[4]      ID: /ias_application_states/chapter4
         Status: with Write Token
         Scope: GLOBAL
[5]      ID: /ias_application_states
         Status: with Read Token
         Scope: GLOBAL
         Child[0]:chapter4
[6]      ID: /gxsessroot//b10739d00c93c172
         Status: with Write Token
         Scope: GLOBAL
         Attribute[GX_CB_KEY_DISABLE]:1
         Attribute[safecounter]:2
         Attribute[GX_CB_KEY_PORT]:10820
         Attribute[GX_CB_KEY_HOST]:-1062731517
         Attribute[GX_SESSION_CB_AE_KEY]:SessionInvalidator
[7]      ID: /EBFoRootNode
         Status: with Write Token
         Scope: GLOBAL
[8]      ID: /gxsessroot
         Status: with Read Token
         Scope: GLOBAL
         Child[0]:
```

The DSYNC client log shows that the client currently has a write token for the b10739d00c93c172 session (which agrees with the information that you read from the DSYNC Primary). All the nodes have the same attribute information that you find in the DSYNC Primary but without all the detailed information showing the state of the node within the cluster.

The DSYNC logs can provide lots of very detailed information about the current state of the DSYNC engine, including all the sessions in flight, but they aren't particularly interesting on a day-to-day basis unless you're trying to troubleshoot a problem with the session manager.

Summary

iPlanet Application Server provides log files to troubleshoot and monitor each of the functions of the application server. Understanding the underlying architecture of iAS helps administrators determine which logs to investigate for any given situation.

Administrators should carefully decide which logs to generate, which to rotate, and how long to archive each log. Some logs are useful only for troubleshooting, whereas you can use others as a historical record of server activity.

Consult the following sources for more information on topics that I cover in this chapter:

Web server administration

- ◆ Online iPlanet Web Server Documentation: `http://docs.iplanet.com/docs/manuals/enterprise.html`
- ◆ WebTrends HTTP Log Analyzer: `www.webtrends.com/products/log/default.htm`
- ◆ Webalizer HTTP Log Analyzer: `www.mrunix.net/webalizer/`

Performance testing software

- ◆ Mercury Interactive's LoadRunner: `www-heva.mercuryinteractive.com/products/loadrunner/`
- ◆ RadView's WebLoad: `www.radview.com/products/webload.asp`

Chapter 15

RMI/IIOP

IN THIS CHAPTER

- ◆ Information on the RMI/IIOP protocol and its strengths and weaknesses
- ◆ Alternatives to RMI/IIOP and when using them is appropriate
- ◆ Troubleshooting tips for using RMI/IIOP with iPlanet Application Server

THE J2EE STANDARD REQUIRES certified application servers to implement RMI over IIOP as a mechanism for remotely invoking Enterprise Java Beans. This mechanism is the only one for remote invocation that the J2EE specification requires, so, despite its drawbacks, developers often use it for remotely invoking Enterprise Java Beans.

RMI/IIOP Basics

One of the critical features of Enterprise Java Beans is their capability for remote execution. The `Stub/Skeleton/Implementation` architecture of EJBs enables you to execute them from remote clients, while the bean's logic still executes on a central server or server cluster. The EJB specification specifies that RMI is the API that you use for these remote invocations and also specifies that IIOP must be one of the transport protocols available. (Some application servers also support additional transport protocols.)

RMI (*R*emote *M*ethod *I*nvocation) is the API that Java uses to enable remote invocation of Java objects. The RMI specification includes details on how to serialize objects between client and server, the `stub/skeleton` model for providing remote interfaces, and an exception model for handling problems with RMI components. Figure 15-1 shows the basic architecture of RMI.

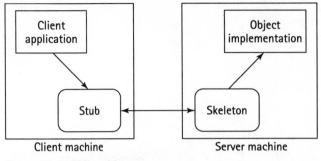

Figure 15-1: RMI architecture

The *IIOP* (*I*nternet *I*nter *O*rb *P*rotocol) transport protocol is the communication protocol designed for use in CORBA. RMI/IIOP is a language- and platform-independent communication protocol for remote invocation of objects that the Object Management Group (OMG) created. The goal of IIOP and CORBA is very similar to that of RMI, as shown in Figure 15-2.

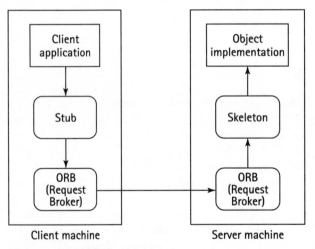

Figure 15-2: CORBA architecture

As you can see, the CORBA architecture is very similar to the RMI architecture but with the addition of an *ORB* (*O*bject *R*equest *B*roker) to broker the client requests. RMI/IIOP combines these two models. By adding a CORBA ORB to the RMI model, RMI/IIOP enables Java developers to use the Java RMI API, while leveraging the interoperability of the CORBA/IIOP model. By using RMI/IIOP as the protocol for communicating with EJBs remotely, non-Java CORBA clients can use CORBA naming and resolution services to communicate with Enterprise Java Beans.

iPlanet sometimes refers to RMI/IIOP as "rich-client" functionality within the application server documentation, because RMI/IIOP is the API that you use to connect rich-client Java applications to iAS.

Disadvantages of Using RMI/IIOP

Although the RMI/IIOP protocol fits well with the EJB architecture, it suffers several disadvantages that may lead you to implement alternative architectures. RMI/IIOP is a suitable technology for many applications, but understanding its weaknesses gives you important information for designing remoteable components.

Many of the disadvantages of RMI/IIOP relate to its relative chattiness and inefficiency as a protocol. Using iPlanet Application Server as a RMI/IIOP server further aggravates this protocol inefficiency because of the CXS architecture that proxies all RMI/IIOP requests.

See Chapter 2 for more information about setting up and configuring a CXS process.

All incoming RMI/IIOP requests first pass through the CXS process, which acts as a proxy into the actual EJB container in the KJS process. This setup has the advantage of enabling RMI/IIOP requests to funnel through a single port listener that the CXS process hosts. Conversely, it also enables you to create multiple CXS processes to satisfy scalability or failover requirements without affecting the KJS architecture. Unfortunately, this CXS architecture also means that the CXS must also proxy all RMI/IIOP requests across process boundaries. This extra overhead is measurable, both in resources that it requires and in response time.

Because of the relative chattiness of RMI/IIOP, architects of RMI-based solutions should attempt to reduce the number of method invocations and the number of arguments to those methods.

One common way to reduce the number of method arguments, for example, is the *Value Object pattern* that Sun's J2EE Design Patterns describe. (See the section at the end of this chapter for a link to the online repository for Sun's J2EE Design Patterns.) This design pattern involves using a custom object to encapsulate several pieces of data within a single argument. Use of this pattern is a good way to optimize network traffic, but it does reduce the convenience of the RMI API. Not only must you populate the custom object with the data before calling the EJB method, but both the client and server also need access to the class for the custom object. This requirement increases the footprint and complexity of the client application as well as the difficulty of client application deployment.

Another problem with RMI/IIOP is that it limits client applications to Java and CORBA clients. Although CORBA is language-independent by design, it does require the use of CORBA infrastructure and certain skills that aren't common in today's marketplace.

Even within Java-based applications, supporting RMI/IIOP is somewhat difficult. iPlanet officially supports only client applications that use the bundled JVM that includes a specially configured ORB. Although configuring other Java 1.2 JVMs to connect to iAS via RMI/IIOP is possible, it's often troublesome as well. Configuring a Java 1.1 or Java 1.3 JVM to connect to iAS via RMI/IIOP is even more difficult, as differences between the Java versions can cause problems.

RMI/IIOP isn't particularly easy to configure firewalls to accept. Although the CXS architecture of iPlanet Application Server enables you to direct all RMI traffic to a single customizable TCP/IP port, most firewalls can't introspect IIOP traffic, and some firewall configurations therefore reject it. And, because the IIOP requires a dedicated port, it often requires you to open a separate port in the firewall.

RMI/IIOP versus Web Services

As programming models for Web services gain popularity, developers obtain additional choices on how to expose components for remote execution. In addition to using RMI/IIOP, developers can now expose components via a variety of Web services protocols, such as SOAP and XML-RPC.

These Web services protocols enable cross-platform and cross-language remote invocation of both Enterprise Java Beans and other Java components. As a result, you should carefully consider your choices about how to remotely expose your components and how to remotely invoke the components that others provide.

 See Chapter 16 for more information about exposing Java components as Web services, as well as information about the advantages and disadvantages of SOAP-based components.

Web-service components avoid many of the disadvantages of RMI/IIOP. Web services are also relatively easy to access from a variety of platforms and languages. Because Web services are based on industry-standard protocols, such as XML, HTTP, and SMTP, many Web service APIs are available to assist in the development and creation of components. From a client-application programmer's point of view, Web services also greatly simplify client configuration. You needn't worry about making sure that your JVM or ORB is compatible with iAS and configured correctly as you're deploying Web services, because SOAP and other Web services protocols are "on-the-wire" protocols that require no specific client software. Web services are also very firewall friendly because of their use of HTTP and other Web standards (such as SMTP) as their transport protocols.

RMI/IIOP, however, does have its appropriate uses. Because RMI/IIOP is the standard for remote execution defined as part of the Enterprise Java Bean protocol, all Enterprise Java Beans are exposed by RMI/IIOP automatically. If RMI/IIOP is sufficient to meet your remotability needs, therefore, the extra work necessary to make your EJBs accessible via alternative methods isn't necessary.

RMI/IIOP is a suitable choice for applications limited to a Java/CORBA environment and with limited scalability and performance requirements. Applications that need to expose their methods outside the firewall to a variety of client application types or that have high scalability requirements are better suited for a Web services-based approach.

Deploy RMI/IIOP Clients

Deploying RMI/IIOP clients is relatively challenging. Testing your Enterprise Java Beans from servlet testing harnesses is always best before attempting to access them remotely from RMI clients. This approach aids in troubleshooting your RMI/IIOP clients, because you're already confident in the actual EJB logic.

Another step to help avoid RMI/IIOP client problems is to first deploy and test the sample Currency Converter application that iAS provides. Testing this simple RMI/IIOP-based application enables you to verify that you've correctly configured your RMI/IIOP infrastructure before attempting to deploy your own applications.

The logical steps to follow to deploy a rich-client application based on RMI/IIOP are as follows:

1. Make sure that a CXS bridge process is running on an iAS server. The client application must know the TCP/IP address of this CXS process to connect to the server. The first section of Chapter 6 in the iPlanet Application Server Administration Guide details the process for creating new iAS processes, including creating a new CXS process.

2. Include the TCP/IP address of the server in the environment properties in creating the initial context for JNDI lookups. The following client code fragment, for example, creates a JNDI context based on a RMI/IIOP connection to port 9010 on chico.thirdnotice.com (where 9010 is the default port for iAS's CXS process):

```
Properties env = new Properties();
env.put("java.naming.factory.initial",
    "com.sun.jndi.cosnaming.CNCtxFactory");
env.put("java.naming.provider.url",
    "iiop://chico.thirdnotice.com:9010");
Context initial = new InitialContext(env);
```

3. Add RMI/IIOP support to the deployment descriptors of the EJBs that you intend to expose remotely. Setting the `iiop` subelement of the `ias-ejb-jar.xml` deployment descriptor instructs the EJB compiler (ejbc) to generate stubs and skeletons for IIOP access. (The EJB compiler must also be given the -iiop option at compile-time in order to properly generate the stubs and skeletons.) This deployment descriptor also prepares the CXS process to accept requests for that component. (Notice that, because the `iiop` descriptor affects the way that the EJB compiler creates the stubs and skeletons, you must set the descriptor before the `EJB` compiler executes.)

4. Deploy the server-side components, which includes generating and packaging the stubs and skeletons for the remotely referenced EJBs. You can deploy EJBs as either an EAR file or as a standalone JAR file. (See Chapter 5 for more information on application packaging.)

5. Create a JAR of the client application, including all necessary helper files, among them the remote and stub classes and home interfaces for the referenced EJBs.

6. Configure the client environment. This step includes adding several JAR files to the `CLASSPATH`, including `iasclient.jar`, `javax.jar`, and, optionally, `iasacc.jar` (if you use Application Client Container features).

7. Execute the client application by using the JVM that iAS provides or an existing JVM that you configure, as the section "Using an Existing JDK," in Chapter 9 of the iPlanet Application Server's Developer's Guide, describes.

You may encounter several common problems in performing these steps. If you encounter problems deploying your client applications, the following tips may help you troubleshoot your problem:

◆ Make sure that your EJBs work if you access them via a Web application. Enterprise Java Beans are easier to troubleshoot from servlets and JSPs.

◆ Make sure that a CXS process is running on the correct port of the server. Grepping the process list for `iiop` is a quick way to determine whether a CXS process is running on a Unix machine.

◆ Make sure that you restart your application server after deploying your EJBs. Although EJB implementations are dynamically reloadable in iPlanet Application Server, home, and remote interfaces require a server restart for deployment.

◆ Make sure that you include all required classes in the client-side JAR. These classes include the home and remote interfaces, stubs, and all helper classes necessary to support those classes and interfaces. In iAS, Web applications are more lenient about this requirement than remote rich clients, because Web applications share the same system CLASSPATH as the EJB container.

◆ Make sure that you include all necessary JARs in the CLASSPATH of the client. Not including iasclient.jar, for example, results in a can't instantiate ORB error.

◆ Make sure that the client code is referring to the correct context factory. Specifying a port or server that the client can't resolve results in a can't connect to ORB error.

◆ Make sure that the JNDI name is correct. Incorrect JNDI names result in Name not Found or Class not Found errors in the log of the CXS process.

ORB Problems and Alternatives

The ORB that comes within iPlanet Application Server is a modified version of the reference Java ORB. This ORB does limit the scalability of using RMI/IIOP to access iPlanet Application Server. Although the iPlanet modifications to the ORB do increase the ORB's capability to handle concurrent requests, you can still crash the ORB by making too many concurrent requests.

You can take several steps that increase the scalability and performance of using RMI/IIOP with iPlanet Application Server (although, as I mention earlier in the "RMI/IIOP versus Web Services" section, using RMI/IIOP alternatives such as SOAP or XML-RPC is another way to increase scalability of remotely invoking Java components). The following list of tuning tips may help you increase the number of concurrent requests that a RMI/IIOP-based application can handle:

◆ *Make sure that you allocate sufficient memory to the CXS process.* The CXS process contains much of the conversational state between client and server and consumes more memory than you may expect. You can adjust the heap memory for the CXS process in the $IAS_ROOT/ias/env/ iasenv.ksh script on Unix.

◆ *Make sure that the operating system has enough file descriptors.* The CXS process can use a large number of them while it's processing requests. To increase the maximum number of file descriptors to 8192, add the following line to your /etc/system file and then reboot your machine:

```
set rlim_fd_max = 8192
```

◆ *Create multiple CXS processes and load balance RMI/IIOP requests across multiple CXS processes.* (You can load balance these RMI/IIOP requests either by using custom client-application code or a DNS load balancer.)

◆ *Use an alternative ORB implementation.* iPlanet currently supports the use of the ORBIX ORB instead of the internal iAS ORB. Other ORBs should work as well, although iPlanet doesn't officially support them. You can find Instructions for using the ORBIX ORB in Chapter 9 of the iPlanet Application Server Developer's Guide.

Client Containers

The J2EE specification includes the concept of *client containers* that provide services to client applications in the same way that EJB containers and Web containers provide services to the server-side of J2EE applications. The goal of the client container is to isolate client-application programmers from the complexity of the naming, security, and transactions of the EJB container.

Unfortunately, the current state of the client-container specification doesn't provide much value to developers. Because of the very limited services that the current version of the client-container specification provides, developers must still develop custom code to connect to the naming, security, and transactions of the server. In addition, the specification gives very little guidance to the EJB container vendor about the interfaces to the client container. Because of this situation, not every vendor's client-container APIs are compatible.

Although iPlanet Application Server does support the application client container development model, iPlanet doesn't generally recommended this development model because of the current state of the specification. The application client container interface doesn't provide any significant value over the RMI API, and the additional packaging necessary to implement the application client container is just another challenge for deploying remote rich-client applications.

If you decide to implement the application client container model in your client application, you must take the following steps in addition to those that I already list for RMI-based applications in the "Deploy RMI/IIOP Clients" section:

1. Include the `iasacc.jar` JAR file in the `CLASSPATH` of the client application.

2. Create two deployment descriptors for the client application. The `app-client.xml` deployment descriptor should include the deployment descriptor elements that Chapter 9.6 of the J2EE specification describes. The `ias-app-client.xml` deployment descriptor should include the vendor-specific deployment-descriptor elements that Chapter 10 of the iPlanet Application Server Developer's Guide describes.

3. Package the client classes in an EAR file along with the deployment descriptors from Step 2.

4. Start the client application by invoking the `com.netscape.ejb.client.`
   `AppContainer` class and passing the name of the EAR file and the name
   of the iAS XML deployment descriptor file, as in the following example:

```
java com.netscape.ejb.client.AppContainer acctest.ear -iasXml
ias-app-client.xml
```

Accessing Non-EJB Resources

iPlanet Application Server exposes Enterprise Java Beans via the RMI/IIOP protocol, as the J2EE specification mandates. I discuss both the disadvantage and advantages of this approach in the section "RMI/IIOP versus Web Services," earlier in this
chapter.

An important point that you need to understand is that iPlanet Application
Server doesn't expose other application-server objects via RMI/IIOP. Unlike with
some other J2EE application servers, you can't access datasources, JMS objects,
user transactions, and other JNDI resources from the client application. Although
it's a convenient feature, providing access to these types of resources isn't part of
the J2EE standard.

The best way to provide access to non-EJB server resources is to create an EJB
session bean to encapsulate the business logic associated with that resource and
then expose the business methods of that session bean to the client application.
This approach provides for a cleaner separation of presentation logic and business
logic. It also keeps the application implementation within the bounds of the J2EE
specification, which means that the application is more portable between J2EE
application servers.

Summary

The J2EE standards body selected RMI/IIOP as a remote invocation protocol to
increase the interoperability of J2EE application-server components. Although
RMI/IIOP is still a valuable mechanism for communication between rich Java
clients and Enterprise Java Beans, other alternatives now exist with SOAP, XML-
RPC, and other Web-service protocols.

Application architects should consider the alternatives carefully. Not only must
architects choose which protocol to implement in their applications, but also the
manner in which they utilize these remote-invocation protocols. Because brokering
these requests between client and server involves significant overhead, you must
give careful consideration to how to use these protocols efficiently.

Consult the following sources for more information on the topics in this chapter:

Official documentation

- ◆ iPlanet Developer's Guide (Chapter 9: Developing and Deploying CORBA-Based clients): `http://docs.iplanet.com/docs/manuals/ias/60/sp4/dg/jpgrichc.htm#11284`

- ◆ Javasoft RMI/IIOP home page: `http://java.sun.com/products/rmi-iiop/index.html`

- ◆ RMI documentation: `http://java.sun.com/j2se/1.3/docs/guide/rmi/spec/rmiTOC.html`

- ◆ IIOP Documentation: `http://cgi.omg.org/cgi-bin/doc?formal/99-10-07`

Sample RMI/IIOP code

- ◆ J2EE Design Patterns: `http://developer.java.sun.com/developer/technicalArticles/J2EE/J2EEpatterns/`

- ◆ RMI/IIOP Samples: `http://developer.iplanet.com/appserver/samples/docs/rmi-iiop.html`

- ◆ Currency Converter Sample: `http://developer.iplanet.com/appserver/samples/j2eeguide/docs/converter.html`

Chapter 16

Web Services

THIS CHAPTER EXPLORES the emerging area of Web services, including the various definitions of Web services and the list of Web-service protocols. It specifically discusses Sun Microsystem's Web-service strategy along with iPlanet Application Server's role in delivering Web services.

Fundamentals of Web Services

No standard definition of Web services is available. Every vendor of Web services (Sun, IBM, Apache, Microsoft, and others) gives you a slightly different definition of what defines Web services. Following, however, are several concepts that most people universally associate with Web services:

◆ **Componentization** – Web services consist of coarsely grained application components that provide remote users access to business logic that's executing on a central server. Web-service advocates suggest that Web services are likely to develop into a marketplace where service providers and enterprises offer access to Web-service components for a fee.

◆ **Remote-method invocation** – SOAP-based remote-method invocation is a central element of virtually every definition of Web services. Web services is a paradigm for distributed computing.

◆ **Dynamic binding** – One unique feature of Web services, in comparison to previous distributed-computing models, is the capability of Web services for self-description. Web services publish their APIs with standards-based descriptors that client application can then use to perform dynamic binding at run time.

◆ **Open standards** – Open TCP/IP standards define Web services. Most frequently, Web services involve SOAP (for remote component invocation), UDDI (Universal Description, Discovery, and Integration) for service discovery and WSDL (Web Service Definition Language) for service description. Some definitions include only SOAP. Some definitions use slightly different protocols, such as XML-RPC instead of SOAP. And some definitions are broader, including data formats such as BizTalk or ebXML. But in general, Web services is synonymous with SOAP/UDDI/WSDL.

◆ **Cross-platform support** – Although other distributed-computing models, such as CORBA, attempt to provide cross-platform capabilities, the Web-services movement is a leap forward in heterogeneous platform support. The on-the-wire, open-standard protocols that form Web services enable them to offer easy interoperability between widely varying platforms and programming languages.

Regardless of each vendor's exact Web-services strategy, the concept of Web services is starting to revolutionize the world of enterprise computing. IT managers see many advantages in Web services. They see Web services as a way to outsource nonessential tasks, because doing so enables them to access remotely hosted services. Conversely, many CIOs also see the possibilities in selling access to Web services. Many also see Web services as an EAI (Enterprise Application Integration) tool, enabling disparate systems to communicate with each other.

At this time, however, Web services are still relatively experimental. Most SOAP implementations currently offer basic functionality. Many aspects of enterprise programming such as authentication and security are poorly defined. Most currently deployed Web services are proof of concepts or academic examples. Despite all the talk in the IT community about Web services, Web services is an emerging technology that is sure to evolve significantly over the next several years.

Web Service Protocols

As I mentioned in the last section, one of the common characteristics of Web services is that they are all based on open TCP/IP- and XML-based protocols. Five of the protocols most commonly associated with Web services are: SOAP, XML-RPC, UDDI, WSDL, and ebXML. These protocols are not exclusive. Most vendors use a combination of these protocols (such as SOAP, UDDI, and WSDL) to form a Web services platform.

SOAP

SOAP (*Simple Object Access Protocol*) is an on-the-wire protocol, based on XML messaging for remote-method invocation. SOAP, which you typically use in combination with HTTP as a transport protocol, is the most common protocol in use today for invoking Web services.

Chapter 11 discusses SOAP, including information about integrating Apache's SOAP RPCRouter with iPlanet Application Server.

SOAP enables clients to remotely execute components that Web-service providers expose. The SOAP specification details the contents of those messages, including enveloping, serialization, and processing instructions. SOAP can support multiple transport protocols, but the one most commonly in use is HTTP.

Application servers typically expose Web services by installing an RPC router application that receives SOAP requests and acts as a proxy to the requested component or components. In effect, the RPC router encapsulates the SOAP implementation details from the components. This encapsulation means that you can SOAP enabled existing components without changing the component code: The RPC router acts as the SOAP listener and constructs and interprets the XML messages.

Several Java-based RPC routers are available; some are commercial products and some are open source. iPlanet Application Server is tested with and includes sample applications for the Apache SOAP RPC router, but other routers (such as WASP Server from Systinet) are also possible for use with iAS.

XML–RPC

XML-RPC (XML Remote Procedure Call) is an alternative method of using XML for remote procedure calls. XML-RPC is similar to SOAP but is simpler in scope. XML-RPC uses only one transport protocol, HTTP, and is much more limited than SOAP in the data types that it can communicate.

Large vendors are more likely to include SOAP rather than XML-RPC in their Web-services strategies. SOAP is more flexible and can solve a wider range of enterprise computing problems. If you need a simpler Web-services strategy, however, XML-RPC may prove an appealing alternative to SOAP.

UDDI

Although the rising popularity of SOAP is providing a powerful methodology for cross-platform and cross-language remote procedure calls, *UDDI* (Universal Description, Discovery, and Integration) is actually the more revolutionary part of Web services. UDDI is a technology that enables you to publish Web-service information, enabling Web-service client applications to dynamically find and connect to Web services. You can envision UDDI as a phone book for Web services. Client applications connect to UDDI registries to find out what services are available and how to connect to them. Some registries may even focus only on internal Web services, such as advertising services that are available on a corporate intranet. As providers better define the payment model for Web services, however, public UDDI registries designed for open consumption are sure to publish more and more Web services.

UDDI is a new technology, and support for UDDI is still new (or missing) in most Web services implementations. This lack of support for UDDI is true of iPlanet Application Server as well. If you create Web services on iPlanet Application Server, you must publish the UDDI for your Web service in your company's UDDI directory yourself. (Although the Sun's Forte for Java IDE does offer the capability to publish UDDI information.) iAS doesn't provide any interfaces for interacting with UDDI, but third-party Java classes that simplify working with UDDI are available. The most popular UDDI Java-class library is UDDI4J, which you can find at www.uddi4j.org.

WSDL

WSDL (Web Services Definition Language) is a subset of the UDDI specification that defines the details of any interaction with Web services. WSDL defines what the Web service is capable of, where you can find the Web service, and how to interact with it. This definition includes all the relevant data types, the operations that the service supports, and the network address where the service is available.

WSDL is very generic in its definition of interfaces, in part because of the transport-independent nature of SOAP. Although most SOAP services utilize the HTTP transport protocol, for example, WSDL uses the neutral term *ports* to describe the location of Web services. A section of the WSDL descriptor then binds the port definitions to the actual transport protocol.

The WSDL term *port* has no relation to a TCP/IP network port. A WSDL port is an abstracted Web-service "endpoint" that it can reuse throughout the WSDL definition. An endpoint is the location of a SOAP service provider. A SOAP port doesn't have any direct relationship to a physical TCP/IP port.

The WSDL descriptor lists all the available data types, operations (known as *ports*), and corresponding message formats. The WSDL also includes the bindings that associate the abstract port definitions with the actual network location that provides the Web service. In WSDL terminology, a Web service is just a grouping of ports. Listing 16-1 is the example from the WSDL specification.

Listing 16-1: Stock Quote WSDL

```
<?xml version="1.0"?>
<definitions name="StockQuote"

targetNamespace="http://example.com/stockquote.wsdl"
        xmlns:tns="http://example.com/stockquote.wsdl"
        xmlns:xsd1="http://example.com/stockquote.xsd"
        xmlns:soap="http://schemas.xmlsoap.org/wsdl/soap/"
        xmlns="http://schemas.xmlsoap.org/wsdl/">
```

```
<types>
    <schema targetNamespace="http://example.com/stockquote.xsd"
          xmlns="http://www.w3.org/2000/10/XMLSchema">
        <element name="TradePriceRequest">
            <complexType>
                <all>
                    <element name="tickerSymbol" type="string"/>
                </all>
            </complexType>
        </element>
        <element name="TradePrice">
            <complexType>
                <all>
                    <element name="price" type="float"/>
                </all>
            </complexType>
        </element>
    </schema>
</types>

<message name="GetLastTradePriceInput">
    <part name="body" element="xsd1:TradePriceRequest"/>
</message>

<message name="GetLastTradePriceOutput">
    <part name="body" element="xsd1:TradePrice"/>
</message>

<portType name="StockQuotePortType">
    <operation name="GetLastTradePrice">
        <input message="tns:GetLastTradePriceInput"/>
        <output message="tns:GetLastTradePriceOutput"/>
    </operation>
</portType>

<binding name="StockQuoteSoapBinding" type="tns:StockQuotePortType">
    <soap:binding style="document" transport="http://schemas.xmlsoap.↵
org/soap/http"/>
    <operation name="GetLastTradePrice">
        <soap:operation soapAction="http://example.com/GetLastTradePrice"/>
        <input>
            <soap:body use="literal"/>
```

Continued

Listing 16-1 *(Continued)*

```
            </input>
            <output>
                <soap:body use="literal"/>
            </output>
        </operation>
    </binding>

    <service name="StockQuoteService">
        <documentation>My first service</documentation>
        <port name="StockQuotePort" binding="tns:StockQuoteBinding">
            <soap:address location="http://example.com/stockquote"/>
        </port>
    </service>
</definitions>
```

This simple WSDL descriptor defines two custom data types (TradePrice and TradePriceRequest), two messages (GetLastTradePriceInput and GetLast TradePriceOutput), one port (StockQuotePortType), one binding for the port (StockQuoteSoapBinding), and one service (StockQuoteService).

Notice that, as I mention earlier in this section., the port here is just an abstraction of an operation. It's the binding definition that actually defines the network location of the services. Notice, too, that the service definition is just a collection of the ports (operations) that are available.

ebXML

ebXML (Electronic Business using XML) is a specification for the definition of business-message formatting. ebXML is based on XML and is an attempt to develop a business-messaging standard that's easier to implement and more flexible than the EDI formatting that's currently dominant.

If you combine ebXML with industry-standards bodies, it defines the message types for common business messages. A major inconvenience would result if everyone who built a Web service that sends or receives an invoice were to define its invoice data types differently. ebXML addresses this problem of defining, sending, and managing these complex business data types.

In addition to determining how to define business documents in XML, ebXML also standardizes the definition of trading partnerships, business processes, and many other elements of conducting business. Even a cursory summary of ebXML is beyond the scope of this book: The specification itself is hundreds of pages long. The key idea to understand, however, is that, as Web services evolve from simple "proof of concept" demonstrations to enterprise applications, more complex message types become necessary. To manage the complexity of these messages, more and more Web services-based applications are sure to involve industry-defined standards such as ebXML.

SunONE

Web Services are a critical part of the Sun's SunONE (Sun Open Net Environment) software strategy. SunONE currently implements Web services with a combination of iPlanet Application Server (with Apache SOAP) along with iPlanet Integration Server, which enables legacy application integration via SOAP and XML transformations. Sun also includes Web services support in its Forte for Java development IDE.

In the future, Sun will expand Java's support for Web services with the Java XML Pack: Java API for XML Messaging (JAXM), Java API for XML Processing (JAXP), Java API for XML Registries (JAXR), and Java API for XML-Based RPC (JAX-RPC). Early access versions of these technologies are already available from Sun. The J also assumes that the Java Community Process (JCP) will include a requirement for Web services support into the J2EE 1.4 specification, which is due for release in 2003.

In general, SunONE is an effort to be one step ahead of the Web services movement. SunONE not only includes support for the basics of Web services (SOAP over HTTP), but it also includes details that enable you to integrate Web services technologies with other technologies, allowing for enterprise application development using Web services. Examples of the enterprise extensions to basic Web services include: using JMS as a transport protocol (instead of HTTP) to enable reliable asynchronous processing; using ebXML for business process definition; and using J2EE Connector Architecture (JCA) for integrating Web services with legacy systems.

One of the defining elements of SunONE is Sun's assertion that J2EE is the premier platform for developing and deploying Web services. SunONE leverages the strength and maturity of the J2EE platform to add enterprise-level functionality to Web services. As Sun's J2EE implementation, iPlanet Application Server is also a key part of the SunONE vision. Using iPlanet Application Server to implement Web services enables you to take advantage of all of the enterprise features of iPlanet Application Server (distributed transactions, load balancing, failover, etc.) from almost any type of client application that has access to TCP/IP.

In short, iPlanet Application Server is Sun's recommended platform for developing and deploying Web services. (iPlanet Integration Server is focused on providing a SOAP wrapper for existing applications.) By combining the strengths of Java as a development language, J2EE as an enterprise platform, iAS as a value-added infrastructure, and SOAP as a cross-platform, vendor-neutral method for distributing computing, you have the advantages of the best features of both the Java and XML worlds.

Summary

Web services are an exciting, new emerging technology for cross-platform-distributed computing. Although the standards for Web services are still emerging, Web services generally center around an XML-based RPC mechanism (such as SOAP or

XML-RPC) and usually UDDI /WSDL for dynamic discovery of those RPC services. Some Web-service strategies may also involve ebXML or other XML standards for data definitions or data access.

In designing a new J2EE application (or upgrading an old one), you should definitely consider the Web-services strategy for that application. Some applications, of course, may not prove appropriate for a Web services approach. But as new developer tools make working with Web services easier and easier, exposing some of the application's APIs via Web services may lead to easier application integration in the future.

You should especially consider web services when building Enterprise Java Beans. Although RMI was previously seen as the RPC service for J2EE application, Web-service protocols offer many advantages over RMI. By adding a SOAP wrapper around your EJBs, you expose them to a much wider range of client applications and generally make invoking your components easier for other applications.

Nonetheless, you must remember that Web services remain essentially a synchronous RPC call mechanism. Finely grained SOAP components have the same network performance problems that any other finely grained distributed object has. Just as many application architects made the mistake of overusing EJBs after they were first introduced, many architects are also likely to make the mistake of overengineering their Web-services strategies. You want to consider Web services as a tool for making your application more accessible and not as a magic silver bullet or panacea.

Consult the following sources for more information on the topics that I present in this chapter:

General Web-service information

- ◆ SunONE: www.sun.com/sunone/
- ◆ Web Services Portal: www.webservices.org/
- ◆ Web Services Primer: www.xml.com/pub/a/2001/04/04/webservices/index.html
- ◆ XML-RPC Resources: www.xml.com/pub/rg/XML_RPC.
- ◆ Comparison of XML-RPC and SOAP: weblog.masukomi.org/writings/xml-rpc_vs_soap.htm
- ◆ Annotated Examples of WSDL and Corresponding SOAP Request/Responses: www.w3.org/2001/03/14-annotated-WSDL-examples

Web-services specifications

- ◆ SOAP: www.w3.org/TR/SOAP/
- ◆ XML-RPC: www.xmlrpc.com/

◆ UDDI: `www.uddi.org/specification.html`

◆ WSDL: `www.w3.org/TR/wsdl`

◆ ebXML: `www.ebxml.org/specs/`

Developer tools

◆ Apache SOAP: `http://xml.apache.org/soap/index.html`

◆ Forte for Java: `www.sun.com/forte/ffj/`

◆ Java XML Pack: `http://java.sun.com/xml/javaxmlpack.html`

◆ Systinet WASP Developer: `www.systinet.com/products/tools/index.html`

◆ UDDI Class Libraries for Java: `www.uddi4j.org`

◆ Directory of Public SOAP Services: `www.xmethods.net/`

Part IV

Best Practices

Chapter 17

Production Architectures

IN THIS CHAPTER

◆ Understanding DMZ (demilitarized zone) architectures and firewall configurations

◆ Learning common cluster configurations

◆ Understanding static content deployment

THIS CHAPTER EXAMINES common best practices for the physical deployment of iPlanet Application Server. After you finish this chapter, you should find that you can explain common best-practice architectures for iPlanet Application Server. You should also find yourself able to discuss the advantages and disadvantages of the alternatives, as well as to make an informed decision about the best architecture for your own applications.

DMZ Architectures and Firewall Configurations

In discussing network design, a *DMZ* (demilitarized zone) is a network segment that resides between the internal network and the Internet. (The term DMZ comes from the buffer zone that was created between North and South Korea at the end of the Korean conflict. A network DMZ is designed to create a similar buffer between the internal network and the uncontrolled internet.) A firewall protects the DMZ from the Internet and gives the outside world only specific, limited rights to access the DMZ. Typically, the firewall permits only HTTP and HTTPS access to the DMZ in the form of TCP/IP connections on specific ports. Depending on what other services you're hosting in your DMZ, the firewall may also enable FTP, SMTP, or SSH traffic as well.

The DMZ is also isolated from the internal network by a firewall in case of a security breach in the DMZ. Access from the DMZ to the internal network is limited to the protocols necessary to generate dynamic content. For iPlanet Application Server, those protocols are LDAP and the proprietary protocols that the iAS Web connector uses. This setup limits the damage that a hacker can cause if he manages to compromise the DMZ.

DMZ design

An ideal DMZ configuration for an iAS application is shown in Figure 17-1. The diagram shows three internal network zones: a DMZ, a protected zone, and an intranet zone. The following list describes these three zones:

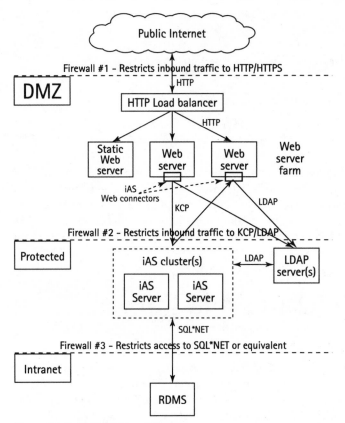

Figure 17-1: Ideal DMZ architecture

◆ The DMZ contains the static and dynamic Web servers. A firewall separates it from the Internet, permitting only HTTP and HTTPS traffic into the DMZ.

◆ The *protected zone* includes the LDAP server or servers, along with the iPlanet Application Server clusters. A firewall isolates the protected zone from the DMZ, permitting only incoming KCP and LDAP traffic. (I provide information on KCP in the next section.) This setup shields the protected zone from compromise should a hacker exploit a security hole in a Web server.

◆ *The intranet zone* houses the RDBMS, as well as any other backend systems. A firewall isolates the intranet zone from the protected zone, permitting only the protocols necessary to retrieve data (such as SQL*Net) from the protected zone.

Not all companies implement the final firewall separating the protected and intranet zones. Because application code is running in the protected zone, however, some companies consider the protected zone subject to compromise. System architects must weigh the value of the third firewall, basing its use on the security policies of their enterprise.

KCP and firewall configuration

KCP (*Kiva Communications Protocol*) is the name of the proprietary protocols that iPlanet Application Server instances use for intercommunication. To configure the firewall between the DMZ (where the iAS Web connectors reside) and the protected zone (where the iAS servers reside), you must understand the TCP/IP ports that KCP uses.

KCP uses multiple channels of TCP/IP communication, and you must configure the firewall to permit each channel. Some communication channels exist only between the server processes, and you use some communication channels for Web connector-to-server communication. Table 17-1 lists all the channels necessary for communication between the Web connector and the application server. These are the channels that must be opened in a firewall between the DMZ and the protected zone.

TABLE 17-1 CHANNELS FOR WEB CONNECTOR TO SERVER COMMUNICATION

Channel	Protocol	Direction	Ports	Explanation
Data requests	TCP/IP	Connector ⇨ Server	KXS port Default=10818	Forwards browser requests to iAS. Required for each iAS in cluster.
Data reply	TCP/IP	Server ⇨ Connector	Ephemeral	Responds to data requests. Outgoing data over an ephemeral port.
LDAP	TCP/IP	Connector ⇨ LDAP	389 (default) 636 for LDAP/SSL	Accesses central registry.
Server Ping	UDP/IP	Connector ⇨ Server	9610	Verifies server status. Required for each iAS in cluster.
Server Ping Return	UDP/IP	Server ⇨ Connector	Ephemeral	Responds to ping. Required for each iAS in cluster.

Ephemeral ports (also known as anonymous ports) are temporary ports used by iAS for return communications. When initiating a reply iAS will request an ephemeral port from the operating system. The operating system will then provide iAS with an unused port from a range of ports that it has reserved for ephemeral communications. The range of ports reserved for ephemeral communication will vary based on the operating system. By default, AIX and Solaris will reserve 32768 through 65535 for ephemeral ports; HP/UX will reserve ports 49152 through 65535; and Windows will reserve ports 1024 through 4999.

TIP Some enterprises don't permit UDP traffic between their DMZ and protected zones. In this case, you can disable iAS's UDP `ping` feature by adding a registry value of `SOFTWARE\\iPlanet\\6.0\\CCSO\\CONN\\DisableEcho` with the value of 1. Disabling the UDP `ping` feature, however, forces the Web connector to rely on TCP/IP timeouts to detect iAS server failures, thereby increasing the amount of time necessary to react to a server failure.

Also note that in addition to the TCP/IP and UDP/IP communication between the Web connectors and the iAS server processes, there is also communication among the iAS servers within a cluster. Since there should not be firewalls between the iAS servers this is generally not an issue. However, it should be noted that the iAS server uses two IP multicasting addressing channels to communicate server load-balancing tables and administrative information. IP multicasting allows for a server to broadcast information to all servers listening on that multicasting channel on the same subnet, much like a party line or chat server.

There are two important things to note about iAS's use of multicasting. The first is that it requires that all iAS servers within a load-balancing group be on the same network subnet, since IP multicasting will not cross subnet boundaries. The second is that if you want to completely isolate iAS servers from each other, you must prevent them from sending each other multicasting messages.

By default, iAS uses ports 9607 and 9608 for IP multicasting. These two ports can be changed with the `Software\iPlanet\Application Server\6.5\GMS\KES\MCastPort` and `Software\iPlanet\Application Server\6.5\GMS\KAS\MCastPort` registry keys, respectively. Isolating servers from each other by changing these IP multicasting ports is never necessary, but it does help performance slightly since it reduces the amount of multicasting messages that must be processed by each iAS server.

Cluster Configuration

You must make the following three essential decisions in planning cluster architectures:

- ◆ Should I use clustering?
- ◆ How many iAS server instances should I configure?
- ◆ How should I partition my application?

The following subsections help you answer these questions based on your application and system requirements.

Cluster requirements

Clustering provides transparent failover for `HttpSession` and stateful session beans. If your application needs to support failover without the loss of session data, you must enable clustering. (Alternatively, you can build your own session failover system, but this approach is typically inadvisable because of iAS's enterprise class, built-in session failover capabilities.)

Review Chapter 10 for information on the technical details of clustering and the alternatives. Chapter 11 provides more information about clustering, as well as details of the failover process.

Optimal number of server instances

The next step, after determining whether there is a need for clustering, is determining the number of server instances that are necessary to support your application. To simplify system maintenance and maximize performance, you should try to minimize the number of server instances while still meeting your system requirements.

All the following factors influence the number of server instances that you need to meet your system requirements:

- ◆ *The physical size of the available hardware.* If your application requires 12 CPUs of processing power and your application server hardware can support only four CPUs per server, you must have at least three server instances.

- ◆ *The vertical scalability of iPlanet Application Server.* Each server instance can support only a limited number of processors effectively. (One well-tuned server instance can typically support eight to 20 CPUs. If your application server has 64 processors, it would be advisable to configure multiple server instances that can use all 64 processors effectively.

♦ *The level of isolation necessary between applications.* Applications that share the same server instance also share the same JVM. If one application crashes the JVM, it can affect all other applications in the same server instance. Critical or unstable applications may warrant their own server instances.

♦ *Failover requirements.* Applications that require hardware (machine) failover without loss of session data require at least two server instances running that application on separate hardware.

Case Study

This case study examines a fictional company, ABCCorp, with one existing iAS application. ABCCorp needs to upgrade its production architecture to handle an upgrade of the existing application and also needs to deploy a new application.

The existing system

Internal customer-service agents use ABCCorp's existing iAS application, ServiceWeb. A single four-processor iAS server hosts ServiceWeb, which has no exposure to the Internet. The company doesn't consider ServiceWeb mission-critical, because customer service agents can access the same information via legacy systems if ServiceWeb fails. Figure 17-2 shows the current ABCCorp iAS production architecture.

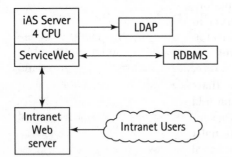

Figure 17-2: ABCCorp's current production architecture

Required system changes

Over the next few months, ABCCorp plans to offer customers access to ServiceWeb via the Internet to facilitate customer self-service. Additionally, the company's deploying an *OLAP* (*OnLine Analytic Processing*) application, ServiceTracker, so that internal employees can analyze the customer-service data.

The capacity-planning analysis for ServiceWeb predicts that the company must quadruple iAS server capacity to 16 CPUs of processing power to handle the additional load from customers. ServiceWeb is to become a mission-critical application after it's available on the Internet, although limited maintenance windows are to remain available during off-hours.

Performance analysis of ServiceTracker indicates that ordinary usage requires only one CPU of processing power. As is true of many OLAP applications, however, ServiceTracker is certain to experience periods of peak usage that consume considerably more resources. ServiceTracker isn't considered mission-critical.

Planned implementation

Enabling customers to access ServiceWeb via the Internet necessitates the creation of a network DMZ to provide a secure environment and to isolate the Web-server zone from the application-server zone.

The change in status to mission-critical requires HttpSession failover. The company determined that using iPlanet Application Server's DSYNC HttpSession Clustering feature is both the easiest solution to implement and the most reliable for HttpSession failover. The change to mission-critical status also necessitates the use of clustering software to make LDAP and RDBMS systems highly available.

The company also decided that a separate server instance is necessary for the ServiceTracker application. It made this decision because the stability of ServiceTracker isn't proven and because the company expects ServiceTracker to consume significant resources during peak periods. By isolating ServiceTracker into its own instance, the company prevents ServiceTracker utilization peaks from affecting ServiceWeb response times. Additionally, any failures in the ServiceTracker application don't affect the mission-critical ServiceWeb application.

The final recommendation is for three server instances: one four-CPU instance for ServiceTracker and two eight-CPU instances for a ServiceWeb cluster. This setup minimizes the number of server instances and enables the company to repurpose the existing four-CPU ServiceWeb application server as a ServiceTracker server.

The planning analysis also recommends that the company cluster all three servers, however, and that they share a common LDAP registry. This setup enables the company to easily bring the ServiceTracker server online as an additional ServiceWeb application server should additional capacity prove necessary in an emergency. As a result, the company plans to install the ServiceTracker application server as a SYNC-LOCAL to make sure that the DSYNC Primary and Backup reside on ServiceWeb machines, to maximize DSYNC cache effectiveness. (Because ServiceTracker isn't mission-critical, it doesn't use DSYNC sessions.)

Figure 17-3 shows the planned implementation. Notice that the company's utilizing multiple Web servers to provide redundancy and that two layers of firewalls protect all corporate data.

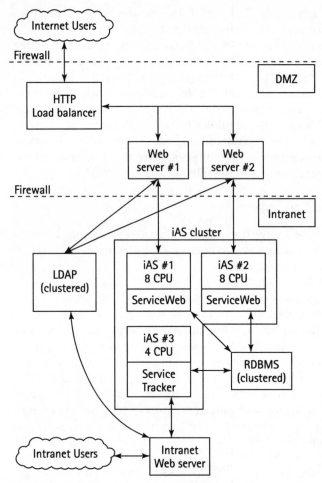

Figure 17–3: ABCCorp planned architecture

The proposed architecture enables ABCCorp to deploy customer-facing applications, maximize the uptime of ServiceWeb, and meet the desired capacity. As an added feature, the new architecture also enables the rapid deployment of additional capacity to the ServiceWeb application by using the ServiceTracker application server as a warm standby for the ServiceWeb application.

Static Content Deployment

The Java Servlet specification encourages developers to package all their static content into their application WAR files. Deploying static content in the WAR file to the application server tier enables WAR files to become more self-contained. As

I discuss in Chapter 9, one goal of EAR and WAR files is to enable you to package applications so that they have no external dependencies.

If you remove an application's dependencies on external static content, however, the workload of serving static content moves from the Web server to the application server. This approach has many disadvantages. Unlike Web servers, application servers aren't designed or tuned for static content. Application servers reside in the protected network rather than in the DMZ, requiring traffic to cross an additional network boundary. Application servers also don't natively support If-Modified-Since HTTP headers and other mechanisms for static content caching. Without these headers browsers and proxy servers cannot effectively cache content, and therefore the number of requests made to the application server will increase. In short, using application servers for the purpose is an extremely inefficient way to deliver static content.

This choice is of particular importance to Web application design, because the typical page of HTML content that a Web application creates references many images, each of which the browser retrieves. The decision to service static content from the application server tier can increase the amount of application server requests by an order of magnitude. (This decision is also important because many companies are outsourcing their static-content delivery to third parties such as Akamai.)

Highly scalable Web sites, therefore, continue to serve their static content from Web servers rather than from Java application servers. So you want to follow several best practices in developing applications that rely on static content outside of the WAR file, as the following list describes:

◆ You should develop a repeatable deployment methodology for synchronizing static and dynamic content.

If you choose to separate static content from the EAR or WAR file, you must develop strong processes and tools to keep the static content synchronized with the dynamic content. Ant scripts to deploy both static and dynamic simultaneously are an example of one tool that you commonly use for content synchronization, although you must combine Ant scripts with integration into SCM tools to devise a complete solution.

◆ Programmatic URL generation should use deployment descriptors to define a URL root. During development the deployment descriptor would be set to null, resulting in relative links. But after product deployment descriptor could be changed to "../../", resulting in a relative link back to the webserver, or to an absolute link such as "http://images.third-notice.com/images/".

Because the location of static URLs may change throughout the life of an application, URLs that you programmatically generate should remain flexible concerning their URL roots, preferably by the developer storing the root of the URL in a deployment descriptor that JNDI accesses. During development, an HTML page may refer to a navigation-bar graphic, for example, as SRC= "navbar.gif". At deployment time, you may deploy the GIF file to a directory dedicated to static images, changing the reference to SRC="../../images/navbar.gif". At some time in the future, you may move the GIF file to a dedicated static-content Web server, changing the reference to SRC="http://images.hungryminds.com/navbar.gif". If you enable the URL root to change from null to ../../images/, to http://images.hungryminds.com/ at deployment time, using a deployment descriptor to define a base URL prevents code changes from becoming necessary to support these static-content changes.

◆ Don't use static HTML.

Use JSPs to generate all HTML content. In addition to enabling you to generate URLs programmatically, this approach also provides more flexibility in application designs. You can dynamically include common site elements — for example, footers, headers, and styles — by using include directives instead of duplicating them in each HTML file.

Summary

This chapter covers a wide variety of topics related to producing J2EE architectures. We discussed network architectures, firewall configurations, cluster topologies, and application architecture. The basic lesson that you can learn from all these discussions is that production architectures need to be planned and tested before the first deployment.

Applications should be tested in an environment that mirrors their production architecture. Testing in a mirror environment helps bring to light architectural problems that otherwise would not appear until the last minute, when they are often most difficult to fix. For example, if an application assumes that all URLs will begin with the default token NASApp, the application is likely to suffer from broken links in a production environment with a customized token.

Because of these dangers, leaving the design of the production architecture until a testing phase, or leaving the design to a separate operations group, is unwise. System architects should design their production architectures as carefully as their application architecture.

Please consult the following sources for more information on the topics in this chapter:

◆ Whatis.com Definition of a Network DMZ: http://whatis.techtarget.com/definition/0,,sid9_gci213891,00.html

◆ Akamai Technologies: www.akamai.com/

Chapter 18

Maintenance Strategies

IN THIS CHAPTER

◆ Describing the goals and challenges of maintenance strategies

◆ Avoiding common misconceptions about iPlanet Application Server and application maintenance

◆ Choosing and implementing a maintenance strategy appropriate to your uptime requirements

MY DEFINITION OF a maintenance strategy is an operational plan to avoid downtime during application and infrastructure upgrades. Maintenance strategies range from the simple, such as maintenance windows, to the complicated, such as transferring users between multiple application clusters. In this chapter, I examine several best practices regarding infrastructure and application maintenance. I also discuss uptime expectations and the role of clustering and hot deployment in maintenance strategies.

Common Misconceptions

Before I discuss best-practice maintenance strategies, I must debunk several misconceptions about maintenance strategies. Understanding what techniques aren't as good maintenance strategies is as important as understanding successful strategies.

Misconception #1: Hot deployment is a maintenance strategy

Hot deployment (also known as *dynamic reloading*) is a solution that people sometimes expect to prove effective for performing application upgrades on production boxes. Hot deployment is always a bad idea for production boxes, however, and you should always disable it on production servers.

Hot deployment is a bad solution for application upgrades, too, because no transitional period is possible between application versions. If a person is using version 1.0 of the application while you're deploying version 1.1, his user interface suddenly changes without warning. He may even find that his application is now a mixture of the two interfaces if all parts of the application don't dynamically reload simultaneously. Even worse, if version 1.1 of the application has expectations about objects in the application or session scope that are different than those of the objects that version 1.0 of the application creates, the application logic may fail completely.

What your maintenance strategy needs to provide for application upgrades is a method for users of version 1.0 to gracefully exit from version 1.0 as you upgrade to version 1.1. You can accomplish this transfer either by waiting for those users to log out or by forcibly exiting them from version 1.0 with an explanatory message. Only after they exit from version 1.0 do you enable them to log in to version 1.1. Because hot deployment can't provide this transition, you should disable it on production boxes. (Another reason to disable hot deployment is that it can affect server performance.) Hot deployment is also completely ineffective for managing infrastructure upgrades, such as service-pack installation on application servers.

Hot deployment is a feature designed for developers to minimize the time that they need to take to test new versions of an application, not as a tool to enable field upgrades of new applications or infrastructure versions.

Misconception #2: iAS clustering is a maintenance strategy

Clustering is a useful tool for providing high availability, but it's not useful for performing application and infrastructure upgrades. Because a cluster shares a central registry of application information, an application server cluster must always agree about the application version in use. If server #1 is running version 1.0 of an application, server #2 in the same cluster must also run version 1.0 of the application. Clustering, therefore, provides no benefit if you're performing application upgrades. You must upgrade applications on every server of a cluster simultaneously.

Each server in a cluster must also run the same version of iPlanet Application Server, because the communication protocol that enables communication between server versions can change between iAS service packs. This strategy prevents you from using clustering to upgrade the iAS version that a cluster uses. iAS server upgrades require a shutdown of the cluster, installation of the service packs, and then a cluster restart.

iPlanet Application Server clustering is designed to support transparent failover of application sessions but not to support the field upgrade of applications or service-pack upgrades.

Misconception #3: Web applications can't have scheduled maintenance windows

Some think that, because of the constant public exposure of Internet applications (24 hours a day and 365 days a year), Web applications can't have downtime. In reality, however, scheduled downtime is a reality for the vast majority of Web applications. Companies must balance the opportunity cost of system downtime versus the hardware and labor costs of implementing a more sophisticated maintenance strategy.

Maintenance Goals

Maintenance strategies have the following three major goals:

◆ Enabling you to install iAS service packs and application upgrades repeatably, verifiably, and revocably. *Repeatably* means that the process for installing updates is known and well-documented. *Verifiably* means that you can verify the success of the install before bringing the new application or service pack into production. *Revocably* means that you can back out of the service pack or application upgrade should a problem occur.

◆ Presenting a predictable and minimally disruptive user interface to end users during the transition. You don't want to present any sudden changes in functionality to the end user without ample warning. Neither do you want a user to lose session information, such as the contents of an active shopping cart, without such warning.

◆ Minimizing or eliminating the amount of time that the application is unavailable.

I don't discuss the first goal in this chapter, as I discuss repeatable deployment, testing, and system rollbacks extensively in Chapters 20, 21, and 22, respectively. It's an important part of maintenance processes, however, as iPlanet Application Server doesn't have the capability to automatically roll back changes to itself or its applications. (No other major application servers have this functionality yet either.)

Keeping a consistent user interface during application upgrades prevents users from becoming stranded on pages with links to functionality that you remove or change. In an ideal world, the user would keep his old version of the application until he logs out. The next time that he logs in to the application, he would get the new version of the application. This type of transition ensures that all links remain valid and also ensures that the user receives a consistent look and feel throughout his use of the application.

Minimizing the amount of downtime has the obvious benefit of reducing the amount of time that the system is unavailable to users. This benefit includes minimizing the amount of time the system is unavailable and also minimizing the amount of time that users lose by your forcing them to log out of the system.

Maintenance Strategies

The following sections describe the goals and challenges of several different maintenance strategies.

Complete shutdown

The simplest methodology for performing maintenance is to shut down the iAS cluster, install the service pack or application upgrade, and then restart the cluster. This approach, of course, involves the very negative effect of forcing your users off the system and leaving the system down for the duration of your upgrade.

Because upgrading an entire cluster to a new service pack can prove a time-consuming process, this strategy can cause significant downtime. Some intranet applications, however, give you the luxury of large maintenance windows. If a large-enough maintenance window is available, the simplest solution is to perform a complete cluster shutdown and not worry about the graceful cutover of users to the new application.

 TIP If you plan on using planned maintenance windows for your application, the wise course is to write code for your application that warns users of an approaching maintenance window. Checking a configuration file for messages to display during specific time windows is easy to implement, and you can use this technique for a variety of purposes.

A complete shutdown isn't very effective in minimizing downtime, but it does ensure that users receive a consistent user interface. It also simplifies the process of repeatable deployment, because you can apply the changes directly to the cluster without needing to worry about the continuing operation of the application. During the shutdown, it is customary to have the Web server redirect traffic to a maintenance page that explains the expected length of the outage and possibly lists the benefits of the pending upgrade.

Single-server cutover

Assuming that you don't have the luxury of a large maintenance window in which to effect a complete shutdown, the best solution is to get the new system ready for operation before shutting down the old system. The single-server cutover strategy uses a single server in the cluster as this preprepared system.

In the single-server cutover strategy, you initially shut down a single server. The system continues normally because of the cluster's failover capabilities, relying on the other servers to continue operation of the system.

You then upgrade the single server with the new application version or service pack at leisure. After you upgrade and test the single server, you shut down the rest of the cluster (presumably with warning to the users). You then restart the single upgraded server. The single server serves the new version of the application until you can upgrade the additional servers and bring them into the new cluster.

The advantage of the single-server cutover strategy is that you largely avoid downtime because you can bring up the new server immediately after the old cluster's shutdown. The disadvantages include the following:

◆ All users lose their sessions as you shut down the old cluster. All users thus lose any work they have in their sessions and must restart a new session on the new server.

◆ The new server must be capable of supporting the workloads of all the users until you can restart the rest of the cluster.

◆ The system upgrade can prove difficult to test on the new server because you can't bring it online until you shut down the old cluster. (Otherwise, the upgraded server attempts to rejoin the old cluster.) The system must remain isolated from the rest of the network if testing is necessary.

The single-server cutoff strategy is good at achieving a consistent user interface and reasonably good at minimizing downtime. The single-server cutoff strategy isn't a very effective tool for making service-pack and application-upgrade installations repeatable, verifiable, and revocable. Testing each upgraded server without disturbing the operating cluster is difficult. The strategy also requires that a single server handle the entire workload, necessitating that you upgrade the additional servers quickly.

Figure 18-1 shows the process of using the single-server cutover strategy with a three-server cluster. First, you separate and upgrade the single server. Second, you cut the system over from the old cluster to the newly upgraded server. Finally, you upgrade the remaining servers and cluster them with the upgraded server.

Using multiple clusters

An alternative strategy to removing a single server from a cluster to host the upgraded application is to use an entirely new cluster to host the new application. You install two clusters and alternate operation between them.

During normal operation, only one cluster is in operation. You use the first cluster to run the application until you need to make an upgrade. You then upgrade the second cluster with the new application. After the upgrade is complete, you shut down the Web servers that link to the first cluster and start the Web servers (running them on the same port) that link to the second cluster. This approach switches the system over to the new application with minimal downtime.

To avoid wasting hardware, you installed both clusters on the same set of hardware. Each server employs two iAS instances: one that belongs to cluster 1 and one that belongs to cluster 2. Each cluster runs with its own set of TCP/IP ports and with its own configuration space within the directory server. (See Chapter 4 of the iPlanet Application Server Installation Guide for the details on installing multiple copies of iPlanet Application Server on a single server.)

Step #1: Bring one server down and upgrade it

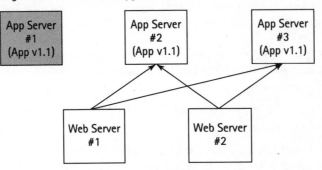

Step #2: Shut down old version and bring up new version

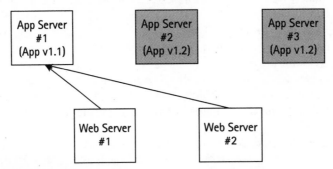

Step #3: Upgrade and restore remaining servers

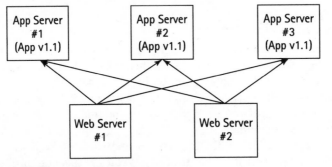

Figure 18-1: Single-server cutover strategy

Figure 18-2 shows the use of the multiple-cluster strategy with a three-server cluster. At first, the top cluster remains active while you upgrade the bottom cluster offline. You then switch operation to the bottom cluster. You can then upgrade the top cluster at leisure. (The top cluster can then serve as a standby system until the next system upgrade.)

Step #1: Upgrade secondary cluster while secondary Web servers offline

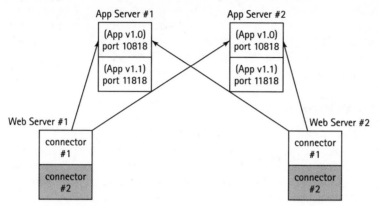

Step #2: Stop initial Web servers and start secondary Web servers–transferring load to secondary cluster

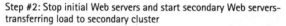

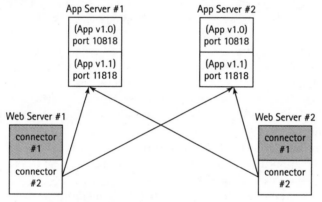

Step #3: Upgrade initial cluster at leisure

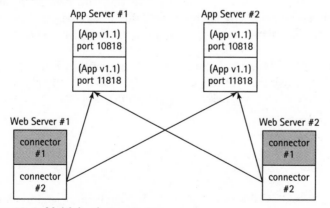

Figure 18-2: Multiple-cluster strategy

The multiple-cluster strategy is good at meeting all your maintenance goals. Its two disadvantages are complexity and the fact that users lose all their sessions during the cutover process. Testing is much easier than if you're using the single-server cutover strategy, because you can test the new cluster thoroughly before cutover. You face no capacity problem during the transition either, because the new cluster is immediately capable of providing as much capacity as the original cluster.

Rolling maintenance

The rolling-maintenance strategy is very similar to the multiple-cluster strategy. Two server instances exist on each physical server, and you configure the servers into two clusters, just as in the multiple-cluster strategy. The difference between the multiple-cluster strategy and the rolling-maintenance strategy is in how you cut over operation from the first cluster to the second cluster.

Many high-end Web load balancers, such as F5 Lab's BigIP and Cisco's ArrowPoint, can perform intelligent sticky load balancing. During ordinary operation, you configure the intelligent sticky load balancer to enable you to create new sessions on any of cluster 1's Web servers. (Sticky loadbalancing is discussed in Chapter 10.)

After you upgrade and test cluster 2, you update the load balancer's configuration to create any new sessions on the Web servers that connect to cluster 2. Because of the sticky load balancing, however, the existing sessions continue to route to cluster 1. Gradually, as existing users log out, less and less traffic routes to cluster 1. Eventually, all traffic routes to cluster 2, and all users are using the new version of the application.

After all traffic is routing to cluster 2, you can shut down and upgrade cluster 1 to the new version of the application. You can then upgrade cluster 1 at leisure and use cluster 2 to service all users.

The rolling-maintenance strategy provides for true 24/7 operation with no disruption to end users. Sessions are never lost and users never experience downtime because of maintenance. It also enables you to test upgrades sufficiently, because internal users can test cluster 2 directly by bypassing the load balancer. After the testing is complete, you can instruct the load balancer to begin transferring the traffic.

The rolling-maintenance strategy is complex to set up initially, however, and depending on your user's usage patterns, transferring the users from the old cluster to the new cluster may take a long time. This strategy can make performing a maintenance upgrade a long process.

Summary

This chapter debunked several of the major myths about application maintenance. Debunking these myths exposed the difficulties of application upgrades and the challenges associated with maintaining uptime during upgrades.

You also explored several strategies for upgrading iAS applications, including the benefits and drawbacks of each. Now you should be able to reasonably evaluate the uptime goals of your applications and evaluate the maintenance strategies needed to meet those goals.

Chapter 19

Automated Builds

IN THIS CHAPTER

- ◆ Learning the benefits of establishing automated builds
- ◆ Understanding the requirements for making an automated-build process successful
- ◆ Creating a plan for introducing an automated-build process into your development environment

THIS CHAPTER'S FOCUS is a time-tested best practice for development: automated builds and continuous integration. I explore the effect that Web development models and J2EE have on continuous integration and how to best implement automated builds by using iPlanet Application Server.

Fundamentals of Automated Builds

An *automated build* is a process whereby you automatically and periodically recreate a software system from the source code. Typically a central server retrieves the latest source code from a central repository, compiles, links, and packages the source code, and then possibly deploys the end result to a test environment. Often the automated-build environment then conducts a series of basic tests to verify that the new build functions correctly and that no existing functionality has broken since the last build. These tests are commonly known as *smoke tests*. The name comes from the idea that you're just plugging the system in and seeing whether smoke comes out. You're testing basic functionality and generally not running the complete suite of QA tests.

The best practice of automated builds is also known as *Daily Builds*, *Daily Build and Smoke Tests*, or *Continuous Integration*, depending on the exact details that you implement. The central element that defines automated builds is the automated creation of software builds that occurs on a regular or continuous basis and requires no human intervention.

A typical automated-build system looks like the logical architecture shown in Figure 19-1. Notice that this diagram is a logical architecture and doesn't always reflect the physical architecture. In some cases, the build server could run one of the developer's workstations during off hours. Frequently the build server uses the same hardware as the smoke-test server. In short, the exact hardware requirements can vary depending on the necessary performance, size of the project, and the available hardware, but the logical architecture should remain the same.

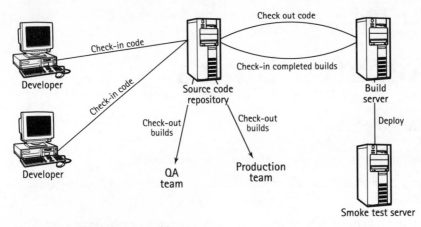

Figure 19-1: Build-system architecture

Figure 19-1 shows that all developers interact only with source-code control. After checking in their code to the central source-code repository, the build server checks out the entire codebase and compiles and packages the application. It then sends the completed build to a smoke-test server for basic testing and checks in the build to source-code control for future use.

Benefits of Automated Builds

The key feature of automated builds is to provide a repeatable process by which you can frequently generate test and production builds. By using the same method for both test and production builds, it ensures that differences between the production and test builds don't cause bugs in the production system.

After you develop a process for creating regular builds, you realize several significant benefits, as the following list describes:

◆ *Developers and QA get immediate feedback from code changes.* After a developer checks code changes into the central repository, the automated build process makes a build that reflects those changes. Both the development and QA teams can then immediately test this build.

◆ *The build process introduces no defects into the software.* Developers are often under great pressure to meet deadlines, and introducing bugs at the last minute through a faulty build process is easy if human intervention is necessary to create a complete build of the software.

◆ *The build process helps to enforce source-code control.* Because the build server can access only the file in the source-code control repository, that helps to ensure that developers include all files in the source-code control repository.

♦ *You can create builds for all deployment platforms automatically.* A developer is unlikely to have all the production environment available on his desktop. By using automated builds, you can detect platform-specific defects early in the development process rather than later during an "integration phase," when making changes to the source code is more difficult. Many developers work on a Windows platform, for example, while production systems are on Solaris. By checking in the code, the automated build system quickly produces a test build on Solaris.

♦ *An automated build system is the first step to an automated test system.* By having the automated build system trigger a series of automated smoke tests on the new build, you can track your project's progress and also help prevent regression bugs.

♦ By archiving all daily builds, you can easily determine when a developer introduced a bug into a system. One common question that developers ask in trying to troubleshoot a bug is "When did this problem start?" By having an archive of previous system builds, you can easily test for when a problem started occurring and can also create a list of what changes were made between the last working build and the first broken build. This method is very effective in determining which changes cause a new bug.

Development benefits

Every project should have automated builds, without exception or excuse. No application is too large or complex for automated builds. Automated builds provide large increases in productivity and reduce risk significantly for a relatively low amount of up-front, one-time setup. The frequency of builds can vary depending on the project needs and the available hardware, but you should always have a single, well-defined automated-build process.

Implementing automated-build environments is even easier in the J2EE environment than in other areas of software development. Following are several characteristics of J2EE that aid in the implementation of automated builds:

♦ You can largely represent a J2EE application as a single file: the EAR archive. The entire concept of J2EE application packaging is designed to make the deployment of applications repeatable.

♦ Many third-party tools are available to help automate the J2EE build process, especially the Ant utility from the Jakarta organization. See the links at the end of this chapter for more information, as well as Appendix B.

♦ J2EE's Write Once Run Anywhere (WORA) paradigm reduces the amount of platform dependencies. Although cross-platform testing is important, the build system can remain largely agnostic about the destination platform.

◆ Because access to J2EE applications occurs via standard on-the-wire protocols such as SOAP, RMI, and HTTP, setting up automated test cases is much easier than setting up a GUI application. A variety of third-party Web-application testing products can easily establish smoke tests for your build process. If these applications are unavailable, however, you can put together an adequate smoke test by using wget, Perl scripts, and other basic tools.

In short, implementing an automated-build system is critical to long-term application success. Automated-build systems provide numerous long- and short-term benefits and are relatively straightforward to implement. Develop your build-system strategy iteratively, beginning with a simple automated process for generating complete builds and progressing toward a complete build/test/deploy system with strong auditing, logging, and reporting features.

Operational benefits

In addition to the significant benefits that automated builds provide the development process, a repeatable build process is equally critical to the group that manages the production servers.

The first and obvious benefit is that the operations group has a known and repeatable methodology for deployment. If the build server uses a repeatable and automated process to deploy applications on the test server, replicating that process on the production servers is generally a straightforward process. You may need to make some slight changes because of network or security differences in the production servers, but the build-deployment system is a good starting point for developing the production-deployment process.

Another very significant advantage to an automated-build process is the archive of tested daily builds. The production group can easily change the production servers to run any build that the build system creates. If it finds a bug in the production code, the production group can use the build-system archive to roll back to the last production build. Or, in an extreme case, the group may use a daily build in production.

Another, less obvious advantage is the decrease in time that packaging and deploying production builds takes. If builds require manual intervention, creating and deploying an application version often takes significant effort and the direct involvement of a buildmaster. If the operations team is dependent on the development team to conduct an application deployment, the operations group can't be effective in its jobs. Discovering how many operation teams can't recreate a production server should you need to redeploy applications can prove very surprising and disturbing.

As a case study, one Fortune 500 company was using iPlanet Application Server to host a dozen Web applications that connected to several backend systems and several databases. Many of the applications were developed by outside consulting firms. When the time came to add an additional production server to the cluster, the operations group claimed that creating a new production server would take six months. They quoted this amount of time for the following reasons:

♦ None of the applications had any documentation about how the group needed to deploy them. In the past, each development group had deployed its own applications via the GUI `deploytool`.

♦ No documentation existed about which datasources and backend systems were necessary for which application. The operations group had never received the XML files to create the iAS datasource definitions.

♦ Several of the applications required specific modifications to the server environment, such as `cron` jobs that should run on the application server and properties files that needed modification to contain the correct data-source or LDAP directory.

♦ No standard set of tests could be run to determine whether the new server was successfully installed. In fact, the operations group often didn't know the logins and passwords necessary to test the applications.

After suffering through this long and painful process of creating a new production server, the Fortune 500 company did document several of the processes necessary to create a new server instance. But many of the problems were difficult to address because the correct infrastructure for automating application deployment didn't exist.

In short, by forcing the development team to conduct an application deployment every day (or even more frequently), the development team naturally develops tools to make that deployment easier. They also must design the application in a way that doesn't require manual intervention for deployment. If the development team conducts application deployments only at the last minute, the details of application builds and application deployments become an afterthought and are hard to repeat effectively.

How to Implement Automated Builds

After you decide to implement an automated-build system, you need to set up the infrastructure to perform the builds and conduct the smoke tests. To be effective, an automated build system must have the following characteristics:

♦ The build system must not require any manual intervention. If you must update a file manually or adjust a server configuration manually, it can't count as a successful automated build.

◆ The results of the build system must be capable of deployment in the production server environment as well as the test environment. One of the purposes of the automated system is to detect platform bugs. If you can't test the results of the build system on the production platform, the build system can't achieve this goal.

◆ The build system must execute frequently – daily at a minimum and continually if possible.

◆ The build system must log its results and alert the buildmaster if problems occur. Typically the build system e-mails the buildmaster (or perhaps the entire team) with the results of a build. Failed builds should be highlighted appropriately.

◆ The build system must at least make basic tests to check to determine whether the build is successful. At a minimum, the build system should make a request to the first page of the application by using wget (or a similar utility) to make sure that deployment is successful.

◆ The development culture must strongly discourage breaking the build. If a developer checks in code that prevents the build system from successfully compiling or deploying a new version, it breaks the cycle of feedback. Until the build system is successful again, no new feedback can go from the build system to the QA or development groups.

 Because breaking the build results in such negative effects, many development groups impose a token "punishment" on developers who break the process of the build server. The group may, for example, force a build breaker to maintain the build system until the next build breakage. Or it may make the build breaker responsible for buying lunch or breakfast for the rest of the team. The "punishments" are usually symbolic because the point isn't really to punish the developer but instead to make sure that breaking the build system is taken seriously.

In setting up an automated-build system you also need to keep several guidelines in mind. The build system should execute at predictable and nonintrusive times. The developers should know when to expect the build system to pick up the code that they check in. This enables developers to plan their work around the availability of new builds and the daily deadlines for checking in code. (If you have only one build a day, lunchtime is often a good time to perform the build as it enables developers to have a build with which to test their changes before leaving for the day.)

If you're new to automated builds, the best way to create your own system is to develop it piece by piece. First create a development environment, documenting all the details and including all the patch and version levels of the tools, operating systems, and servers necessary to create a complete version of the application. Next, take your existing `makefile` or Ant build file and automate any steps that currently require manual intervention. If you currently use Ant to compile and package your application, for example, adding Ant targets to deploy your application and restart the server is simple.

See Appendix B for more information about Ant and how to integrate Ant with iPlanet Application Server.

After you have a script that can build your application from scratch, create a scheduler or `cron` job to run the build periodically on whatever hardware you have available. You can then add additional functionality, such as logging and testing, piece by piece until your build system has all the functionality that you need. I list several third-party tools at the end of this chapter that can help you build out this advanced functionality.

Build-System–Source-Code-Control Integration

I've already mentioned source-code control several times in this chapter. Establishing good source-code control practices is essential before even beginning to implement an automated-build process. The source-code control repository is necessary for several reasons. The first is that the build server needs some central place to obtain the latest version of the application source code. The second reason is that the source-code repository can also serve as a good storage location for the completed builds. (Some prefer to rename completed builds by date and time instead of using a source-code control system to archive, but using your source-code control system reduces clutter and also gives you more functionality, such as the capability to tag releases.)

Source-code control can also help you perform blame analysis for your build system. *Blame analysis* is the process of determining who causes a build to fail. So if a build fails, the build system may query the source-code control system for a list of developers who've submitted changes since the last successful build. It would then send that list of developers, along with the build error messages, to the buildmaster. The buildmaster could then use that information to determine who's most likely at fault for the problem with the build.

TIP   On a Unix machine, you can determine who modified a CVS repository by
using the following command:

`cvs history -e -D "1 day ago" | cut -d" " -f5 | sort -u`

The `-e` option tells CVS to report on the `commit` commands that people
have made during the specified time period by using the `-D` option. The `cut`
command extracts out the usernames, and the `sort` command alphabet-
izes the results and removes duplicates.

Source-code control is also useful in determining whether a build is necessary. If
your build system runs frequently or continually, the build system should check the
source-code control logs to determine whether any changes were made since the
last build. This checkup prevents the build system from generating a multitude of
duplicate builds on holidays and weekends.

The build system should also interact with the source-code control system to tag
builds appropriately. One solution is to have the build system place a version tag on
the source code associated with each build that it makes. The build system then
places a matching tag on the completed build. This methodology makes recon-
structing a build after the fact easy, which is useful in working with branches and
troubleshooting previous builds. This method does, however, result in a very large
number of version control tags, which can become unwieldy if your automated
build system generates builds frequently.

Another alternative method is to create a log file that contains the exact date
and time stamp of each build. You can then use this timestamp to recreate the build,
if necessary. This method is less convenient, especially if you have multiple
branches in the source-code repository, but it reduces the amount of version tags
that the build system stores in the repository.

Summary

Automating the build, test, and deployment phases is a well-known best practice
for all types of software development. The nature of J2EE programming lends itself
very well to the effective deployment of this best practice, and every development
organization should automate its build and test environment.

A variety of third party tools can make constructing an automated build system
easier, including build tools, testing tools, and source-code control tools. By incre-
mementally building an automated-build environment using these building blocks,
a design team can speed development, increase the reliability and repeatability of
the deployment process, and decrease integration time.

Consult the following sources for more information on the topics that I cover in
this chapter:

Benefits of automated builds

◆ "Daily Builds are Your Friend," by Joel Spolsky: `www.joelonsoftware.com/articles/fog0000000023.html`

◆ "CxOne Best Practice: Daily Build and Smoke Test," by Construx Software: `www.construx.com/cxone/Construction/CxBest_DailyBuild.pdf`

◆ "Continuous Integration," by Martin Fowler: `www.martinfowler.com/articles/continuousIntegration.html`

◆ "CVS Best Practices, Chapter 8: Build Early Build Often," by Vivek Venugopalan: `www.ibiblio.org/mdw/REF/CVS-BestPractices/CVS-BestPractices.pdf`

Automated build tools

◆ Ant (Java Build Tool): `http://jakarta.apache.org/ant/index.html`

◆ Cactus (Java Unit Test Tool): `http://jakarta.apache.org/cactus/index.html`

◆ GNU wget: `http://wget.sunsite.dk/`

◆ Finalbuilder (GUI Scripting Tool Focused on Automated Builds): `www.atozedsoftware.com/finalbuilder.html`

Source code control systems (SCM)

◆ Concurrent Versions System (CVS): `www.cvshome.org/`

◆ Merant PVCS: `www.merant.com/pvcs/index.asp`

◆ Microsoft Visual SourceSafe: `http://msdn.microsoft.com/ssafe/`

◆ MKS Source Integrity: `www.mks.com/products/sis/`

◆ Perforce P4: `www.perforce.com/perforce/products.html`

◆ Rational ClearCase: `www.rational.com/products/clearcase/index.jsp`

Chapter 20

Quality-Assurance Strategies

IN THIS CHAPTER

- ◆ Learning the goals of quality assurance
- ◆ Understanding the unique challenges of testing J2EE applications
- ◆ Designing architectures conducive to quality assurance
- ◆ Understanding benefits of testing automation

THIS CHAPTER PRESENTS advice about how to increase the quality of your enterprise applications. Implementing a quality-assurance (QA) plan for J2EE applications offers several additional challenges to desktop and client/server developers who may be new to J2EE development.

Quality assurance should be more than just a set of tests that you execute at the end of a project. Implementing a quality plan at the beginning of a project also increases developer understanding of the functionality that you need, increases visibility into the progress of the project, and greatly simplifies debugging. A QA plan can also serve as an excellent communication tool between the developers and the end users because the QA plan defines what you must accomplish to make the software application complete.

Quality-Assurance Goals

Although people most commonly associate QA testing with testing an application for functional defects (bugs), quality assurance actually involves many elements. A good quality-assurance program should check for several application characteristics, as follows:

- ◆ *Correctness:* As it's the most straightforward of QA goals, a quality-assurance program should ensure that the application correctly performs the tasks that the functional specifications define.

- ◆ *Robustness:* Not only should an application respond correctly to correct requests, but it should also degrade gracefully if it receives bad data. If you give it meaningless or contradictory inputs, the application

433

should respond with appropriate errors and/or messages. The application should avoid cryptic end-user messages and should log application errors appropriately.

◆ *Security:* The application should prevent unauthorized activity and should log inappropriate requests appropriately. A quality-assurance plan should ensure that the application takes reasonable precautions to preserve its own integrity.

◆ *Performance:* The application should be capable of handling the expected user loads on an appropriate amount of hardware. The definition of *appropriate* varies from project to project. For some projects, the amount of hardware may be predetermined, and you must tune the application to meet that constraint.

◆ *Reliability:* The application must continue to provide repeatable, correct results even under stressful and unusual conditions. This characteristic includes making sure that the application preserves transactional integrity, if appropriate.

◆ *Usability:* An application should prove easy to use by its end users. Users should be able to efficiently and correctly interact with the system. You should test both graphical user interfaces and system interfaces for usability. Technical excellence is worthless if users can't or won't use the system.

Notice that these quality-assurance goals offer a significant challenge that you can't accomplish with simple human unit and system testing. A good QA plan includes well-defined application functionality (to enable correctness and robustness testing), performance and uptime requirements (for reliability, security, and performance tests), and usability studies (which you should feed back into functional requirements). A QA of this scope requires upfront planning, recognition of QA as a primary goal, and an application architecture designed for effective testing. Projects that consider quality assurance only retroactively, at the end of the project, can't effectively meet these six goals.

Challenges of J2EE Testing

J2EE development offers QA challenges that are different than the QA challenges of client/server and desktop development. Desktop and client/server applications (especially shrink-wrap applications), for example, often face such challenges as the fact that the application platform is an unknown quantity. Certain bugs may become evident only on certain versions of the OS or if you use it with certain third-party library combinations. J2EE applications rarely face this problem because the production platform is generally well known and well defined. You can easily test JDK bugs or operating system inconsistencies by testing the application on a mirror of the production system.

J2EE, however, offers its own testing challenges. Three of these challenges — indirection, multithreading, and performance — I discuss in the following sections. I also discuss a strategy for mitigating the difficulty of each challenge.

Indirection

J2EE applications are typically *n-tiered applications*, meaning that presentation logic is separate from business logic, which is, in turn, separate from data logic. Many J2EE applications also take advantage of development frameworks such as Struts. These levels of indirection are helpful to application flexibility and maintenance, but can add difficulty to debugging and testing. The following steps may, for example, prove necessary to process a single request:

1. A *controller* servlet receives and routes the request based on HTTP request parameters.

2. The controller passes the request to a JavaBean, which validates the input parameters.

3. After validation, the controller passes control to another JavaBean, which instantiates an session EJB.

4. The session EJB invokes one or more entity beans to collect data from a backend datasource.

5. The Entity Beans access stored procedures written in PL/SQL to retrieve data rows.

6. The stored procedure filters and sorts the data.

7. The Entity and Session beans return the processed data to the JavaBean.

8. The controller servlet passes the resultant data to a JSP.

9. The JSP merges the resultant data with an HTML template.

10. The JSP includes header and footer JSPs, which add additional presentation to the end results.

11. Client-side JavaScript code executes to enable the user to dynamically interact with the resulting data.

A bug in application logic can occur in any one of these steps. The various steps occur in multiple languages and on multiple platforms. In most cases, different developers are responsible for each of the different steps. These multiple layers of indirection can make stepping through the application difficult, if not impossible.

Multithreading

All J2EE applications are implicitly *multithreaded*. Although the J2EE container tries to isolate the developer from the complexity of developing multithreaded applications, developers must still take the normal precautions in developing such applications. Neglecting to consider a race condition or deadlock possibility can result in a difficult-to-reproduce and difficult-to-diagnose bug.

A test plan must include testing to ensure that the components are correctly threadsafe. Generally, testing for thread safety means using automated testing tools, because a single human user generally isn't capable of generating the rapid sequences of events that can cause threading problems. Automated code analyzers can also prove useful in detecting some threading problems.

But even if developers succeed in making their code completely threadsafe, the multithreaded nature of J2EE application servers makes diagnosing bugs more difficult. In a production environment, a single application server instance hosts multiple applications in several JVM instances, each containing many threads. If the JVM crashes, you have no easy way to tell which application is causing the JVM crash. As another example, if an application forgets to release its database connections and exhausts all the connections in the database connection pool, determining which application is causing the problem is difficult.

Performance

The *performance* considerations of designing a J2EE application are very different than those of designing the desktop or client/server applications. A desktop application exclusively controls its resources, many of which remain idle during user think time. Performance-tuning desktop applications generally focuses on improving response time.

In contrast, a J2EE server application may need to divide its resources between many thousands of active sessions and hundreds of concurrent requests. J2EE performance tuning generally focuses more on improving total server throughput than on decreasing the response time of any single request. Because of this need, many desktop tuning techniques, such as caching the user's state and asynchronous processing, are often counterproductive in designing J2EE applications.

Ensuring adequate performance is part of a quality-assurance plan. The test environment is the first opportunity to ensure that the application can meet the performance requirements. Tracking the performance of the application over the course of development prevents last-minute surprises about the scalability of the application. Additionally, keeping performance metrics throughout the course of development can also help predict how much time, if any, you need to dedicate to tuning application performance.

Quality Plans

Creating a written *quality plan* is the first and most critical step toward increasing the quality of a project. Documenting the expected levels of testing not only gives guidelines for executing tests, but also enforces the message that quality is a critical project goal and not just a last-minute task.

Quality plans also help to estimate the amount of work that you need to accomplish to create testing infrastructures. The best practices that I lay out in this chapter take time to both design and implement. If the project plan doesn't include a quality plan that details the necessary quality infrastructure, the project schedule is unlikely to include time for building that infrastructure.

A quality plan should include the following:

◆ A summary of the quality goals for the project, including measurable metrics for as many goals as possible.

◆ An outline of how you intend to build code, including, at a minimum, standards for design reviews, standards for code reviews, exception-handling guidelines, build procedures, and general coding guidelines.

◆ An outline of how you intend to test code, including, at a minimum, how you're going to define test cases, unit-testing requirements, system-testing requirements, and general guidelines on how developers will interact with the testing infrastructure.

◆ A defined procedure for recording and managing bugs. Many powerful off-the-shelf and open-source bug-tracking applications are available. Even the smallest project needs to utilize bug-tracking software.

◆ A flowchart for the bug's life cycle, including how developers and testers communicate bug information with one another. The developer who fixes a bug, for example, generally shouldn't be able to close a bug. Either another developer or, preferably, a dedicated tester should independently verify all bug fixes.

◆ A list of all the testing tools and infrastructure.

◆ A flowchart for the project's life cycle, including what tasks you must complete for each phase of the life cycle. Moving from the design phase to the development phase, for example, may require only that the technical lead and project manager both agree to move forward. But moving from the testing phase to beta release may require the joint approval of several groups and to close all severe bugs.

◆ A list of final acceptance criteria — a detailed account of all the deliverables that you must complete before the project is completely done.

As you can see, building a quality plan requires careful consideration about the project's needs. Documenting this information up front, however, is always better than creating your plan ad hoc. The quality plan prevents arguments about which tasks are which team's responsibility. It helps ensure that the tools and infrastructure are available as you need them. Most important, the quality plan establishes measurable goals that you can use to track and manage the progress of the application.

Design Testable Architectures

Although testing is only one part of software quality, it's a critical part. Creating an effective testing environment not only enables you to detect bugs in your code, but also increases the effectiveness of a development team. If you define test cases as part of the functional specification, for example, that not only makes the tester's job easier, but also clarifies the functionality that you want to the developer.

Similarly, making a component easy to test benefits both the developer and the testers. A component that you design for testability has the following characteristics:

◆ You can test it outside of the complexity of the entire application. This capability enables the tester to incrementally test each component as you develop it. It also enables developers to troubleshoot problems much more quickly because isolating the problem down to a single malfunctioning component is easier.

◆ You can integrate it into an automated testing solution. This capability obviously increases the efficiency of the tester and also benefits the developer, as I describe in Chapter 19.

◆ It has a clearly defined success criteria. A test case that defines the correct behavior of the component helps both the developer and the tester.

◆ You can easily monitor it for test regressions. Regression tests help developers make sure that their changes don't adversely affect anyone else's code. Testers obviously benefit as well, because regression tests help them ensure that additional functionality doesn't introduce bugs into existing components.

Component-level testing

The first element of designing your components for quality assurance is to integrate your components by using a test harness. A test harness is a program designed to test other components without the complexity of the surrounding application. If your component is an entity EJB that the application can access only via a session EJB, for example, a test harness is a simple servlet that tests the entity bean directly.

Test harnesses enable you to pass arbitrary values into the methods of your component and interactively view the results that the component returns. In the example of the entity bean, the test harness is the only method to effectively test the component. Testing the entity bean through the session bean would test only the parts of the entity bean that the session bean uses. In addition, if the session bean returns an incorrect value, the bug may exist in either the entity bean or the session bean.

Test harnesses are necessary for effective automated testing and also improve the quality of unit testing at the developer level. Test harnesses also enable developers to build each component independently. Without a test harness, the entity bean developer couldn't test his component at all until the session bean developer completes his component.

SERVLET TEST HARNESSES

Because you can call servlets directly via a browser, they may seem not to need test harnesses. This assumption is often untrue, however, because servlets often vary their behavior on the state of a user's session or other application state. A servlet test harness is a tool that enables the tester to arbitrarily build that application state before invoking the servlet.

A servlet test harness may, for example, place arbitrary values into the HttpSession or ServletContext. You can find an example of such a test harness in Listing 20-1.

Listing 20-1: Simple servlet test harness

```
package com.hungryminds.ias.chapter20;

import java.io.*;
import java.text.*;
import java.util.*;
import javax.servlet.*;
import javax.servlet.http.*;
import java.net.*;


public class Harness extends HttpServlet {

    public void doGet(HttpServletRequest req,
        HttpServletResponse resp)
        throws IOException, ServletException {

        HttpSession session = req.getSession();
        PrintWriter out=resp.getWriter();
        String msg="unknown request type";

        resp.setContentType("text/html");

        String button = req.getParameter("ACTION");

        if (button==null) {
            msg="<br>";
        }
```

Continued

Listing 20-1 *(continued)*

```java
        else if (button.equals("INVALIDATE")) {
            session.invalidate();
            session=req.getSession();
            msg="Session Invalided";
        }
        else if (button.equals("ADDVALUE")) {
            try {
                session.setAttribute(
                    req.getParameter("NEWDATANAME"),
                    Integer.valueOf(req.getParameter("NEWDATAVALUE")));
                msg="Session attribute added/modified";
            }
            catch (NumberFormatException e) {
                msg="Cannot add non-numeric value";
            }
        }
        else if (button.equals("SETCOUNTER")) {
            try {
                AppInfo.unsafeCounter=Integer.valueOf(
                    req.getParameter("COUNTERVALUE")).intValue();
                msg="Counter updated";
            }
            catch (NumberFormatException e) {
                msg="Cannot add non-numeric value";
            }
        }

        out.println("<html>");
        out.println("<body bgcolor=\"white\">");
        out.println("<head>");

        out.println("<title>Chapter 20 Test Servlet Harness</title>");
        out.println("</head>");
        out.println("<body>");
        out.println(msg + "<br>");
        out.println("<h1>Chapter 20 Test Servlet Harness</h1>");
        out.println("<h2>Current session contents</h2>");

        Enumeration sessValues = session.getAttributeNames();

        if (sessValues.hasMoreElements()) {
            String attrName;
```

```
        String attrValue;

        out.println("<ul>");
        while (sessValues.hasMoreElements()) {
            attrName = (String) sessValues.nextElement();
            attrValue = session.getAttribute(attrName).toString();
            out.println("<li>" + attrName + " = " + attrValue + "</li>");
        }
        out.println("</ul>");
    }
    else {
        out.println("<p>none</p>");
    }

    out.print("<form action=\"");
    out.print("Harness\" ");
    out.println("method=GET>");
    out.println("New session attribute: ");
    out.println("<input type=text size=20 name=NEWDATANAME>");
    out.println("<br><br>");
    out.println("New session value: ");
    out.println("<input type=text size=20 name=NEWDATAVALUE>");
    out.println("<br><br>");
    out.println("New counter value: ");
    out.println("<input type=text size=20 name=COUNTERVALUE>");
    out.println("<br><br>");
    out.println("This version of the test harness can only add Integer");
    out.println("values to the session. Entering non-integer values ");
    out.println("will cause an error to occur.<br>");
    out.println("<input type=submit name=\"ACTION\" value=\"ADDVALUE\">");
    out.println("<input type=submit name=\"ACTION\" value=\"INVALIDATE\">");
    out.println("<input type=submit name=\"ACTION\" value=\"SETCOUNTER\">");
    out.println("</form>");
    out.println("<a href=\"Harness\">Reload this page</a><br>");
    out.println("<a href=\"AppInfo\">Test AppInfo</a>");
    out.println("</body></html>");
    out.close();
}

public void doPost(HttpServletRequest req,
    HttpServletResponse resp)
    throws IOException, ServletException {

    doGet(req,resp);
}
}
```

This simple test harness is designed to work with a slightly modified version of
the AppInfo servlet that I introduce in Chapter 4. (The only difference is that this
version of AppInfo exposes the `unsafeCounter` variable as public and static so that
the harness can modify it.) The test harness has three functions: adding `Integer`
attributes to the `HttpSession`, invalidating the `HttpSession`, and modifying the
`unsafeCounter` variable of the AppInfo servlet.

You can find the source code for the new version of AppInfo in Listing 20-2.
(I've removed some comments for brevity.)

Listing 20-2: Modified version of AppInfo

```
package com.hungryminds.ias.chapter20;

import java.io.*;
import java.util.*;
import javax.servlet.*;
import javax.servlet.http.*;
import java.net.*;

public class AppInfo extends HttpServlet {

    String myHostName;
    public static int unsafeCounter;

    public void init (ServletConfig config) throws ServletException {

        super.init(config);

        System.out.println("Chapter20 : init method of AppInfo");

        try {
            InetAddress theAddress = InetAddress.getLocalHost();
            myHostName = theAddress.getHostName();
        }
        catch (Exception e) {
            myHostName = "N/A";
            System.out.println("Hostname not available");
        }

        unsafeCounter=1;
    }

    public void doGet(HttpServletRequest req,
                    HttpServletResponse resp)
```

```
throws IOException, ServletException {

//Log requests
System.out.println("Chapter20 : AppInfo processing request");

//Get objects from request and session
HttpSession session = req.getSession();
PrintWriter out = resp.getWriter();
Integer safeCounter = (Integer) session.getAttribute("safecounter");
String userAgent = req.getHeader("User-Agent");
if (safeCounter==null) {
    System.out.println("Chapter20 : Initializing safeCounter");
    safeCounter=new Integer(1);
}
if (userAgent==null) {
    userAgent="No User Agent HTTP header provided.";
}

//Send results to client
resp.setContentType("text/html");
out.println("<html>");
out.println("<head><title>Chapter20 : AppInfo</title></head>");
out.println("<body bgcolor=\"white\">");
out.println("<h1>Chapter20 Sample</h1>");
out.println("<h3>Host : " + myHostName);
out.println("<h3>User Agent : " + userAgent);
out.println("<br>Session ID: " + session.getId());
out.println("<br>");
out.println("Session Start: ");
out.println(new Date(session.getCreationTime()) + "<br>");
out.println("Session Last Accessed: ");
out.println(new Date(session.getLastAccessedTime()));
out.println("<br>");
out.println("<br>Safe Counter :" + safeCounter.toString());
out.println("<br>Unsafe counter :" + unsafeCounter);
out.println("</body></html>");
out.close();

// Update counters
unsafeCounter++;
safeCounter=new Integer(safeCounter.intValue()+1);
session.setAttribute("safecounter",safeCounter);

System.out.println("Chapter20 : AppInfo finished processing request");
```

Continued

Listing 20-2 *(continued)*

```
    }

    /**
     * This sample makes no distinction between GET and POST requests,
     * forwarding all doPost requests to doGet for processing.
     *
     * @param req     HttpServletRequest object required by superclass
     * @param resp    HttpServletResponse object required by superclass
     */

    public void doPost(HttpServletRequest req, HttpServletResponse resp)
        throws IOException,ServletException {

        doGet(req,resp);
    }
}
```

You can use the test harness to set arbitrary values for both the safe and unsafe counters of AppInfo. Additionally, because the harness is an ordinary servlet, automated testing tools can access the harness easily. A test script may call the harness by using `wget` to set the counters to starting values, for example, and then call AppInfo by using `wget` and compare the HTML that returns with the expected results. If you expand the harness servlet to have the capability to modify more sophisticated state information, such as backend databases, you could utilize the same basic code to test much more sophisticated applications.

 Because the test harness servlet, by definition, has the capability to arbitrarily modify application state, you should never deploy it to the production environment. Even if access to the servlet is protected, the risk of damaging production data is too great to risk deploying such a servlet into production.

EJB TEST HARNESSES

Unlike a servlet that you can access easily by using command line tools such as `wget` or from an interactive browser, Enterprise Java Beans are much more complicated to invoke. You need to look them up, instantiate them, cast them appropriately, and then invoke business methods.

At first, EJB developers may think to build a simple Java application to test Enterprise Java Beans via their RMI/IIOP interfaces. Although this idea is appealing because it provides an easy way to test Enterprise Java Beans from the command line, it generally doesn't work well in practice (at least for iPlanet Application Server).

Setting up and utilizing RMI/IIOP is likely to introduce too much complexity. Additionally, some EJB features such as authentication and transaction management don't work the same way over RMI/IIOP as they do from within the same JVM.

Your best course, therefore, is to test Enterprise Java Beans the same way that you plan on utilizing them. If you plan on accessing them remotely via RMI/IIOP, go ahead and create standalone Java applications to test them. But if you intend on accessing your EJBs from within the iAS Web container, create a simple JSP or servlet for each EJB as a test harness.

The TestEJB servlet from Chapter 9 is an example of a simple EJB test harness. I don't provide the TestEJB source code either here or in Chapter 9, but I include it on the supplemental CD.

TestEJB instantiates the NoopEJB EJB and prints the results of its `getEJBMsg` business method. It also prints copious status messages as it instantiates and invokes the EJB.

HELPER CLASS TEST HARNESSES

Make sure that you make test harnesses for your helper classes as well. Although every class may not need a test harness, any class that contains business logic should have a test harness that enables you to test the logic.

You can take any of the following three approaches to developing test harnesses:

♦ *Build a servlet that acts as a test harness.* Using a servlet test harness simplifies testing because it can use the same infrastructure that you use to test EJBs and servlets. You can use a single set of scripts and utilities that calls servlet URLs and compares the results to the expected results, regardless of the type of component that you're testing.

♦ *Build a standalone application as a test harness.* Using a standalone Java application to test your Java classes simplifies the testing process because testing can occur outside the iAS container. It also enables you to build the logic of verifying the test results directly into the test harness. Of course, you can't test helper classes that depend on the servlet container outside of iAS in this way.

♦ *Include a built-in test harness within helper classes.* By giving each helper class a `main` method, you can invoke helper classes directly as a mechanism for running a test harness. This method effectively employs the same strategy as the previous one (with the same advantages and disadvantages), except that you integrate the test harness with each class. You can place reusable testing logic in a superclass from which all testable helper classes derive.

To minimize the overhead of developing testing infrastructure, your project should select one methodology for testing helper classes. Doing so enables you to utilize one set of testing tools across the entire application.

Assertions

Many languages have the concept of an *assertion*. An assertion is a function that verifies an assumption and terminates execution of the program if that assumption isn't true. In some languages, the assertion function always checks the assumption; in other languages, it may check the assumption only if you compile the program with a debugging flag. The details range from language to language, but the central concept is the same. Assertions give developers a way to document and verify certain assumptions that they're making in their code.

A method that determines the average revenue per day in a given month, for example, generally assumes that the number of days in each month is greater than zero. This assumption is generally a good one. Because all months have at least 28 days, you'd have no chance for a division by zero error. But a careful programmer may place this assumption in an assertion, as shown in the following pseudocode:

```
daysInMonth=findDaysInMonth(thisMonth);
assert(daysInMonth>0,"Days in month not a positive value.");
avgRevenue = monthlyRevenue / daysInMonth;
```

By adding this assertion, the developer is guarding against findDaysInMonth incorrectly initializing the value of daysInMonth. Imagine that the findDays InMonth function contains a bug and returns a negative value. Without the assertion, the bug in the findDaysInMonth code would make the avgRevenue negative, which may affect something somewhere else in the code, causing a ripple effect throughout the program. By the time that the user receives the results, the error may become difficult to spot. The assert statement enables you to detect errors early, thereby making the process of debugging that error easier.

The Java language didn't incorporate assertions until JDK 1.4, which is still in testing and isn't compatible with iPlanet Application Server version 6.*x*. (I include a link to the JDK 1.4 documentation about assertions at the end of this chapter.) So if you want to use assertions in iAS, you must build your own assertion function. The following code is a very simple assertion method that you can add to a base class or utility class:

```
public static final void checkAssertion(boolean condition,
    String msg) {
    if (!condition) {
        log("assertion failure : " + msg);
        throw new java.lang.Error("assertion failure : " + msg);
    }
}
```

Notice that the `assert` method throws an `Error` rather than a subclass of `Exception`. This subclassing of `Error` prevents every class from needing to declare an assertion exception in its `throws` clause. It also prevents `try/catch` blocks from inadvertently catching the exception. (Remember that assertions should stop program execution.) In this method, the `checkAssertion` method evaluates the condition as one of the arguments, so using `checkAssertion` causes the method to evaluate the condition even if you comment out the function itself. This type of assertion function, therefore, affects the performance of your application even if you attempt to disable the assertion facility by removing the method body.

 The assertion facility in JDK 1.4 uses *assert* as a new keyword. To ensure forward compatibility with JDK 1.4, a good idea is to name your assertion methods by using a name other than *assert*.

Using assertions helps software quality by giving developers a method of verifying and commenting the assumptions that they're making in developing code. Because the JDK bundled with iPlanet Application Server doesn't include assertion support, developers must balance the benefits of building their own assertion facility with the possible performance implications.

Automate Your Testing

Testing automation is now a critical element to software quality. Because of the complexity of J2EE applications, testing most J2EE applications effectively by hand isn't feasible. Additionally, many J2EE projects' testing groups are understaffed, or the project may even lack a dedicated testing team altogether.

The solution to this lack of manpower is automated testing tools. Automated testing tools range from expensive suites of tools that enable developers to define test cases via point and click (Mercury and RadView) to open-source testing frameworks (JMeter and Cactus), to hand-built scripts and applications.

Using automated testing offers the following advantages:

♦ The requirement to define test cases as test scripts forces you to define those test cases thoroughly.

♦ Automated testing enables you to execute many more tests than is possible if you do so manually.

♦ Automation removes human error from evaluating test results.

♦ After you define automated tests correctly, you can re-execute them easily. These tests enable extremely effective regression testing, because you can re-execute the suite of test cases after every build.

◆ You can reuse functional tests as performance tests merely by changing the parameters of the testing tool.

One great place to find information about automated testing is in the Extreme Programming methodology (see the link at the end of the chapter). Extreme Programming is a new software-development methodology that focuses on simplicity, team-based development, and strong unit testing.

Regardless of whether your team utilizes the Extreme Programming (XP) methodology or even whether you agree with its somewhat controversial ideas about development, Extreme Programming's focus on unit testing results in effective tools for managing testing environments.

Summary

Planning for quality is critical for both project success and developer productivity. Although setting up a testing infrastructure involves some upfront work and requires a certain amount of discipline to enforce testing policies, a well-designed quality plan can greatly improve efficiency, accountability, and predictability.

Despite the unique challenges of the J2EE environment, the most important aspect of a quality plan is the forethought that creating such a plan requires. By forcing you to make quality planned activity that all affected parties agree to instead of an ad hoc activity that you conduct with the remaining time in the project, a written quality plan enhances all aspects of project quality.

Consult the following sources for more information on the topics that I cover in this chapter.

General information

◆ CxOne Quality Plan Checklist: www.construx.com/cxone/Quality/Management/CxCheck_QualityPlan.pdf

◆ JDK 1.4 Assertions: http://java.sun.com/j2se/1.4/docs/guide/lang/assert.html

Testing tools

◆ Cactus Testing Framework: http://jakarta.apache.org/cactus/index.html

◆ JMeter: http://jakarta.apache.org/jmeter/index.html

◆ JProbe Threadalyzer: www.sitraka.com/software/jprobe/jprobethreadalyzer.html

- ◆ **Mercury Interactive:** www-heva.mercuryinteractive.com/
- ◆ **RadView:** www.radview.com/default.asp

Extreme programming

- ◆ **XProgramming.com:** www.xprogramming.com/
- ◆ **Extreme Programming:** www.extremeprogramming.org/

Chapter 21

Backups and Restores

IN THIS CHAPTER

◆ Listing the various iAS components that you need to back up

◆ Using and describing tools that are useful for iAS backups

◆ Selecting an appropriate backup schedule for your iAS implementation

THE CAPABILITY TO BACK UP and restore iPlanet Application Server instances in an accurate, repeatable, and timely fashion is a critical skill that developers often overlook. In this chapter, I look at some best practices regarding backing up and restoring the various components of iPlanet Application Server.

Backup Components

An iPlanet Application Server installation involves several elements, and each component exhibits characteristics that require individual treatment. Some elements use data that change frequently, and some use data that change infrequently. Some elements use data that you can back up by using simple file-system backup commands, and others require special tools. In the following sections, I examine each major component of iAS and discuss the backup requirements and challenges for each.

Custom application code

A novice administrator may consider the custom application code residing under the APPS directory the most important part of the application server to back up. Typically, after spending a long time testing and tweaking an application to work correctly, the administrator wants to take a file-system snapshot of the APPS directory, thinking that such a snapshot enables him to quickly restore the applications in case of emergency.

Ironically, the APPS directory is possibly the least important component of an iAS backup strategy. If the novice administrator attempts to restore an application by restoring the APPS directory, he likely finds that his application is now irrevocably broken because the application is out of sync with the registry, the server environment, the static content, or the backend systems. (More information can be found about the registry in Chapter 13.)

451

Ideally, you shouldn't need to back up your custom application code at all. You should find that you can recreate the APPS directory easily by quickly redeploying your applications. The redeployment ensures that all your datasources, infrastructure, and registry entries correctly synchronize with your application code.

Chapter 20 discusses the importance of this repeatable deployment process. It also details strategies for success with automated build and deploy systems.

If your organization hasn't mastered repeatable deployments, and you need backups of the APPS directory, you should always match them with backups of the rest of the system. This enables you to restore the rest of the system in sync with the application code.

You can back up the custom code in the APPS directory easily by using any file-system backup utility. Because the application code changes only during application deployment, the files change relatively infrequently, and you can back them up either periodically or as part of the deployment process. In production, you should always stop the application server processes during a file-system restoration.

Static Web-server content

If you deploy static content to the Web-server tier instead of to the application-server tier, you often neglect the static content as part of application backups. Although many organizations periodically back up their Web-server content, these backups aren't always in sync with the backup of application-server content. This discrepancy can make restoration difficult because you need to restore the static content and dynamic content in sync.

The section "Static content deployment," in Chapter 17, discusses the benefits of deploying static content to the Web-server tier. That section also discusses some of the strategies that you need to employ to overcome the additional complexity of static-content deployment.

Backing up static content is simple, because you store static content as ordinary files on the file system. Restorations are typically simple for static content, because the Web server automatically checks the time and date stamp of any cached files. (In restoring the file system with older versions of content, you should cycle the Web server to make sure that the Web server's cache is clear.)

Registry data

The application-server configuration registry is the most complex part of backing up an iPlanet Application Server implementation for the following reasons:

◆ You store the registry in two parts: one part either in a flat file (in Unix) or the Windows registry and the second part in an LDAP server. If you don't back up and restore simultaneously the two parts, registry corruption can result.

◆ The LDAP portion of the registry may exist remotely, so a backup involves synchronizing backups and restores across multiple machines.

◆ The LDAP portion of the registry is a transactional database – you don't store it as a flat file. The LDAP portion of the registry, therefore, requires special tools to effectively back up and restore.

◆ In a Windows install, you store the local portion of the registry in the Windows directory, which requires special tools to back up and restore effectively.

As you can see, the configuration registry requires special care. This situation is unfortunate because registry backups are critical. A corrupted registry can prove crippling, because without a good backup, the only reliable way to recreate the registry information is to completely reinstall the cluster and redeploy all the applications.

Backing up the configuration registry involves simultaneously backing up the local registries of all the servers, along with all the LDAP servers that you're using as configuration registries.

BACKING UP LOCAL REGISTRIES

Backing up local registries is relatively straightforward. In Unix, simply back up the reg.dat file in $IAS_ROOT/ias/registry/reg.dat. (This file also exists on Web-connector installations in Unix.) On Windows-based systems, you can back up the local registry by making a backup of the SOFTWARE\\iPlanet key of the Windows Registry. All Windows backup utilities include the capability to back up the Windows Registry. The important part of backing up local registries is to ensure that you back them up simultaneously and in synchronization with the LDAP registry.

Restoring local registries is as simple as stopping the relevant server (Web server or appserver) and then restoring the file or Windows Registry. After restart, the server picks up the new version of the registry.

BACKING UP LDAP REGISTRIES

Because iPlanet Directory Server is a transaction database, it requires special tools to back up and restore. You have two choices in making backups of iPlanet Directory Server.

The first backup option is db2bak, which takes a snapshot of the LDAP directory and stores copies of all the database files in a backup directory. This option is the most efficient way of backing up the directory. For most users, this option is probably the best as it's fast and convenient. db2bak can either take a backup directory as an argument or automatically create a directory with a default name based on the current date and time.

The alternative is to use db2ldif, which takes a snapshot of the LDAP directory and stores the result as an *LDIF* (*LDAP Data Interchange Format*) file. LDIF is a standards-based text format for saving and exchanging directory information. Because LDIF is a text-based format and because db2ldif generates a single file instead of a directory of files, db2ldif is easier to work with in some circumstances — for example, if you're analyzing the results of the backup by using a diff utility or storing them in a version-control repository. For large directories, db2ldif is considerably slower than db2bak, however, so use db2ldif instead of db2bak only if you have a compelling reason to do so — for example, the need to use this backup as an input to another LDAP system.

If a backup program captures the transaction log files and database files instantaneously, iPlanet Directory Server can use them to recover. The amount of time that such a recovery takes, however, depends on the amount of time that's passed since a database checkpoint. Additionally, most file-system backup utilities don't take instantaneous snapshots and may capture the transaction log files and data files out of sync. In such a case, recovery isn't possible.

In most cases you need only to back up one LDAP directory. If multiple LDAP directory servers exist, they should all contain identical data anyway. (See Chapter 22 for details of architectures that utilize multiple LDAP directories.)

Log files

People sometimes forget log files in making backups and restores. Log files, however, are instrumental for diagnosing problems. In the case of a system failure, a complete set of log files can prove useful in determining the cause of that failure. If you lose the log files as part of that failure, however, or if they're overwritten as part of the file-system restore, they're not available to aid in troubleshooting.

In short, you should include log files as part of system backups. Retention periods for log files vary from company to company. In some companies, file-system backups may even serve as a good methodology for archiving old log files.

The iAS console logs and iAS file logs are just ordinary text files that you can back up by using any file-system backup utility. The same is true for Web-server and Web-connector logs.

Application binaries

Most companies back up all application binaries as part of their file-system backups. Although this practice is somewhat redundant, because you could restore the application binaries from the installation media, restoring the application binaries from a file-system snapshot is generally faster and more convenient.

Restoring from tape instead of installation media means that you don't need to repeat all customizations. You'd need to restore changes to the JVM parameters in the $IAS_ROOT/ias/env/iasenv.ksh script by hand, for example, if you reinstall iAS from the original installation media. A complete file-system snapshot also means that you don't need to reinstall database drivers, backend connectivity, and other infrastructure modifications. (Don't overlook these files in performing backups and restores.)

Nonetheless, the capability to reinstall from the installation media if necessary is important. In some cases, for example, an application binary or system configuration gets corrupted or damaged, and no one notices the problem until after the same corruption gets into the backups as well. In general, the capability to restore application from either a file-system backup or the original installation media, as the condition warrants, is important.

The iPlanet Application Server installer modifies some of the application binaries during installation. Specifically, the installer adds the installation directory into some of the libraries that iAS uses.

This somewhat unusual behavior means that you can't simply copy iAS from one directory to another after installation and also that you must restore iAS into the same directory from which you back it up.

Application data

You also need to back up your application data appropriately. Whether you store that data in an LDAP directory, a relational database, or in flat files, application data is a critical part of application state. You can't restore a system unless you can restore the data as well.

Restoring application data, however, poses one unique challenge: Application data often contains both application configuration information and transactional data. If you're rolling back from version 4.05 to 4.04 of your custom application because a bug turns up in version 4.05, you may need to roll back parts of your database to reflect the difference in the application versions. But you don't want to roll back customer transactions or data.

This problem has no easy solution. It should, however, serve as a warning to application architects to keep the following points in mind:

◆ *Keep application configuration information separate from transactional data.* Although storing application-configuration data (such as lookup tables) in a relational database is convenient, you need to make a clean demarcation between that configuration data and transactional data that you never want to roll back.

◆ *Avoid schema changes whenever possible.* You also want schemas that are backward and forward compatible, whenever possible (meaning that version 4.04 of an application can use the database schema from version 4.05). This compatibility not only simplifies migration, but also makes backing out of an application version easier.

◆ *Document dependencies clearly.* Clearly mark configuration files or data so that you can determine with which application to associate that data. Restoring and backing up applications is much easier if you can easily identify all parts of that application.

Backup Strategies

Some companies back up their application server infrastructure only if they're going to make a change to the server configuration. This policy gives a lot of flexibility to the operational team. During major changes to server infrastructure, you can take snapshots of the system frequently. But after a system is stable, only the application data and logs change, so you need to back up only these elements.

In contrast, many companies back up their systems whether the underlying data changes or not. Although this policy is less flexible and more wasteful of backup storage, this methodology also offers certain advantages. Most important, it eliminates the capacity for human error. In the "on-demand" strategy, forgetting to back up the system after a "minor" change is all too easy. On the other hand, creating a regular backup schedule ensures that the backup process is automated and completely repeatable.

Which methodology is best for you depends on how frequently you make changes to your system and to your existing backup systems and standards. Erring on the side of caution, however, is always better. Even if the system remains largely static, frequent backups incur very little incremental cost.

Summary

A well-thought-out backup strategy is a critical element in any operational plan. Understanding the various components of iAS and how they interact is imperative to building that backup strategy. Restoring only one component out of sync with the other components is likely to cause more problems than it solves.

Understanding the iAS registry is especially important for developing a backup plan for iAS. The multiple components to the registry and the transactional nature of the LDAP directory component of the registry mean that a standard file-system backup is insufficient to back up this core component of iAS. Operational teams who assume that just backing up the server file systems is an adequate backup strategy are mistaken.

For more information on the topics that I cover in this chapter, consult the following sources:

◆ LDIF Standard Definition: www.faqs.org/rfcs/rfc2849.html

◆ Backup and Restore Utilities for iPlanet Directory Server:
http://docs.iplanet.com/docs/manuals/directory/51/html/cli/
scripts.htm#23510

Chapter 22

High-Availability Architectures

IN THIS CHAPTER

♦ Examining iAS infrastructure for single points of failure

♦ Deciding where HA infrastructure is appropriate for your application

♦ Implementing HA infrastructure at the Web-, directory-, and application-server tiers

THIS CHAPTER EXAMINES ways to reduce or eliminate single points of failure in an iPlanet Application Server environment. This process of creating redundant systems is typically known as *high availability* (*HA*) or *clustering*. Because the term *clustering* has special and specific meaning for both the Sun Cluster product and iPlanet Application Server, I use the more generic term of high availability in this chapter.

Chapters 10, 11, and 17 of this book examine the clustering and failover features of iPlanet Application Server and how you can implement them to make the application-server tier highly available. The application server, however, is only one part of making an entire iAS architecture highly available. This chapter focuses on the elements necessary to remove single points of failure from the entire architecture.

Benefits and Drawbacks of High Availability

The primary reason for reducing the number of single points of failure is to increase the uptime of the system. (Hence the term *high availability*.) High-availability design is essentially planning for Murphy's Law. By ensuring that the architecture is completely dependent on no single component, you ensure that the complete system can withstand Murphy's Law that "anything that can go wrong will."

High-availability architectures, however, have several drawbacks. Introducing redundant system elements increases system complexity. Not only do redundant elements increase the number of system components, but they also require that you add a mechanism for switching between the redundant elements.

> ## Mean Time Between Failure
>
> You can also increase the uptime of a system by increasing the reliability of each of the system components: what you usually measure as "*mean time between failure (MTBF)*." MTBF is simply the amount of time that you can expect a system component to remain available. MTBF is relatively easy to measure and predict for hardware components. You can test a hard drive, for example, to determine its reliability and durability and then use that data to calculate a MTBF. Software components are much harder to measure. The MTBF of a Java Virtual Machine depends on the code that's executing within that virtual machine. In short, a JVM is only as reliable as the code that you ask it to execute.
>
> This chapter focuses on increasing uptime by increasing system redundancy. Increasing uptime by increasing MTBF, however, is also valuable. The best way to increase software MTBF is by creating a good test plan. (See Chapter 20 for tips on creating test plans.) You can increase hardware MTBF by purchasing quality components, following maintenance and usage guidelines, and maintaining a good operating environment.

In general, high-availability architectures also add a significant cost. Redundant hardware is an added expense, as is the software that you need to perform failover between redundant components.

In considering adding a redundant component to a system, always consider the following questions:

◆ What are the business requirements for availability?

◆ Is system availability sufficient without the redundant component?

◆ How much complexity do you add by introducing the redundant component? Is the extra availability worth the extra complexity?

◆ How much additional cost do you incur by introducing the redundant component? Is the extra availability worth the extra cost and effort?

◆ Are any alternative methods of increasing availability more efficient.

The rest of this chapter explores several common single points of failure in iPlanet Application Server systems and the typical methods for removing those single points of failure. It also explores the relative complexity and cost of adding redundancy, including methodologies for minimizing these drawbacks.

High-Availability Web Servers

Typically, a Web server first receives requests to the application server. (RMI/IIOP requests are the exception.) So if you have only a single Web server, the Web server can become a single point of failure for the entire system.

Resolving this single point of failure is relatively simple. A wide variety of hardware and software solutions can introduce failover and load balancing across multiple Web servers. I provide a short list of common solutions in the Summary section, at the end of this chapter. These products greatly simplify the process of administrating the load-balancing and failover process. On the other hand, increasing the number of Web servers does increase the number of physical servers that you need to patch, install, and maintain.

The cost of introducing failover at the Web-server level is relatively low. The cost of the Web load-balancing products is relatively low, and their capability of distributing traffic evenly prevents redundant Web-server hardware from remaining idle.

High-Availability Application Servers

I discuss distributing application-server workload among multiple servers in Chapter 10 and explore failover between iPlanet Application Server instances in Chapter 11, so I'm not repeating that information in this chapter. In short, however, iAS is designed to make the process of load balancing and failover relatively transparent. You can add additional servers into an iAS cluster on the fly, and the Web servers automatically begin routing traffic to these new servers. Similarly, the iAS webconnector automatically detects and routes around failed servers.

The cost of introducing failover at the application server level is low. You need no additional software to manage the load balancing and failover. And any additional hardware that you add to the cluster for redundancy it uses for load balancing, so you waste no hardware dollars on idle servers.

High-Availability Directory Servers

iPlanet Application Server depends on an iPlanet Directory Server to store its central repository of configuration information. In addition, some iAS applications may depend on this directory server for their authentication or authorization information. The directory server is, therefore, a possible single point of failure. You have several methodologies for eliminating this single point of failure. Each methodology offers its own advantages and disadvantages, as I describe in the following section.

Dedicated directory servers

This high-availability methodology involves setting up one directory server for each application server, each pair typically residing on the same hardware. (This methodology assumes multiple application servers.) Because each application server is using its own dedicated instance of iPlanet Directory Server, the maximum effect of a directory-server failure is the loss of one application server.

The major advantage of this methodology is its initial setup simplicity and the fact that even a registry corruption can't disrupt the entire cluster, because each application-server/directory-server pair is a complete silo that's well isolated from all of the other machines in the cluster.

This methodology very much depends, however, on keeping the information in the directories in sync. Because the directory servers are completely independent, no automatic propagation of information occurs between them. If an administrator changes a registry value on one server, he must make absolutely certain that he makes the same changes on all the other servers. Having conflicting information in the directories can create difficult-to-diagnose problems.

Figure 22-1 illustrates one example of this methodology. Each of three application-server instances is running a directory server on the same physical server to which it connects to get its configuration information. Not shown on this diagram are the iAS Web connectors. The Web connectors should connect to differing directories as well so that a directory server failure doesn't disable all the Web connectors.

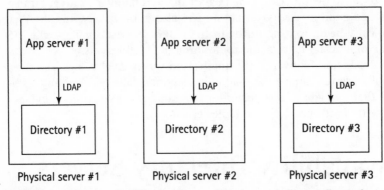

Figure 22-1: High-availability directory architecture — dedicated directories

Supplier/consumer failover

iPlanet Application Server offers the built-in capability to failover to an alternative directory if the connection to the first directory server fails. This methodology takes advantage of that feature by establishing one primary directory server and one backup directory server that uses iPlanet Directory Server's supplier/consumer replication to maintain a mirror image of the primary's data. The backup directory server is limited to read-only access because of the nature of iPlanet Directory Server's replication, but this read-only access is enough for normal operation of iPlanet Application Server.

This methodology adds relatively little complexity to daily operation. iPlanet Application Server automatically handles the failover process. The iPlanet Directory Server replication takes care of synchronizing the directory server's data. Additional cost is limited as well, because the directory servers can generally exist on existing application-server hardware.

The primary disadvantage of this methodology is the initial complexity of setup. You must set up several replication agreements between the directory servers to replicate the various parts of the directory tree that you need for iPlanet Application Server operation. Another slight disadvantage is that damage to the primary directory server's data propagates automatically to the backup server as well. If a bug in application code or a malicious hacker deletes part of iAS's configuration in the directory, for example, the directory server replicates that same deletion to the backup data.

Figure 22-2 shows an implementation of this methodology. Three iAS instances all connect to a single directory server for configuration information. All three iAS instances are also configured with the location of a backup directory server in case connection to the first server is lost.

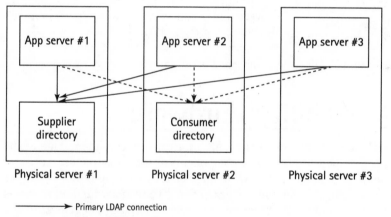

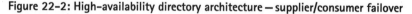
Primary LDAP connection

- - - - - - - - ► Failover LDAP connection

Figure 22-2: High-availability directory architecture — supplier/consumer failover

Hardware clustering

Sun Microsystems offers a Sun Cluster module for iPlanet Directory Server. You can use this Sun Cluster module to monitor and failover the configuration directory of an iAS configuration directory. The clustering module enables two physical servers to share a common array of disks. Should one of the servers fail, the Sun Cluster module detects the failure and switches over to the backup server.

This configuration is relatively simple to set up in comparison to iDS replication and still requires little additional daily maintenance. Because the data exists only on the shared disk no data synchronization is necessary. (Sun Cluster uses the features of the shared disk to maintain high availability of the actual physical storage.)

This methodology, however, involves significant hardware and software costs. You need to move the directory servers to their own physical machines, and you must acquire a shared disk array and Sun Cluster monitoring server as well. Figure 22-3 shows this configuration. Notice that, unlike for previous methodologies, each server in this diagram runs on dedicated hardware.

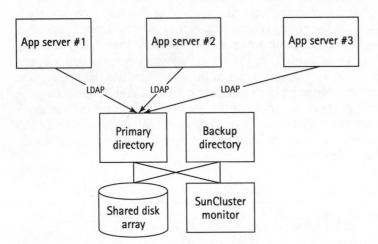

Figure 22-3: High-availability directory architecture — hardware clustering

High-Availability Hardware

In addition to making the software parts of iAS infrastructure redundant, high availability can also benefit physical hardware components of the infrastructure. Low-end servers may offer several single points of failure, such as a single power supply or hard drive. More expensive server hardware may feature built-in redundant elements such as multiple power sources, RAID arrays, and even multiple system clocks.

Operating-system software is also critical in terms of responding to hardware failures. Solaris, for example, can handle hot swappable CPU units. A multiprocessor Solaris box, therefore, can suffer the loss of a CPU without causing system failure or even any downtime to replace the failed unit.

In short, in examining the high availability of your software components, you should also examine the redundancies in your physical hardware. Redundant disk arrays, multiple power supplies, or hot swappable CPUs all increase the MTBF of your individual servers. In some cases, this increase in MTBF may reduce the amount of redundancy that you need in the software components.

High-Availability Network Infrastructure

Another hardware consideration that you must take into account is network infrastructure. If your system infrastructure relies on a single ISP, firewall, or router, the application server's network inaccessibility may prove a more serious problem than hardware or software failures.

Highly available network infrastructure is outside the scope of this book. Designing a highly available IP network for use by an iPlanet Application Server system is the same as designing a highly available IP network for any other IP-based system. Most companies already have this type of infrastructure in place, and those that don't generally don't expect their iAS infrastructures to meet HA requirements.

Summary

iPlanet Application Server is designed so that you can make each software element redundant if necessary. Nonetheless, evaluating your own high-availability requirements is important so that you can design an architecture that's appropriate for your own needs. Although redundant Web servers, application servers, and directory servers can increase your system uptime, they can also increase the complexity and cost of your infrastructure. In designing a highly available system, a software architect should also consider other factors, such as increasing mean time between failures and increasing reliability of the underlying hardware and networking components.

Planning for high availability also means planning for system recovery and system maintenance. Meeting planned downtime requirements is equally as important as meeting unplanned downtime requirements. Consult Chapters 18 and 21 for information about maintenance planning and failure recovery.

For more information on the topics that I cover in this chapter, consult the following sources:

Web load-balancing products

- Cisco LocalDirector: www.cisco.com/univercd/cc/td/doc/pcat/ld.htm
- F5 BigIP: www.f5.com/BIGIP5K/index.html
- Resonate Central Dispatch: www.Resonate.com/solutions/products/central_dispatch/cd_data_sheet.php

Hardware clustering products

- Sun Cluster: www.sun.com/software/cluster/
- Veritas Cluster: www.veritas.com/products/category/ProductDetail.jhtml?productId=clusterserver

What's on the CD-ROM

THIS APPENDIX PROVIDES you with information about the contents of the CD that accompanies this book. For the latest and greatest information, please refer to the ReadMe file that you find at the root of the CD. Here is what you find on the CD:

◆ System Requirements

◆ Using the CD with Windows and Solaris

◆ CD Contents

◆ Troubleshooting

System Requirements

Make sure that your computer meets the minimum system requirements that I list in this section. If your computer doesn't match up to most of these requirements, you may have a problem using some of or all the contents of the CD.

For Windows 2000 SP2 or Windows NT4 SP6a:

◆ PC with a Pentium III (or compatible) processor running at 866 Mhz or faster

◆ At least 512MB of total RAM on your computer

◆ Ethernet network interface card (NIC)

◆ A fixed IP address (with DNS entries correctly configured)

◆ A CD-ROM drive

For SPARC/Solaris:

◆ Sun UltraSPARC II processor running at 500 MHz or faster

◆ At least 512MB of total RAM

◆ A fixed IP address (with DNS entries correctly configured)

◆ A CD-ROM drive

Using the CD with Windows

To install the items from the CD to your hard drive, follow these steps:

1. Insert the CD into your computer's CD-ROM drive.

2. A window appears displaying the following options: Install, Explore, Links, and Exit. These options perform the following functions:

   ■ **Install:** Gives you the option to install the supplied software and/or the author-created samples on the CD-ROM.

   ■ **Explore:** Enables you to view the contents of the CD-ROM in its directory structure.

   ■ **Links:** Opens a hyperlinked page of Web sites.

   ■ **Exit:** Closes the autorun window.

If you don't have autorun enabled or if the autorun window doesn't appear, follow these steps to access the CD:

1. Click Start→ Run.

2. In the Run dialog box that appears, type **d:\setup.exe**, where *d* is the letter of your CD-ROM drive. This action opens the autorun window as I describe in the preceding steps.

3. Choose the Install, Explore, Links, or Exit option from the menu. (See Step 2 in the preceding list for a description of these options.)

Using the CD with Solaris

To install the items from the CD to your hard drive, follow these steps:

1. Log in as root.

2. Insert the CD into your computer's CD-ROM drive.

3. If your computer has AutoMount enabled, wait for the CD to mount. Otherwise, follow one of these steps:

   ■ *Command-line instructions:* At the command prompt, type the following line:

   ```
   mount /dev/cdrom /mnt/cdrom
   ```

(This action mounts the cdrom device to the `mnt/cdrom` directory. If your device has a different name, exchange `cdrom` with that device name – for example, `cdrom1`.)

- *Graphical instructions*: Right-click the CD-ROM icon on the desktop and choose Mount CD-ROM from the pop-up menu. This action mounts your CD-ROM.

4. Browse the CD and follow the individual installation instructions for the products that I list in the section "Applications," a little later in this appendix.

5. To remove the CD from your CD-ROM drive, follow one of these steps:

- *Command-line instructions*: At the command prompt, type the following line:

```
umount /mnt/cdrom
```

- *Graphical instructions*: Right-click the CD-ROM icon on the desktop and choose UMount CD-ROM from the pop-up menu. This action mounts your CD-ROM.

CD Contents

The following sections provide a summary of the software and other materials that you find on the CD.

Author-created materials

All author-created material from the book, including code listings and samples, are on the CD in the Author folder. Each chapter listing that contains sample code has a subdirectory within the Author folder. Each chapter's sample directory includes its own Ant `build.xml` file and is organized into subdirectories similar to the samples that come with iPlanet Application Server. I include a compiled EAR file in the subdirectory for each sample. You can find the source code and build files that you need to generate that EAR file in an `src` subdirectory for each sample.

Applications

The following applications are on the CD:

JAVA 2 SOFTWARE DEVELOPMENT KIT VERSION 1.4 FOR WINDOWS
This is a software development kit for Java standard edition required for developing Java applications.

ANT, FROM APACHE SOFTWARE FOUNDATION

Ant is a build tool designed specifically for Java applications. Version 1.2 of Ant is bundled with iPlanet Application Server. All of the samples provided with this book and with iPlanet Application Server itself support version 1.2 of Ant. However, the iAS extensions to Ant (see below) require version 1.4 of Ant, and therefore I have included version 1.4 of Ant on the CD-ROM for the readers who wish to use the iAS extensions.

FORTE FOR JAVA, RELEASE 3.0, COMMUNITY EDITION, FROM SUN MICROSYSTEMS

Forte for Java is an IDE (Integrated Development Environment) that includes support for developing iPlanet Application Server applications. You can upgrade the Community Edition that I include on the CD-ROM to the Enterprise Edition (which includes iAS support) by using the Update Center feature of Forte for Java.

You can find more information, including upgrade instructions, at wwws.sun.com/software/Developer-products/ffj/.

IPLANET APPLICATION SERVER ANT EXTENSIONS, FROM ICSYNERGY

The ICSynergy Ant extensions are a series of custom Ant tasks that simplify the process of creating Ant build scripts for iAS projects. Features of the ICSynergy Ant extensions include EJB stub generation, module packaging, deployment, and a method for controlling an iAS instance.

You can find installation instructions and documentation for the custom Ant task in the antExtDocs.html file.

IPLANET APPLICATION SERVER, FROM SUN MICROSYSTEMS

A copy of iPlanet Application Server version 6.5 is included on the CD-ROM. See Chapter 2 for iAS installation instructions.

IPLANET WEB SERVER ENTERPRISE EDITION, FROM SUN MICROSYSTEMS

iPlanet Web Server is the Web server that you most commonly use with iPlanet Application Server. See Chapter 2 for installation instructions.

Downloadable Software

IPLANET DIRECTORY SERVER, FROM SUN MICROSYSTEMS

iPlanet Directory Server can be downloaded in a standalone version from http://wwws.sun.com/software/download/inter_ecom.html. This enables you to upgrade your directory server independently from your application server. See the installation instructions at http://docs.iplanet.com/docs/manuals/ for instructions on installing a standalone copy of iPlanet Directory Server.

Troubleshooting

If you experience any difficulty installing or using any of the materials on the companion CD, try the following solutions:

◆ **Turn off any antivirus software that you may have running.** Installers sometimes mimic virus activity and can make your computer incorrectly believe that a virus is infecting it. (Make sure that you turn the antivirus software back on later.)

◆ **Close all running programs.** The more programs that you're running, the less memory is available to other programs. Installers also typically update files and programs; if you keep other programs running, installation may not work correctly.

◆ **Reference the ReadMe file.** Please refer to the ReadMe file, which you find at the root of the CD-ROM, for the latest product information at the time of publication.

If you still have trouble with the CD, please call the Wiley phone number: (800) 762-2974. Outside the United States, call 1 (317) 572-3994. You can also contact Wiley Customer Service by e-mail at techsupdum@wiley.com. Wiley provides technical support only for installation and other general quality-control items; for technical support on the applications themselves, consult the program's vendor or author.

Appendix B

Third-Party Products

This appendix lists several third-party products that people often use in conjunction with iAS. I discuss several of them elsewhere in this book as well. None of them are necessary to use with iPlanet Application Server, and Sun does not offer support for any of them. (JATO and Forte are exceptions, as they are both Sun products.)

Ant

Ant is a build tool that the Jakarta Project of the Apache Software Foundation specifically produces for Java-based development. Version 1.2 of Ant comes with iPlanet Application Server, and I provide version 1.2-compatible Ant build files for all of the iPlanet sample applications in this book. Some iAS-specific extensions are even available that enable Ant to easily integrate with such iAS functions as ejbc and iasdeploy.

 Newer versions of Ant are available, and you can use them with iAS, but the build.xml files that I provide in the samples in this book aren't compatible with these newer Ant versions.

Ant is an open-source project available under the Apache license. You can download it from the Project home page at http://jakarta.apache.org/ant/index.html.

CocoBase

CocoBase is a CMP plug-in from Thought, Inc. CocoBase's object-to-relational mapping features are much more sophisticated than the built-in basic CMP features of iPlanet Application Server. CocoBase enables you to build much more complex relationships between entity beans and relational tables. The CocoBase engine also optimizes database calls to greatly improve CMP performance.

CocoBase is a commercial project. You can download an evaluation edition from the CocoBase home page at http://www.thoughtinc.com/cber_index.html.

Diamelle Components

Diamelle is a leading EJB component vendor that provides suites of prebuilt EJBs for e-commerce and e-CRM (customer relationship management). These components can provide the foundation for many types of business applications by providing reusable services for user management, catalog management, order management, personalization, invoicing, and many other common business functions.

Diamelle components are commercial products. You can download evaluation copies of the Diamelle components (customized for iPlanet Application Server) from the Diamelle site at www.diamelle.com/iplanet.

Forte for Java

Forte for Java is a Java IDE that Sun Microsystems produces. The enterprise edition of Forte for Java includes built-in support for building and deploying iPlanet Application Server applications. This support includes both code-generation wizards and deployment wizards.

Forte for Java is a commercial product that Sun bases on open-source core. You can download a trial version of Forte for Java Enterprise Edition from the Forte for Java home page at http://forte.sun.com/ffj/. Forte for Java Enterprise Edition comes with the iPlanet Application Server Developer Pack.

Introscope

Introscope is an application-monitoring tool that Wiley Technologies produces. Introscope enables administrators to collect real-time performance and health information from production applications. Unlike a Java profiler, Introscope works within the regular Java JVM that iPlanet Application Server utilizes and only minimally affects system performance. This architecture enables Introscope to remain enabled, even on production systems.

You can use Introscope as a performance-tuning tool, because it can help you spot which components and methods are consuming the majority of system resources, and also as a health-monitoring tool for your applications. Introscope provides a "dashboard" that monitors the health of Web applications and that can provide appropriate alerts if an application fails or reaches unacceptable performance levels.

Introscope is commercially licensed. You can request a trial copy from the Introscope home page at www.wileytechnologies.com/solutions.html. iPlanet Application Server provides built-in hooks to support the Introscope technology.

JATO

JATO (J2EE Assisted Takeoff) is a framework for building Web applications that iPlanet provides. As do many other development frameworks, JATO utilizes a Model-View-Controller paradigm that utilizes servlets and JSP technology. Although not as widely utilized as some other frameworks, JATO offers many features that aren't available in other frameworks. For a comparison of JATO to other frameworks, see the JATO white paper at `http://developer.iplanet.com/tech/appserver/framework/wpapers/jato_overview.html`. Many iPlanet products use JATO behind the scenes, and it's designed for both functionality and performance.

JATO is commercially licensed but is free and includes a source distribution. You can download the JATO framework from the JATO home page at `http://developer.iplanet.com/tech/appserver/framework/index.jsp`.

JBuilder

JBuilder is a Java IDE that Borland produces. The latest version of JBuilder includes support for integrating it with iPlanet Application Server.

JBuilder is a commercial product. You can download a trial version of JBuilder from the JBuilder home page at `www.borland.com/jbuilder/`.

JProbe

JProbe is a Java profiler that Sitraka produces. JProbe enables you to execute your application within a special JVM that enables you to introspect how your application executes at run time. This product helps you to spot bottlenecks and possible problems within your application. Java profilers are especially helpful in detecting memory and threading issues.

JProbe is commercially licensed. A free trial copy is available from the JProbe home page at `www.sitraka.com/software/jprobe/index.html`.

Log4J

Log4J is a class library that provides a sophisticated logging API for Java developers. Log4J is designed so that you can configure the level of logging detail at run time by modifying configuration files. This capability, combined with a focus on logging performance, enables logging comments to remain in product code without adversely affecting application performance.

Log4J also provides great flexibility in the destination of log messages. Log4J supports logging to files, databases, dedicated logging servers, the NT event log, the Unix syslog, and several other destinations. It also supports multiple categories of log messages, so you can control the verbosity and destination of log messages on a finely grained level.

Log4J is an open-source project available under the Apache license. You can download it from the project home page at `http://jakarta.apache.org/log4j/index.html`.

OptimizeIt

OptimizeIt is a Java profiler that Borland produces. OptimizeIt, like other Java profilers, executes your application in a custom JVM. The run time characteristics of your application can be monitored within this custom JVM, allowing you to spot both application bugs and performance bottlenecks. Because Java profilers allow you to see behind the scenes of the JVM, they are particularly helpful in observing memory and threading.

OptimizeIt is commercially licensed. A free trial copy is available from the OptimizeIt home page at `www.optimizeit.com/products/index.html`.

Struts

Struts is a framework for building J2EE applications that the Jakarta Project of the Apache Software Foundation produces. Struts provides a Model-View-Controller paradigm for Web development, using a servlet for the controller, Java classes for the model, and JSPs as a view mechanism. Struts also provides numerous utilities helpful in building Web applications, including utilities for working with Web forms and validating user data.

Struts is an open-source project available under the Apache license. You can download it from the project home page at `http://jakarta.apache.org/struts/index.html`.

 A starter Struts app for iPlanet is available at
`www.icsynergy.com/downloads/index.html#struts-example`.

VisualCafé

VisualCafé is a Java IDE that WebGain produces. An iPlanet Application Server plug-in (co-developed by WebGain and iPlanet) is available for VisualCafé that adds support for building and deploying iPlanet Application Server applications. This support includes both code-generation wizards and deployment wizards.

VisualCafé is a commercial product. You can download a trial version from the VisualCafé home page at `www.webgain.com/products/visual_cafe/`. The iAS plug-in is a free (but commercially licensed) product that you can download from `www.webgain.com/download/visual_cafe/application_server_plugin.html`. The plug-in also comes in the iPlanet Application Server Developer Pack.

Index

Symbols
backward slash (\\), 277
forward slash (/), 277

A
ABCCorp, production architecture case study, 408–410
abnormal clusters
  manual inspection of, 328–329
  no brain clusters, 327
  recovery from, 327–328
  split brain clusters, 327
abstract accessor methods, adding to classes, 251
access entity EJBs
  compound keys, 236
  finder methods, 235
  primary keys, 235–236
access log files, 359–361
accessing
  Ant tool, 473
  CocoBase, 473
  Daimelle, 474
  Forte for Java, 474
  Introscope, 474
  JBuilder, 475
  JProbe, 475
  Log4J, 475–476
  OptimizeIt, 476
  session beans, 216–218
actions
  `action.jsp` listing, 164
  `CRCBean.java` file, listing of, 165–167
  `fallback`, 163
  `forward`, 163
  `getProperty`, 163, 165, 167, 179
  `include`, 163, 197
  overview, 162–163
  `param`, 163
  `plugin`, 163
  `setProperty`, 163, 165, 167, 179
  `useBean`, 163, 165, 167, 177
Add/Troubleshoot Device radio button, 25–26
`ADMIN 159` message log, 289
`ADMIN` privileges, 285–286
Administration Port prompt (Solaris installation), 44
Administration Services Components screen (Solaris installation), 41
administrative servers, starting and stopping, 9–10
administrative tools, directory server, starting and stopping, 7
Akamai Technologies Web site, 412
alias, lookup, 228
All Registered Servers icon, 48
anonymous ports, 406
Ant tool
  accessing, 473
  creating stubs using, 227
  example listings of, 146–149
  extensions, downloading, 145
  overview, 144
Apache
  Apache Software Foundation, 336
  Tomcat, 5
  Web site, 118, 343
AppInfo sample servlet. *See also* servlets
  `init` method, 113–114
  requests, processing, 115–116
  sample output form, 113
  source code, 110–112
application assembler
  Ant tool usage, 144
  command line tool usage, 139
  defined, 123
  deployment tool usage, 143
  IDE tool usage, 150

continued

continued

continued

Terms and conditions of the license and export for Java™ 2 SDK, Standard Edition 1.4.0 Sun Microsystems, Inc. Binary Code License Agreement

READ THE TERMS OF THIS AGREEMENT AND ANY PROVIDED SUPPLEMENTAL LICENSE TERMS (COLLECTIVELY "AGREEMENT") CAREFULLY BEFORE OPENING THE SOFTWARE MEDIA PACKAGE. BY OPENING THE SOFTWARE MEDIA PACKAGE, YOU AGREE TO THE TERMS OF THIS AGREEMENT. IF YOU ARE ACCESSING THE SOFTWARE ELECTRONICALLY, INDICATE YOUR ACCEPTANCE OF THESE TERMS BY SELECTING THE "ACCEPT" BUTTON AT THE END OF THIS AGREEMENT. IF YOU DO NOT AGREE TO ALL THESE TERMS, PROMPTLY RETURN THE UNUSED SOFTWARE TO YOUR PLACE OF PURCHASE FOR A REFUND OR, IF THE SOFTWARE IS ACCESSED ELECTRONICALLY, SELECT THE "DECLINE" BUTTON AT THE END OF THIS AGREEMENT.

1. LICENSE TO USE. Sun grants you a non-exclusive and non-transferable license for the internal use only of the accompanying software and documentation and any error corrections provided by Sun (collectively "Software"), by the number of users and the class of computer hardware for which the corresponding fee has been paid.

2. RESTRICTIONS. Software is confidential and copyrighted. Title to Software and all associated intellectual property rights is retained by Sun and/or its licensors. Except as specifically authorized in any Supplemental License Terms, you may not make copies of Software, other than a single copy of Software for archival purposes. Unless enforcement is prohibited by applicable law, you may not modify, decompile, or reverse engineer Software. You acknowledge that Software is not designed, licensed or intended for use in the design, construction, operation or maintenance of any nuclear facility. Sun disclaims any express or implied warranty of fitness for such uses. No right, title or interest in or to any trademark, service mark, logo or trade name of Sun or its licensors is granted under this Agreement.

3. LIMITED WARRANTY. Sun warrants to you that for a period of ninety (90) days from the date of purchase, as evidenced by a copy of the receipt, the media on which Software is furnished (if any) will be free of defects in materials and workmanship under normal use. Except for the foregoing, Software is provided "AS IS". Your exclusive remedy and Sun's entire liability under this limited warranty will be at Sun's option to replace Software media or refund the fee paid for Software.

4. DISCLAIMER OF WARRANTY. UNLESS SPECIFIED IN THIS AGREEMENT, ALL EXPRESS OR IMPLIED CONDITIONS, REPRESENTATIONS AND WARRANTIES, INCLUDING ANY IMPLIED WARRANTY OF MER- CHANTABILITY, FITNESS FOR A PARTICULAR PURPOSE OR NON- INFRINGEMENT ARE DISCLAIMED, EXCEPT TO THE EXTENT THAT THESE DISCLAIMERS ARE HELD TO BE LEGALLY INVALID.

5. LIMITATION OF LIABILITY. TO THE EXTENT NOT PROHIBITED BY LAW, IN NO EVENT WILL SUN OR ITS LICENSORS BE LIABLE FOR ANY LOST REVENUE, PROFIT OR DATA, OR FOR SPECIAL, INDIRECT, CONSEQUEN- TIAL, INCIDENTAL OR PUNITIVE DAMAGES, HOWEVER CAUSED REGARDLESS OF THE THEORY OF LIABILITY, ARISING OUT OF OR RELATED TO THE USE OF OR INABILITY TO USE SOFTWARE, EVEN IF SUN HAS BEEN ADVISED OF THE POSSIBILITY OF SUCH DAMAGES. In no event will Sun's liability to you, whether in contract, tort (including negligence), or otherwise, exceed the amount paid by you for Software under this Agreement. The foregoing limitations will apply even if the above stated warranty fails of its essential purpose.

6. Termination. This Agreement is effective until terminated. You may termi- nate this Agreement at any time by destroying all copies of Software. This Agreement will terminate immediately without notice from Sun if you fail to comply with any provision of this Agreement. Upon Termination, you must destroy all copies of Software.

7. Export Regulations. All Software and technical data delivered under this Agreement are subject to US export control laws and may be subject to export or import regulations in other countries. You agree to comply strictly with all such laws and regulations and acknowledge that you have the responsibility to obtain such licenses to export, re-export, or import as may be required after delivery to you.

8. U.S. Government Restricted Rights. If Software is being acquired by or on behalf of the U.S. Government or by a U.S. Government prime contractor or subcontractor (at any tier), then the Government's rights in Software and accompanying documentation will be only as set forth in this Agreement; this is in accordance with 48 CFR 227.7201 through 227.7202-4 (for Department of Defense (DOD) acquisitions) and with 48 CFR 2.101 and 12.212 (for non-DOD acquisitions).

9. Governing Law. Any action related to this Agreement will be governed by California law and controlling U.S. federal law. No choice of law rules of any jurisdiction will apply.

10. Severability. If any provision of this Agreement is held to be unenforce- able, this Agreement will remain in effect with the provision omitted, unless omission would frustrate the intent of the parties, in which case this Agreement will immediately terminate.

11. Integration. This Agreement is the entire agreement between you and Sun relating to its subject matter. It supersedes all prior or contemporaneous oral or written communications, proposals, representations and warranties and prevails over any conflicting or additional terms of any quote, order, acknowledgment, or other communication between the parties relating to its subject matter during the term of this Agreement. No modification of this Agreement will be binding, unless in writing and signed by an authorized representative of each party.

JAVA™ 2 SOFTWARE DEVELOPMENT KIT (J2SDK), STANDARD EDITION, VERSION 1.4.X SUPPLEMENTAL LICENSE TERMS

These supplemental license terms ("Supplemental Terms") add to or modify the terms of the Binary Code License Agreement (collectively, the "Agreement"). Capitalized terms not defined in these Supplemental Terms shall have the same meanings ascribed to them in the Agreement. These Supplemental Terms shall supersede any inconsistent or conflicting terms in the Agreement, or in any license contained within the Software.

1. Software Internal Use and Development License Grant. Subject to the terms and conditions of this Agreement, including, but not limited to Section 4 (Java Technology Restrictions) of these Supplemental Terms, Sun grants you a non-exclusive, non-transferable, limited license to reproduce internally and use internally the binary form of the Software complete and unmodified for the sole purpose of designing, developing and testing your Java applets and applications intended to run on the Java platform ("Programs").

2. License to Distribute Software. Subject to the terms and conditions of this Agreement, including, but not limited to Section 4 (Java Technology Restrictions) of these Supplemental Terms, Sun grants you a non-exclusive, non-transferable, limited license to reproduce and distribute the Software, provided that (i) you distribute the Software complete and unmodified (unless otherwise specified in the applicable README file) and only bundled as part of, and for the sole purpose of running, your Programs, (ii) the Programs add significant and primary functionality to the Software, (iii) you do not distribute additional software intended to replace any component(s) of the Software (unless otherwise specified in the applicable README file), (iv) you do not remove or alter any proprietary legends or

notices contained in the Software, (v) you only distribute the Software subject to a license agreement that protects Sun's interests consistent with the terms contained in this Agreement, and (vi) you agree to defend and indemnify Sun and its licensors from and against any damages, costs, liabilities, settlement amounts and/or expenses (including attorneys' fees) incurred in connection with any claim, lawsuit or action by any third party that arises or results from the use or distribution of any and all Programs and/or Software. (vi) include the following statement as part of product documentation (whether hard copy or electronic), as a part of a copyright page or proprietary rights notice page, in an "About" box or in any other form reasonably designed to make the statement visible to users of the Software: "This product includes code licensed from RSA Security, Inc.", and (vii) include the statement, "Some portions licensed from IBM are available at http://oss.software.ibm.com/icu4j/".

3. License to Distribute Redistributables. Subject to the terms and conditions of this Agreement, including but not limited to Section 4 (Java Technology Restrictions) of these Supplemental Terms, Sun grants you a non-exclusive, non-transferable, limited license to reproduce and distribute those files specifically identified as redistributable in the Software "README" file ("Redistributables") provided that: (i) you distribute the Redistributables complete and unmodified (unless otherwise specified in the applicable README file), and only bundled as part of Programs, (ii) you do not distribute additional software intended to supersede any component(s) of the Redistributables (unless otherwise specified in the applicable README file), (iii) you do not remove or alter any proprietary legends or notices contained in or on the Redistributables, (iv) you only distribute the Redistributables pursuant to a license agreement that protects Sun's interests consistent with the terms contained in the Agreement, (v) you agree to defend and indemnify Sun and its licensors from and against any damages, costs, liabilities, settlement amounts and/or expenses (including attorneys' fees) incurred in connection with any claim, lawsuit or action by any third party that arises or results from the use or distribution of any and all Programs and/or Software, (vi) include the following statement as part of product documentation (whether hard copy or electronic), as a part of a copyright page or proprietary rights notice page, in an "About" box or in any other form reasonably designed to make the statement visible to users of the Software: "This product includes code licensed from RSA Security, Inc.", and (vii) include the statement, "Some portions licensed from IBM are available at http://oss.software.ibm.com/icu4j/".

4. Java Technology Restrictions. You may not modify the Java Platform Interface ("JPI", identified as classes contained within the "java" package or any subpackages of the "java" package), by creating additional classes within the JPI or otherwise causing the addition to or modification of the classes in the JPI. In the event that you create an additional class and

associated API(s) which (i) extends the functionality of the Java platform, and (ii) is exposed to third party software developers for the purpose of developing additional software which invokes such additional API, you must promptly publish broadly an accurate specification for such API for free use by all developers. You may not create, or authorize your licensees to create, additional classes, interfaces, or subpackages that are in any way identified as "java", "javax", "sun" or similar convention as specified by Sun in any naming convention designation.

5. Notice of Automatic Software Updates from Sun. You acknowledge that the Software may automatically download, install, and execute applets, applications, software extensions, and updated versions of the Software from Sun ("Software Updates"), which may require you to accept updated terms and conditions for installation. If additional terms and conditions are not presented on installation, the Software Updates will be considered part of the Software and subject to the terms and conditions of the Agreement.

6. Notice of Automatic Downloads. You acknowledge that, by your use of the Software and/or by requesting services that require use of the Software, the Software may automatically download, install, and execute software applications from sources other than Sun ("Other Software"). Sun makes no representations of a relationship of any kind to licensors of Other Software. TO THE EXTENT NOT PROHIBITED BY LAW, IN NO EVENT WILL SUN OR ITS LICENSORS BE LIABLE FOR ANY LOST REV-ENUE, PROFIT OR DATA, OR FOR SPECIAL, INDIRECT, CONSEQUENTIAL, INCIDENTAL OR PUNITIVE DAMAGES, HOWEVER CAUSED REGARDLESS OF THE THEORY OF LIABILITY, ARISING OUT OF OR RELATED TO THE USE OF OR INABILITY TO USE OTHER SOFTWARE, EVEN IF SUN HAS BEEN ADVISED OF THE POSSIBILITY OF SUCH DAMAGES.

7. Trademarks and Logos. You acknowledge and agree as between you and Sun that Sun owns the SUN, SOLARIS, JAVA, JINI, FORTE, and iPLANET trademarks and all SUN, SOLARIS, JAVA, JINI, FORTE, and iPLANET-related trademarks, service marks, logos and other brand designations ("Sun Marks"), and you agree to comply with the Sun Trademark and Logo Usage Requirements currently located at http://www.sun.com/policies/trademarks. Any use you make of the Sun Marks inures to Sun's benefit.

8. Source Code. Software may contain source code that is provided solely for reference purposes pursuant to the terms of this Agreement. Source code may not be redistributed unless expressly provided for in this Agreement.

9. Termination for Infringement. Either party may terminate this Agreement immediately should any Software become, or in either party's opinion be likely to become, the subject of a claim of infringement of any intellectual property right.

For inquiries please contact: Sun Microsystems, Inc. 901 San Antonio Road, Palo Alto, California 94303
(LFI#109998/Form ID#011801)

Forte for Java, release 3.0, Community Edition, English

To obtain Forte for Java, release 3.0, Community Edition, English, you must agree to the software license below.

Sun Microsystems, Inc. Binary Code License Agreement

READ THE TERMS OF THIS AGREEMENT AND ANY PROVIDED SUPPLEMENTAL LICENSE TERMS (COLLECTIVELY "AGREEMENT") CAREFULLY BEFORE OPENING THE SOFTWARE MEDIA PACKAGE. BY OPENING THE SOFTWARE MEDIA PACKAGE, YOU AGREE TO THE TERMS OF THIS AGREEMENT. IF YOU ARE ACCESSING THE SOFTWARE ELECTRONICALLY, INDICATE YOUR ACCEPTANCE OF THESE TERMS BY SELECTING THE "ACCEPT" BUTTON AT THE END OF THIS AGREEMENT. IF YOU DO NOT AGREE TO ALL THESE TERMS, PROMPTLY RETURN THE UNUSED SOFTWARE TO YOUR PLACE OF PURCHASE FOR A REFUND OR, IF THE SOFTWARE IS ACCESSED ELECTRONICALLY, SELECT THE "DECLINE" BUTTON AT THE END OF THIS AGREEMENT.

1. LICENSE TO USE. Sun grants you a non-exclusive and non-transferable license for the internal use only of the accompanying software and documentation and any error corrections provided by Sun (collectively "Software"), by the number of users and the class of computer hardware for which the corresponding fee has been paid.

2. RESTRICTIONS. Software is confidential and copyrighted. Title to Software and all associated intellectual property rights is retained by Sun and/or its licensors. Except as specifically authorized in any Supplemental License Terms, you may not make copies of Software, other than a single copy of Software for archival purposes. Unless enforcement is prohibited by applicable law, you may not modify, decompile, or reverse engineer Software. You acknowledge that Software is not designed, licensed or intended for use in the design, construction, operation or maintenance of any nuclear facility. Sun disclaims any express or implied warranty of fitness for such uses. No right, title or interest in or to any trademark, service mark, logo or trade name of Sun or its licensors is granted under this Agreement.

3. LIMITED WARRANTY. Sun warrants to you that for a period of ninety (90) days from the date of purchase, as evidenced by a copy of the receipt, the media on which Software is furnished (if any) will be free of defects in materials and workmanship under normal use. Except for the foregoing, Software is provided "AS IS". Your exclusive remedy and Sun's entire liability under this limited warranty will be at Sun's option to replace Software media or refund the fee paid for Software.

4. DISCLAIMER OF WARRANTY. UNLESS SPECIFIED IN THIS AGREEMENT, ALL EXPRESS OR IMPLIED CONDITIONS, REPRESENTATIONS AND WARRANTIES, INCLUDING ANY IMPLIED WARRANTY OF MERCHANTABILITY, FITNESS FOR A PARTICULAR PURPOSE OR NON-INFRINGEMENT ARE DISCLAIMED, EXCEPT TO THE EXTENT THAT THESE DISCLAIMERS ARE HELD TO BE LEGALLY INVALID.

5. LIMITATION OF LIABILITY. TO THE EXTENT NOT PROHIBITED BY LAW, IN NO EVENT WILL SUN OR ITS LICENSORS BE LIABLE FOR ANY LOST REVENUE, PROFIT OR DATA, OR FOR SPECIAL, INDIRECT, CONSEQUENTIAL, INCIDENTAL OR PUNITIVE DAMAGES, HOWEVER CAUSED REGARDLESS OF THE THEORY OF LIABILITY, ARISING OUT OF OR RELATED TO THE USE OF OR INABILITY TO USE SOFTWARE, EVEN IF SUN HAS BEEN ADVISED OF THE POSSIBILITY OF SUCH DAMAGES. In no event will Sun's liability to you, whether in contract, tort (including negligence), or otherwise, exceed the amount paid by you for Software under this Agreement. The foregoing limitations will apply even if the above stated warranty fails of its essential purpose.

6. Termination. This Agreement is effective until terminated. You may terminate this Agreement at any time by destroying all copies of Software. This Agreement will terminate immediately without notice from Sun if you fail to comply with any provision of this Agreement. Upon Termination, you must destroy all copies of Software.

7. Export Regulations. All Software and technical data delivered under this Agreement are subject to US export control laws and may be subject to export or import regulations in other countries. You agree to comply strictly with all such laws and regulations and acknowledge that you have the responsibility to obtain such licenses to export, re-export, or import as may be required after delivery to you.

8. U.S. Government Restricted Rights. If Software is being acquired by or on behalf of the U.S. Government or by a U.S. Government prime contractor or subcontractor (at any tier), then the Government's rights in Software and accompanying documentation will be only as set forth in this Agreement; this is in accordance with 48 CFR 227.7201 through 227.7202-4 (for Department of Defense (DOD) acquisitions) and with 48 CFR 2.101 and 12.212 (for non-DOD acquisitions).

9. Governing Law. Any action related to this Agreement will be governed by California law and controlling U.S. federal law. No choice of law rules of any jurisdiction will apply.

10. Severability. If any provision of this Agreement is held to be unenforceable, this Agreement will remain in effect with the provision omitted, unless omission would frustrate the intent of the parties, in which case this Agreement will immediately terminate.

11. Integration. This Agreement is the entire agreement between you and Sun relating to its subject matter. It supersedes all prior or contemporaneous oral or written communications, proposals, representations and warranties and prevails over any conflicting or additional terms of any quote, order, acknowledgment, or other communication between the parties relating to its subject matter during the term of this Agreement. No modification of this Agreement will be binding, unless in writing and signed by an authorized representative of each party.

FORTE™ FOR JAVA™, RELEASE 3.0, COMMUNITY EDITION SUPPLEMENTAL LICENSE TERMS

These supplemental license terms ("Supplemental Terms") add to or modify the terms of the Binary Code License Agreement (collectively, the "Agreement"). Capitalized terms not defined in these Supplemental Terms shall have the same meanings ascribed to them in the Agreement. These Supplement contained within the Software.

1. Software Internal Use and Development License Grant. Subject to the terms and conditions of this Agreement, including, but not limited to Section 4 (Java™ Technology Restrictions) of these Supplemental Terms, Sun grants you a non-exclusive, non-transferable, limited license to reproduce internally and use internally the binary form of the Software complete and unmodified for

2. License to Distribute Software. Subject to the terms and conditions of this Agreement, including, but not limited to Section 4 (Java ™ Technology Restrictions) of these Supplemental Terms, Sun grants you a non-exclusive, non-transferable, limited license to reproduce and distribute the Software in binary code form only, provided that (i) you distribute the Software complete and unmodified and only bundled as part of, and for the sole purpose of running, your Programs, (ii) the Programs add significant and primary functionality to the Software, (iii) you do not distribute

additional software intended to replace any component(s) of the Software, (iv) for a particular version of the Java platform, any executable output generated by a compiler that is contained in the Software must (a) only be compiled from source code that conforms to the corresponding version of the OEM Java Language Specification; (b) be in the class file format defined by the corresponding version of the OEM Java Virtual Machine Specification; and (c) execute properly on a reference runtime, as specified by Sun, associated with such version of the Java platform, (v) you do not remove or alter any proprietary legends or notices contained in the Software, (v) you only distribute the Software subject to a license agreement that protects Sun's interests consistent with the terms contained in this Agreement, and (vi) you agree to defend and indemnify Sun and its licensors from and against any damages, costs, liabilities, settlement amounts and/or expenses (including attorneys' fees) incurred in connection with any claim, lawsuit or action by any third party that arises or

3. License to Distribute Redistributables. Subject to the terms and conditions of this Agreement, including but not limited to Section 4 (Java Technology Restrictions) of these Supplemental Terms, Sun grants you a non-exclusive, non-transferable, limited license to reproduce and distribute the binary form of those files specifically identified as redistributable in the Software "RELEASE NOTES" file ("Redistributables") provided that: (i) you distribute the Redistributables complete and unmodified (unless otherwise specified in the applicable RELEASE NOTES file), and only bundled as part of Programs, (ii) you do not distribute additional software intended to supersede any component(s) of the Redistributables, (iii) you do not remove or alter any proprietary legends or notices contained in or on the Redistributables, (iv) for a particular version of the Java platform, any executable output generated by a compiler that is contained in the Software must (a) only be compiled from source code that conforms to the corresponding version of the OEM Java Language Specification; (b) be in the class file format defined by the corresponding version of the OEM Java Virtual Machine Specification; and (c) execute properly on a reference runtime, as specified by Sun, associated with such version of the Java platform, (v) you only distribute the Redistributables pursuant to a license agreement that protects Sun's interests consistent with the terms contained in the Agreement, and (v) you agree to defend and indemnify Sun and its licensors from and against any damages, costs, liabilities, settlement amounts and/or expenses (including attorneys' fees) incurred in connection with any claim, lawsuit or action by any third party that arises or results from the use or distribution of any and all Programs and/or Software.

4. Java Technology Restrictions. You may not modify the Java Platform Interface ("JPI", identified as classes contained within the "java" package or any subpackages of the "java" package), by creating additional classes within the JPI or otherwise causing the addition to or modification of the

classes in the JPI. In the event that you create an additional class and associated API(s) which (i) extends the functionality of the Java platform, and (ii) is exposed to third party software developers for the purpose of developing additional software which invokes such additional API, you must promptly publish broadly an accurate specification for such API for free use by all developers. You may not create, or authorize your licensees to create, additional classes, interfaces, or subpackages that are in any way identified as "java", "javax", "sun" or similar convention as specified by Sun in any naming convention designation.

5. Java Runtime Availability. Refer to the appropriate version of the Java Runtime Environment binary code license (currently located at http://www.java.sun.com/jdk/index.html) for the availability of runtime code which may be distributed with Java applets and applications.

6. Trademarks and Logos. You acknowledge and agree as between you and Sun that Sun owns the SUN, SOLARIS, JAVA, JINI, FORTE, and iPLANET trademarks and all SUN, SOLARIS, JAVA, JINI, FORTE, and iPLANET-related trademarks, service marks, logos and other brand designations ("Sun Marks"), and you agree to comply with the Sun Trademark and Logo Usage Requirements currently located at http://www.sun.com/policies/trademarks. Any use you make of the Sun Marks inures to Sun's benefit.

7. Source Code. Software may contain source code that is provided solely for reference purposes pursuant to the terms of this Agreement. Source code may not be redistributed unless expressly provided for in this Agreement.

8. Termination for Infringement. Either party may terminate this Agreement immediately should any Software become, or in either party's opinion be likely to become, the subject of a claim of infringement of any intellectual property right.

For inquiries please contact: Sun Microsystems, Inc. 901, San Antonio Road, Palo Alto, California 94303
(LFI#91205/Form ID#011801)